OXFOR

General I
Associate General Editors.

FOUR JACOBEAN SEX TRAGEDIES

JACOBEAN tragedy handled sexual topics with exceptional frankness, showing the tensions between the disruptive energies of sex
and the social, cultural, and political values of early seventeenth-
century Europe. *The Insatiate Countess* (1610), written by William
Barksted and Lewis Machin from an incomplete draft by John
Marston, is a study in obsessive nymphomania and the reprisals
which the male establishment takes. *The Maid's Tragedy* (1611), by
Francis Beaumont and John Fletcher, reveals dark sexual secrets at
the heart of the royal court, and emphasizes the political instability
which ensues their discovery. Thomas Middleton's *The Maiden's
Tragedy* (1611) provides an overtly Christian dimension to the conflict between lust and chastity, and John Fletcher's *The Tragedy of
Valentinian* (1614) is a chilling portrayal of rape as the exercise of
absolute power. Each of the plays raises difficult questions about
conventional moral and social attitudes to sexuality which remain
relevant today.

MARTIN WIGGINS is a Fellow of the Shakespeare Institute and
Lecturer in English at the University of Birmingham. His published
work ranges from Shakespeare and Webster to Dennis Potter and
television censorship, and includes *Journeymen in Murder: The
Assassin in English Renaissance Drama* (1991) and an edition of
Christopher Marlowe's *Edward the Second* (New Mermaids, 1997).
He is completing a book on *Shakespeare and the Drama of his Time*.

MICHAEL CORDNER is Reader in the Department of English and
Related Literature at the University of York. His editions include
George Farquhar's *The Beaux' Stratagem*, the *Complete Plays* of Sir
George Etherege, *Four Comedies* of Sir John Vanbrugh, and *Four
Restoration Marriage Comedies*. He is completing a book on *The
Comedy of Marriage 1660–1737*.

PETER HOLLAND is Professor of Shakespeare Studies and Director of the Shakespeare Institute, University of Birmingham.

OXFORD ENGLISH DRAMA

J. M. Barrie
Peter Pan and Other Plays

Aphra Behn
The Rover and Other Plays

George Farquhar
The Recruiting Officer and Other Plays

John Ford
'Tis Pity She's a Whore and Other Plays

Ben Jonson
The Alchemist and Other Plays

Christopher Marlowe
Doctor Faustus and Other Plays

John Marston
The Malcontent and Other Plays

Thomas Middleton
*A Mad World, My Masters and
Other Plays*

Arthur Wing Pinero
Trelawny of the 'Wells' and Other Plays

Richard Brinsley Sheridan
*The School for Scandal and
Other Plays*

J. M. Synge
*The Playboy of the Western World and
Other Plays*

John Webster
*The Duchess of Malfi and
Other Plays*

Oscar Wilde
*The Importance of Being Earnest and
Other Plays*

William Wycherley
The Country Wife and Other Plays

Court Masques
ed. David Lindley

Four Jacobean Sex Tragedies
ed. Martin Wiggins

Four Restoration Marriage Comedies
ed. Michael Cordner

Four Revenge Tragedies
ed. Katharine Maus

*The Lights o' London and
Other Plays*
ed. Michael R. Booth

*The New Woman and
Other Emancipated Woman Plays*
ed. Jean Chothia

Trilby and Other Plays
Four Plays for Victorian Star Actors
ed. George Taylor

OXFORD WORLD'S CLASSICS

Four Jacobean Sex Tragedies

WILLIAM BARKSTED and LEWIS MACHIN
(from a draft by JOHN MARSTON)
The Insatiate Countess

FRANCIS BEAUMONT and JOHN FLETCHER
The Maid's Tragedy

THOMAS MIDDLETON
The Maiden's Tragedy

JOHN FLETCHER
The Tragedy of Valentinian

Edited with an Introduction and Notes by
MARTIN WIGGINS

Oxford   New York
OXFORD UNIVERSITY PRESS
1998

Oxford University Press, Great Clarendon Street, Oxford OX2 6DP

Oxford New York

Athens Auckland Bangkok Bogota Bombay Buenos Aires
Calcutta Cape Town Dar es Salaam Delhi Florence Hong Kong Istanbul
Karachi Kuala Lumpur Madras Madrid Melbourne Mexico City
Nairobi Paris Singapore Taipei Tokyo Toronto Warsaw

and associated companies in
Berlin Ibadan

Oxford is a trade mark of Oxford University Press

Editorial Matter © Martin Wiggins 1998

First published as an Oxford World's Classics paperback 1998

British Library Cataloguing in Publication Data

Data available

Library of Congress Cataloging in Publication Data

Four Jacobean sex tragedies / edited with an introduction by Martin Wiggins.
(Oxford world's classics)
Includes bibliographical references (p.   ).
Contents: The insatiate countess / William Barksted and Lewis
Machin (from a draft by John Marston)—The maid's tragedy /
Francis Beaumont and John Fletcher—The maiden's tragedy / Thomas
Middleton—The tragedy of Valentinian / John Fletcher.
1. English drama—17th century. 2. English drama (Tragedy).
3. Sex—Drama. I. Wiggins, Martin. II. Series: Oxford world's
classics (Oxford University Press)
PR1265.3.F68 1998   822'.0512083538—dc21   97–38296
ISBN 0–19–282320–5

1 3 5 7 9 10 8 6 4 2

Typeset by Best-set Typesetter Ltd., Hong Kong
Printed in Great Britain by
Caledonian International Book Manufacturing Ltd.
Glasgow

CONTENTS

ACKNOWLEDGEMENTS

MY paramount debt is to the general editor, Michael Cordner, whose 'right happy and copious industry' has saved me from many an embarrassing blunder; he is not, of course, responsible for any that remain. Thanks are also due to my Shakespeare Institute colleagues: to Stanley Wells for an unstinting supply of practical wisdom about editorial matters, to John Jowett for long theoretical discussions of many textual conundrums, to Russell Jackson for advice on theatre history, and especially to Susan Brock, the Queen of academic librarians, for everything from palaeographical guidance to enlightened rule-bending. The Institute's play-reading group enabled me to hear all four plays, and I have learned a lot from the members of my MA seminar on English Renaissance tragedy. I am grateful to Irena Cholij, who traced the seventeenth-century settings of three of the songs in *The Tragedy of Valentinian*, and to Paul Edmondson, Victoria Stec, and Suzanne Davis, who performed them for me. Other contributions, great and small though all appreciated, and ranging from stage history to horticultural knowledge, came from Cynthia Bonar, George Costigan, David Gould, Jacqueline Hanham, Margaret Jane Kidnie, Jane Kingsley-Smith, Sue Knott, Simon Leake, Mary McGuigan, Gordon McMullan, Dawn Massey, Sergio Mazzarelli, Brian Meredith, Gail McCracken Price, Niky Rathbone, Nicholas Robins, James Shaw, and Solitaire Townsend. I owe a special debt of gratitude to Eugene Giddens, who checked the entire edition with characteristic skill and precision. At OUP, Judith Luna's contribution, dispensing clearheaded advice whenever needed, has been vital. The last word (without wrong last to be named) is for Kelley Costigan, who put up with everything, even when it took Mycerinus' methods to get it all finished.

M. J. W.

INTRODUCTION

It is difficult, even today, to discuss a work of art's treatment of sexual matters in terms which are neither salacious nor censorious; but the plays in this collection require just that open-mindedness. Around 1610, Jacobean tragedy began to turn increasingly towards themes arising out of human sexuality. All four plays were written at about this time, and in each of them, tragic events develop out of the carnal feelings of one or more of the principal characters. Their sexual behaviour, which includes such obsessive extremes as nymphomania, rape, and necrophilia, is portrayed with a frankness unprecedented in English drama, and rarely seen since.

It is sometimes assumed that this emphasis on sexual topics in later Jacobean drama is a sign of 'decadence'. Beaumont and Fletcher wrote *The Maid's Tragedy* and plays like it 'for people who were too dumb to dig Shakespeare', readers of the *Daily Express* were told apropos of a production in 1964; 'The play's contemporary equivalent would be a lurid paperback novelette with a bosomy illustration on the cover.'[1] Of course, it's quite normal to have a prurient interest in sex (no doubt that's why more than a few people first picked up this book), but it is lazy to assume that the plays, as products of the commercial theatre, merely seek to exploit this tendency, and that they may therefore be dismissed as nothing more than dirty-minded drama for dirty-minded audiences.

Such audiences might well find a degree of titillation in the sequence of *The Maid's Tragedy* where the bride Evadne prepares for bed. In a modern production, her gradual undressing by her ladies-in-waiting could take on the quality of striptease, no doubt leaving the more voyeuristic playgoers disappointed when she goes to finish in off-stage privacy. But such a response was less available in Jacobean performances, because clothes literally made the woman: female roles were played by male actors, usually teenage boys (though adult men sometimes took the parts of older women), and the audiences knew it. The point is not that the regular use of boy actors rendered the plays proof against the sexual fantasies of the theatre's patrons (in some cases, obviously, the contrary was true), but that in these circumstances

[1] Herbert Kretzmer, *Daily Express*, 5 June 1964.

a directly sexual response would be entirely irrelevant.[2] Evadne is supposed to be an exceptionally attractive woman, and her new husband Amintor is looking forward to having sex with her. With an actress in the role, any erotic feelings excited by this scene might conceivably be said to be to the point; they certainly aren't if their object is a young man. If the play here teases its audience with anything, it is with the prospective breakdown of the dramatic illusion, not the tawdry expectation of female nudity: the disrobing, if completed, would only reveal an unequivocally male leading lady.

The broader point is that the audience's own erotic feelings can draw them into a closer and not entirely appropriate engagement with the sexually fixated characters on the stage (and this is obviously a greater risk in a modern production with actresses rather than boys). The court society in which *The Maid's Tragedy* takes place is shown to be explicitly and exceedingly interested in sex. The characters, men and women alike, are seen to enjoy swapping jokes and gossip about the subject: in the case of Amintor and Evadne the King may abrogate the bawdy custom of putting the bride and groom to bed together, but the lewd chatter of the ladies-in-waiting in the undressing sequence, and the courtiers' baiting of Amintor on the morning after, both illustrate why that custom should be usual and appreciated in this environment. Amintor himself is not immune: later in the play, he fobs off his friend Melantius, who wants a serious conversation, by offering a presumably indecent anecdote about another courtier and a lady. But the play does not ask us to identify totally with this consuming interest. One of the most arresting moments comes when Evadne refuses to consummate the marriage, and meets Amintor's bland assumption that she is over-attached to her virginity with the cynical, mocking riposte, 'A maidenhead, Amintor, at my years?' (2.1.173) The double standard—a lubricious interest in other people's sex lives combined with romantic notions about pre-marital chastity in one's own wife—stands starkly exposed.

The truth about Amintor's marriage, that it has been arranged by the King as a cover for his own furtive relationship with Evadne, begs an important but unspoken question. The stratagem is politically ill-conceived: not only does it entail humiliating Amintor, a courtier with powerful friends, but also offending the family of Aspatia, the fiancée he was obliged to jilt; the ultimate outcome is the King's own death.

---

[2] On sexual responses to boy actors, see Lisa Jardine, *Still Harping on Daughters. Women and Drama in the Age of Shakespeare* (1983), ch. 1

But it is also unnecessary: since the King is a bachelor, why doesn't he just marry Evadne himself?

One recurrent emphasis in these plays is the contrast between the evanescence of sexual pleasure and the longevity or permanence of other areas of human experience; the audience is never encouraged to embrace uncritically what Middleton called, in *The Revenger's Tragedy* (1606), 'the poor benefit of a bewitching minute'.[3] In *The Tragedy of Valentinian*, the Emperor's quest for short-term ecstasy is juxtaposed with other characters' sense of honour, which will last beyond their deaths and determine their eventual existence as respected figures in history, whereas Valentinian will be remembered only as a dissolute rapist. In the Christian context of *The Maiden's Tragedy*, it is more an issue of personal survival into the next world: heaven and hell are a prominent context for the action, and in the final scene, the simulta-neous presence on stage of the Lady's ghost and her decaying body, the latter still the object of the Tyrant's fleshly desire, underlines the incorruptibility of the soul and so the superiority of spiritual to mater-ial pursuits. All this illuminates the reluctance of the King in *The Maid's Tragedy* to commit himself permanently to Evadne by making her his queen. Her future, her brother points out, will be that of any discarded whore:

> When his cool majesty hath laid you by,
> To be at pension with some needy sir
> For meat and coarser clothes. (4.1.153–5)

Sex is brief, but marriage is lifelong: in matching his lover with Amintor, the King is keeping his own options open.

From here it would be easy to argue that these three plays (let's exclude *The Insatiate Countess* for now) adopt a moralistic, censorious attitude to extramarital sex. Each of them addresses the problems which arise from the conjunction of supreme political power with the mastering force of male sexual desire: the situation at the root of them all is a ruler's sexual interest in a prominent female subject, which leads on to tyrannical behaviour. Evadne is the only willing partner: in *The Maiden's Tragedy*, the Lady is subjected to an extreme form of sexual harassment, while in *Valentinian* the Emperor actually rapes Lucina; in these cases sexual misconduct and the abuse of power are coextensive.

---

[3] Thomas Middleton, *The Revenger's Tragedy*, 3.5.74, in Katharine Eisaman Maus (ed.), *Four Revenge Tragedies* (1995).

The ultimate consequence of such tyranny, in all three plays, is deposition, and the later stages of the action duly strip away the mystique of power to reveal its true foundation in the control of the army or, in *The Maid's Tragedy*, of a strategically significant fort. Earlier on, however, the mystique is crucial: the ruler can get away with his sexual vices—can indeed be aided and abetted in them—because his empowerment removes, or at least complicates, his subjects' right of redress. When violated Lucina says she will cry for justice, the imperial rapist chillingly assures her, 'Justice shall never hear ye: I am justice' (3.1.34); the only remonstrance she or the Lady can make against such undisciplined absolutism is suicide. The problem is not so much that people can be terrorized by naked force into submission, but that power can distort the perceptions in a way apparent in poor, confused Amintor's reaction to the knowledge that Evadne's lover is the King: it 'wipes away | All thoughts revengeful' (2.1.286–7), he says, and much of the middle movement of the play deals with his reluctant conversion from loyalty to reprisal. The King is right even when he's wrong, and for subjects less personally compromised this can make for active collusion: in *Valentinian*, the imperial court includes a vast bureaucracy of professional procurers, all working to corrupt chaste Lucina in the play's first movement, and the emissaries who hope to tempt the Lady into the Tyrant's bed in *The Maiden's Tragedy* include her own father; the subversion of the family relationship makes the starkest possible illustration of the delusions engendered by the glamour of power.

It is in rejecting that glamour, and so claiming an objective, undistorted perspective on the rulers' behaviour, that the plays make available a censorious attitude to some sexual mores. This is only partly generated by a negative view of the monarchs themselves; it also entails a response to the female protagonists whom they desire. Valentinian, for example, is odious not only in what he does but, more importantly, in his calculating, self-confident attitude both before and after his crime; an audience's sympathies are bound to swing towards Lucina. From there it is easy to read the play in terms of a binary opposition between chastity and promiscuity, with chastity obviously the approved alternative. 'We cannot reverence chastity too much,' remarks the rightful King, Govianus, after enthroning the Lady's dead body at the end of *The Maiden's Tragedy* (5.2.200), and even Evadne comes to regard herself as the King's victim rather than his sexual partner, transformed from a chaste virgin into a whore. It is a reading consistent with Jacobean official culture, many aspects of which still survive today, and no doubt many playgoers did go home from the

Globe and the Blackfriars, the theatres where the three plays were originally staged, feeling they had seen sexual decency upheld and incontinence fitly punished. I want to suggest that it is as lazy and reductive to see the plays in these terms as to think them simply titillating, and that there are other ways than the merely judgemental in which works of art, particularly tragedies, may deal seriously with sexual behaviour.

The play which initially seems least promising in this respect is *The Insatiate Countess*: with a crackle of bawdy innuendo running through the dialogue, it doesn't *sound* like a play which takes sex seriously. Rutting is a focus of obsessive fascination for all the principal characters, both for the usual reasons and, in the comic sub-plot, as a weapon in a long-standing family feud; the Countess herself, Isabella, gets through four lovers in the course of the action, one of them only just off-stage, before being beheaded in the penultimate scene. It all begins to seem uncomfortably reminiscent of the collocation of prudery and prurience familiar today from tabloid newspapers' handling of sex 'scandals': sensational subject-matter rendered innocuous by an overlay of moral conservatism assuring us that it is all utterly shocking. Isabella gives us a lot of salacious entertainment, but our morals are in no danger because eventually she's properly punished for it—so the argument might run.

The trouble is, the condemnation of Isabella's promiscuity which is expressed within the play is always shown to be fatally compromised. Her most persistent critic is Rogero: he censures her in the opening scene for taking a second husband before she had finished mourning her first, and later he circulates bitter verses attacking her promiscuity. But on the first occasion he is a disappointed rival and on the second a superseded paramour: he too came to woo Isabella in her bereavement, and would presumably have accepted her apostasy if it had been in his favour; and he later becomes the first of her extramarital lovers, with whom she flees her second husband, and so is hardly in a position to attack her when she rejects him in turn. In any event, the criticism costs him his life, and it is for his murder that Isabella is arraigned and executed. Perhaps the rights and wrongs of the case are less absolutely clear-cut than they seemed.

A number of visual and verbal elements in the execution scene itself serve to create an unsettling echo effect: when Isabella's second husband Roberto kneels and embraces her on the scaffold, the stage image recalls her earlier kneeling embrace of her chosen killer, Don

Sago; and when the presiding figure of authority, the Duke of Medina, declares that he would execute even his 'father's daughter' for the sake of justice (5.1.111), we may remember Sago's earlier declaration, 'To gain your love my father's blood I'll spill.' (4.2.209) The scene sets up an uncomfortable association between the operations of crime and of punishment—Don Sago has even called the murder an 'act of justice' (4.4.14)—which must make us at least open-minded about the execution's claim to just impartiality. This is proclaimed at the end of the scene by Medina, who didn't even bother to stay and witness the execution, and he takes a defensive, protesting-too-much tone:

> None here, I hope, can tax us of injustice.
> She died deservedly, and may like fate
> Attend all women so insatiate. (5.1.227–9)

The emphasis on lustful women is especially revealing: it seems that Isabella is killed as much for her promiscuity as for her part in Rogero's death, while Don Sago, who actually committed the murder, is pardoned. Again the double standard is apparent.

Apparent to us, of course, but what about the Jacobeans? It is never easy to differentiate between texts which deliberately represent misogyny and those which merely participate in it, and we should never underestimate any play's capacity merely to confirm its audience's prejudices. Equally, we should beware of making unsupported assumptions about what those prejudices might have been. It is clear that misogyny is an important part of the social and cultural fabric of all these plays. Several characters, both male and female, voice negative opinions of women in general: we hear that women are inferior to men in virtue, have no souls, and are actually incapable of doing good; they are, in fact, the cause of all men's downfall.[4] One thing that is striking about *The Insatiate Countess*, however, is the range and variety of its female characters. Isabella is not presented in isolation but in relation to the other three principal women: although the plots remain largely independent of one another, there are some structural touches which encourage comparisons, such as the way the third act opens with Lady Lentulus at her window and closes with Isabella at hers, the only times the upper acting area is used. None of them would support the generalizations that are made about female depravity: the witty Abigail and the pragmatic Thais are notable for their resourceful common sense in frustrating their idiotic husbands' wife-swapping revenge

---

[4] *Maiden*, 1.2.58–9; *Countess*, 3.4.178–9, 5.2.35–6; *Maid*, 4.1.256; *Countess*, 3.4.175.

plots, while Lady Lentulus is conscientious in her impossible struggle to reconcile her widow's vows with her feelings for Mendosa.

It is especially important that all the female characters are explicitly shown to be interested in sex. One of the ways in which women are dominated in misogynistic societies is by defining female virtue in extraordinarily limited terms; usually the definition centres on sexual modesty. This is why, in *Valentinian* and *The Maiden's Tragedy*, Lucina and the Lady have no viable alternative to suicide: any other response to their particular situation would entail their being branded as whores. It is also why Isabella is executed: Rogero's murder supplies the legal pretext, but her greater offence lies in her sexual appetite and the active role she takes in satisfying it. The play itself does not acquiesce in this procedure, however. It would have been very easy to present the Countess in antithesis to a chaste sub-plot heroine (*The Maiden's Tragedy* does something similar in contrasting the incorruptible Lady with Anselmus' all too susceptible wife in its sub-plot); but in making its overtly good women sexual creatures too, the play undermines the assumed distinction between good and evil female behaviour on which her condemnation rests.

Moreover, Isabella is a more complex figure than her bad reputation might suggest, and one who is allowed a degree of audience sympathy. It is revealing that many of the play's classical allusions draw on material from Ovid's *Metamorphoses*, partly because Ovid was the most erotic poet in general circulation in the period, his creative energies magnificently aligned with Isabella's experience rather than the puritanical response to her; but partly too because the poem's theme of the transformations wrought by extremes of passion is also one of the play's fundamental concerns. Change is central to Isabella's career of nymphomaniac promiscuity: changes of heart, changes of lover, changes of location. It is an extreme example of a recognized condition: the idea that love and sexual feelings transform people was a familiar theme in Renaissance fiction.[5] Isabella evidently wishes for constancy and stability—she promises Gniaca, her third lover,

> My faith to thee, like rocks, shall never move;
> The sun shall change his course ere I my love. (3.4.101–2)

—but the bewitching minute disappears every time. This is one reason why the play is so very full of bawdy puns: the language becomes

---

[5] See R. S. White, 'Metamorphosis by Love in Elizabethan Romance, Romantic Comedy, and Shakespeare's Early Comedies', *Review of English Studies*, 35 (1984), 14–44.

unstable, shimmering with secondary meanings which have no relation to objective reality and which vanish as quickly as the sexual pleasure to which they refer. They are the verbal equivalent of the mayfly affairs through which the insatiate Countess passes en route to the ultimate stability she achieves on the scaffold.

In this respect Isabella is not simply an unscrupulous pleasure-seeker who sleeps her way across Italy with a flagrant disregard for the feelings of others; she is also shown to be a victim of her own sexuality. There is an obsessive quality in her pursuit of sexual pleasure which makes her ignore not only her matrimonial obligations but also deeper cultural taboos. She can imagine herself participating in inter-generational sex with old Father Time, for instance—

> Do this, gentle Time,
> And I will curl thine agèd silver lock
> And dally with thee in delicious pleasure. (3.4.5–7)

—and her desire for Gniaca is so strong that even incest would be no inhibition: 'I'll clip him, were 't my brother' (3.2.48). It is telling that she expresses herself not only willing to embrace such an excess, but also aware that it *is* excessive. Throughout the play she is represented as someone powerlessly watching herself spin out of control: she regularly speaks of the forces which drive her—Cupid, Desire, Revenge—in personified terms which establish her sense of them as external. Unable to govern them, she can only submit in the hope that they will wear themselves out:

> Desire, thou quenchless flame that burn'st our souls,
> Cease to torment me.
> The dew of pleasure shall put out thy fire
> And quite consume thee with satiety.
> Lust shall be cooled with lust, wherein I'll prove
> The life of love is only saved by love. (3.4.18–23)

Her sense of calculating self-definition as she embraces promiscuity is as deluded as the notion that she can extinguish a quenchless flame; what the speech brings out is not only the pity of her condition, enslaved by sexual obsession, but also the terrible fact that there can be no escape.

The Maiden's Tragedy is the most explicitly Christian and morally conservative of the four plays, but it too is open to ambiguous judgements and unexpected sympathies. The political situation at the start seems to invite a clear-cut moral response: the rightful King, Govianus, has been deposed by a conspiracy of disaffected nobles, and a usurper installed in his place. The broad similarities with *Hamlet*, the fact that the usurper has no personal name but (on the page at least) only the damning label 'Tyrant', and perhaps a historical awareness of Jacobean royalism, all incline readers to interpret the play in black-and-white terms which favour Govianus. He will prove to be an exceptionally flawed hero.

Why was Govianus deposed? It is the play's great unasked question, and one which could scarcely be addressed directly: the Jacobean censor would not have looked kindly on the idea that dethroning a king could ever be justified. Yet if the situation is to be at all plausible, the Tyrant must initially seem a better ruler than Govianus could be. In the first half of the play, there is much to be said against the ex-King. At first he mistakenly believes his betrothed, the Lady, to be venally ambitious, and assumes that she will reject him now that he is no longer King:

> O she's a woman, and her eye will stand
> Upon advancement, never weary yonder;
> But when she turns her head by chance and sees
> The fortunes that are my companions,
> She'll snatch her eyes off and repent the looking. (1.1.63–7)

Evidently his judgement of people is unreliable, and it is no more secure on moral issues. When noblemen-panders arrive to tempt the Lady, his interventions, though technically correct, are unduly aggressive: Helvetius only escapes with his life because he is the Lady's father, he says, and if at this point he more resembles the posturing Bonario of Ben Jonson's *Volpone* (1605) than the dangerously outraged hero he would like to be, he does later succeed in killing the old sycophant Sophonirus, who comes with an army on the same mission. He then props the body up against the door so that it will look as if the soldiers have killed him breaking in:

> I'll plant this bawd
> Against the door, the fittest place for him
> That, when with ungoverned weapons they rush in,
> Blinded with fury, they may take his death
> Into the purple number of their deeds
> And wipe it off from mine. (3.1.180–5)

This is both sly and crass: both attempting to shift the appearance of guilt and believing that doing so will also shift the burden of moral responsibility. Govianus acts and thinks more like a confused adolescent than a king, and that's probably what cost him his crown.[6]

Conversely, the Tyrant is not quite the degenerate villain we might expect. He could be seen as a kind of empowered stalker who won't leave the Lady alone even though she has made it abundantly clear that she is not in the least interested in him. But in the early stages he is far less dangerous than that: more of a lovesick Orsino than a potential rapist. As a monarch he has the power of life and death (Sophonirus talks nervously about the risk of being beheaded or having his body treated like butcher's meat), but he is strikingly reluctant to use that power: he explicitly decides *not* to execute Govianus in the first act and Helvetius in the second. And when rape is proposed to him as an option, he rejects it:

> That had been done before thy thought begot it
> If my affection could be so hard-hearted
> To stand upon such payment. It must come
> Gently and kindly like a debt of love,
> Or 'tis not worth receiving. (1.1.185–9)

Persuasion is the better alternative because he is genuinely concerned that the Lady should be a willing long-term partner. He may be misguided, but he is not entirely monstrous.

The political action of the play gradually reverses the two men's relative positions. The Tyrant's hold on power deteriorates as his obsession with the Lady escalates: he grows increasingly irritable, and increasingly prone to use force, with every setback. When he steals the Lady's body from her tomb, the scene is punctuated with bawdily incredulous comments from his soldiers, which serve to emphasize his psychotic alienation from normal sexuality such as theirs. By the end of the play Govianus is clearly the preferable candidate for the throne and is duly elected king by the same nobles who previously deposed him. But this is arguably more a function of the Tyrant's deterioration than of any corresponding amelioration in Govianus himself.

After he kills the usurper, Govianus does not look to resume his former place on the throne, but merely to join the Lady in death. This can be seen as an egocentric avoidance of political responsibility. Throughout the later stages of the action, the immature confusion which the first half established in general terms is more precisely

---

[6] This is not to say that he actually is an adolescent; his brother Anselmus, who seems more mature though no less fallible in judgement, is presumably the younger of the two.

focused as an excessive devotion to the person of his beloved: when she resolves to choose death before dishonour, he cannot bring himself to kill her, so that she has to do the job herself, and later, when her ghost appears to him, he says that he would happily endure all the pains of hell if they came in her shape; he even considers putting off dealing with the Tyrant so that the ghost will come back and nag him. There is an obsessive distortion here which neglects or misconstrues all wider considerations—moral, political, and spiritual—when they interfere with his love. In this he is uncomfortably close to his antagonist: 'Does all things end with death and not thy lust?' (5.2.122) he asks the Tyrant, but it is also his paramount concern to continue his relationship with the Lady, albeit on the other side of the grave. It is both apt and disconcerting that his first act as king should be to enthrone and crown her body, to the ghost's evident disapproval and, incidentally, the alarm of the Jacobean censor: the distance between him and the necrophiliac Tyrant narrows to a hair's breadth. This is the idolatrous context for his concluding declaration that we cannot reverence chastity too much.

The paradox is that what discredits Govianus is his distance from the wider values which motivate the Lady: she wants to be killed, wants her body to be reburied, and his failure or reluctance to comply is our index of his ethical confusion. So by treating the representative of chastity as a figure of absolute spiritual authority, we make it impossible to read the most explicit statement in favour of that chastity without an element of undermining irony: the play's overt moral orientation, powerfully backed by appeal to the Christian eschatology which was central to orthodox belief in the period, ultimately wrong-foots itself. But then, are we *really* going to condemn Govianus because he won't murder his girlfriend? According to Helvetius, the Lady was 'too resolute' (5.2.181): as in Shakespeare's *The Rape of Lucrece* (1594), the surviving father considers suicide an excessive response to the situation. Her relentless chastity is as remote from ordinary human standards as the Tyrant's body-snatching. It may be that one is bound for heaven and the other for hell, but the play becomes more complex and more satisfying if we do not respond to them solely in those terms.

Compared with Isabella or the Tyrant, both the King of Rhodes and the Emperor Valentinian are relatively under-characterized, their unorthodox sexual lives presented, in different ways, as secrets which are discovered as the stories unfold. What is striking about the first act of *The Maid's Tragedy* is the sheer normality of the situation: nothing occurs that would not ordinarily happen at a court wedding in the period. This serves two purposes. First, it sets up the dramatic reversal in the second act when, nearly half an hour into the play, Evadne refuses to consummate the marriage: the action's entire trajectory has moved, with exceptional frankness, towards an event which then does not take place. It has, in fact, already taken place, but with the King rather than Amintor as partner—and that makes the play's initial ordinariness not just a context for this unexpected development, but also a constructed façade concealing the extraordinary truth.

The King's affair with Evadne is seen to be a well-kept secret partly because the play devotes more attention to his senior courtiers than to the gentlemen attending his bedchamber who briefly appear in the last act and are evidently in the know. *Valentinian* gives more stage time to such figures, who ply Lucina unsuccessfully with temptations in the opening act. This serves partly to make the Emperor seem more powerful, less dependent on the good will of his most prominent subjects and so able to act with greater impunity. Secrecy is for him a last resort, after direct persuasion has failed. Whereas *The Maid's Tragedy* begins with the veneer, *Valentinian* uses the relative openness of the initial approach to Lucina to set in relief the terrible sense of the unspoken in the sequence leading up to the rape: the panders' brittle socializing conceals a horror which is simultaneously unarticulated but known, and even half-suspected by Lucina herself. It is the play's most brilliantly sustained piece of writing.

In both plays, the exposition of the rulers' sexual irregularities falls mainly to the accomplices in them: respectively, Evadne and the panders. Together with the plays' emphasis on the secrecy of those irregularities, this has the effect of characterizing the King and Valentinian more from the outside: they are defined not by the kind of emotional engagement with their actions seen in the sexually transgressive characters of *The Insatiate Countess* and *The Maiden's Tragedy*, but simply by the deeds themselves and the hypocrisy with which they conceal them. This means that the plays' concern is more with the political response to tyrannous lust than with the lust itself; but again there is a signal avoidance of simple moral judgements.

The possibility of taking revenge against a monarch was the touchiest subject in Jacobean politics: that is why, though the King and Valentinian are portrayed as uncomplicatedly vicious, Evadne's brother Melantius and Lucina's husband Maximus can take their reprisals only after extended debate with confidants who advocate less radical action. In Melantius' case, this is Amintor, who has been even more directly wronged by the King, but whose instinctive response is to accept the situation:

> it is my fate
> To bear and bow beneath a thousand griefs
> To keep that little credit with the world. (3.1.254–6)

Part of the difference between them is their degree of engagement with the court environment and its habitual modes of behaviour: Amintor is a full-time courtier and here seems to be sucked even deeper into the King's world of secrecy and sham honour, whereas Melantius is more at home on the battlefield than among the jests and compliments of the society he defends. In the period, soldiers such as he were often considered dangerous forces who brought back with them the aggression and killing of the front, but the play negates any possible royalist bid to explain his support for regicide in these terms. Melantius bristles with suppressed violence, particularly over his feud with Calianax: he comes repeatedly to the brink of combat, drawing his sword so often that it almost becomes a part of the scenic form of 3.2, but he never actually fights; he doesn't even manage to commit suicide at the end. When the King is eventually murdered, it is Evadne, not he, who does it: it cannot be seen as an eruption of soldierly barbarism into the centre of a civilized society.

Melantius' other principal difference from Amintor is the one that ultimately determines the outcome: he is an older man, more mature in judgement and more magnetic in personality than his suggestible young friend. As an outsider in the court, he has the advantage of a degree of objectivity, but it is his charisma and clear-headedness which eventually converts Amintor. The weight of the argument, and of the audience's sympathies, falls on the side of direct action—something as monstrous to Jacobean official culture as any of the sexual practices these plays represent.

The issue is more delicately balanced in *Valentinian*, because it is the only thing separating Maximus from his friend and general, Aëtius. Both men are critics of the Emperor from the start: Maximus rails against his vices in private, whereas Aëtius takes the riskier course of repeating such criticisms to Valentinian's face in the hope of reforming him. Neither approach achieves very much, but Aëtius at least acquires the audience's respect: his candour may not avert the rape, but it demands a degree of honesty and moral courage which Maximus, who slinks away when the Emperor arrives, significantly seems to lack. The distinction is fundamental to their subsequent development: in the aftermath of the rape, Aëtius rises to a noble death, contrived because Maximus fears his persuasive opposition, while Maximus himself gradually descends to odium, too ready to support Lucina in her determination on suicide and too devoted to devious hole-in-corner methods in pursuit of his revenge, before finally being poisoned himself by way of counter-revenge.

In this respect *Valentinian* must have been far more palatable to the Jacobean authorities than *The Maid's Tragedy*: presenting a situation in which there is no right answer, no course of action that is both morally acceptable and politically effective, it at least ensures that censure is appropriately distributed between rapist and regicide. But when the new king ends *The Maid's Tragedy* by trying to interpret the action in similar terms—

> on lustful kings
> Unlooked-for sudden deaths from God are sent;
> But cursed is he that is their instrument (5.3.289–91)

—we are uneasily aware that this formulation better suits contemporary political orthodoxy than it does the actual circumstances: there has been no previous indication that Melantius and his fellow-conspirators are the unwitting agents of providential action, and from the point of view of audience sympathy they are, though perhaps equivocal, nonetheless far from cursed. The questions which the play has raised cannot be so glibly resolved.

We have to get out of the habit of reading Jacobean tragedies prescriptively. It is too easy to interpret these plays as complacently royalist, complacently Christian, complacently misogynistic or sex-hating, but equally reductive to read them as manifestos for revolution, whether political or sexual. The insatiate Countess is neither a disgraceful whore rightfully executed nor an innocent victim of sexually intolerant patriarchy: the play is more open-minded than that. In *The Maid's Tragedy*, Amintor naïvely assumes there must be a solution, if only the gods would supply it:

> You powers above, if you did ever mean
> Man should be used thus, you have thought a way
> How he may bear himself and save his honour. (2.1.222–4)

But there is no answer—no fixed, reliable point of view for us to take. The plays all deal with unresolvable situations created by the interaction of some of the basic social and cultural norms of Renaissance

Europe: the supposed wickedness of promiscuity, the restricted freedom of women, the power of the crown.

Jacobean tragedies are concerned with the circumscription of freedom not only by the characters' previous actions and psychological make-up, but also by the worlds in which they live. Amintor's horrified first reaction to Evadne's wedding-night revelation is to hush it up lest the knowledge should put later generations off marriage and precipitate the collapse of civilization into a chaos of irresponsible fornication. Wrong again. His rejected fiancée Aspatia declares that, in view of the irreconcilable differences between the sexes, 'It is unjust | That men and women should be matched together.' (5.3.29–30) It is the play's most radical criticism of the social order which enfolds, and restricts, the characters; but, coming as it does from someone whose exclusion from marriage has relegated her to the margins of her society and brought her to the brink of annihilation, it is utterly ineffectual. Social institutions don't break: people do. The birth of tragedy is the failure of the art of the possible.

NOTE ON THE TEXTS

ALL four plays in this edition have been freshly edited from the ear-
liest available copies. The paramount concern, as with all editions in
this series, is to transmit to a reader, as far as is possible, the experience of the plays in the theatres for which they were written. The early
editions, in Quarto, Folio, and manuscript, are treated not as authoritative documents whose every material feature must be punctiliously
preserved, but as textual witnesses from which an editor attempts to
reconstruct the plays as they were offered to the theatregoers of their
time.

Accordingly, the most important components of any written play-
text are the words of the dialogue, the part of the play which is identical in both media. The least important are bibliographical features
such as title-pages or colophons, which have no bearing on any aspect
of a performance and are not transcribed here. (The reader is, however,
provided with the usual convenience of a list of the characters of each
play, compiled afresh in every case whether or not such a list appeared
in the early editions.) Somewhere in between are the stage directions,
which represent but do not in themselves reproduce elements of the
performed text.

In this edition I assume that, while stage directions are significant
indicators of non-verbal action, their precise wording in the original
editions is not textually substantive. On occasion, indeed, it can interfere with a play's literary effect. For example, the original stage direction at *The Insatiate Countess* 3.4.31 reads '*Enter Gniaca in his hunting
weeds*', but the phrase 'hunting weeds' also appears in the dialogue two
lines later. The sense of repetitiveness this creates is no part of the
theatrical experience of the play, and can legitimately be eliminated by
minor editorial revision. (In this edition, the stage direction in question reads '. . . *hunting clothes*'.) Similarly, in the final act of *The Maid's
Tragedy*, a number of characters '*kill*'—as the original stage directions
have it—themselves and others; yet incongruously the victims remain
sentient and articulate for some time afterwards. The word '*kills*' obviously refers to the giving of a death-wound, but this is to prejudge the
outcome: what we see in the theatre is a stabbing which becomes a
killing retrospectively once the victim is dead. This edition seeks to
represent in print the real-time experience of the plays in the theatre,

so the stage directions have been adjusted to read '*stabs*'. Other original stage directions are revised or expanded to clarify the action for a modern reader, without underestimating the texts' openness to interpretation; however, the original wording has not been altered without a positive reason for doing so. Minor adjustments of this kind have been made silently, but square brackets are used to indicate substantive, editorially introduced items of stage action.

The plays were all written for theatres which used act-divisions, and in each case the five acts are clearly indicated in the control-texts. Formal scene-divisions had no place in Jacobean theatrical practice, but they are included here for convenience (and are supplied silently when they are not present in the control-texts).

Spelling and punctuation have been modernized according to the principles set out by Stanley Wells in *Modernizing Shakespeare's Spelling* (1979), using the lemma forms of the *Oxford English Dictionary* as standard. Contractions are represented by the equivalent modern contraction of the root words, e.g. 'sh'av' becomes 'she've' (*Maiden*, 1.2.287), 'y'are' becomes 'you're', ''t'as' becomes 'it's'. Obsolete forms of inflected verbs are similarly transformed to their modern equivalent, e.g. 'risse' becomes 'rose' (*Maiden*, 1.1.112). Where appropriate, proper names are regularized to their accepted historical forms, e.g. 'Aecius' becomes Aëtius (*Valentinian*). The rules have obliged me to retain some outmoded words, intimately related to modern equivalents but listed by the *OED* as distinct forms; I hope that nobody using this edition as the basis for a performance will feel they need to be equally scrupulous in retaining such orthographic dinosaurs as *chirurgeon* (for *surgeon*) or *rampires* (for *ramparts*).

The textual apparatus is necessarily limited to emendations introduced in this edition; emendations which are already part of the editorial tradition are generally adopted silently. However, all emendations are discussed where they are relevant to points of literary interpretation, and textual variants are documented when they reveal the process of revision.

In the course of its movement from pen to stage to print, a text will exist in many different versions as it is refined, revised, censored, and so on. Usually only one of those versions will survive, as is the case with *The Tragedy of Valentinian*, and the editor's only major textual labour will be to emend away misprints. However, the other three plays all exist in states which reveal more than one stage in their development, and which consequently require fundamental editorial choices. In making those choices, I have been guided by the principle that a play-text is not complete when it leaves the author but when it is enacted on the stage. Accordingly I have sought to produce texts as close as possible—which in one case is still not at all close—to the state of each play as it was first performed.

To apply this principle with absolute consistency, however, would entail accepting *every* change made for the theatre: adjustments made by the acting company to ensure that a particular scene would be possible in performance would be taken to have as much validity as changes made for moral or political reasons on the instructions of the censor. All Jacobean plays were subject to scrutiny and possible censorship by a court official, the Master of the Revels; at the time of the plays in this volume the post was held by Sir George Buc, whose hand is traceable in both *The Maid's Tragedy* and *The Maiden's Tragedy*. To accept his deletions would result in an authentic reconstruction of both plays as they were originally performed, but also in artistically disempowered texts with many of their more trenchant passages missing.

Accordingly, my principle has been to accept alterations, additions, and deletions except where they are attributable to censorship (including cuts, such as the removal of oaths, made by persons other than Buc in anticipation of or response to his demands). The aim has been to preserve intentional changes made by the theatre company, and to undo involuntary ones imposed upon them by outside forces. The resultant texts are, admittedly, versions of the plays which could not legally have been performed in the early seventeenth century; but, I hope, ones which the authors and the company would have preferred to stage had circumstances allowed.

The Insatiate Countess is an unfinished play, at least in the form in which it was published by Thomas Archer in the first Quarto of 1613. This was printed from copy which seems to have been a rough draft of the play in several different hands, and sometimes to have been illegible to boot: Q contains an exceptionally large number of obvious misprints (including, for 5.2.222, 'The poxe is vnto Panders giuen', a misreading as glorious as it is inept); we cannot be confident that there are no other errors lurking undetected in apparently sensible readings. Two later Quartos were issued, in 1616 and 1631 respectively, but Q1 served as the copy for both. Consequently, although Q2 introduced many emendations of varying accuracy, there is no independent textual witness to the play's later development into a workable stage version. (The title-pages of Q1 and Q3 attest to the fact that it was performed at the Whitefriars Theatre.) Q1 is, by default, the control-text for this edition.

In 1984, the Revels edition by Giorgio Melchiori offered a thorough analysis of the play's textual problems, and a hypothesis about its textual provenance, with which I have broadly concurred; without Melchiori's exemplary labours my task as editor would have been far more difficult. The printer's copy for Q1, Melchiori argued, derived from several different stages in the composition of the text. The play was begun by John Marston, who wrote relatively full versions of 1.1 and 2.1.1–103, and sketchier outlines of the rest. The play was still incomplete on 8 June 1608, when Marston was imprisoned; he was never again to write for the theatre.[1] At some later point, the actor William Barksted and his associate Lewis Machin took over the play and began to develop it for the stage, writing up the missing scenes and changing some of the characters' names; though it is impossible to assign precise shares to each collaborator, it appears that Barksted took particular responsibility for the tragic plot and Machin for the comic. Later still, some or all of their early working papers were acquired, possibly illicitly, by a third party, who made some attempt to cast them into good order before they passed to the printer; it is possible that this entailed writing anew an essential scene (5.2) missing from the papers, though Melchiori's argument on this point is founded more on subjective literary judgement than on adducible evidence. This provenance may explain why the character of Guido disappears after the second act, and why the plot of Mendosa and Lady Lentulus fizzles out unfinished: these parts of the play may simply not have been written at the time the working papers were produced.

One of the most problematic aspects of the text is the revisers' treatment of three characters' names. In Marston's original draft, Isabella's second lover was named Guido, Thais's husband was Rogero, and the bawdy, satirical commentator was Mizaldus. Barksted and Machin, however, swapped the names around: Marston's 'Rogero' became Mizaldus (they seem also to have flirted with the idea of naming him Mendosa), 'Guido' became Rogero, and 'Mizaldus' in turn became Guido. Consequently Q calls these characters by different names in different parts of the play, corresponding to different sections of the underlying copy. Finally the person preparing the tangle

---

[1] It is not universally accepted that the play was Marston's last work for the theatre. Michael Scott has suggested that it was begun and abandoned at a much earlier stage of his career: 'Marston's Early Contribution to *The Insatiate Countess*', *Notes and Queries*, 222 (1977), 116–17.

of papers for the press cast a further patina of obscurity over the text with an incomplete attempt to restore the original names intended by Marston and featured in the opening scene.

An editor has a straight choice between the names originally intended by Marston and those adopted in the revision by Barksted and Machin—to retain Q's confusions simply will not do. Melchiori chose Marston, on the reasoning that it required fewer alterations to the Q readings. However, Q is not an authentic representation of *The Insatiate Countess* as it was eventually seen on the Jacobean stage: once it is recognized as an unsatisfactory, intermediate state of the play, Melchiori's textually conservative argument loses its potency. To privilege the intentions of Marston, who left the play unfinished, over those of the men finally responsible for preparing it for the theatre, is to create a text which never existed—unless you believe, as neither I nor Melchiori do, that Q's incomplete reimposition of Marston's names represents the revisers' second thoughts or the work of some theatre functionary. Accordingly, I have systematically (and, for reasons of space, silently) adopted Barksted and Machin's choice of names.

This edition also departs from scholarly tradition in attributing the play primarily to Barksted and Machin rather than to Marston. The authorship was evidently the subject of controversy in the early seventeenth century, when concerted efforts were made to obliterate evidence of Marston's connection with the play, or at least with the version that appeared in print. Three of the eight surviving copies of Q1 have his name snipped out of the title-page, while a fourth has a cancel title-page naming Machin and 'William Bacster' as the authors; Q2, apparently an edition with a small print-run undertaken to avoid legal action rather than for profit, studiously avoids naming any author on its title-page; and as late as the 1630s, Q3 again had to remove a title-page naming Marston and substitute a cancel which survives in one of the extant copies and which gives 'Barksteed' as the sole author. The play was not included in the collected edition of Marston's *Tragedies and Comedies* which appeared in 1633. Whatever circumstances lie behind this bibliographical evidence, it seems clear that someone with an interest in the play either wanted the names of Barksted and Machin to appear on the title-page, or (more probably) wanted the name of Marston not to; it further seems likely that the play was presented at the Whitefriars as the work of these two dramatists and not that of John Marston.

With this play, conventional editorial techniques cannot hope to produce a version of the text which corresponds with the finished play that was staged in the early seventeenth century. In this edition I have tried at least to take it a little of the way. I hope that anyone using the edition with a view to producing the play will not feel inhibited from going further: it is, as John Arden's fictitious theatre director Jack Pogmoor puts it, 'a corrupt text that craves clever adapting'.[2]

The Maid's Tragedy first appeared in print in 1619. A second edition followed in 1622, and the play was one of a core group of 'Beaumont and Fletcher' texts which remained popular through the seventeenth century: it appeared in seven more Quarto editions before 1700, as well as in the second Beaumont and Fletcher Folio of 1679. However, only the first two Quartos have any textual authority. Each presents a substantively different version of the play: Q2 contains passages amounting to about 80 lines which are not present in Q1, and Q1 contains a few shorter passages missing from Q2; there are also numerous minor verbal variants. All editors agree that Q2 offers, in broad terms, the better text: it was printed from a copy of Q1 annotated with reference to a manuscript, possibly in Beaumont's hand. It is further agreed that a different manuscript was the copy for Q1. The editorial problem is to identify the nature and relationship of these two underlying manuscripts.

This edition is based on the new hypothesis that Q1 was an unauthorized edition, printed from a manuscript which was probably a hurried transcript of an illicitly acquired prompt-book, and that Q2 is a non-theatrical text derived from a revision, possibly by Beaumont, of the dramatists' foul papers. This analysis, presented in detail elsewhere, turns on two points.[3] First, some passages present in Q2 but not in Q1 seem to have been censorship cuts and to be attributable to Buc: the type of material removed is similar to passages he deleted from the manuscript of *The Maiden's Tragedy* (see below). It follows that Q1 cannot derive from an early draft, as editors used to believe, and that Q2 cannot be a theatrical version, since it includes the censored passages. However, the very rough, almost paraphrased nature of the Q1 text is plainly inferior to that of Q2; this was evident to the original publisher, Francis Constable, who must have considered it worth the expense and trouble of procuring a new text for the second

[2] John Arden, *Jack Juggler and the Emperor's Whore* (1995), 556.
[3] Martin Wiggins, '*The Maid's Tragedy* Q1 Reconsidered', forthcoming.

edition. Q1 can hardly be the play as it was staged by the King's Men; but that version could easily have been corrupted through an inadequate transcript of the kind which also lies behind the first Quarto of another Beaumont and Fletcher play, *Philaster*, produced the following year by the same printer, Nicholas Okes, and again replaced by a superior second edition in 1622.

None of the Q2-only passages are essential for the play's narrative or its practical staging, and a number of them cannot convincingly be identified as censorship cuts. Their absence from Q1 may be explained in three ways: omission, whether inadvertent or deliberate, by the transcriber; theatrical cutting by the King's Men; or subsequent authorial revision. At least one passage (printed here as Additional Passage C) seems clearly to be an insertion into an already existing scene, and there is also some indication of revision at work in the masque (see note to 1.2.230–2). If so, then someone must at some point have produced a second version of the play (and, if it was indeed Beaumont, this must have been before 1616, when he died); he must have worked with reference to a copy, probably foul papers, which retained intact the material cut by the acting company and the censor; and the revision must have been done for literary rather than theatrical purposes.

If this hypothesis is correct, Q1 represents the overall shape of the play as it was originally performed, but suffers from extensive corruption in the actual words. My aim has been to prefer Q2 readings over Q1 readings where they correct errors by the Q1 transcriber or compositor, and where they restore censorship cuts; but to prefer Q1 readings over Q2 readings where the latter seem to represent compositorial errors, material cut by the King's Men for theatrical reasons, or changes made in revision. In general, beeause Q1 is the more corrupt and more prone to error of the two texts, Q2 readings have been adopted where there seemed no positive case for preferring Q1— though admittedly it is difficult to distinguish between corrections and revisions at the level of single words. Five substantial additions in Q2 are printed at the end of the text as Additional Passages, and are cued in the notes. A supplementary appendix records instances where I have adopted Q1 readings and not implemented Q1 cuts.

I am especially indebted to the work of the following modern editors of the play: Howard B. Norland (Regents Renaissance Drama, 1968); Andrew Gurr (Fountainwell Drama Texts, 1969); Robert Kean Turner (in *The Dramatic Works in the Beaumont and Fletcher Canon*, vol. ii, gen. ed. Fredson Bowers, 1970); and T. W. Craik (Revels Plays, 1988).

The Maiden's Tragedy survives in a single manuscript, which is now held in the British Museum and catalogued as Lansdowne MS 807. It was originally the property of the King's Men, and may have been one of the plays which the company sold to the printer Humphrey Moseley after the theatres were closed in 1642; in 1653, Moseley entered it in the Stationers' Register, but did not publish an edition. The play was first printed in 1824, but only the manuscript has any textual authority.

The manuscript appears to be a scribal copy of the text which has been marked up for use as a prompt-book. Accordingly, it contains several strata of textual revision and adaptation: there is the original state of the text as transcribed from, presumably, the author's manuscript; there are minor additions and deletions in at least four different hands, identified by W. W. Greg (who edited a diplomatic transcript for the Malone Society in 1910) as the scribe, a 'literary corrector', a 'playhouse reviser', and Sir George Buc; six longer passages appear on five inserted slips of paper, and there are also five substantial deletions.[4] The difficulty for the editor is that the beginning and end of the process can be identified, but not the various interim stages of revision. Either one can remove all the changes imposed on the manuscript (except for the scribe's mechanical corrections of his own errors), to reconstruct the original state of the text as the author delivered it to the theatre; or one can implement all of those changes to produce the state of the text as it was eventually performed. What one cannot do with any confidence is identify any intermediate state, because there is no certain way of knowing the sequence in which the various alterations were made.

The play's first modernized and annotated edition appeared in 1978 in the Revels Plays series. Its editor, Anne Lancashire, evidently worked on the principle that more is better. She chose to edit 'backwards' to the authorial text rather than 'forward' to the theatrical one, but also incorporated the additions. The problem with this procedure is that it ignores the historical dimension of the text's development, a development which entailed making deletions as well as additions. Lancashire's text includes every element of the play available in the manuscript, except in cases of substitution where that would obviously be impossible; but some of these elements would almost certainly not

---

[4] A tentative case has been made for identifying Shakespeare (in his capacity as the company's in-house dramatist) as the author of the additions: Eric Rasmussen, 'Shakespeare's Hand in *The Second Maiden's Tragedy*', *Shakespeare Quarterly*, 40 (1989), 1–27.

have coincided at any stage of the play's transformation from an authorial to a theatrical text. In other words, the Revels edition reconstructs a version of the text which probably never existed.

In contrast, this edition attempts to edit the play 'forward' towards a theatrical text, accepting many of the manuscript's alterations, additions, and deletions. This includes five major cuts, which are printed as additional passages, and a number of shorter ones, which are mentioned in the notes. Alterations and cuts attributable to the censor, however, have been undone. The notes include some comments on the process of revision; other important variants, attributable to both revision and censorship, are listed in a supplementary appendix.

The inherent problem is, of course, that the identification of censorship is to some degree a subjective matter. Where material is substituted for the original, Buc's handwriting is identifiable, but even without his spoor it is possible to discern some patterns of likely censorship in the manuscript's many deletions. Evidently Buc considered the play politically sensitive: many of the alterations tone down or remove altogether the play's criticisms of corrupt courtiers and of lustful kings, and its concern with tyrannicide. The final scene, in which the Tyrant is poisoned by Govianus, was especially heavily cut, reducing Govianus' gloating over his action and eradicating altogether the nobles' plot to depose the Tyrant on their own account. This brings the play into line with contemporary conservative opinion on tyrannicide, whereby the right of redress against a usurper was confined to the rightful monarch alone; in the censored version there is no suggestion that courtiers are justified in rebellion even against a usurper.

This edition retains only one textual detail which is certainly attributable to Sir George Buc: the title. The manuscript bore no title when it was submitted to him for censorship late in October 1611, as he noted in licensing it for performance: 'This second *Maiden's Tragedy* (for it hath no name inscribed) may, with the reformations, be acted publicly.' Buc was, of course, remembering *The Maid's Tragedy*, which he had recently licensed for the same company, though Middleton's play has no narrative connection with Beaumont and Fletcher's. The association seems to have stuck, for when the manuscript later came into Moseley's possession, he entered it in the Stationers' Register as '*The Maid's Tragedy, 2nd Part*'.

Until recently, the play has been known to scholars, including the Revels and Malone Society editors, as *The Second Maiden's Tragedy*, following the title inscribed on the last leaf of the manuscript, probably in the late seventeenth century. As a title, however, this has scarcely more authority than the conjectural ascriptions to Thomas Goffe, George Chapman, and William Shakespeare which were made by the same hand. The Lady is not a 'second maiden'; as used by Buc, the adjective refers to the play as a whole. It has come to be known as *The Second Maiden's Tragedy*, then, through a misunderstanding: Buc meant to call it *The Maiden's Tragedy*. Even this is inauthoritative, of course, and the play's most recent editor, in the Oxford edition of Middleton's *Complete Works*, chose to rename it *The Lady's Tragedy*. In contrast, I have retained Buc's title because, though it too is an invention, it is at least one which was assigned by a careful and conscientious reader of the play at a time close to its composition.

The Tragedy of Valentinian first appeared in print in the first Folio edition of the *Comedies and Tragedies* of Francis Beaumont and John Fletcher, published by Humphrey Moseley in 1647. It is by far the least textually complex of the plays in this volume. The Folio is the only authoritative early edition, and is accordingly the control-text. The play later appeared in the enlarged second Folio of 1679, which introduced a number of emendations. The most important and scholarly of the subsequent editions is that of Robert K. Turner, jun., in volume iv of *The Dramatic Works in the Beaumont and Fletcher Canon*, gen. ed. Fredson Bowers (1979), to which I am especially indebted.

The copy for the Folio text was probably a scribal transcript of authorial papers. The printer, Susan Islip, seems to have done a reasonably accurate job, although on two occasions, one of her two compositors (the one designated 'B' by Turner) exercised minor censorship by substituting long ruled lines for words—apparently 'Pox' (4.4.109) and 'damnèd' (5.2.63)—which were presumably deemed offensive; the words are duly restored in this edition.

Seventeenth-century musical settings survive for three of the songs: 'Now the lusty spring' (2.5.5–24); 'Care-charming sleep' (5.2.13–22); and 'God Lyaeus' (5.8.37–47). (Music for a fourth, 'Hear ye ladies', 2.5.25–44, appeared on the now missing page xix of the incomplete New York Public Library manuscript Drexel 4175.) 'Now the lusty spring' and 'God Lyaeus' were set by John Wilson (1595–1674), who worked for the King's Men from the 1610s until 1634, and later became Professor of Music at Oxford in 1656; the settings appear in Edinburgh University MS Dc.I.69, pp. 76 and 148 respectively, and were also published (in arrangements for three voices) in Wilson's *Cheerfull Ayres or Ballads* (1660). 'Care-charming sleep' was especially popular, and two different settings survive. One was composed by Robert Johnson, musician to King James I, and was probably used in the original production; Johnson also provided music for productions of *Macbeth*, *The Winter's Tale*, and *The Tempest*. This version appears in three different manuscript collections: (*a*) London: British Library, Add. MS 11608 fos. 16ᵛ–17; (*b*) Oxford: Bodleian Library, MS Don. c. 57 fo. 19ᵛ; (*c*) Cambridge: Fitzwilliam Museum, MS 52 D. 25, fo. 109ᵛ. (The other, anonymous setting appears in Oxford: Christ Church MS 87 fos. 5ᵛ–6.) The lyrics given with each of these settings contain a number of textual variants, some of which are evidently revisions introduced in circulation (e.g. 'Care-charming sleep' is made applicable to non-royal listeners by the substitution of 'wight' for 'prince' in line 15); others, however, provide necessary emendations to F. I have assumed that the settings by Wilson and Johnson, both of them associated with the King's Men, were those used in the original production; in choosing between F and MS readings, I have accordingly been guided by the phrasing of the music.

SELECT BIBLIOGRAPHY

ACADEMIC studies dealing in general terms with English Renaissance drama's treatment of sexuality are of varying merit and comprehensibility. Especially useful volumes include Mary Beth Rose, *The Expense of Spirit* (1988) and Carole Levin and Karen Robertson (eds.), *Sexuality and Politics in Renaissance Drama* (1991), though neither deals directly with any of the plays in this collection. *The Maid's Tragedy* (as a 'tragedy of false romantic love') and *The Maiden's Tragedy* (as a 'tragedy of courtly love') are among the wide range of plays covered by Leonora Leet Brodwin in her study of *Elizabethan Love Tragedy* (1971). David Farley-Hills has no brief for sex in *Jacobean Drama* (1988), but the book offers a readable introductory survey including short accounts of *The Maid's Tragedy*, *The Maiden's Tragedy*, and *Valentinian*.

The Insatiate Countess has attracted relatively little critical attention, perhaps partly because of a dismissive paragraph by T. S. Eliot in his essay on John Marston (*Selected Essays*, 3rd edn., 1951, 226). An illuminating account of the play's relationship with its sources is scattered through Max Bluestone's *From Story to Stage* (1974), and Marliss C. Desens discusses the sub-plot in *The Bed-Trick in English Renaissance Drama* (1994). The play is also briefly noticed in four books on Marston: Anthony Caputi, *John Marston, Satirist* (1961); Philip J. Finkelpearl, *John Marston of the Middle Temple* (1969); Michael Scott, *John Marston's Plays* (1978); and George L. Geckle, *John Marston's Drama* (1980). Information about the other two authors, Barksted and Machin, may be found in Giorgio Melchiori's 'Attore drammaturgo e repertorio in una compagnia di ragazzi', *Le forme del teatro*, vol. ii (1981), 101–37. It should be noted that all these books use a different recension of the text from the one adopted in this edition, and that consequently the names of some characters are interchanged.

Clifford Leech's *The John Fletcher Plays* (1962) remains an accessible general introduction to the 'Beaumont and Fletcher' canon; other rewarding studies include Philip J. Finkelpearl's 'Beaumont, Fletcher, and "Beaumont and Fletcher": Some Distinctions', *English Literary Renaissance*, 1 (1971), 144–64, and Kathleen McLuskie's feminist analysis in *Renaissance Dramatists* (1989). Specialized scholarly interest in the plays has concentrated on two issues: their politics and their imaginative engagement with Shakespeare. Similarities between the works of Shakespeare and of Beaumont and Fletcher are painstakingly if unimaginatively documented by Daniel Morley McKeithan in *The Debt to Shakespeare in the Beaumont-and-Fletcher Plays* (1938). Lawrence Bergmann Wallis offers a fuller study of the plays' literary and cultural origins in *Fletcher, Beaumont and Company: Entertainers to the Jacobean Gentry* (1947), while H. Neville Davies, 'Beaumont and Fletcher's *Hamlet*' in Kenneth Muir et al. (eds.), *Shakespeare, Man of the Theater* (1983), 173–81, and Marco Mincoff, 'Shakespeare, Fletcher and Baroque Tragedy', *Shakespeare Survey*, 20 (1967), 1–15, discuss the Shakespearian presence in *The Maid's Tragedy* and *Valentinian* respectively.

One of the limitations of Wallis's book is its underestimation of the plays' seriousness and political sophistication. A classic early statement of their engagement with the seventeenth-century crisis of absolutism appears in John F. Danby's *Poets on Fortune's Hill* (1952), reprinted as *Elizabethan and Jacobean Poets* (1964). More recent writers on the subject include Ronald Broude, 'Divine Right and Divine Retribution in Beaumont and Fletcher's *The Maid's Tragedy*', in W. R. Elton and William B. Long (eds.), *Shakespeare and Dramatic Tradition* (1989), 246–63; Robert Y. Turner, 'Responses to Tyranny in John Fletcher's Plays', *Medieval and Renaissance Drama in England*, 4 (1989), 123–41; Philip J. Finkelpearl, *Court and Country Politics in the Plays of Beaumont and Fletcher* (1990); and Gordon McMullan, *The Politics of Unease in the Plays of John Fletcher* (1994). Robert D. Hume's '*The Maid's Tragedy* and Censorship in the Restoration Theatre', *Philological Quarterly*, 61 (1982), 484–90, demonstrates that play's continuing political relevance later in the century.

Other important studies of *The Maid's Tragedy* include Robert Ornstein's *The Moral Vision of Jacobean Tragedy* (1960); Michael Neill's ' "The Simetry, Which Gives a Poem Grace": Masque, Imagery, and the Fancy of *The Maid's Tragedy*', *Renaissance Drama*, NS 3 (1970), 111–35; and William Shullenberger's ' "This for the Most Wronged of Women": A Reappraisal of *The Maid's Tragedy*', *Renaissance Drama*, NS 13 (1982), 131–56. *Valentinian*, too often a target of throwaway abuse, was favoured by W. Bridges-Adams with an enthusiastic account over several pages of his general history of English drama, *The Irresistible Theatre* (1957); the play is also discussed in detail by Marco Mincoff in 'Fletcher's Early Tragedies', *Renaissance Drama*, 7 (1964), 70–94, and by Nancy Cotton Pearse in *John Fletcher's*

Chastity Plays: Mirrors of Modesty (1973). The Restoration adaptation of the play appears in Frank H. Ellis's edition of the Earl of Rochester's *Complete Works* (1994).

Although the manuscript had attracted scholarly interest from the nineteenth century on, critical commentary on *The Maiden's Tragedy* was virtually non-existent when Samuel Schoenbaum published a general account of the play in *Middleton's Tragedies* (1955); major subsequent studies include Richard Levin's exposition of the relationship between the two plots in *The Multiple Plot in English Renaissance Drama* (1971), Anne Lancashire's allegorical reading in '*The Second Maiden's Tragedy*: A Jacobean Saint's Life', *Review of English Studies*, 25 (1974), 267–79, and David M. Bergeron's analysis of the play's thematic exploitation of theatrical self-consciousness in 'Art within *The Second Maiden's Tragedy*', *Medieval and Renaissance Drama in England*, 1 (1984), 173–86. Two important books include discussions of the play's censorship by Sir George Buc: Janet Clare's '*Art Made Tongue-Tied by Authority'*: *Elizabethan and Jacobean Dramatic Censorship* (1990) and Richard Dutton's *Mastering the Revels: The Regulation and Censorship of English Renaissance Drama* (1991). Much of this material is usefully synthesized in Swapan Chakravorty's *Society and Politics in the Plays of Thomas Middleton* (1996).

A CHRONOLOGY OF THE PLAYS

Note: All productions listed took place in London unless otherwise stated.

The Insatiate Countess

1526   Execution in Milan of Bianca Maria, Countess of Challant, the historical original of Isabella (20 October).

1554   Publication of Matteo Bandello's *Novelle*, including an account of the Countess of Challant's life; later translated into French by François Belleforest (1565).

1567   Publication of the second volume of William Painter's *The Palace of Pleasure*, a collection of novellas, containing the story of the Countess (no. 24), translated directly from Belleforest; this was the play's immediate narrative source. The volume also contained the source of the sub-plot (no. 26).

*c.*1575   Birth of John Marston in Oxfordshire.

*c.*1599   Marston began to write for the stage.

1608   Marston wrote a draft of part of the play but abandoned it after his imprisonment on 8 June. (Some scholars date this stage of the composition about eight years earlier.)

*c.*1610   The actor William Barksted and his associate Lewis Machin completed the play for production at the Whitefriars Theatre. Barksted used extensive material from his non-dramatic poems *Myrrha* and *Hiren* (published 1607 and 1611 respectively).

1613   First publication (Q1).

1634   Death of Marston (25 June).

1679   Publication of a loose prose adaptation (with a German setting) in *God's Revenge against the Abominable Sin of Adultery*.

The Maid's Tragedy

1579   Birth of John Fletcher in Rye, Sussex (December).

*c.*1584   Birth of Francis Beaumont in Leicestershire.

*c.*1606   Beaumont and Fletcher began to collaborate as dramatists.

1611   The first production by the King's Men (before 31 October), at the Blackfriars Theatre; the production probably also played at the Globe. The cast included John Lowin (Melantius). In the wedding masque, the company may have been able to use sea-gods' costumes originally designed for Samuel Daniel's court masque, *Tethys' Festival* (5 June 1610). The play remained in the company's repertory until the 1630s, and was performed at court in 1613, 1630, and 1636. In later performances the cast included Stephen Hammerton (Amintor).

*c.*1613   Beaumont married the heiress Ursula Isley and gave up writing for the stage.

1616   Death of Beaumont (6 March).

1619   First publication (Q1).

1622   Publication of a different version (Q2).

1625   Death of Fletcher (August).

1660   Production by the King's Company at the Vere Street Theatre. The play remained in the company's repertory through the decade (playing at Drury Lane after 1662). The cast in this period included Charles Hart (Amintor), Michael Mohun (Melantius), and Elizabeth Boutell (Aspatia); William Wintershall played both Evadne (in 1660) and the King (in later performances), and subsequent Evadnes were the sisters Anne Marshall and Rebecca Marshall.

1672   Publication of *The Testy Lord*, a 'droll' (short comic play) adapted from scenes featuring Calianax, especially 4.2, and said to have been illicitly performed during the 1650s.

*c.*1680–3 The play may have been banned by the authorities during the exclusion crisis.

1687   Production by the United Company.

1690   Posthumous publication of two alternative fifth acts by Edmund Waller, each with a happy ending. (These may have been written as early as *c.*1664.)

1698   Production by Thomas Betterton's company; Betterton may have played Melantius.

1704   Production at Drury Lane with additional dancing; the masque was performed to music by Henry Purcell.

1706–10 In repertory at the Queen's Theatre; the cast included Thomas Betterton (Melantius), Robert Wilks (Amintor), Elizabeth Barry (Evadne), John Mills (the King), and, in some performances, Anne Bracegirdle (Aspatia).

1715–28 In repertory at Drury Lane; the cast included Barton Booth

(Melantius), Robert Wilks (Amintor), Mary Porter (Evadne), and John Mills (the King).

1729-33   In repertory at Lincoln's Inn Fields and (in 1733) Covent Garden; the cast included James Quin (Melantius) and Lacy Ryan (Amintor).

1735   Production at Drury Lane; the cast included James Quin (Melantius), Sarah Thurmond (Evadne), and William Mills (the King).

1744-5   Production at Covent Garden; the cast included James Quin (Melantius) and Hannah Pritchard (Evadne).

1746   French adaptation by P. A. de la Place, *La Pucelle* (The Maid).

1765   German translation by H. W. von Gerstenberg, *Die Braut* (The Bride).

1831   Adaptation, *The Bridal*, by W. C. Macready and James Sheridan Knowles (published 1837). This version, a vehicle for Macready's own performance as Melantius, was produced at Dublin in 1834 (with Laura Allison as Aspatia), at the Haymarket Theatre, London in 1837 (with Mary Huddart as Evadne, Edward Elton as Amintor, and Harriet Taylor as Aspatia), and in America in 1843-4 (with Charlotte Cushman).

1844-5   Production of *The Bridal* at Sadler's Wells Theatre; the cast included Samuel Phelps (Melantius), Mary Warner, née Huddart (Evadne), Fanny Cooper (Aspatia), and Henry Marston (Amintor). The play was in the theatre's repertory in seven subsequent seasons.

1873   Production of *The Bridal* at the Standard Theatre; the cast included William Creswick (Melantius), Mrs Charles Viner (Evadne), Charles Creswick (Amintor), and George Hamilton (the King).

1875   Production of *The Bridal* at Holborn Amphitheatre; the cast included Mr Pennington (Melantius), Mr Moxon (Amintor), and Miss Leighton (Evadne).

1904   Production at the Royalty Theatre, produced by Philip Carr; the cast included W. H. Kemble (Melantius) and Dora Hole (Evadne).

1908   Production at the Court Theatre, produced by Clarence Derwent; the cast included W. Edwyn Holloway (Amintor), H. A. Saintsbury (Melantius), and Esmé Beringer (Evadne).

1921   Production by the Phoenix Society at the Lyric, Hammersmith, produced by Allan Wade; the cast included Sybil Thorndike (Evadne), Isabel Jeans (Aspatia), Ion Swinley (Amintor), and George Skillan (Melantius).

1925   Production at the Scala Theatre, produced by Frank Cellier; the cast included Edith Evans (Evadne), Baliol Holloway (Melantius), George Zucco (the King), Ion Swinley (Amintor), and Rose Quong (Aspatia).

1954   BBC radio production by Peter Watts (4 April); the cast included Maxine Audley (Evadne), Valentine Dyall (Melantius), and Baliol Holloway (Calianax).

1962   BBC radio production by R. D. Smith (23 November); the cast included Nicolette Bernard (Evadne), Ralph Truman (Melantius), and Anthony Jacobs (the King).

1964   Production at the Mermaid Theatre, directed by Bernard Miles; the cast included Irene Hamilton (Evadne), Ronald Hines (Melantius), Peter Halliday (the King), and David Bird (Calianax).

1972   Production at the Equity Library Theatre, New York.

1979   Production at the Citizen's Theatre, Glasgow, directed by Philip Prowse; the cast included Julia Blalock (Evadne), Mark Lewis (Melantius), and Pierce Brosnan (the King).

1980   Production by the RSC at the Other Place, Stratford-upon-Avon, directed by Barry Kyle; the cast included Sinead Cusack (Evadne), Rob Edwards (Amintor), John Carlisle (the King), and Tom Wilkinson (Melantius).

1985   Production at the Guildhall School of Drama, directed by Peter Clough; the cast included Caroline Johnson (Evadne).

1997   Production at the reconstructed Globe Theatre, directed by Lucy Bailey; the cast included Patrick Godfrey (Calianax), Nicholas Le Prevost (the King), and Geraldine Alexander (Evadne).

The Maiden's Tragedy

1580   Birth of Thomas Middleton, London (April).

1602   Middleton began to write for the stage.

1605   Publication at Madrid of *Don Quixote* by Miguel de Cervantes, containing the story of the 'curious impertinent' which is the source of the play's sub-plot; the story was later translated into French in 1608 and the entire work into English *c.*1607 (but not published until 1612).

1610   Arabella Stuart, a potential claimant to the thrones of

England and Scotland, secretly married William Seymour, also of royal blood, on 21 June; they were imprisoned on 8 July. The case may have influenced Middleton's conception of the main plot.

1611   The first production by the King's Men (after 31 October), probably at the Blackfriars Theatre; the cast included Richard Robinson (the Lady) and Robert Gough (Memphonius).

1627   Death of Middleton (July).

1642   Closure of the London theatres (2 September); at some time in the next eleven years the publisher Humphrey Moseley acquired the manuscript of the play, probably by direct purchase from the King's Men.

1807   Manuscript bought by the British Museum.

1824   First published edition, under the title *The Second Maiden's Tragedy*.

1829   German translation by Dorothea Tieck and Wolf von Baudissin, *Der Tyrann, oder die zweite Jungfrauen-Tragoedie* (*The Tyrant, or The Second Maiden's Tragedy*).

1984   Production (under the title *The Tyrant*) at the Upstream Theatre, directed by Andrew Wickes; the cast included Siobhan Willis (the Lady), Clive Simpson (the Tyrant), and Christopher Webber (Govianus).

1994   Production (under the title *The Lady's Tragedy*) at the Hen and Chicken, Bristol, directed by Alan Coveney; the cast included Miriam Cooper (the Lady), David Forrester (Govianus), and Coveney himself (the Tyrant).

The Tragedy of Valentinian

AD 455   Murder of the Roman Emperor Valentinian III after he had contrived the assassination of his general Aëtius and raped Lucina, wife of Petronius Maximus. Maximus succeeded to the emperorship but was himself murdered a few months later.

1579   Birth of John Fletcher.

1610   Publication at Paris of the 'Histoire d'Eudoxe, Valentinian, et Ursace', the play's main narrative source, in Part 2 of Honoré D'Urfé's *L'Astrée* (February).

c.1614   The first production by the King's Men at the Globe and Blackfriars Theatres (before 16 December); the cast included Richard Burbage, Henry Condell, John Lowin, William Ostler, and John Underwood.

1625   Death of Fletcher.

1641   The play was in the current repertory of the King's Men.

1647   First publication, in the Beaumont and Fletcher Folio.

1669   The play was assigned to the King's Company for performance.

1670s Adaptation by John Wilmot, Earl of Rochester (published 1685), apparently performed by the King's Company; the cast included Charles Hart (Valentinian), Rebecca Marshall (Lucina), Michael Mohun (Aëtius), and William Wintershall (Maximus),

1684   Rochester's adaptation was performed at court by the United Company (11 February); the cast included Elizabeth Barry (Lucina), Cardell Goodman (Valentinian), Thomas Betterton (Aëtius), Edward Kynaston (Maximus), and Phillip Griffin (Pontius). The adaptation continued in the company's repertory until the early 1690s, with George Powell in the title role.

1704   Production of Rochester's adaptation at Lincoln's Inn Fields; the cast included Elizabeth Barry (Lucina).

1706   Production at Drury Lane; the cast included Robert Wilks (Valentinian) and Anne Oldfield (Lucina). Another production at the Queen's Theatre featured Elizabeth Barry (Lucina), Thomas Betterton (Aëtius), Barton Booth (Maximus), and John Verbruggen (Valentinian).

1710–11 Production of Rochester's adaptation at Drury Lane; the cast included George Powell (Valentinian), Barton Booth (Maximus), Theophilus Keene (Aëtius), and Lucretia Bradshaw (Lucina).

1715   Production of Rochester's adaptation at Lincoln's Inn Fields; the cast included John Thurmond (Valentinian), Jane Rogers (Lucina), and Theophilus Keene (Aëtius).

1959   BBC radio production by Raymond Raikes (5 August); the cast included Anthony Jacobs (Valentinian), Howard Marion Crawford (Maximus), Francis de Wolff (Aëtius), Jack May (Pontius), and Sylvia Coleridge (Ardelia).

	included Richard Burbage, Henry Condell, John Lowin, William Ostler, and John Underwood.
1625	Death of Fletcher.
1642	The play was in the current repertory of the King's Men.
1647	First publication, in the Beaumont and Fletcher Folio.
1660	The play was assigned to the King's Company for performance.
1675	Adaptation by John Wilmot, Earl of Rochester (published 1685), apparently performed by the King's Company; the cast included Charles Hart (Valentinian), Rebecca Marshall (Lucina), Michael Mohun (Aecius), and William Wintershall (Maximus).
1684	Rochester's adaptation was performed at court by the United Company (11 February); the cast included Elizabeth Barry (Lucina), Cardell Goodman (Valentinian), Thomas Betterton (Aecius), Edward Kynaston (Maximus), and Philip Griffin (Pontius). The adaptation continued in the company's repertory until the early 1690s, with George Powell in the title role.
1704	Production of Rochester's adaptation at Lincoln's Inn Fields; the cast included Elizabeth Barry (Lucina).
1706	Production at Drury Lane; the cast included Robert Wilks (Valentinian) and Anne Oldfield (Lucina). Another production at the Queen's Theatre featured Elizabeth Barry (Lucina), Thomas Betterton (Aecius), Barton Booth (Maximus), and John Verbruggen (Valentinian).
1710-11	Production of Rochester's adaptation at Drury Lane; the cast included George Powell (Valentinian), Barton Booth (Maximus), Theophilus Keene (Aecius), and Lacerta Bradshaw (Lucina).
1715	Production of Rochester's adaptation at Lincoln's Inn Fields; the cast included John Thurmond (Valentinian), Jane Rogers (Lucina), and Theophilus Keene (Aecius).
1930	BBC radio production by Raymond Raikes (5 August); the cast included Anthony Jacobs (Valentinian), Howard Marion Crawford (Maximus), Francis de Wolff (Aecius), Jack May (Pontius), and Sylvia Coleridge (Ardelia).

THE INSATIATE COUNTESS

WILLIAM BARKSTED *and* **LEWIS MACHIN**
from a draft by **JOHN MARSTON**

THE PERSONS OF THE PLAY

Isabella, Countess of Swevia°
Anna, her maidservant
Her Page

Roberto, Count of Cyprus, later Isabella's second husband
His Servants
Lord Cardinal, a guest at his wedding

Rogero, Count of Arsena and Massino, later Isabella's lover
His Servants
A Doctor

Gniaca, Count of Gazia, Rogero's friend, later Isabella's lover
His Page
His Attendants

Signor Claridiana,° an apothecary's son
Abigail,° his wife
Their Maidservant
Guests at their wedding

Signor Mizaldus, a Jew°
Thais,° his wife
Their Maidservant
Guests at their wedding

Lady Lentulus,° a widow
Mendosa° Foscari, Amago's nephew
His Page

Signor Guido, a friend of Rogero and Claridiana

Amago, Duke of Venice
The Captain of the Watch at Venice
Officers of the Watch under his command
Venetian Senators
A Friar

Don Sago,° a Spanish colonel, later Isabella's lover
His Lieutenant
His Soldiers

The Duke of Medina, ruler of Pavia
The Captain of the guard at Pavia
His Soldiers
A Cardinal, present at Isabella's execution
A Messenger
An Executioner

1.1

Isabella, the Countess of Swevia is discovered,° dressed in
mourning clothes and sitting at a table covered with black, on
which stand two black tapers lighted. Enter Roberto, Count of
Cyprus, Rogero, Count of Arsena, and Signor Guido

GUIDO What should we do in this Countess's dark hole?° She's sul-
lenly retired. As the turtle,° every day has been a black day with her
since her husband died, and what should we unruly members° make
here?

ROGERO As melancholy night masks up heaven's face,   5
So doth the evening star present herself
Unto the careful shepherd's gladsome eyes,
By which unto the fold he leads his flock.

GUIDO Zounds,° what a sheepish beginning is here! 'Tis said true,
'Love is simple',° and it may well hold, and thou art a simple   10
lover.

ROBERTO See how yon star-like beauty in a cloud°
Illumines darkness and beguiles the moon
Of all her glory in the firmament.

GUIDO Well said, Man i' the Moon.° Was ever such astronomers?   15
Marry, I fear none of these will fall into the right ditch.°

ROBERTO Madam.

ISABELLA Ha! Anna, what, are my doors unbarred?

GUIDO I'll assure you the way into your ladyship° is open.

ROBERTO And God defend that any profane hand   20
Should offer sacrilege to such a saint.
    [*He kisses her*]
Lovely Isabella, by this duteous kiss
(That draws part of my soul along with it),°
Had I but thought my rude intrusion
Had waked the dove-like spleen harboured within you,°   25
Life and my first-born should not satisfy
Such a transgression, worthy of a check.°
But that immortals wink at my offence
Makes me presume more boldly: I am come°
To raise you from this so infernal sadness.   30

ISABELLA My lord of Cyprus, do not mock my grief:

Tears are as due a tribute to the dead
As fear to God and duty unto kings,
Love to the just or hate unto the wicked.
ROBERTO Surcease.   35
　Believe it is a wrong unto the gods:
　They sail against the wind that wail the dead,
　And since his heart hath wrestled with death's pangs
　(From whose stern cave none tracts a backward path),
　Leave to lament this necessary change   40
　And thank the gods, for they can give as good.
ISABELLA [aside] I wail his loss! Sink him ten cubits deeper,°
　I may not fear his resurrection.°
　I will be sworn upon the holy writ,
　I mourn thus fervent 'cause he died no sooner.   45
　He buried me alive,
　And mewed me up like Cretan Daedalus,
　And with wall-eyed jealousy kept me from hope
　Of any waxen wings to fly to pleasure.°
　But now his soul her Argus eyes hath closed,°   50
　And I am free as air. You of my sex,
　In the first flow of youth use you the sweets
　Due to your proper beauties, ere the ebb°
　And long wane of unwelcome change shall come.
　Fair women play: she's chaste whom none will have.°   55
　Here is a man of a most mild aspect,°
　Temperate, effeminate, and worthy love,°
　One that with burning ardour hath pursued me.
　A donative he hath of every god:
　Apollo gave him locks, Jove his high front,   60
　The god of eloquence his flowing speech.
　The feminine deities strewed all their bounties
　And beauty on his face: that eye was Juno's,
　Those lips were hers that won the golden ball,°
　That virgin blush Diana's: here they meet,°   65
　As in a sacred synod. [Aloud] My lords, I must entreat°
　A while your wished forbearance.
ALL We obey you, lady.
　　　　Exeunt Rogero and Guido. [Roberto makes to go, but Isabella
　　　　stops him]
ISABELLA My lord, with you I have some conference.

I pray, my lord, do you woo every lady   70
In this phrase you do me?

ROBERTO   Fairest, till now
Love was an infant in my oratory.

ISABELLA   And kiss thus too?°
    [*She kisses him*]

ROBERTO I ne'er was so kissed. Leave thus to please,
Flames into flames, seas thou pour'st into seas.°

ISABELLA Pray frown, my lord, let me see how many wives   75
You'll have. Heigh-ho, you'll bury me, I see.°

ROBERTO In the swan's down, and tomb thee in mine arms.

ISABELLA Then folks shall pray in vain to send me rest.°
Away, you're such another meddling lord.

ROBERTO By heaven, my love's as chaste as thou art fair,   80
And both exceed comparison. By this kiss
(That crowns me monarch of another world°
Superior to the first), fair, thou shalt see,°
As unto heaven, my love so unto thee.°
    [*He kisses her*]

ISABELLA Alas, poor creatures, when we are once o' the falling
        hand°   85
A man may easily come over us.°
It is as hard for us to hide our love
As to shut sin from the creator's eyes.
I' faith, my lord, I had a month's mind unto you,°
As tedious as a full-riped maidenhead.°   90
And, Count of Cyprus, think my love as pure
As the first opening of the blooms in May.
You're Virtue's man. Nay, let me not blush to say so.°
And see, for your sake thus I leave to sorrow.
Begin this subtle conjuration with me,   95
And as this taper, due unto the dead,
I here extinguish, so my late dead lord
I put out ever from my memory,
        She puts out one of the tapers
That his remembrance may not wrong our love,
As bold-faced women when they wed another
Banquet their husbands with their dead loves' heads.°   100

ROBERTO And as I sacrifice this to his ghost,
With this expire all corrupt thoughts of youth,
That same insatiate devil jealousy,

6

And all the sparks that may bring unto flame   105
Hate betwixt man and wife, or breed defame.°
    [*He puts out the other taper.*] *Enter Guido and Rogero*

GUIDO Marry, amen, I say. Madam, are you, that were in for all day,
now come to be in for all night? How now, Count Arsena?

ROGERO Faith, signor, not unlike the condemned malefactor
That hears his judgement openly pronounced.°   110
But I ascribe to fate. Joy swell your love,
Cyprus, and willow grace my drooping crest.°

ROBERTO We do intend our hymeneal rites
With the next rising sun. Count Arsena,
Next to our bride, the welcom'st to our feast.   115
    [*Exeunt Isabella and Roberto. The traverse curtains are drawn
    across the discovery space*°]

ROGERO *Sancta Maria*, what think'st thou of this change?
A player's passion I'll believe hereafter,
And in a tragic scene weep for old Priam
When fell revenging Pyrrhus with supposed
And artificial wounds mangles his breast,°   120
And think it a more worthy act to me
Than trust a female mourning o'er her love.
Nought that is done of woman shall me please,
Nature's step-children, rather her disease.°

GUIDO Learn of a well-composèd epigram   125
A woman's love, and thus 'twas sung to us:
'The tapers that stood on her husband's hearse
Isabel advances to a second bed.
Is it not wondrous strange for to rehearse
She should so soon forget her husband dead   130
One hour? For if the husband's life once fade,
Both love and husband in one grave are laid.'
But we forget ourselves. I am for the marriage
Of Signor Claridiana and the fine Mistress Abigail.

ROGERO I for his arch-foe's wedding, Signor Mizaldus and the spruce 135
Mistress Thais. But see, the solemn rites are ended, and from their
several temples they are come.

GUIDO A quarrel,° on my life.
    *Enter at one door Signor Claridiana, Abigail his wife, the
    Lady Lentulus with rosemary° as from church. At the other
    door° enter Signor Mizaldus and Thais his wife, Mendosa
    Foscari, nephew to the Duke, from the bridal. [Both parties are*

*accompanied by male Wedding Guests.°]   Claridiana and
Mizaldus see one another and draw their swords. Rogero,
Guido, and others step between them*

CLARIDIANA [*to Guido*] Good my lord, detain me not: I will tilt
   at him.°

ROGERO [*to Claridiana*] Remember, sir, this is your wedding day,   140
   And that triumph belongs only to your wife.

MIZALDUS [*to Rogero*] If you be noble, let me cut off his head.

GUIDO° [*to Mizaldus*] Remember, o' the other side, you have a maidenhead of your own to cut off.

MIZALDUS I'll make my marriage day like to the bloody bridal   145
   Alcides by the fiery centaurs had.°

THAIS Husband, dear husband!

MIZALDUS Away with these caterwaulers. Come on, sir.

CLARIDIANA Thou son of a Jew—

ROGERO [*to Thais*] Alas, poor wench, thy husband's circumcised.°   150

CLARIDIANA —Begot when thy father's face was toward the East
   To show that thou wouldst prove a caterpillar.°
   His Messiah shall not save thee from me.
   I'll send thee to him in collops.

ROGERO O fry not in choler so, sir.°   155

MIZALDUS Mountebank with thy pedantical action,°
   Rinatrix, bugle-ox, rhinoceros.°

MENDOSA Gentlemen, I conjure you, by the virtues of men.

MIZALDUS Shall any broken quacksalver's bastard oppose him to me
   in my nuptials? No, but I'll show him better metal° than e'er the   160
   gallimaufry his father used. Thou scum of his melting pots (that
   wert christened in a crusoile with Mercury's water,° to show thou
   wouldst prove a stinging aspis°—for all thou spitt'st is aquafortis,
   and thy breath is a compound of poison's stillatory): if I get within°
   thee, hadst thou the scaly hide of a crocodile (as thou art partly of   165
   his nature), I would leave thee as bare as an anatomy° at the second
   viewing.

CLARIDIANA Thou Jew of the tribe of Gad,° that sure (were there
   none here but thou and I) wouldst teach me the art of breathing;
   thou wouldst run like a dromedary.°   170

MIZALDUS Thou that art the tallest° man of Christendom—when
   thou art alone, if thou dost maintain this to my face, I'll make thee
   skip like an ounce.

MENDOSA Nay, good sir, be you still.

MIZALDUS Let the quacksalver's son be still.   175

8

His father was still, and still, and still again.°

CLARIDIANA By the almighty, I'll study nigromancy but I'll be
    revenged.°

ROGERO Gentlemen, leave these dissensions.
    Signor Mizaldus, you are a man of worth.   180

CLARIDIANA True, all the city points at him for a knave.

ROGERO You are of like reputation, Signor Claridiana.
    The hatred 'twixt your grandsires first began:
    Impute it to the folly of that age.
    These your dissensions may erect a faction   185
    Like to the Capulets and Montagues.°

MENDOSA Put it to equal arbitration, choose your friends;
    The senators will think 'em happy in 't.

MIZALDUS I'll ne'er embrace the smoke of a furnace, the quintessence
    of mineral or simples, or, as I may say more learnedly, nor the spirit   190
    of quicksilver.°

CLARIDIANA Nor I such a centaur, half a man, half an ass, and all
    a Jew.

ROGERO Nay, then, we will be constables, and force a quiet. Gentle-
    men, keep 'em asunder, and help to persuade 'em.   195
        *Exeunt Claridiana, Mizaldus, Rogero, Guido, and the other
        men except Mendosa, who remains with Lady Lentulus,
        Abigail, and Thais*

MENDOSA Well, ladies, your husbands behave 'em as lustily on their
    wedding days as e'er I heard any. [*To Lady Lentulus*] Nay, lady
    widow, you and I must have a falling.° You're of Signor Guido's
    faction,° and I am your vowed enemy, from the bodkin to the
    pincase.° Hark in your ear.   200
        [*Mendosa and Lady Lentulus talk apart*]

ABIGAIL Well, Thais, O you're a cunning carver. We two that any
    time these fourteen years have called sisters, brought and bred
    up together; that have told one another all our wanton dreams,
    talked all night long of young men, and spent many an idle hour;
    fasted upon the stones on Saint Agnes' night° together, practised   205
    all the petulant amorousnesses that delights young maids; yet
    have you concealed not only the marriage but the man. And well
    you might deceive me, for I'll be sworn you never dreamed of him,
    and it stands against all reason you should enjoy him you never
    dreamed of.   210

THAIS Is not all this the same in you? Did you ever manifest your
    sweetheart's nose, that I might nose him by 't? Commended his calf,

9

or his nether lip?—apparent signs that you were in love or wisely
covered it. Have you ever said, 'Such-a-man goes upright' or 'has
a better gait than any of the rest'; as indeed, since he is proved a   215
magnifico, I thought thou wouldst have put it into my hands°
whate'er 't had been.

ABIGAIL Well, wench, we have cross fates: our husbands such invet-
erate foes, and we such entire friends. But the best is, we are neighbours, and our back-arbours may afford visitation freely. Prithee let   220
us maintain our familiarity still, whatsoever thy husband do unto
thee, as I am afraid he will cross it i' the nick.°

THAIS Faith, you little one, if I please him in one thing, he shall please
me in all, that's certain. Who shall I have to keep my counsel if I
miss thee? Who shall teach me to use the bridle when the reins are   225
in mine own hand? What to long for, when to take physic, where to
be melancholy? Why, we two are one another's grounds, without
which would be no music.

ABIGAIL Well said, wench, and the prick-song° we use shall be our
husbands'.   230

THAIS I will long for swine's flesh o' th' first child.

ABIGAIL Wilt 'ou, little Jew? And I to kiss thy husband upon the
least belly-ache.° This will mad 'em.

THAIS I kiss thee, wench, for that, and with it confirm our
friendship.   235

[*Abigail and Thais talk apart*]

MENDOSA By these sweet lips, widow.

LADY LENTULUS Good my lord, learn to swear by rote.°
Your birth and fortune makes my brain suppose
That, like a man heated with wines and lust,
She that is next your object is your mate,°   240
Till the foul water have quenched out the fire.°
You, the Duke's kinsman, tell me I am young,
Fair, rich, and virtuous. I myself will flatter
Myself, till you are gone, that are more fair,
More rich, more virtuous, and more debonair,   245
All which are ladders to an higher reach.°
Who drinks a puddle that may taste a spring,
Who kiss a subject that may hug a king?

MENDOSA Yes, the camel always drinks in puddle-water,°
And as for huggings, read antiquities.   250
Faith, madam, I'll board thee one of these days.°

LADY LENTULUS Ay, but ne'er bed me, my lord. My vow is firm:

10

Since God hath called me to this noble state,
Much to my grief, of virtuous widowhood,
No man shall ever come within my gates.°   255
MENDOSA Wilt thou ram up thy port-hole? O widow, I perceive
    You're ignorant of the lover's legerdemain.
    There's a fellow that by magic will assist
    To murder princes invisible; I can command his spirit.°
    Or what say you to a fine scaling-ladder of ropes?   260
    I can tell you, I am a mad waghalter.
    But by the virtue I see seated in you,
    And by the worthy fame is blazoned of you,
    By little Cupid that is mighty named°
    And can command my looser follies down,   265
    I love, and must enjoy; yet with such limits
    As one that knows enforcèd marriage
    To be the Furies' sister. Think of me.°
ABIGAIL and THAIS Ha ha ha!
MENDOSA How now, lady, does the toy take you, as they say?   270
ABIGAIL No, my lord, nor do we take your toy, as they say. This is a
    child's birth, that must not be delivered before a man, though your
    lordship might be a midwife for your chin.°
MENDOSA Some bawdy riddle, is 't not? You long till 't be night.
THAIS No, my lord, women's longing comes after their marriage   275
    night.° Sister, see you be constant° now.
ABIGAIL Why, dost think I'll make my husband a cuckold? O, here
    they come.
            Enter Guido with Claridiana; at another door, Rogero with
            Mizaldus; Mendosa meets them
MENDOSA Signor Mizaldus, are you yet qualified?
MIZALDUS Yes. Does any man think I'll go like a sheep to the slaugh-   280
    ter? Hands off, my lord, your lordship may chance come under
    my hands. If you do, I shall show myself a citizen, and revenge
    basely.
CLARIDIANA I think if I were receiving the holy sacrament
    His sight would make me gnash my teeth terribly.°   285
    [*Aside, seeing Thais*] But there's the beauty without parallel
    In whom the graces and the virtues meet.
    In her aspect mild honour sits and smiles,
    And who looks there, were it the savage bear,
    But would derive new nature from her eyes?   290
    But to be reconciled simply for him,

11

Were mankind to be lost again, I'd let it,
And a new heap of stones should stock the world.°
In heaven and earth this power beauty hath:
It inflames temp'rance and temp'rates wrath.   295
Whate'er thou art, mine art thou, wise or chaste.
I shall set hard upon thy marriage vow
And write revenge high in thy husband's brow,
In a strange character. [*To Mendosa*] You may begin, sir.°

MENDOSA Signor Claridiana, I hope Signor Mizaldus   300
Thus employed me about a good office.
'Twere worthy Cicero's tongue, a famous oration now;°
Let friendship, that is mutually embracèd of the gods°
And is Jove's usher to each sacred synod
(Without the which he could not reign in heaven),°   305
Quench these hot flames of rage, that else will be
As fire midst your nuptial jollity,
Burning the edge off from your present joy,
And keep you 'wake to terror.

CLARIDIANA I have not yet swallowed the 'rinatrix', nor the 'ono-   310
centaur': the 'rhinoceros' was monstrous.°

ROGERO Sir, be you of the more flexible nature, and confess an
error.

CLARIDIANA I must, the gods of love command,
And that bright star, her eye, that guides my fate.   315
Signor Mizaldus, joy then, Signor Mizaldus.

MIZALDUS 'Signor', sir? O devil!°

THAIS Good husband, show yourself a temp'rate man.
Your mother was a woman, I dare swear;
No tiger got you, nor no bear was rival   320
In your conception. You seem like the issue°
The painters limn leaping from Envy's mouth,
That devours all he meets.°

MIZALDUS Had the last or the least syllable
Of this more-than-immortal eloquence   325
Commenced to me when rage had been so high
Within my blood that it o'er-topped my soul,
Like to the lion when he hears the sound
Of Dian's bow-string in some shady wood,
I should have couched my lowly limb on earth   330
And held my silence a proud sacrifice.°

CLARIDIANA Slave, I will fight with thee at any odds;

Or, name an instrument fit for destruction,
That e'er was made to make away a man,
I'll meet thee on the ridges of the Alps,   335
Or some inhospitable wilderness,
Stark naked, at push of pike or keen cutlass,°
At Turkish sickle, Babylonian saw,
The ancient hooks of great Cadwalader,°
Or any other heathen invention.   340

THAIS O God bless the man!

LADY LENTULUS Counsel him, good my lord.

MENDOSA Our tongues are weary, and he desperate.
He does refuse to hear. What shall we do?

CLARIDIANA I am not mad: I can hear, I can see, I can feel.   345
But a wise rage in man, wrongs past compare,
Should be well nourished, as his virtues are.
I'd have it known unto each valiant sprite,
He wrongs no man that to himself does right.
Cazzo! I ha' done, Signor Mizaldus, I ha' done.   350

ROGERO By heaven, this voluntary reconciliation, made
Freely and of itself, argues unfeigned
And virtuous knot of love. So, sirs, embrace.

MIZALDUS Sir, by the conscience of a Catholic man,
And by our mother church that binds   355
And doth atone in amity with God
The souls of men, that they with men be one,
I tread into the centre all the thoughts°
Of ill in me toward you, and memory
Of what from you might aught disparage me;°   360
Wishing unfeignedly it may sink low
And, as untimely births, want power to grow.°

MENDOSA Christianly said. Signor, what would you have more?

CLARIDIANA And so I swear: you're honest, 'onocentaur'.

ROGERO Nay, see now, fie upon your turbulent spirit!   365
Did he do 't in this form?

CLARIDIANA If you think not this sufficient, you shall command
me to be reconciled in another form, as a 'rinatrix', or a
'rhinoceros'.

MENDOSA 'Sblood, what will you do?   370

CLARIDIANA Well, give me your hands first, I am friends with you, i'
faith. [*He shakes Mizaldus' hand*] Thereupon I embrace you, kiss
your wife, and (*to Thais*) God give us joy.

THAIS You mean me and my husband.

CLARIDIANA You take the meaning better than the speech, lady. 375

MIZALDUS The like wish I, but ne'er can be the like,
    And therefore wish I thee—
        [*Claridiana and Thais speak apart*]

CLARIDIANA By this bright light that is derived from thee—

THAIS So, sir, you make me a very light creature.

CLARIDIANA But that thou art a blessèd angel, sent 380
    Down from the gods t' atone mortal men,
    I would have thought deeds beyond all men's thoughts,
    And executed more upon his corpse.
    O let him thank the beauty of this eye
    And not his resolute sword or destiny. 385

ROGERO What say'st thou, Guido? Come, applaud this jubilee, a
    day these hundred years before not truly known to these divided
    factions.

CLARIDIANA [*aside*] No, nor this day had it been falsely borne,
    But that I mean to sound it with his horn.° 390

GUIDO [*to Rogero*] I liked the former jar better: then they showed like
    men and soldiers; now, like cowards and lechers.

ROGERO Well said, Guido, thou art like a bass-viol in a consort: let the
    other instruments wish and delight in your highest sense, thou art
    still grumbling. 395

        Mizaldus gives a letter to Abigail. [They talk apart]

MIZALDUS Nay, sweet, receive it, and in it my heart.
    And when thou read'st a moving syllable,
    Think that my soul was secretary to 't.
    It is my love, and not the odious wish
    Of my revenge in styling him a cuckold, 400
    Makes me presume thus far. Then read it fair;°
    My passion's ample as your beauties are.

ABIGAIL Well, sir, we will not stick with you.°

ROGERO And, gentlemen, since it hath happed so fortunately,
    I do entreat we may all meet tomorrow 405
    In some heroic masque to grace the nuptials
    Of the most noble Count of Cyprus.

MENDOSA Who does the young Count marry?

ROGERO O sir, who but the very heir of all her sex,
    That bears the palm of beauty from 'em all: 410
    Others compared to her show like faint stars

To the full moon of wonder in her face:°
The lady Isabella, the late widow
To the deceased and noble Viscount Hermes.

MENDOSA [*to Lady Lentulus*] La you there, widow: there's one of
    the last edition,°   415
    Whose husband yet retains in his cold trunk
    Some little airing of his noble guest,°
    Yet she a fresh bride as the month of May.

LADY LENTULUS Well, my lord, I am none of these
    That have my second husband bespoke: 420
    My door shall be a testimony of it.°
    And but these noble marriages incite me,
    My much abstracted presence should have showed it.°
    If you come to me (hark in your ear, my lord),
    [*Whispers*] Look your ladder of ropes be strong,   425
    For I shall tie you to your tackling.°

ROGERO Gentlemen, your answer to the masque.

ALL Your honour leads, we'll follow.
      [*Rogero, Guido, Mizaldus, Abigail, Mendosa, and Lady*
      Lentulus make to go; Claridiana holds back with Thais]

MIZALDUS Signor Claridiana.

CLARIDIANA   I attend you, sir.

THAIS [*to Claridiana*] You'll be constant.

CLARIDIANA   Above the adamant: 430
    The goat's blood shall not break me.°
      Exeunt all except Claridiana
    Yet shallow fools, and plainer mortal men,
    That understand not what they undertake,
    Fall in their own snares or come short of vengeance.
    No, let the sun view with an open face   435
    And afterward shrink in his blushing cheeks
    Ashamed, and cursing of the fixed decree
    That makes his light bawd to the crimes of men.
    When I have ended what I now devise,
    Apollo's oracle shall swear me wise:°   440
    Strumpet his wife, branch my false-seeming friend,°
    And make him foster what my hate begot:
    A bastard, that when age and sickness seize him,
    Shall be a corsive to his griping heart.°
    I'll write to her; for what her modesty   445

15

Will not permit, nor my adulterate forcing,
That blushless herald shall not fear to tell.
Mizaldus shall know that yet his foe's a man,
And what is more, a true Italian.°
        Exit

2.1

[*Seats are set out for the masque.*] *Enter Torch-Bearers*
attending Roberto, Lord Cardinal, Isabella, Lady Lentulus,
Abigail, and Thais

ROBERTO My grave lord Cardinal, we congratulate
    And zealously do entertain your love,
    That from your high and divine contemplation°
    You have vouchsafed to consummate a day
    Due to our nuptials. O may this knot you knit,   5
    This individual Gordian grasp of hands°
    In sight of God so fairly intermixed,
    Never be severed, as heaven smiles at it,
    By all the darts shot by infernal Jove.°
    Angels of grace, amen, amen say to 't.   10
    [*To Isabella*] Fair lady, widow, and my worthy mistress,
    Do you keep silence for a wager?
THAIS Do you ask a woman that question, my lord,
    When she enforcedly pursues what she's forbidden?°
    I think if I had been tied to silence,   15
    I should have been worthy the cucking-stool ere this time.°
ROBERTO You shall not be my orator, lady, that pleads thus for
    yourself.
    [*Enter a Servant*]
SERVANT My lord, the masquers are at hand.
ROBERTO Give them kind entertainment.   20
    [*Exit Servant*]
    [*To the Cardinal*] Some worthy friends of mine, my lord, unknown
    to me, too lavish of their loves, bring their own welcome in a solemn
    masque.
    [*They take their seats for the masque*]
ABIGAIL I am glad there's noblemen i' the masque with our husbands,
    to overrule them: they had shamed us all else.   25
THAIS Why? For why, I pray?
ABIGAIL Why? Marry, they had come in with some city show° else;
    hired a few tinsel coats at the vizard-makers, which would ha' made
    them look for all the world like bakers in their linen bases and mealy
    vizards, new come from bolting. I saw a show once at the marriage   30
    of a magnifico's daughter, presented by Time; which Time was an

old bald thing—a servant 'twas. The best man, he was a dyer, and
came in likeness of the rainbow in all manner of colours to show
his art; but the rainbow smelt of urine, so we were all afraid the
property was changed, and looked for a shower.° Then came in after   35
him one that, it seemed, feared no colours,° a grocer that had
trimmed up himself handsomely; he was Justice, and showed
reasons why. And I think this grocer, I mean this Justice, had borrowed a weather-beaten balance from some Justice of a conduit,°
both which scales were replenished with the choice of his ware, and   40
the more liberally to show his nature, he gave every woman in the
room her handful.°

THAIS O great act of Justice! Well, an my husband come cleanly off
with this, he shall ne'er betray his weakness more but confess
himself a citizen hereafter, and acknowledge their wit, for alas they   45
come short.°

> *Enter in the masque*° *Rogero the Count of Arsena, Mendosa,*
> *Mizaldus, Claridiana, and Torch-Bearers.*° [*They are all*
> *masked*] *and carrying shields which they deliver to their several*
> *mistresses: Mendosa to the Lady Lentulus; Claridiana to*
> *Thais; Rogero to Isabella; Mizaldus to Abigail*

ISABELLA [*to the Cardinal*] Good my lord, be my expositor.°

CARDINAL The sun setting, a man pointing at it;
  The motto, *Sensi tamen ipse calorem.*°
  Fair bride, some servant of yours, that here intimates°   50
  To have felt the heat of love bred in your brightness;
  But setting thus from him, by marriage,
  He only here acknowledgeth your power,
  And must expect beams of a morrow sun.°

LADY LENTULUS [*to Roberto*] Lord bridegroom, will you interpret
  me?   55

ROBERTO A sable shield; the word, *Vidua spes.*°
  What, the forlorn hope in black despairing?°
  Lady Lentulus, is this the badge of all your suitors?

LADY LENTULUS Ay, by my troth, my lord, if they come to me.

ROBERTO I could give it another interpretation. Methinks this lover   60
has learned of women to deal by contraries. If so, then here he says,
the widow is his only hope.

LADY LENTULUS No, good my lord, let the first stand.

MIZALDUS Enquire of him, and he'll resolve the doubt.

ABIGAIL What's here? A ship sailing nigh her haven?   65
  With good ware, belike: 'tis well ballast.°

THAIS O, this your device smells of the merchant. What's your ship's name, I pray? *The Forlorn Hope?*

ABIGAIL No, *The Merchant Royal.*

THAIS And why not *Adventurer?*°   70

ABIGAIL You see no likelihood of that: would it not fain be in the haven? The word, *Ut tangerem portum.*° Marry, for aught I know, God grant it. What's there?

THAIS Mine's an azure shield. Marry, what else? I should tell thee more than I understand, but the word is, *Aut pretio, aut*   75 *precibus.*°

ABIGAIL Ay, ay, some common council° device.

> *The masquers take the women and dance the first change*

MENDOSA Fair widow, how like you this change?

LADY LENTULUS I changed° too lately to like any.

MENDOSA O, your husband! You wear his memory like a death's
head.°   80
For heaven's love think of me as the man
Whose dancing days, you see, are not yet done.

LADY LENTULUS Yet you sink apace,° sir.

MENDOSA That fault's in my upholsterer,° lady.

CLARIDIANA Thou shalt as soon find Truth telling a lie,   85
Virtue a bawd, Honesty a courtier,
As me turned recreant to thy least design.
Love makes me speak, and he makes love divine.°

THAIS Would Love could make you so; but 'tis his guise
To let us surfeit ere he ope his eyes.°   90

> *Mizaldus holds Abigail by the hand*

ABIGAIL You grasp my hand too hard, i' faith, fair sir.

MIZALDUS Not as you grasp my heart, unwilling wanton.°
Were but my breast bare and anatomized,°
Thou shouldst behold there how thou tortur'st it;
And as Apelles limned the Queen of Love,°   95
In her right hand grasping a heart in flames,
So may I thee, fairer, but crueller.

ABIGAIL Well, sir, your visor gives you colour for what you say.

> [*He offers her a ruby ring*]

MIZALDUS Grace me to wear this favour ('tis a gem
That vails to your eyes, though not to th' eagle's),°   100
And in exchange give me one word of comfort.

ABIGAIL Ay, marry. [*Aside*] I like this wooer well,
He'll win 's pleasure out o' the stones.°

The second change; Isabella falls in love° with Rogero when the changers speak

ISABELLA Change is no robbery; yet in this change°
　　Thou robb'st me of my heart. Sure Cupid's here,   105
　　Disguisèd like a pretty torch-bearer,
　　And makes his brand a torch, that with more sleight°
　　He may entrap weak women. Here the sparks
　　Fly as in Etna from his father's anvil.°
　　O powerful boy! My heart's on fire, and unto mine eyes   110
　　The raging flames ascend, like to two beacons,
　　Summoning my strongest powers, but all too late:°
　　The conqueror already opes the gate.
　　I will not ask his name.

ABIGAIL [*to Mizaldus*] You dare put it into my hands.   115

MIZALDUS Zounds, do you think I will not?

ABIGAIL Then thus, tomorrow. You'll be secret, servant?

MIZALDUS All that I do, I'll do in secret.

ABIGAIL My husband goes to Murano° to renew the farm he has.

MIZALDUS Well, what time goes the jakes-farmer?   120

ABIGAIL He shall not be long out, but you shall put in,° I
　　warrant you. Have a care that you stand just i' the nick° about
　　six o'clock in the evening. My maid shall conduct you up. To
　　save mine honour you must come up darkling, and to avoid
　　suspicion.   125

MIZALDUS Zounds, hoodwinked, an if you'll open all,° sweet lady.

ABIGAIL But if you fail to do 't——

MIZALDUS The sun shall fail the day first.

ABIGAIL Tie this ring fast, you may be sure to know.°
　　You'll brag of this, now you have brought me to the bay.° 130

MIZALDUS [*aside*] Pox o' this masque! Would 'twere done,
　　　I might
　　To my apothecary's for some stirring meats.

THAIS Methinks, sir, you should blush e'en through your visor.
　　I have scarce patience to dance out the rest.

CLARIDIANA The worse my fate that ploughs a marble quarry.° 135
　　Pygmalion, yet thy image was more kind,°
　　Although thy love not half so true as mine.
　　Dance they that list, I sail against the wind.

THAIS Nay, sir, betray not your infirmities:
　　You'll make my husband jealous by and by.   140
　　We will think of you, and that presently.

ROGERO The spheres ne'er danced unto a better tune.°
Sound music there!

ISABELLA   'Twas music that he spake.
    They dance the third change, after which the Ladies fall off°

ROBERTO Gallants, I thank you, and begin a health°
To your mistresses.
    [*He drinks to them*]

MENDOSA, CLARIDIANA, *and* MIZALDUS Fair thanks, sir
bridegroom.°   145
    [*They drink to Roberto*]

ISABELLA [*indicating Rogero*] He speaks not to this pledge; has he no
mistress?°
Would I might choose one for him; but 't may be
He doth adore a brighter star than we.°

ROBERTO Sit, ladies, sit, you have had standing long.
    The Ladies sit down. Rogero dances a lavolta, or a galliard,°
    and in the midst of it, falleth into the bride's lap, but straight
    leaps up and danceth it out

MENDOSA Bless the man, sprightly and nobly done.   150

THAIS What, is your ladyship hurt?

ISABELLA   O no, an easy fall.
    [*Aside*] Was I not deep enough, thou god of lust,
But I must further wade? I am his now,
As sure as Juno's Jove's. Hymen take flight,
And see not me: 'tis not my wedding night.   155
    Exit Isabella

CARDINAL The bride's departed, discontent, it seems.

ROBERTO We'll after her. Gallants, unmask, I pray,
And taste a homely banquet we entreat.°
    Exeunt Roberto and the Cardinal, attended by Torch-Bearers.
    [*Claridiana, Mizaldus, and Mendosa remove their masks,*
    but Rogero keeps his on.° *The seats are removed*°]

CLARIDIANA Candied eringoes, I beseech thee.

MENDOSA Come, widow, I'll be bold to put you in.°   160
My lord, will you have a sociate?°
    Exeunt Thais, Lady Lentulus, Abigail, [and Mendosa]

ROGERO Good gentlemen, if I have any interest in you,
Let me depart unknown; 'tis a disgrace
Of an eternal memory.

MIZALDUS What, the fall, my lord? As common a thing as can be: the   165
stiffest° man in Italy may fall between a woman's legs.

CLARIDIANA Would I had changed places with you, my lord; would it
    had been my hap!

ROGERO What cuckold laid his horns in my way?° Signor
    Claridiana, you were by the lady when I fell: do you think I hurt   170
    her?

CLARIDIANA You could not hurt her, my lord, between the legs.

ROGERO What was 't I fell withal?

MIZALDUS A cross-point,° my lord

ROGERO Cross-point, indeed.   175
    Well, if you love me, let me hence unknown,
    The silence yours, the disgrace mine own.
        *Exeunt Claridiana and Mizaldus. Enter Isabella with a gilt
        goblet; she meets Rogero*

ISABELLA Sir, if wine were nectar I'll begin a health
    To her that were most gracious in your eye.
        [*She drinks*]
    Yet deign, as simply 'tis the gift of Bacchus,   180
    To give her pledge that drinks. This god of wine
    Cannot inflame me more to appetite,
    Though he be co-supreme with mighty Love,°
    Than thy fair shape.

ROGERO [*aside*] Zounds, she comes to deride me.   185
        [*Isabella kisses the goblet*]

ISABELLA   That kiss shall serve°
    To be a pledge, although my lips should starve.
    [*Aside*] No trick to get that visor from his face?

ROGERO [*aside*] I will steal hence, and so conceal disgrace.°
        [*He makes to leave*]

ISABELLA Sir, have you left nought behind?   190

ROGERO Yes, lady, but the Fates will not permit°
    (As gems once lost are seldom or never found)
    I should convey it with me. Sweet, goodnight.°
    [*Aside*] She bends to me: there's my fall again.°
        Exit Rogero

ISABELLA He's gone, that lightning that awhile doth strike   195
    Our eyes with amazèd brightness, and on a sudden
    Leaves us in prisoned darkness. Lust, thou art high.
    My similes may well come from the sky.°
    [*Calls*] Anna, Anna!
        Enter Anna

ANNA Madam, did you call?   200

22

ISABELLA Follow yon stranger, prithee learn his name:
  We may hereafter thank him.

       Exit Anna

                    How I dote!
  Is he not a god
  That can command what other men would win
  With the hard'st advantage? I must have him,°   205
  Or shadow-like follow his fleeting steps.
  Were I as Daphne, and he followed chase,
  Though I rejected young Apollo's love
  And like a dream beguile his wand'ring steps,°
  Should he pursue me through the neighbouring grove   210
  Each cowslip stalk should trip a willing fall
  Till he were mine, who till then am his thrall.°
  Nor will I blush, since worthy is my chance.°
  'Tis said that Venus with a satyr slept,°
  And how much short came she of my fair aim?   215
  Then, Queen of Love, a precedent I'll be
  To teach fair women learn to love of me.

       Enter Anna

  Speak music, what's his name?°

ANNA Madam, it was the worthy Count Massino.

ISABELLA Blessed be thy tongue: the worthy Count indeed, 220
  The worthiest of the Worthies. Trusty Anna,°
  Hast thou packed up those moneys, plate, and jewels
  I gave direction for?

ANNA Yes, madam, I have trussed up them, that many
  A proper man has been trussed up for.°   225

ISABELLA I thank thee: take the wings of night,°
  Belovèd secretary, and post with them to Pavia;°
  There furnish up some stately palace,
  Worthy to entertain the King of Love;°
  Prepare it for my coming and my love's.   230
  Ere Phoebus' steeds once more unharnessed be,
  Or ere he sport with his belovèd Thetis,
  The silver-footed goddess of the sea,°
  We will set forward. Fly like the northern wind,
  Or swifter, Anna, fleet like to my mind.°   235

ANNA I am just of your mind, madam, I am gone.

       Exit Anna

ISABELLA So to the house of death the mourner goes,

That is bereft of what his soul desired,
As I to bed, I to my nuptial bed,
The heaven on earth. So to thought slaughters went°   240
The pale Andromeda bedewed with tears,°
When every minute she expected grips
Of a fell monster, and in vain bewailed
The act of her creation. Sullen Night,
That look'st with sunk eyes on my nuptial bed,   245
With ne'er a star that smiles upon the end,
Mend thy slack pace and lend the malcontent,
The hoping lover, and the wishing bride
Beams that too long thou shadowest; or if not,°
In spite of thy fixed front when my loathed mate   250
Shall struggle in due pleasure for his right,
I'll think 't my love, and die in that delight.°

    Exit

2.2

Enter at several doors Abigail and Thais, each carrying a letter

ABIGAIL Thais, you're an early riser. I have that to show will make
    your hair stand on end.

THAIS Well, lady, and I have that to show you will bring your courage
    down. What would you say, an I would name a party saw your
    husband court, kiss—nay, almost go through for the hole?°   5

ABIGAIL How, how, what would I say? Nay, by this light, what would
    I not do? If ever Amazon fought better, or more at the face° than
    I'll do, let me never be thought a new-married wife. Come, unmask
    her. 'Tis some admirable creature, whose beauty you need not paint.
    I warrant you, 'tis done to your hand.°   10

THAIS Would any woman but I be abused to her face?
    [*She hands Abigail the letter*]
    Prithee read the contents. Know'st thou the character?

ABIGAIL 'Tis my husband's hand, and a love-letter. But for the con-
    tents, I find none in it. Has the lustful monster, all back and belly,°
    starved me° thus? What defect does he see in me? I'll be sworn,   15
    wench, I am of as pliant and yielding body to him, e'en which way
    he will: he may turn me° as he list himself. [*Reads*] What? '. . . and
    dedicate to thee . . .' Ay marry, here's a style so high° as a man

cannot help a dog o'er it. He was wont to write to me in the city
phrase, 'My good Abigail'. Here's 'astonishment of nature, unpar-   20
alleled excellency, and most unequal rarity of creation'.° Three
such words will turn any honest° woman in the world whore, for
a woman is never won till she know not what to answer°—and
beshrew me if I understand any of these. You are the party, I perceive, and here's a white sheet° that your husband has promised to   25
do penance in. You must not think to dance the shaking of the
sheets° alone.

    [She hands Thais a letter]

Though there be not such rare phrases in 't, 'tis more to the matter.
A legible hand, but for the dash, or the '(he)' and '(as)'; short, bawdy
parentheses° as ever you saw, to the purpose. He has not left out a   30
prick,° I warrant you, wherein he has promised to do me any good,
but the law's in mine own hand.°

THAIS I ever thought by his red beard he would prove a Judas.° Here
am I bought and sold: he makes much of me° indeed. Well, wench,
we were best wisely in time seek for prevention. I should be loath   35
to take drink° and die on° 't, as I am afraid I shall that he will° lie
with thee.

ABIGAIL To be short, sweetheart, I'll be true to thee, though a liar to
my husband. I have signed your husband's bill like a woodcock° (as
he is held), persuaded him—since nought but my love can assuage   40
his violent passions—he should enjoy, like a private friend, the pleasures of my bed. I told him my husband was to go to Murano today,
to renew a farm he has, and in the meantime he might be tenant at
will, to use mine. This false fire has so took with him, that he's ravished afore he come. I have had stones on him all red;° dost know   45
this?

    She points to her ring

THAIS Ay, too well; it blushes for its master.

ABIGAIL Now my husband will be hawking about° thee anon an thou
canst meet him closely.°

THAIS By my faith, I would be loath in the dark, an he knew° me.   50

ABIGAIL I mean thus. The same occasion will serve him too: they are
birds of a feather, and will fly together,° I warrant thee, wench.
Appoint him to come: say that thy husband's gone to Murano, and
tell me anon if thou madest not his heart-blood spring for joy in
his face.   55

THAIS I conceive you not all this while.

ABIGAIL Then thou'rt a barren woman, and no marvel if thy husband

love thee not. The hour for both to come is six, a dark time fit for
purblind lovers; and with cleanly conveyance° by the nigglers° our
maids, they shall be translated into our bedchambers, your husband   60
into mine and mine into yours.

THAIS But you mean they shall come in at the back-doors.

ABIGAIL Who, our husbands? Nay, an they come not in at the
fore-doors there will be no pleasure in 't. But we two will climb
over our garden-pales° and come in that way (the chastest that   65
are in Venice will stray for a good turn), and thus wittily will we
be bestowed, you into my house to your husband, and I into your
house to my husband; and I warrant thee, before a month come
to an end they'll crack° louder of this night's lodging than the
bedsteads.   70

THAIS All is, if our maids keep secret.

ABIGAIL Mine is a maid,° I'll be sworn; she has kept her secrets
hitherto.

THAIS Troth, and I never had any sea-captain boarded° in my
house.   75

ABIGAIL Go to, then; and the better to avoid suspicion, thus we must
insist: they must come up darkling, recreate themselves with their
delight an hour or two, and, after a million of kisses or so—

THAIS But is my husband content to come darkling?

ABIGAIL What not, to save mine honour? He that will run through   80
fire, as he has professed, will by the heat of his love grope in the
dark. I warrant him, he shall save mine honour.

THAIS I am afraid my voice will discover me.

ABIGAIL Why then, you're best say nothing, and take it thus quietly
when your husband comes.   85

THAIS Ay, but you know a woman cannot choose but speak° in these
cases.

ABIGAIL Bite in your nether lip, and I warrant you;
Or make as if you were whiffing tobacco,
Or puke like me. *Cazzo*, I hear your husband!   90
        Exit Abigail

THAIS Farewell, wise woman.
        Enter Mizaldus

MIZALDUS [*aside*] Now 'gins my vengeance mount high in my lust.
'Tis a rare creature, she'll do 't i' faith;
And I am armed at all points. A rare whiblin,
To be revenged and yet gain pleasure in 't: 95
One height above revenge. Yet what a slave am I!

Are there not younger brothers enough, but we must
Branch one another? O, but mine's revenge,°
And who on that doth dream
Must be a tyrant ever in extreme.   100
[*Aloud*] O my wife Thais, get my breakfast ready.
I must into the country to a farm I have
Some two miles off, and, as I think,
Shall not come home tonight. [*Calls off stage*] Jaques, Jaques,°
Get my vessel ready to row me down the river.°   105
[*To Thais*] Prithee make haste, sweet girl.
        Exit Mizaldus

THAIS So, there's one fool shipped away. Are your cross-points discovered? Get your breakfast ready! By this light, I'll tie you to hard
fare.° I have been too sparing of that you prodigally offer voluntary
to another. Well, you shall be a tame fool hereafter.   110
The finest sleight is when we first defraud;°
Husband, tonight 'tis I must lie abroad.
        Exit

2.3

Enter Isabella, with a letter, and a Page

ISABELLA Here, take this letter, bear it to the Count.
    But boy, first tell me, think'st thou I am in love?
PAGE Madam, I cannot tell.
ISABELLA Canst thou not tell? Dost thou not see my face?
    Is not the face the index of the mind?   5
    And canst not thou distinguish love by that?
PAGE No, madam.
ISABELLA Then take this letter and deliver it
    Unto the worthy Count. No, fie upon him,
    Come back again. Tell me, why shouldst thou think   10
    That same's a love-letter?
PAGE I do not think so, madam.
ISABELLA I know thou dost, for thou dost ever use
    To hold the wrong opinion. Tell me true,
    Dost thou not think that letter is of love?   15
PAGE If you would have me think so, madam, yes.
ISABELLA What, dost thou think thy lady is so fond?

27

Give me the letter: thyself shall see it.
Yet I should tear it in the breaking ope,
And make him lay a wrongful charge on thee,   20
And say thou brok'st it open by the way,
And saw what heinous things I charge him with.
But 'tis all one, the letter is not of love.
Therefore deliver it unto himself
And tell him he's deceived, I do not love him;   25
But if he think so, bid him come to me
And I'll confute him straight. I'll show him reasons;
I'll show him plainly why I cannot love him.
And if he hap to read it in thy hearing,
Or chance to tell thee that the words were sweet,   30
Do not thou then disclose my lewd intent°
Under those siren words, and how I mean
To use him when I have him at my will;
For then thou wilt destroy the plot that's laid,
And make him fear to yield when I do wish   35
Only to have him yield. For when I have him,
None but myself shall know how I will use him.
Begone: why stay'st thou?
        [*The Page makes to go*]
                            Yet return again.
PAGE [*coming back*] Ay, madam?
ISABELLA Why dost thou come again? I bade thee go: 40
If I say go, never return again.
        Exit Page
My blood, like to a troubled ocean
Cuffed with the winds, incertain where to rest,
Butts at the utmost shore of every limb.
My husband's not the man I would have had.   45
O my new thoughts to this brave sprightly lord
Was fixed by that hid fire lovers feel.°
Where was my mind before, that refined judgement,
That represents rare objects to our passions?
Or did my lust beguile me of my sense,   50
Making me feast upon such dangerous cates
For present want, that needs must breed a surfeit?
How was I shipwrecked? Yet, Isabella, think
Thy husband is a noble gentleman,
Young, wise, and rich. Think what fate follows thee,   55

And nought but lust doth blind thy worthy love.
I will desist. O no, it may not be.
Even as a headstrong courser bears away
His rider, vainly striving him to stay;
Or as a sudden gale thrusts into sea   60
The haven-touching bark, now near the lea:
So wavering Cupid brings me back amain,
And purple Love resumes his darts again.
Here of themselves thy shafts come as if shot:
Better than I thy quiver knows 'em not.   65
        Enter Rogero and the Page
PAGE Madam, the Count.
ROGERO So fell the Trojan wanderer on the Greek°
    And bore away his ravished prize to Troy.
    For such a beauty brighter than his Danaë°
    Jove should methinks now come himself again.   70
    Lovely Isabella, I confess me mortal,
    Not worthy to serve thee in thought, I swear;
    Yet shall not this same overflow of favour
    Diminish my vowed duty to your beauty.
ISABELLA Your love, my lord (I blushingly proclaim it),°   75
    Hath power to draw me through a wilderness,
    Were 't armed with Furies as with furious beasts.°
    Boy, bid our train be ready; we'll to horse.
        Exit Page
    My lord, I should say something, but I blush:
    Courting is not befitting to our sex.   80
ROGERO I'll teach you how to woo: say you have loved me long,°
    And tell me that a woman's feeble tongue
    Was never tuned unto a wooing string;
    Yet for my sake you will forget your sex
    And court my love with strained immodesty;   85
    Then bid me make you happy with a kiss.
ISABELLA Sir, though women do not woo, yet for your sake
    I am content to leave that civil custom
    And pray you kiss me.
ROGERO Now use some unexpected ambages   90
    To draw me further into Vulcan's net.°
ISABELLA You love me not so well as I love you.
ROGERO Fair lady, but I do.
ISABELLA   Then show your love.

ROGERO Why, in this kiss I show 't, and in my vowed service.
    [*He kisses her*]
  This wooing shall suffice: 'tis easier far   95
  To make the current of a silver brook
  Convert his flowing backward to his spring
  Than turn a woman wooer. There's no cause
  Can turn the settled course of nature's laws.
ISABELLA My lord, will you pursue the plot?°   100
ROGERO The letter gives direction here for Pavy.
  To horse, to horse: thus once Eurydice,
  With looks regardant, did the Thracian gaze,°
  And lost his gift while he desired the sight;°
  But wiser I, led by more powerful charm,   105
  I'd see the world win thee from out mine arm.°
      Exeunt Isabella and Rogero. A trampling of horses is heard
      off-stage. Enter at several doors Claridiana and Guido°
GUIDO Zounds, is the hurricano coming? Claridiana, what's the
  matter?
CLARIDIANA The Countess of Swevia has new taken horse.
    [*To himself*] Fly, Phoebus, fly, the hour is six o'clock.°   110
GUIDO Whither is she going, signor?
CLARIDIANA [*to himself*] Even as Jove went to meet his Semele—°
    [*To Guido*] To the Devil, I think.
GUIDO   You know not wherefore?
CLARIDIANA To say sooth, I do not.
    [*To himself*] So in immortal wise shall I arrive—   115
GUIDO At the gallows. What, in a passion, signor?
CLARIDIANA Zounds, do not hold me, sir!
    [*To himself*] Beauteous Thais, I am all thine wholly.
  The staff is now advancing for the rest,°
  And when I tilt, Mizaldus, aware thy crest.°   120
      Exit Claridiana
GUIDO What's here? The cap'ring cod's-head tilting in the air?°
      Enter Roberto in his cap and nightgown, with Servants. He
      kneels down
ROBERTO The gods send her no house, a poor old age,
  Eternal woe, and sickness' lasting rage.
GUIDO My lord, you may yet o'ertake 'em.
ROBERTO Furies supply that place, for I will not. No,   125
  She that can forsake me when pleasure's in the full,
  Fresh and untired, what would she on the least barren coldness?

I warrant you she has already got
Her bravoes and her ruffians: the meanest whore°
Will have one buckler, but your great ones more.   130
The shores of Sicily retains not such a monster,
Though to galley-slaves they daily prostitute.
To let the nuptial tapers give light to her new lust!
Who would have thought it? She that could no more
Forsake my company than could the day   135
Forsake the glorious presence of the sun
(When I was absent, then her gallèd eyes
Would have shed April showers and out-wept
The clouds in that same o'er-passionate mood
When they drowned all the world), yet now forsakes me.   140
Women, your eyes shed glances like the sun:
Now shines your brightness, now your light is done.
On the sweetest flowers you shine: 'tis but by chance,
And on the basest weed you'll waste a glance.
Your beams, once lost, can never more be found   145
Unless we wait until your course run round
And take you at fifth hand. Since I cannot
Enjoy the noble title of a man,
But after ages (as our virtues are°
Buried whilst we are living), will sound out   150
My infamy and her degenerate shame;°
Yet in my life I'll smother 't if I may,
And, like a dead man, to the world bequeath
These houses of vanity, mills, and lands
(Take what you will, I will not keep among you, servants)°   155
And welcome some religious monastery:
A true-sworn beadsman I'll hereafter be,
And wake the morning cock with holy prayers.
SERVANTS Good my lord! Noble master!
ROBERTO Dissuade me not, my will shall be my king.   160
I thank thee, wife, a fair change thou hast given:
I leave thy lust to woo the love of heaven.
        Exeunt Roberto and his Servants
GUIDO This is conversion, is 't not? As good as might have been: he
turns religious upon his wife's turning courtesan. This is just like
some of our gallant prodigals: when they have consumed their pat-   165
rimonies wrongfully, they turn capuchins° for devotion.
        Exit

31

3.1

Enter Claridiana and Mizaldus at several° doors. Being in a
readiness, each goes to the other's house, where he is received by
the Maid. [Exeunt Claridiana and Mizaldus, each into the
other's house, with the Maids.] Then enter Mendosa with a
Page, to the Lady Lentulus' window°

MENDOSA Night like a solemn mourner frowns on earth,
  Envying that day should force her doff her robes
  Or Phoebus chase away her melancholy.°
  Heaven's eyes look faintly through her sable mask°
  And silver Cynthia hies her in her sphere,°   5
  Scorning to grace black Night's solemnity.
  Be unpropitious, Night, to villain thoughts,
  But let thy diamonds shine on virtuous love.
  This is the lower house of high-built heaven,
  Where my chaste Phoebe sits, enthroned 'mong thoughts°   10
  So purely good, brings her to heaven on earth.°
  Such power hath souls in contemplation.
  Sing, boy, though night yet, like the morning's lark:
  A soul that's clear is light, though heaven be dark.
      Music plays. [The Page sings.] Enter Lady Lentulus above at
      her window
LADY LENTULUS Who speaks in music to us?   15
MENDOSA Sweet, 'tis I. Boy, leave me, and to bed.
      Exit Page
LADY LENTULUS I thank you for your music. Now goodnight.
MENDOSA Leave not the world yet, Queen of Chastity:
  Keep promise with thy love Endymion,°
  And let me meet thee there on Latmus' top.   20
  'Tis I whose virtuous hopes are firmly fixed
  On the fruition of thy chaste-vowed love.°
LADY LENTULUS My lord,
  Your honour made me promise your ascent
  Into my house, since my vow barred my doors,   25
  By some wit's engine made for theft and lust.
  Yet for your honour, and my humble fame,
  Check your blood's passions and return, dear lord.
  Suspicion is a dog that still doth bite

Without a cause. This act gives food to envy: 30
Swoll'n big, it bursts and poisons our clear flames.
MENDOSA Envy is stingless when she looks on thee.
LADY LENTULUS Envy is blind, my lord, and cannot see.
MENDOSA If you break promise, fair, you break my heart.
LADY LENTULUS Then come. Yet stay. Ascend. Yet let us part.   35
   I fear, yet know not what I fear:
   Your love is precious, yet mine honour's dear.
MENDOSA If I do stain thy honour with foul lust,
   May thunder strike me to show Jove is just.
LADY LENTULUS Then come, my lord, on earth your vow is given.   40
   This aid I'll lend you.
         He throws up a ladder of cords, which she makes fast to some
         part of the window. He ascends
MENDOSA   Thus I mount my heaven.
   Receive me, sweet.
         He reaches the top, and falls°
LADY LENTULUS   O me, unhappy wretch!
   How fares your honour? Speak, fate-crossèd lord.
   If life retain his seat within you, speak;
   Else like that Sestian dame, that saw her love°   45
   Cast by the frowning billows on the sands
   And lean death swoll'n big with the Hellespont
   In bleak Leander's body: like his love
   Come I to thee. One grave shall serve us both.
         [*She makes to leap from the window*]
MENDOSA Stay, miracle of women, yet I breathe.   50
   Though death be entered in this tower of flesh,
   He is not conqueror: my heart stands out
   And yields to thee, scorning his tyranny.
LADY LENTULUS My doors are vowed shut and I cannot help you.
   Your wounds are mortal; wounded is mine honour   55
   If there the town guard find you. Unhappy dame:
   Relief is perjured, my vow kept, shame.°
   What hellish destiny did twist my fate?
MENDOSA Rest seize thine eyelids, be not passionate.
   Sweet, sleep secure, I'll remove myself.   60
   That viper envy shall not spot thy fame:°
   I'll take that poison with me, my soul's rest,°
   For like a serpent I'll creep on my breast.
LADY LENTULUS Thou more than man! Love-wounded, joy and grief

33

Fight in my blood. Thy wounds and constancy   65
Are both so strong none can have victory.

MENDOSA Darken the world, earth's queen, get thee to bed.
The earth is light where those two stars are spread:°
Their splendour will betray me to men's eyes.
Veil thy bright face, for if thou longer stay   70
Phoebus will rise to thee and make night day.

LADY LENTULUS To part and leave you hurt my soul doth tear.

MENDOSA To part from hence I cannot, you being there.

LADY LENTULUS We'll move together: then fate love controls,
And as we part, so bodies part from souls.   75

MENDOSA Mine is the earth, thine the refinèd fire.
I am mortal, thou divine: then, soul, mount higher.

LADY LENTULUS Why then, take comfort, sweet. I'll see 'ou
tomorrow.

MENDOSA My wounds are nothing: thy loss breeds my sorrow.
        Exit Lady Lentulus
See, now 'tis dark.   80
Support your master, legs, a little further.
Faint not, bold heart, with anguish of my wound.
Try further yet.
        He staggers on, and then falls down
                Can blood weigh down my soul?
Desire is vain without ability.
Thus falls a monarch if fate push at him.   85
        Enter a Captain and the Watch,° [with lights]

CAPTAIN Come on, my hearts, we are the city's security. I'll give you
your charge, and then like courtiers every man spy out. Let no man
in my company be afraid to speak to a cloak lined with velvet, nor
tremble at the sound of a jingling spur.°

FIRST WATCHMAN May I never be counted a cock of the game° if I   90
fear spurs, but be gelded like a capon for the preserving of my
voice.°

CAPTAIN I'll have none of my band refrain to search a venereal
house, though his wife's sister be a lodger there; nor take two
shillings of the bawd to save the gentlemen's credits that are aloft,°   95
and so like voluntary panders leave them, to the shame of all
halberdiers.°

SECOND WATCHMAN Nay, for the wenches, we'll tickle° them, that's
flat.

CAPTAIN If you meet a *shevoiliero*° (that's in the gross phrase, a   100
    knight) that swaggers in the street and, being taken, has no money
    in his purse to pay for his fees,° it shall be a part of your duty to
    entreat me to let him go.

FIRST WATCHMAN O marvellous! Is there such *shevoiliers*?

SECOND WATCHMAN Some two hundred,° that's the least that are   105
    revealed.

         Mendosa groans

CAPTAIN What groan is that? Bring a light. Who lies there?
    It is the lord Mendosa, kinsman to the Duke.
    Speak, good my lord, relate your dire mischance.
        [*Mendosa does not reply*]
    Life like a fearful tyrant flies his master.   110
    Art must atone them, or th' whole man is lost.°
    Convey him to a surgeon's, then return.
    No place shall be unsearched until we find
    The truth of this mischance. Make haste again.
        [*Exeunt some Watchmen, carrying Mendosa*]
    Whose house is this stands open? In, and search   115
    What guests that house contains, and bring them forth.
        Exeunt the rest of the Watch° [*into Claridiana's and*
          Mizaldus' houses°]
    This nobleman's misfortune stirs my quiet
    And fills my soul with fearful fantasies.
    But I'll unwind this labyrinth of doubt,
    Else industry shall lose part of itself's labour.°   120
        Enter the Watch, with Claridiana and Mizaldus, taken in one
        another's houses in their shirts and nightgowns. They see one
        another
    Who have we there? Signors, cannot you tell us
    How our prince's kinsman came wounded to death
    Nigh to your houses?

MIZALDUS [*to Claridiana*] Hey-day! Cross-ruff at midnight! Is 't
    Christmas,°
    You go a-gaming to your neighbour's house?   125

CLARIDIANA Dost make a mummer of me, ox-head?

CAPTAIN Make answer, gentlemen, it doth concern you.

MIZALDUS 'Ox-head' will bear an action.° I'll ha' the law; I'll not be
    yoked! Bear witness, gentlemen, he calls me ox-head.

CAPTAIN Do you hear, sir?   130

CLARIDIANA [*to Mizaldus*] Very well, very well. Take law,° and hang
thyself, I care not. Had she° no other but that good face to dote
upon? I'd rather she had dealt with a dangerous° Frenchman than
with such a pagan.

CAPTAIN Are you mad? Answer my demand.   135

MIZALDUS [*to Claridiana*] I am as good a Christian as thyself,
Though my wife hath now new-christened me.°

CAPTAIN Are you deaf? You make no answer.

CLARIDIANA [*to Mizaldus*] Would I had had the circumcising of thee,
Jew, I'd ha' cut short your cuckold-maker, I would i' faith, I would   140
i' faith!

CAPTAIN Away with them to prison, they'll answer better there.
        [*The Watchmen start to hustle off Claridiana and Mizaldus*]

MIZALDUS Not so fast, gentlemen. What's our crime?

CAPTAIN Murder of the Duke's kinsman, Signor Mendosa.

CLARIDIANA *and* MIZALDUS Nothing else? We did it, we did it, we did   145
it!

CAPTAIN Take heed, gentlemen, what you confess.

CLARIDIANA I'll confess anything since I am made a fool by a knave.
I'll be hanged like an innocent—that's flat!

MIZALDUS I'll not see my shame. Hemp instead of a quacksalver, you   150
shall put out mine eyes, and my head shall be bought to make ink-
horns of.°

CAPTAIN You do confess the murder?

CLARIDIANA   Sir, 'tis true,
Done by a faithless Christian and a Jew.

CAPTAIN To prison with them, we will hear no further: 155
The tongue betrays the heart of guilty murder.
        Exeunt

3.2

Enter Count Rogero, Isabella, Anna, and Servants

ROGERO Welcome to Pavy, sweet, and may this kiss
Chase melancholy from thy company.
Speak, my soul's joy, how fare you after travel?

ISABELLA Like one that scapeth dangers on the seas,
Yet trembles with cold fears being safe on land   5
With bare imagination of what's past.

ROGERO Fear keep with cowards: air stars cannot move.°

36

ISABELLA Fear in this kind, my lord, doth sweeten love.

ROGERO To think fear joy, dear, I cannot conjecture.

ISABELLA Fear's fire to fervency, which makes love's sweet prove
    nectar.°   10
  Trembling desire, fear, hope, and doubtful leisure
  Distil from love the quintessence of pleasure.

ROGERO Madam, I yield to you: fear keeps with love.
  My oratory is too weak against you.
  You have the ground of knowledge, wise experience,   15
  Which makes your argument invincible.

ISABELLA You are time's scholar, and can flatter weakness.°

ROGERO Custom allows it, and we plainly see,
  Princes and women maintain flattery.°

ISABELLA Anna, go see my jewels and my trunks   20
  Be aptly placèd in their several rooms.

     Exit Anna [and Servants]. Enter Gniaca, Count of Gazia,
     with Attendants

  My lord, know you this gallant? 'Tis a complete gentleman.

ROGERO I do, 'tis Count Gniaca, my endearèd friend.

GNIACA Welcome to Pavy; welcome, fairest lady.
  Your sight, dear friend, is life's restorative: 25
  This day's the period of long-wished content,°
  More welcome to me than day to the world,
  Night to the wearied, or gold to the miser.
  Such joy feels friendship in society.
     [*He kisses Isabella°*]

ISABELLA [*aside*] A rare-shaped man. Compare them both
    together—   30

ROGERO Our loves are friendly twins, both at a birth:
  The joy you taste, that joy do I conceive.
  This day's the jubilee of my desire.

ISABELLA [*aside*] —He's fairer than he was when I first saw him.°
  This little time makes him more excellent.   35

GNIACA Relate some news. Hark you, what lady's that?
  Be open-breasted, so will I to thee.
     Rogero and Gniaca whisper to one another

ISABELLA [*aside*] Error did blind him that paints Love blind,
  For my love plainly judges difference.
  Love is clear-sighted, and with eagle's eyes°   40
  Undazzled looks upon clear sun-beamed beauty.
  Nature did rob herself when she made him,

Blushing to see her work excel herself.
'Tis shape makes mankind fumitory.°
Forgive me, Rogero: 'tis my fate   45
To love thy friend and quit thy love with hate.°
I must enjoy him. Let hope thy passions smother.
Faith cannot cool blood. I'll clip him, were 't my brother.
Such is the heat of my sincere affection;
Hell nor earth can keep love in subjection.   50

GNIACA [to Isabella] I crave your honour's pardon; my ignorance
Of what you were may gain a courteous pardon.

ISABELLA There needs no pardon where there's no offence.
[Aside] His tongue strikes music, ravishing my sense:
I must be sudden, else desire confounds me.   55

ROGERO What sport affords this climate for delight?

GNIACA We'll hawk and hunt today; as for tomorrow,
Variety shall feed variety.

ISABELLA [aside] Dissimulation women's armour is:
Aid love belief, and female constancy.°   60
[Aloud] O I am sick, my lord, kind Rogero, help me.

ROGERO Forfend it, heaven! Madam, sit. How fare you?
My life's best comfort, speak, O speak, sweet saint.

ISABELLA Fetch art to keep life; run, my love, I faint.
My vital breath runs coldly through my veins.   65
I see lean death with eyes imaginary
Stand fearfully before me. Hear my end:
A wife unconstant, but thy loving friend.

ROGERO As swift as thought fly I to fetch thee aid.
                    Exit Rogero [with Attendants°]

ISABELLA [aside] Thus innocence by craft is soon betrayed.   70
[Aloud] My lord Gniaca, 'tis your art must heal me.
I am lovesick for your love; love, love, for loving.°
I blush for speaking truth. Fair sir, believe me,
Beneath the moon nought but your frown can grieve me.

GNIACA Lady, by heaven, methinks this fit is strange.   75

ISABELLA Count not my love light for this sudden change.
By Cupid's bow I swear, and will avow,
I never knew true perfect love till now.

GNIACA Wrong not yourself, me, and your dearest friend:
Your love is violent, and soon will end.°   80
Love is not love unless love doth persèver:
That love is perfect love that loves forever.

ISABELLA Such love is mine, believe it, well-shaped youth;
 Though women use to lie, yet I speak truth.
 Give sentence for my life or speedy death: 85
 Can you affect me?
GNIACA I should belie my thoughts to give denial,
 But then to friendship I must turn disloyal.
 I will not wrong my friend, let that suffice.
ISABELLA I'll be a miracle: for love a woman dies.   90
  She tries to stab herself
GNIACA Hold, madam, these are soul-killing passions.°
 I'd rather wrong my friend, than you yourself.
ISABELLA Love me, or else, by Jove, death's but delayed.
 My vow is fixed in heaven, fear shall not move me:
 My life is death with tortures 'less you love me.   95
GNIACA Give me some respite and I will resolve you.
ISABELLA My heart denies it.
 My blood is violent, now or else never
 Love me, and like Love's Queen I'll fall before thee,°
 Enticing dalliance from thee with my smiles,   100
 And steal thy heart with my delicious kisses.
 I'll study art in love, that in a rapture
 Thy soul shall taste pleasures excelling nature.
 Love me, both art and nature in large recompense
 Shall be profuse in ravishing thy sense.   105
GNIACA You have prevailed: I'm yours from all the world.
 Thy wit and beauty have entranced my soul.
 I long for dalliance: my blood burns like fire;
 Hell's pain on earth is to delay desire.
ISABELLA I kiss thee for that breath. [*Kisses him*] This day you
  hunt: 110
 In midst of all your sports leave you Rogero;
 Return to me whose life rests in thy sight,
 Where pleasure shall make nectar our delight.
GNIACA I condescend to what thy will implores me.°
 He that but now neglected thee, adores thee.   115
  Enter Rogero, Anna, and a Doctor
 But see, here comes my friend. Fear makes him tremble.
ISABELLA [*to Gniaca*] Women are witless that cannot dissemble:
 Now I am sick again. [*Aloud*] Where's my lord Rogero?
 His love and my health's vanished both together.
ROGERO Wrong not thy friend, dear friend, in thy extremes.   120

39

Here's a profound Hippocrates, my dear,°
To minister to thee the spirit of health.

ISABELLA Your sight to me, my lord, excels all physic.
I am better far, my love, than when you left me:
Your friend was comfortable to me at the last.   125
'Twas but a fit, my lord, and now 'tis past.
Are all things ready, sir?

ANNA Yes, madam, the house is fit.

GNIACA Desire in women is the life of wit.

> *Exeunt*

3.3

> *Enter Abigail and Thais at several doors*

ABIGAIL O partner, I am with child of laughter, and none but you can
be my midwife. Was there ever such a game at noddy?°

THAIS Our husbands think they are foremen of the jury;° they hold
the heretic point of predestination,° and, sure, they are born to be
hanged.°   5

ABIGAIL They are like to prove men of judgement,° but not for killing
of him that's yet alive and well recovered.

THAIS As soon as my man saw the watch come up, all his spirit was
down.°

ABIGAIL But though they have made us good sport in speech,   10
They did hinder us of good sport in action.°
O wench, imagination is strong in pleasure.

THAIS That's true: for the opinion my goodman had of enjoying you
made him do wonders.

ABIGAIL Why should weak man, that is so soon satisfied, desire   15
variety?

THAIS Their answer is, to feed on pheasants continually would breed
a loathing.

ABIGAIL Then if we seek for strange flesh, that have stomachs, at
will,° 'tis pardonable.   20

THAIS Ay, if men had any feeling of it, but they judge us by themselves.

ABIGAIL Well, we will bring them to the gallows, and then, like kind
virgins, beg their lives,° and after live at our pleasures, and this
bridle shall still rein them.   25

THAIS Faith, if we were disposed, we might sin as safe as if we had the broad seal° to warrant it; but that night's work will stick by me this forty weeks. Come, shall we go visit the discontented Lady Lentulus, whom, the Lord Mendosa has confessed to his chirurgeon, he would have robbed? I thought great men would but° have 30 robbed the poor, yet he the rich.

ABIGAIL He thought that the richer purchase, though with the worse conscience; but we'll to comfort her, and then go hear our husbands' lamentations. They say mine has compiled an ungodly volume of satires against women, and calls his book *The Snarl*.° 35

THAIS But he's in hope his book° will save him.

ABIGAIL God defend that it should, or any that snarl in that fashion.°

THAIS Well, wench, if I could be metamorphosed into thy shape, I should have my husband pliant to me in his life, and soon rid 40 of him; for, being weary with his continual motion, he'd die of a consumption.°

ABIGAIL Make much of him, for all our wanton prize:
Follow the proverb, 'Merry be and wise.'°

Exeunt

3.4

Enter Isabella, Anna, and Servants

ISABELLA [*aside*] Time, that devourest all mortality,
Run swiftly these few hours and bring Gniaca
On thy agèd shoulders, that I may clip°
The rarest model of creation.
Do this, gentle Time, 5
And I will curl thine agèd silver lock°
And dally with thee in delicious pleasure;
Medea-like I will renew thy youth.°
But if thy frozen steps delay my love,
I'll poison thee, with murder curse thy paths, 10
And make thee know a time of infamy.
[*Aloud*] Anna, give watch, and bring me certain notice
When Count Gniaca doth approach my house.

ANNA Madam, I go.
[*Aside*] I am kept for pleasure, though I never taste it; 15

For 'tis the usher's office still to cover°
His lady's private meetings with her lover.

Exit Anna

ISABELLA [*aside*] Desire, thou quenchless flame that burn'st our
    souls,
Cease to torment me.
The dew of pleasure shall put out thy fire   20
And quite consume thee with satiety.
Lust shall be cooled with lust, wherein I'll prove
The life of love is only saved by love.

Enter Anna

ANNA Madam, he's coming.

ISABELLA   Thou blessed Mercury,
Prepare a banquet fit to please the gods.   25
Let sphere-like music breathe delicious tones°
Into our mortal ears. Perfume the house
With odoriferous scents, sweeter than myrrh
Or all the spices in Panchaia.°
His sight and touching we will recreate   30
That his five senses shall be five-fold happy.

[*Exit Anna and the Servants.*] *Enter Gniaca in his hunting
clothes, [with a Page°]*

His breath, like roses, casts out sweet perfume.
Time now with pleasure shall itself consume.°
How like Adonis in his hunting weeds°
Looks this same goddess-tempter.°   35
[*To Gniaca*] And art thou come? This kiss entrance thy soul.
[*She kisses him.*]
Gods, I do not envy you, for know this:
Joy's here on earth complete, excels your bliss;°
I'll not change this night's pleasure with you all.

GNIACA Thou creature made by love, composed of pleasure,   40
That mak'st true use of thy creation:
In thee both wit and beauty's resident,
Delightful pleasure, unpeered excellence.
This is the fate fixed fast unto thy birth:
That thou alone shouldst be man's heaven on earth.   45
If I alone may but enjoy thy love,
I'll not change earthly joy to be heaven's Jove;
For though that women-haters now are common,
They all shall know earth's joy consists in woman.

ISABELLA My love was dotage till I lovèd thee,   50
    For thy soul truly tastes our petulance,
    Conditioned lover, Cupid's intelligencer,°
    That makes man understand what pleasure is.
    These are fit attributes unto thy knowledge;
    For women's beauty o'er men bear that rule,   55
    Our power commands the rich, the wise, the fool.
    Though scorn grows big in man in growth and stature
    Yet women are the rarest works in nature.°
GNIACA I do confess the truth, and must admire°
    That women can command rare man's desire.   60
ISABELLA Cease admiration, sit to Cupid's feast,
    The preparation to Paphian dalliance.°
    Harmonious music, breathe thy silver airs
    To stir up appetite to Venus' banquet,
    That breath of pleasure that entrances souls,   65
    Making that instant happiness a heaven
    In the true taste of love's deliciousness.
GNIACA Thy words are able to stir cold desire
    Into his flesh that lies entombed in ice,
    Having lost the feeling use of warmth in blood;   70
    Then how much more in me, whose youthful veins,
    Like a proud river, overflow their bounds?
    Pleasure's ambrosia, or love's nourisher,
    I long for privacy. Come, let us in:
    'Tis custom and not reason makes love sin.   75
ISABELLA I'll lead the way to Venus' paradise
    Where thou shalt taste that fruit that made man wise.°
      Exit Isabella
GNIACA [*to his Page*] Sing notes of pleasure to elate our blood.
    Why should heaven frown on joys that do us good?
    I come, Isabella, keeper of love's treasure,   80
    To force thy blood to lust, and ravish pleasure.
      Exit Gniaca. The Page sings a short song, [and exits.] Enter
      Isabella and Gniaca again, she hanging about his neck
      lasciviously
GNIACA Still I am thy captive, yet thy thoughts are free:°
    To be love's bondman is true liberty.
    I have swum in seas of pleasure without ground;
    Vent'rous desire past depth itself hath drowned.   85
    Such skill has beauty's art in a true lover

That dead desire to life it can recover.
Thus beauty our desire can soon advance,
Then straight again kill it with dalliance.
Divinest women, your enchanting breaths   90
Give lovers many lives and many deaths.°

ISABELLA May thy desire to me forever last,
Not die by surfeit on my delicates;°
And as I tie this jewel about thy neck,
So may I tie thy constant love to mine,   95
Never to seek weaking variety,
That greedy curse of man's and woman's hell
Where nought but shame and loathed diseases dwell.°

GNIACA You counsel well, dear: learn it then,
For change is given more to you than men.°   100

ISABELLA My faith to thee, like rocks, shall never move;
The sun shall change his course ere I my love.

        Enter Anna

ANNA Madam, the Count Rogero knocks.

ISABELLA Dear love, into my chamber till I send
My hate from sight.

GNIACA   Lust makes me wrong my friend.   105

        Exit Gniaca

ISABELLA Anna, stand here, and entertain Lord Rogero.
I from my window straight will give him answer.
The serpent's wit to woman rest in me:°
By that man fell, then why not he by me?
Feigned sighs and tears dropped from a woman's eye   110
Blinds man of reason, strikes his knowledge dumb.
Wit arms a woman; Count Rogero come.

        Exit Isabella

ANNA My office still is under; yet in time°
Ushers prove masters, degrees make us climb.°

        Rogero knocks within

Who knocks? Is 't you, my noble lord?   115

        Enter Rogero in his hunting weeds

ROGERO Came my friend hither, Count Gniaca?

ANNA No, my good lord.

ROGERO Where's my Isabella?

ANNA In her chamber.

ROGERO Good. I'll visit her.   120

ANNA The chamber's locked, my lord. She will be private.

ROGERO Locked against me, my saucy malapert?

ANNA Be patient, good my lord, she'll give you answer.

ROGERO Isabella, life of love, speak: 'tis I that calls.

Enter Isabella above at her window

ISABELLA I must desire your lordship pardon me.   125

ROGERO 'Lordship'? What's this? Isabella, art thou blind?

ISABELLA My lord, my lust was blind, but now my soul's clear-
  sighted,
  And sees the spots that did corrupt my flesh,
  Those tokens sent from hell, brought by desire,
  The messenger of everlasting death.   130

ANNA My lady's in her pulpit, now she'll preach.

ROGERO Is not thy lady mad? In verity,
  I always took her for a puritan,°
  And now she shows it.

ISABELLA Mock not repentance: profanation   135
  Brings mortals laughing to damnation.
  Believe it, lord, Isabella's ill past life,
  Like gold refined, shall make a perfect wife.
  I stand on firm ground now, before on ice;
  We know not virtue till we taste of vice.   140

ROGERO [*to Anna*] Do you hear dissimulation, woman sinner?

ISABELLA Leave my house, good my lord, and for my part,
  I look for a most wished reconciliation
  Betwixt myself and my most wrongèd husband.
  Tempt not contrition then, religious lord.   145

ROGERO Indeed I was one of your family once;°
  But do not I know these are but brain-tricks?
  And where the devil has the fee-simple,°
  He will keep possession. And will you halt°
  Before me that yourself has made a cripple?   150

ISABELLA Nay, then you wrong me; and, disdainèd lord,
  I paid thee for thy pleasures vendible,
  Whose mercenary flesh I bought with coin.
  I will divulge thy baseness, 'less with speed
  Thou leave my house and my society.   155

ROGERO Already turned apostate, but now all pure!°
  Now damned your faith is, and loves endure
  Like dew upon the grass: when pleasure's sun
  Shines on your virtues, all your virtue's done!°
  I'll leave thy house and thee. Go, get thee in,   160

45

Thou gaudy child of pride, and nurse of sin.

ISABELLA Rail not on me, my lord; for if you do,
My hot desire of vengeance shall strike wonder;
Revenge in woman falls like dreadful thunder.

    Exit Isabella

ANNA Your lordship will command me no further service?   165

ROGERO I thank thee for thy watchful service past,
Thy usher-like attendance on the stairs,
Being true signs of thy humility.

ANNA I hope I did discharge my place with care.

ROGERO Ushers should have much wit, but little hair;°   170
Thou hast of both sufficient. Prithee leave me.
If thou hast an honest lady, commend me to her—
But she is none.

    Exit Anna

Farewell, thou private strumpet, worse than common.°
Man were on earth an angel but for woman: 175
That seven-fold branch of hell from them doth grow:°
Pride, lust, and murder they raise from below,
With all their fellow sins. Women were made
Of blood without souls: when their beauties fade°
And their lust's past, avarice or bawdry   180
Makes them still loved. Then they buy venery,
Bribing damnation, and hire brothel-slaves.
Shame's their executors, infamy their graves.
Your painting will wipe off, which art did hide,°
And show your ugly shape in spite of pride.   185
Farewell, Isabella, poor in soul and fame,
I leave thee rich in nothing but in shame.
Then soulless women know, whose faiths are hollow,
Your lust being quenched, a bloody act must follow.°

    Exit

4.1

Enter the Duke Amago, the Captain and the rest of the
Watch,° with the Senators

AMAGO Justice, that makes princes like the gods,
    Draws us unto the Senate,°
    That with unpartial balance we may poise
    The crimes and innocence of all offenders.
    Our presence can chase bribery from laws;   5
    He best can judge that hears himself the cause.°
FIRST SENATOR True, mighty Duke, it best becomes our places
    To have our light from you, the sun of virtue.
    Subject authority, for gain, love, or fear,°
    Oft quits the guilty and condemns the clear.   10
AMAGO The land and people's mine: the crimes being known,
    I must redress; the subject's wrong's mine own.°
    Call for the two suspected for the murder
    Of Mendosa, our endearèd kinsman,
    These voluntary murderers that confess   15
    The murder of him that is yet alive.
    We'll sport with serious justice for a while:
    In show we'll frown on them that make us smile.
SECOND SENATOR Bring forth the prisoners, we may hear their
    answers.
       Officers bring in Claridiana and Mizaldus
AMAGO Stand forth, you vipers, that have suckèd blood°   20
    And lopped a branch sprung from a royal tree.
    What can you answer to escape tortures?
MIZALDUS We have confessed the fact, my lord, to God and man,
    Our ghostly father and that worthy captain.
    We beg not life but favourable death.   25
AMAGO On what ground sprung your hate to him we loved?
CLARIDIANA Upon that curse laid on Venetians: jealousy.°
    We thought he, being a courtier, would have made us
    magnificoes of the right stamp,° and have played at primero
    in the presence,° with gold of the city brought from our   30
    Indies.
MIZALDUS Nay, more, my lord, we feared that your kinsman for a
    mess of sonnets would have given the plot of us and our wives to

some needy° poet, and for sport and profit brought us in some
Venetian comedy upon the stage.°   35

AMAGO Our justice dwells with mercy; be not desperate.

FIRST SENATOR His highness fain would save your lives if you would
see it.

MIZALDUS All the law in Venice shall not save me; I will not be saved.

CLARIDIANA Fear not, I have a trick to bring us to hanging in spite of   40
the law.

MIZALDUS Why, now I see thou lov'st me; thou hast confirmed
Thy friendship forever to me by these words.
Why, I should never hear lanthorn and candle called for°
But I should think it was for me and my wife.   45
I'll hang for that! Forget not thy trick,
Upon 'em with thy trick: I long for sentence.

SECOND SENATOR Will you appeal for mercy to the Duke?

CLARIDIANA Kill not thy justice, Duke, to save our lives:
We have deservèd death.   50

MIZALDUS Make not us precedents for after wrongs.°
I will receive punishment for my sins:
It shall be a means to lift us towards heaven.

CLARIDIANA Let's have our desert; we crave no favour.

AMAGO Take them asunder.
    [*The Officers separate Mizaldus and Claridiana*]
                              Grave justice makes us mirth.   55
That man is soulless that ne'er sins on earth.°
Signor Mizaldus, relate the weapon you killed him with, and the
manner.

MIZALDUS My lord, your lustful kinsman (I can title him no better)
came sneaking to my house like a promoter to spy flesh in the Lent.°   60
Now, I, having a Venetian spirit,° watched my time, and with my
rapier ran him through, knowing all pains are but trifles to the horn
of a citizen.

AMAGO [*to an Officer*] Take him aside.—Signor Claridiana, what
weapon had you for this bloody act? What dart° used death?   65

CLARIDIANA My lord, I brained him with a lever° my neighbour lent
me, and he stood by and cried, 'Strike home,° old boy!'

AMAGO [*to the Senators*] With several instruments. [*To the Officers*]
Bring them face to face. [*To Claridiana and Mizaldus*] With what
killed you our nephew?   70

MIZALDUS With a rapier, liege.

CLARIDIANA   'Tis a lie.

48

I killed him with a lever, and thou stood'st by.

MIZALDUS Dost think to save me and hang thyself? No, I scorn it. Is this the trick thou said'st thou hadst? I killed him, Duke. He only gave consent;° 'twas I that did it.   75

CLARIDIANA Thou hast always been cross° to me, and wilt be to my death. Have I taken all this pains to bring thee to hanging, and dost thou slip° now?

MIZALDUS We shall never agree in a tale till we come to the gallows; then we shall jump.°   80

CLARIDIANA I'll show you a cross–point,° if you cross me thus, when thou shalt not see it.

MIZALDUS I'll make a wry mouth° at that, or it shall cost me a fall. 'Tis thy pride to be hanged alone, because thou scorn'st my company; but it shall be known I am as good a man as thyself, and   85
in these actions will keep company with thy betters, Jew.°

CLARIDIANA Monster!

MIZALDUS Dog-killer!

CLARIDIANA Fencer!°

Claridiana and Mizaldus bustle

AMAGO Part 'em, part 'em.   90

MIZALDUS Hang us and quarter° us; we shall ne'er be parted till then.

AMAGO You do confess the murder done by both?

CLARIDIANA [*aside*] But that I would not have the slave laugh at me and count me a coward, I have a very good mind to live. But I am resolute: 95
'Tis but a turn. [*Aloud*] I do confess.

MIZALDUS   So do I,°
Pronounce our doom: we are prepared to die.

FIRST SENATOR We sentence you to hang till you be dead.
Since you were men eminent in place and worth,
We give a Christian burial to you both.   100

CLARIDIANA Not in one grave together, we beseech you. We shall ne'er agree.

MIZALDUS He scorns my company till the Day of Judgement;° I'll not hang with him.

AMAGO You hang together: that shall make you friends;   105
An everlasting hatred death soon ends.
To prison with them till the day of death.
Kings' words, like fate, must never change their breath.°

MIZALDUS You malice-monger, I'll be hanged afore thee, an 't be but to vex thee.   110

CLARIDIANA I'll do you as good a turn, or the hangman and I shall
fall out.

> *Exeunt Mizaldus and Claridiana, guarded, [with the Captain*
> *of the Watch], who returns° with Mendosa in his nightgown*
> *and cap, guarded*

AMAGO Now to our kinsman, shame to royal blood:
Bring him before us.
Theft in a prince is sacrilege to honour: 115
'Tis Virtue's scandal, death of royalty.
I blush to see my shame. Nephew, sit down.
Justice that smiles on those on him must frown.
Speak freely, captain, where found you him wounded?

CAPTAIN Between the widow's house and these cross neighbours';   120
Besides, an artificial ladder made of ropes
Was fastened to her window, which he confessed
He brought to rob her of jewels and coin.
My knowledge yields no further circumstance.

AMAGO Thou know'st too much. Would I were past all knowledge;   125
I might forget my grief springs from my shame.
[*To Mendosa*] Thou monster of my blood, answer in brief
To these assertions made against thy life.
Is thy soul guilty of so base a fact?

MENDOSA I do confess I did intend to rob her;   130
In the attempt I fell and hurt myself.
[*Aside*] Law's thunder is but death: I dread it not,
So my Lentulus' honour be preserved°
From black suspicion of a lustful night.

AMAGO Thy head's the forfeit for thy heart's offence: 135
Thy blood's prerogative may claim that favour.°
Thy person then to death doomed by just laws,
Thy death is infamous, but worse the cause.
[*Exeunt*]

4.2

> *Enter Isabella alone, [carrying a paper,] Gniaca following her*

ISABELLA O heavens, that I was born to be hate's slave!
The food of rumour that devours my fame!
I am called 'insatiate countess', 'lust's paramour',

'A glorious devil', and 'the noble whore'.
I am sick, vexed, and tormented. O revenge!   5
GNIACA On whom would my Isabella be revenged?
ISABELLA Upon a viper that does get mine honour.°
I will not name him till I be revenged.
See, here's the libels are divulged against me,
An everlasting scandal to my name,   10
And thus the villain writes in my disgrace:
[Reads] 'Who loves Isabella the insatiate
Needs Atlas' back for to content her lust:°
That wand'ring strumpet and chaste wedlock's hate
That renders Truth deceit for loyal trust;°   15
That sacrilegious thief to Hymen's rights,
Making her lust her god, heav'n her delights.'
Swell not, proud heart, I'll quench thy grief in blood:
Desire in woman cannot be withstood.
GNIACA I'll be thy champion, sweet, 'gainst all the world.   20
Name but the villain that defames thee thus.
ISABELLA Dare thy hand execute whom my tongue condemns,
Then thou art truly valiant, mine forever;
But if thou feign'st, hate must our true love sever.
GNIACA By my dead father's soul, my mother's virtues,   25
And by my knighthood and gentility,
I'll be revenged on all the authors of
Your obloquy. Name him.
ISABELLA   Rogero.
GNIACA   Ha!
ISABELLA What, does his name affright thee, coward lord?
Be mad, Isabella, curse on thy revenge.   30
This lord was knighted for his father's worth,
Not for his own.
Farewell, thou perjured man, I'll leave you all:
You all conspire to work mine honour's fall.
GNIACA Stay, my Isabella, were he my father's son,   35
Composed of me, he dies.°
Delight still keep with thee: go in.
ISABELLA   Thou art just.
Revenge to me is sweeter now than lust.
      [Exit Isabella.] Enter Rogero. He and Gniaca see one another,
      draw their swords, and make a pass. Then enter Anna
ANNA What mean you, nobles, will you kill each other?

GNIACA *and* ROGERO Hold!   40

ROGERO Thou shame to friendship, what intends thy hate?

GNIACA Love arms my hand, makes my soul valiant.
  Isabella's wrongs now sits upon my sword
  To fall more heavy to thy coward's head
  Than thunderbolts upon Jove's rifted oaks.   45
  Deny thy scandal or defend thy life.

ROGERO What? Hath thy faith and reason left thee both,
  That thou art only flesh without a soul?
  Hast thou no feeling of thyself and me?
  Blind rage that will not let thee see thyself!   50

GNIACA I come not to dispute but execute,
  And thus comes death.

ROGERO And thus I break thy dart. Here's at thy whore's face!°
     They fight another pass

GNIACA 'Tis missed. Here's at thy heart! Stay, let us breathe.

ROGERO Let reason govern rage, yet let us leave.   55
  Although most wrong be mine, I can forgive.
  In this attempt thy shame will ever live.

GNIACA Thou hast wronged the Phoenix, of all women rarest,°
  She that's most wise, most loving, chaste, and fairest.

ROGERO Thou dotest upon a devil, not a woman,   60
  That has bewitched thee with her sorcery
  And drowned thy soul in Lethy faculties.°
  Her useless lust has benumbed thy knowledge,°
  Thy intellectual powers oblivion smothers,
  That thou art nothing but forgetfulness.   65

GNIACA What's this to my Isabella? My sin's mine own;
  Her faults were none until thou mad'st 'em known.°

ROGERO Leave her, and leave thy shame where first thou found'st it;
  Else live a bond-slave to diseasèd lust,
  Devourèd in her gulf-like appetite,   70
  And infamy shall write thy epitaph:
  Thy memory leaves nothing but thy crimes,
  A scandal to thy name in future times.

GNIACA Put up your weapon, I dare hear you further.
  Insatiate lust is sire still to murder.   75

ROGERO Believe it, friend, if her heart blood were vexed,
  Though you kill me, new pleasure makes you next.
  She loved me dearer than she loves you now;
  She'll ne'er be faithful has twice broke her vow.°

This curse pursues female adultery: 80
They'll swim through blood for sin's variety,
Their pleasure like a sea, groundless and wide;
A woman's lust was never satisfied.

GNIACA Fear whispers in my breast. I have a soul
That blushes red for tending bloody facts.° 85
Forgive me, friend, if I can be forgiven:
Thy counsel is the path leads me to heaven.

ROGERO I do embrace thy reconcilèd love—

GNIACA —That death or danger now shall ne'er remove.°
Go tell thy insatiate Countess, Anna, 90
We have escaped the snares of her false love,
Vowing forever to abandon her.

ROGERO You have heard our resolution; pray be gone.

ANNA My office ever rested at your pleasure;
I was the Indian, yet you had the treasure.° 95
My faction often sweats, and oft takes cold;
Then gild true diligence o'er with gold.

GNIACA Thy speech deserves it: there's gold.

He gives her money

Be honest now, and not love's noddy,
Turned up and played on whilst thou keep'st the stock.° 100
Prithee, formally, let's ha' thy absence.

ANNA Lords, farewell.

Exit Anna

ROGERO 'Tis whores and panders that makes earth like hell.

GNIACA Now I am got out of lust's labyrinth,
I will to Venice for a certain time 105
To recreate my much abusèd spirits,
And then revisit Pavy and my friend.

ROGERO I'll bring you on your way, but must return.°
Lust is like Etna, and will ever burn;
Yet now desire is quenched flamed once in height.° 110
Till man knows hell, he never has firm faith.

Exeunt Rogero and Gniaca. Enter Isabella raving, and Anna

ISABELLA Out, screech-owl, messenger of my revenge's death!°
Thou dost belie Gniaca, 'tis not so.

ANNA Upon mine honesty they are united.

ISABELLA Thy honesty? Thou vassal to my pleasure, take that! 115

She strikes her

Dar'st thou control me when I say no?

Art not my footstool, did not I create thee,
And made thee gentle, being born a beggar?
Thou hast been my woman-pander for a crown,°
And dost thou stand upon thy honesty? 120

ANNA I am what you please, madam. Yet 'tis so.

ISABELLA Slave, I will slit thy tongue 'less thou say no.

ANNA No, no, no, madam!

ISABELLA I have my humour, though they now be false.
Faint-hearted coward, get thee from my sight. 125
When, villain! Haste, and come not near me.°

ANNA Madam, I run. Her sight like death doth fear me.°
Exit Anna

ISABELLA Perfidious cowards, stain of nobility!
Venetians, and be reconciled with words?
O that I had Gniaca once more here, 130
Within this prison made of flesh and bone,°
I'd not trust thunder with my fell revenge,
But mine own hands should do the dire exploit,
And fame should chronicle a woman's acts.°
My rage respects the persons, not the facts:° 135
Their place and worths had power to defame me;
Mean hate is stingless, and does only name me,
I not regard it; 'tis high blood that swells.°
Give me revenge, and damn me into hells.
Enter Don Sago, a Colonel, with a band of Soldiers and a
Lieutenant
A gallant Spaniard; I will hear him speak. 140
Grief must be speechless ere the heart can break.

SAGO Lieutenant, let good discipline be used
In quartering of our troops within the city.
Not separated into many streets:
That shows weak love, but not sound policy. 145
Division in small numbers makes all weak;
Forces united are the nerves of war,
Mother and nurse of observation,
Whose rare, ingenious sprite fills all the world,
By looking on itself with piercing eyes 150
Will look through strangers' imbecilities:°
Therefore be careful.

LIEUTENANT All shall be ordered fitting your command,
For these three gifts which makes a soldier rare

54

Is love and duty with a valiant care.   155
   Exit Lieutenant with the Soldiers. Don Sago sees Isabella

SAGO [*aside*] What rarity of women feeds my sight
  And leads my senses in a maze of wonder?
  Bellona, thou wert my mistress till I saw that shape,
  But now my sword I'll consecrate to her,
  Leave Mars and become Cupid's martialist.   160
  Beauty can turn the ruggèd face of War
  And make him smile upon delightful Peace,
  Courting her smoothly like a femalist.
  I grow a slave unto my potent love,
  Whose power change hearts, make our fates remove.°   165

ISABELLA [*aside*] Revenge, not pleasure, now o'er-rules my blood.°
  Rage shall drown faint love in a crimson flood,
  And were he caught, I'd make him murder's hand.°

SAGO [*aside*] Methinks 'twere joy to die at her command.
  I'll speak to hear her speech, whose powerful breath   170
  Is able to infuse life into death.

ISABELLA [*aside*] He comes to speak. He's mine; by love he is mine.

SAGO Lady, think bold intrusion courtesy,
  'Tis but imagination alters them;°
  Then 'tis your thoughts, not I, that do offend.   175

ISABELLA Sir, your intrusion yet's but courtesy
  Unless your future humour alter it.

SAGO Why then, divinest woman, know my soul
  Is dedicated to thy shrine of beauty,
  To pray for mercy and repent the wrongs   180
  Done against love and female purity.
  Thou abstract drawn from Nature's empty storehouse,°
  I am thy slave, command my sword, my heart;
  The soul is tried best by the body's smart.

ISABELLA You are a stranger to this land and me;   185
  What madness is 't for me to trust you then?
  To cozen women is a trade 'mongst men:
  Smooth promises, feigned passions with a lie
  Deceives our sex of fame and chastity.
  What danger durst you hazard for my love?   190

SAGO Perils that never mortals durst approve:
  I'll double all the works of Hercules;°
  Expose myself in combat 'gainst an host;
  Meet danger in a place of certain death,

55

Yet never shrink or give way to my fate;   195
Bare-breasted meet the murderous Tartar's dart°
Or any fatal engine made for death.
Such power has love and beauty from your eyes.
He that dies resolute does never die:
'Tis fear gives death his strength, which aye resisted,°   200
Death is but empty air the Fates have twisted.°

ISABELLA Dare you revenge my quarrel 'gainst a foe?

SAGO Then ask me if I dare embrace you thus,
    Or kiss your hand, or gaze on your bright eye
    Where Cupid dances on those globes of love.   205
    Fear is my vassal: when I frown, he flies;
    A hundred times in life a coward dies.

ISABELLA I not suspect your valour but your will.

SAGO To gain your love my father's blood I'll spill.

ISABELLA Many have sworn the like, yet broke their vow.   210

SAGO My whole endeavour to your wish shall bow.
    I am your plague to scourge your enemies.

ISABELLA Perform your promise, and enjoy your pleasure:
    Spend my love's dowry, that is women's treasure.
    But if thy resolution dread the trial,   215
    I'll tell the world a Spaniard was disloyal.

SAGO Relate your grief, I long to hear their names
    Whose bastard spirits thy true worth defames.
    I'll wash thy scandal off when their hearts bleeds.
    Valour makes difference betwixt words and deeds.   220
    Tell thy fame's poison, blood shall wash thee white.°

ISABELLA My spotless honour is a slave to spite.
    These are the monsters Venice doth bring forth,
    Whose empty souls are bankrupt of true worth:
    False Count Rogero, treacherous Gniaca,   225
    Counties of Gazia and of rich Massino.
    Then if thou be'est a knight, help the oppressed:
    Through danger safety comes, through trouble, rest,
    And so my love.

SAGO Ignoble villains, their best blood shall prove   230
    Revenge falls heavy that is raised by love.

ISABELLA Think what reproach is to a woman's name,
    Honoured by birth, by marriage, and by beauty.
        [She kneels°]
    Be God on earth and revenge innocence:

O worthy Spaniard, on my knees I beg,   235
Forget the persons, think on their offence.

SAGO By the white soul of honour, by heaven's Jove,
They die if their death can attain thy love.

ISABELLA Thus will I clip thy waist, embrace thee thus,
Thus dally with thy hair, and kiss thee thus.°   240
Our pleasures, Protean-like in sundry shapes,°
Shall with variety stir dalliance.

SAGO I am immortal! O divinest creature,
Thou dost excel the gods in wit and feature.
False Counts, you die: revenge now shakes his rods.°   245
Beauty condemns you, stronger than the gods.

ISABELLA Come, Mars of lovers, Vulcan is not here.°
Make vengeance like my bed, quite void of fear.

SAGO My senses are entranced, and in this slumber
I taste heaven's joys, but cannot count the number.   250

　　　Exeunt

4.3

Enter Lady Lentulus, Abigail, and Thais

ABIGAIL Well, madam, you see the destiny that follows marriage: our
husbands are quiet now, and must suffer the law.

THAIS If my husband had been worth the begging, some courtier
would have had him. He might be begged well enough, for he knows
not his own wife from another.°   5

LADY LENTULUS O you're a couple of trusty wenches to deceive your
husbands thus.

ABIGAIL If we had not deceived them thus, we had been trussed
wenches.

THAIS Our husbands will° be hanged, because they think themselves   10
cuckolds.

ABIGAIL If all true cuckolds were of that mind, the hangman would
be the richest occupation, and more wealthy widows than there be
younger brothers° to marry them.

THAIS The Merchant Venturers would be a very small company.   15

ABIGAIL 'Tis twelve to one of that; however the rest scape, I shall fear
a massacre.

THAIS If my husband hereafter for his wealth chance to be dubbed,
I'll have him called the Knight of the Supposed Horn.

ABIGAIL Faith, and it sounds well.   20

LADY LENTULUS Come, madcaps, leave jesting, and let's deliver them
out of their earthly purgation. You are the spirits that torment
them; but my love and lord, kind Mendosa, will lose his life to preserve mine honour, not for hate to others.

ABIGAIL By my troth, if I had been his judge, I should have hanged   25
him for having no more wit. I speak as I think, for I would not be
hanged for ne'er a man under the heavens.

THAIS Faith, I think I should for my husband. I do not hold the
opinion of the philosopher that writes we love them best that we
enjoy first,° for I protest I love my husband better than any that did 30
know° me before.

ABIGAIL So do I, yet life and pleasure are two sweet things to a
woman.

LADY LENTULUS He that's willing to die to save mine honour, I'll die
to save his.   35

ABIGAIL Tut: believe it who that list. We love a lively° man, I grant
you, but to maintain that life I'll ne'er consent to die.
This is a rule I still will keep in breast:
Love well thy husband, wench, but thyself best.

THAIS I have followed your counsel hitherto, and mean to do still.   40

LADY LENTULUS Come, we neglect our business. 'Tis no jesting,
tomorrow they are executed 'less we reprieve them.
We be their destinies to cast their fate.
Let's all go.

ABIGAIL   I fear not to come late.°

          Exeunt

          4.4

          Enter Don Sago alone, with a case of pistols

SAGO Day was my night, and night must be my day.
The sun shined on my pleasure with my love,
And darkness must lend aid to my revenge.
The stage of heav'n is hung with solemn black,
A time best fitting to act tragedies.°   5
The night's great queen, that maiden governess,°

58

Musters black clouds to hide her from the world,
Afraid to look on my bold enterprise.
Cursed creatures, messengers of death, possess the world.
Night-ravens, screech-owls, and voice-killing mandrakes,° 10
The ghosts of misers that imprisoned gold
Within the harmless bowels of the earth,
Are night's companions: bawds to lust and murder,
Be all propitious to my act of justice
Upon the scandalizers of her fame 15
That is the life-blood of deliciousness
Deemed: Isabella, Cupid's treasurer,°
Whose soul contains the richest gifts of love.
Her beauty from my heart fear doth expel:
They relish pleasure best that dread not hell. 20
     Enter Count Rogero
Who's there?
ROGERO A friend to thee, if thy intents be just and honourable.
SAGO Count Rogero, speak; I am the Watch.
ROGERO My name is Rogero; dost thou know me?
SAGO Yes, slanderous villain, nurse of obloquy, 25
    Whose poisoned breath has speckled clear-faced virtue
    And made a leper of Isabella's fame°
    That is as spotless as the eye of heav'n.°
    Thy vital thread's a–cutting. Start not, slave:
    He's sure of sudden death heav'n cannot save. 30
ROGERO Art not Gniaca turned apostata?
    Has pleasure once again turned thee a devil?
    Art not Gniaca, ha?
SAGO O that I were, then would I stab myself,
    For he is marked for death as well as thee. 35
    I am Don Sago, thy mortal enemy,
    Whose hand love makes thy executioner.
ROGERO I know thee, valiant Spaniard, and to thee
    Murder's more hateful than is sacrilege.
    Thy actions ever have been honourable. 40
SAGO And this the crown of all my actions,
    To purge the earth of such a man turned monster.
ROGERO I never wronged thee, Spaniard, did I? Speak:
    I'll make thee satisfaction like a soldier,
    A true Italian, and a gentleman.° 45
    Thy rage is treachery without a cause.

SAGO My rage is just, and thy heart blood shall know,
    He that wrongs beauty must be honour's foe.
    Isabel's quarrel arms the Spaniard's spirit.
ROGERO Murder should keep with baseness, not with merit.   50
    I'll answer thee tomorrow, by my soul,
    And clear thy doubts or satisfy thy will.°
SAGO He's war's best scholar can with safety kill:°
    Take this tonight.
           He shoots Rogero
               Now meet with me tomorrow!
    I come, Isabella; half thy hate is dead.   55
    Valour makes murder light, which fear makes lead.°
    Enter a Captain with a band of Soldiers
CAPTAIN The pistol was shot here. Seize him!
    Bring lights. What, Don Sago, colonel of the horse?
    Ring the alarum bell, raise the whole city!
    His troops are in the town: I fear treachery.   60
    Who's this lies murdered? Speak, bloodthirsty Spaniard.
SAGO I have not spoiled his face: you may know his phys'nomy.
CAPTAIN 'Tis Count Rogero. Go, convey him hence.
    [*Exeunt some of the Soldiers with the body*]
    Thy life, proud Spaniard, answers this offence.
    A strong guard for the prisoner, 'less the city's powers°   65
    Rise to rescue him.
           Don Sago is surrounded by Soldiers
SAGO   What needs this strife?
    Know, slaves, I prize revenge above my life.
    Fame's register to future times shall tell
    That by Don Sago Count Rogero fell.
           Exeunt

5.1

[*A scaffold is discovered.*°] *Enter the Duke of Medina with soldiers, some of whom are carrying the dead body of Rogero; Don Sago guarded; and an Executioner*

MEDINA Don Sago, quak'st thou not to behold this spectacle,°
This innocent sacrifice, murdered nobleness,
When blood, the Maker ever promiseth,
Shall though with slow yet with sure vengeance rest?°
It is a guerdon earned, and must be paid,   5
As sure revenge as it is sure a deed:
I ne'er knew murder yet but it did bleed.°
Canst thou (after so many fearful conflicts
Between this object and thy guilty conscience),
Now thou art freed from out the serpent's jaws—   10
That vile adulteress, whose sorceries
Doth draw chaste men into incontinence,
Whose tongue flows over with harmful eloquence—
Canst thou, I say, repent this heinous act
And learn to loathe that killing cockatrice?°   15
SAGO [*to the corpse*] By this fresh blood that from thy manly breast
I cowardly sluiced out, I would in hell,
From this sad minute till the day of doom,
To reinspire vain Aesculapius°
And fill these crimson conduits, feel the fire°   20
Due to the damnèd and this horrid fact.°
MEDINA Upon my soul, brave Spaniard, I believe thee.
SAGO [*to the corpse*] O cease to weep in blood, or teach me too.
The bubbling wounds do murder for revenge.°
This is the end of lust, where men may see   25
Murder's the shadow of adultery,
And follows it to death.
MEDINA But, hopeful lord, we do commiserate
Thy bewitched fortunes, a free pardon give°
On this thy true and noble penitence.   30
        [*Exit the Executioner*°]
Withal we make thee colonel of our horse
Levied against the proud Venetian state.
SAGO Medina, I thank thee not. Give life to him

61

That sits with Risus and the full-cheeked Bacchus,
The rich and mighty monarchs of the earth.   35
To me life is ten times more terrible
Than death can be to me. O break, my breast!
Divines and dying men may talk of hell,
But in my heart the several torments dwell.
What Tanaïs, Nilus, or what Tigris swift,   40
What Rhenus fiercer than the cataract—?
Although Maeotis cold, the waves of all the northern sea
Should flow forever through these guilty hands,
Yet the sanguinolent stain would extant be.°

MEDINA God pardon thee; we do.   45
        Enter a Messenger. There is a shout off stage

MESSENGER The Countess comes, my lord, unto the death;
        But so unwillingly and unprepared
        That she is rather forced, thinking the sum
        She sent to you of twenty thousand pound
        Would have assurèd her of life.

MEDINA   O heavens!   50
Is she not weary yet of lust and life?
Had it been Croesus' wealth, she should have died.°
Her goods by law are all confiscate to us,
And die she shall. Her lust
Would make a slaughter-house of Italy.°   55
Ere she attained to four-and-twenty years,
Three earls, one viscount, and this valiant Spaniard
Are known to ha' been the fuel to her lust,
Besides her secret lovers, which charitably
I judge to have been but few, but some they were.   60
        [*He indicates Rogero's body*]
Here is a glass wherein to view her soul,°
A noble but unfortunate gentleman,
Cropped by her hand, as some rude passenger
Doth pluck the tender roses in the bud.
Murder and lust, the least of which is death,   65
And hath she yet any false hope of breath?
        Enter the Executioner, followed by Isabella with her hair
        hanging down, a chaplet of flowers on her head, a nosegay in
        her hand, and with her a Cardinal

ISABELLA What place is this?
CARDINAL   Madam, the castle green.°

62

ISABELLA There should be dancing on a green, I think.

CARDINAL Madam, to you none other than your dance of death.

ISABELLA Good my lord Cardinal, do not thunder thus.   70
    I sent today to my physician,
    And as he says, he finds no sign of death.

CARDINAL Good madam, do not jest away your soul.

ISABELLA (*to Sago*) O servant, how hast thou betrayed my life?
    Thou art my dearest lover, now I see.   75
    Thou wilt not leave me till my very death.
    Blessed be thy hand: I sacrifice a kiss
    To it and vengeance. Worthily thou didst.
    He died deservedly: not content to enjoy
    My youth and beauty, riches and my fortune,   80
    But, like a chronicler of his own vice,
    In epigrams and songs he tuned my name,
    Renowned me for a strumpet in the courts
    Of the French king and the great Emperor.°
    Didst thou not kill him drunk?

MEDINA   O shameless woman!   85

ISABELLA Thou shouldst, or in the embraces of his lust;°
    It might have been a woman's vengeance.
    Yet I thank thee, Sago, and would not wish him living
    Were my life instant ransom.

CARDINAL O madam, in your soul have charity.   90

      Isabella gives him money

ISABELLA There's money for the poor.

CARDINAL O lady, this is but a branch of charity,
    An ostentation or a liberal pride.
    Let me instruct your soul, for that, I fear,
    Within the painted sepulchre of flesh°   95
    Lies in a dead consumption. Good madam, read.

      He gives her a book

ISABELLA You put me to my book, my lord; will not that save me?

CARDINAL Yes, madam, in the everlasting world.

SAGO Amen, amen.

ISABELLA While thou wert my servant, thou hast ever said   100
    Amen to all my wishes, witness this spectacle.
    Where's my lord Medina?

MEDINA Here, Isabella. What would you?

ISABELLA May we not be reprieved?

MEDINA Mine honour's passed: you may not.   105

63

ISABELLA No, 'tis my honour past.

MEDINA Thine honour's passed indeed.°

ISABELLA Then there's no hope of absolute remission?

MEDINA For that your holy confessor will tell you.
Be dead to this world, for I swear you die   110
Were you my father's daughter.

ISABELLA Can you do nothing, my lord Cardinal?

CARDINAL More than the world, sweet lady: help to save°
What hand of man wants power to destroy.

ISABELLA You're all for this world, then why not I?   115
Were you in health and youth like me, my lord,
Although you merited the crown of life
And stood in state of grace assured of it,
Yet in this fearful separation,
Old as you are, e'en till your latest gasp,   120
You'd crave the help of the physician
And wish your days lengthened one summer longer.
Though all be grief, labour, and misery,
Yet none will part with it that I can see.

MEDINA Up to the scaffold with her, 'tis late.   125

ISABELLA Better late than never, my good lord, you think.
You use square dealing, Medina's mighty Duke,
Tyrant of France, sent hither by the devil.°

        She ascends the scaffold

MEDINA The fitter to meet you.

CARDINAL Peace! Good my lord, in death do not provoke her.   130

ISABELLA (*to Sago*) Servant, low as my destiny I kneel to thee,
Honouring in death thy manly loyalty;
And whatsoe'er become of my poor soul,
The joys of both worlds evermore be thine.°
Commend me to the noble Count Gniaca,   135
That should have shared thy valour and my hatred;
Tell him I pray his pardon.
And, Medina (art yet inspired from heav'n?),°
Show thy creator's image: be like him,
Father of mercy.

MEDINA   Headsman, do thine office.   140

ISABELLA Now God lay all thy sins upon thy head
And sink thee with them to infernal darkness,
Thou teacher of the Furies' cruelty.°

CARDINAL O madam, teach yourself a better prayer:

64

This is your latest hour.

ISABELLA   He is mine enemy;   145
His sight torments me! I shall not die in quiet.

MEDINA I'll be gone. Off with her head, there!
        Exit Medina

ISABELLA Tak'st thou delight to torture misery?
Such mercy find thou in the Day of Doom.
        Enter Roberto, Count of Cyprus, in friar's weeds

SOLDIER My lord, here is a holy friar desires   150
To have some conference with the prisoners.

ROBERTO It is in private what I have to say,
With favour of your fatherhood.

CARDINAL Friar, in God's name, welcome.
        Roberto ascends the scaffold to Isabella

ROBERTO Lady, it seems your eye is still the same,   155
Forgetful of what most it should behold.
Do not you know me then?

ISABELLA Holy sir, so far you are gone from my memory,
I must take truce with time ere I can know you.°

ROBERTO Bear record, all you blessèd saints in heav'n,   160
I come not to torment thee in thy death,
(For of himself he's terrible enough),°
But to call to mind a lady like yourself,
And think how ill in such a beauteous soul
Upon the instant morrow of her nuptials°   165
Apostasy and vile revolt would show.
Withal imagine that she had a lord,
Jealous the air should ravish her chaste looks,
Doting like the creator in his models,
Who views them every minute, and with care   170
Mixed in his fear of their obedience to him.
Suppose her sung through famous Italy,
More common than the looser songs of Petrarch,°
To every several zany's instrument;
And he, poor wretch, hoping some better fate   175
Might call her back from her adulterate purpose,
Lives in obscure and almost unknown life,
Till, hearing that she is condemned to die,
For he once loved her, lends his pinèd corpse°
Motion to bring him to her stage of honour   180
Where, drowned in woe at her so dismal chance,

65

He clasps her: thus he falls into a trance.°
      [*He kneels, embracing her*]
ISABELLA O my offended lord, lift up your eyes;
    But yet avert them from my loathèd sight.
    Had I with you enjoyed the lawful pleasure   185
    To which belongs nor fear nor public shame,
    I might have lived in honour, died in fame.
          [*She kneels to him*]
    Your pardon on my falt'ring knees I beg,
    Which shall confirm more peace unto my death
    Than all the grave instructions of the church.   190
ROBERTO Pardon belongs unto my holy weeds:
    Freely thou hast it. Farewell, my Isabella.
    Let thy death ransom thy soul: O die a rare example.°
    The kiss thou gav'st me in the church here take.°
          [*He kisses her*]
    As I leave thee, so thou the world forsake.   195
      Exit Roberto
CARDINAL Rare accident, ill welcome, noble lord.°
    Madam, your executioner desires you to forgive him.
ISABELLA Yes, and give him too.
      [*She gives him money*]
                              What must I do, my friend?°
EXECUTIONER Madam, only tie up your hair.
ISABELLA   O these golden nets
    That have ensnared so many wanton youths!   200
    Not one but has been held a thread of life
    And superstitiously depended on.
    Now to the block we must vail. What else?
EXECUTIONER Madam, I must entreat you blind your eyes.
ISABELLA I have lived too long in darkness, my friend, 205
    And yet mine eyes with their majestic light
    Have got new Muses in a poet's sprite.°
    They have been more gazed at than the god of day,
    Their brightness never could be flatterèd;
    Yet thou command'st a fixèd cloud of lawn   210
    To eclipse eternally these minutes of light.°
    What else?
EXECUTIONER Now madam, all's done,
    And when you please I'll execute my office.
ISABELLA We will be for thee straight.   215

66

Give me your blessing, my lord Cardinal.
Lord, I am well prepared.
Murder and lust, down with my ashes sink,
But, like ingrateful seed, perish in earth°
That you may never spring against my soul   220
Like weeds to choke it in the heav'nly harvest.
I fall to rise. Mount to thy maker, spirit:
Leave here thy body. Death has her demerit.
[To the Executioner] Strike.°
                    [Isabella is executed°]
CARDINAL An host of angels be thy convoy hence.   225
                    [Enter Medina]
MEDINA To funeral with her body and this lord's.
None here, I hope, can tax us of injustice.
She died deservedly, and may like fate
Attend all women so insatiate.
            Exeunt [with Rogero's body. The traverse curtain is drawn over
            the scaffold°]

5.2

            Enter Duke Amago, the Watch,° and Senators
AMAGO I am amazèd at this maze of wonder,
    Wherein no thread or clew presents itself°
    To wind us from the obscure passages.
    What says my nephew?
WATCHMAN Still resolute, my lord, and doth confess the theft.   5
AMAGO We'll use him like a felon, cut him off
    For fear he do pollute our sounder parts.
    Yet why should he steal,
    That is a loaden vine? Riches to him
    Were adding sands into the Libyan shore,°   10
    Or far less charity. What say the other prisoners?
WATCHMAN Like men, my lord, fit for the other world,
    They take 't upon their death they slew your nephew.
AMAGO And he is yet alive. Keep them asunder.
    We may scent out the wile.   15
            Enter Claridiana and Mizaldus, bound, with a Friar and
            Officers

MIZALDUS [*to an Officer*] My friend, is it the rigour of the law
   I should be tied thus hard? I'll undergo it.
   If not, prithee then slacken. Yet I have deserved it:
   This murder lies heavy on my conscience.

CLARIDIANA Wedlock, ay, here's my wedlock: O whore, whore, whore!   20

FRIAR O sir, be qualified.

CLARIDIANA Sir, I am to die a dog's death, and will snarl a little at
   the old signor. You are only a parenthesis which I will leave out
   of my execrations. But first to our *quondam* wives, that makes
   us cry our vowels in red capital letters: 'I, O, U'° are cuckolds.   25
   O may bastard-bearing with the pangs of childbirth be doubled
   to 'em. May they have ever twins and be three weeks in travail
   between. May they be so rivelled with painting by that time
   they are thirty, that it may be held a work of condign merit but
   to look upon 'em. May they live to ride in triumph in a dung-   30
   cart° and be crowned with all the odious ceremonies belonging to
   't. May the cucking-stool° be their recreation, and a dungeon their
   dying-chamber. May they have nine lives like a cat, to endure this
   and more. May they be burnt for witches of a sudden. And lastly,
   may the opinion of philosophers prove true, that women have no   35
   souls.°

      Enter Thais and Abigail

ABIGAIL What, husband? At your prayers so seriously?

CLARIDIANA Yes, a few orisons. Friar, thou that standest between the
   souls of men and the devil, keep these female spirits away, or I will
   renounce my faith else.   40

THAIS O husband, I little thought to see you in this taking.°

MIZALDUS O whore, I little thought to see you in this taking. I am
   governor of this castle of cornutes;° my grave will be stumbled at.
   Thou adulterate whore, I might have lived like a merchant.

THAIS So you may still, husband.   45

MIZALDUS Peace, thou art very quick with me.

THAIS Ay, by my faith, and so am I, husband: belike you know I am
   with child.

MIZALDUS A bastard, a bastard, a bastard! I might have lived like a
   gentleman, and now I must die like a hanger-on,° show tricks upon   50
   a wooden horse,° and run through an alphabet of scurvy faces.° Do
   not expect a good look from me.

THAIS O me unfortunate!

CLARIDIANA O to think, whilst we are singing the last hymn and ready
   to be turned off, some new tune is inventing by some metre-monger,   55

to a scurvy ballad of our death. Again at our funeral sermons to
have the divine divide his text into fair branches.° O! Flesh and
blood cannot endure it, yet I will take it patiently like a grave man.
Hangman, tie not my halter of a true lover's knot;° I shall burst it
if thou dost.   60

ABIGAIL Husband, I do beseech you on my knees
I may but speak with you. I'll win your pardon,
Or with tears like Niobe bedew a—°

CLARIDIANA Hold thy water, crocodile,° and say I am bound to do
thee no harm: were I free, yet I could not be looser than thou,   65
for thou art a whore. Agamemnon's daughter° that was sacrificed
for a good wind felt but a blast of the torments thou shouldst
endure. I'd make thee sound oftener than that fellow that by his
continual practice hopes to become drum major.° What sayest
thou to tickling to death with bodkins? But thou hast laughed too 70
much at me already, whore. Justice, O Duke, and let me not hang
in suspense.

ABIGAIL Husband,
I'll nail me to the earth but I'll win your pardon.°
My jewels, jointure, all I have shall fly;   75
Apparel, bedding, I'll not leave a rug
So you may come off fairly.

CLARIDIANA I'll come off° fairly—then beg my pardon. I had rather
Chirurgeons' Hall° should beg my dead body for an anatomy than
thou beg my life. Justice, O Duke, and let us die!   80

AMAGO Signor, think, and dally not with heaven,
But freely tell us, did you do the murder?

MIZALDUS I have confessed it to my ghostly father
And done the sacrament of penance for it.
What would your highness more?   85

CLARIDIANA The like have I: what would your highness more?
And here before you all take 't on my death.

AMAGO In God's name, then, on to the death with them.
For the poor widows that you leave behind,
Though by the law their goods are all confiscate,   90
Yet we'll be their good lord and give 'em them.

CLARIDIANA O hell of hells! Why did we not hire some villain to fire
our houses?

MIZALDUS I thought not of that: my mind was altogether of the
gallows.   95

CLARIDIANA May the wealth I leave behind me help to damn her,

And, as the cursèd fate of a courtesan,
What she gleans with her traded art
May one as a most due plague cheat from her
In the last dotage of her tirèd lust   100
And leave her an unpitied age of woe.

MIZALDUS Amen, amen!

WATCHMAN I never heard men pray more fervently.

MIZALDUS O that a man had the instinct of a lion! He knows when
the lioness plays false to him; but these solaces, these women, they   105
bring man to grey hairs before he be thirty; yet they cast out such
mists of flattery from their breath that a man's lost again. Sure I
fell into my marriage bed drunk like the leopard;° well, with sober
eyes would I have avoided it.

Come, grave, and hide me from my blasted fame;   110
O that thou couldst as well conceal my shame!

Exeunt Mizaldus and Claridiana with Officers. Thais and
Abigail kneel to Duke Amago

THAIS Your pardon and your favour, gracious Duke,
At once we do implore, that have so long
Deceived your royal expectation,
Assurèd that the comic knitting-up   115
Will move your spleen unto the proper use
Of mirth, your natural inclination,
And wipe away the wat'ry-coloured anger
From your enforcèd cheek. Fair lord, beguile°
Them, and vouchsafe 't with a pleasing smile.   120

AMAGO Now by my life, I do. Fair ladies, rise:
I ne'er did purpose any other end
To them and these designs. I was informed
Of some notorious error as I sat in judgement,
And (do you hear?) these night-works require   125
A cat's eyes to impierce dejected darkness.—
Call back the prisoners.

Enter Claridiana and Mizaldus, with Officers

CLARIDIANA Now what other troubled news, that we must back thus?
Has any senator begged my pardon upon my wife's prostitution to
him?   130

MIZALDUS What a spite's this! I had kept in my breath of purpose,
thinking to go away the quieter, and must we now back?

AMAGO Since you are to die, we'll give you winding-sheets

Wherein you shall be shrouded alive,
By which we wind out all these miseries.   135
Signor Mizaldus, bestow a while your eye
And read here of your true wife's chastity.
   He gives Mizaldus a letter

MIZALDUS Chastity! I will sooner expect a Jesuit's recantation°
   Or the Great Turk's conversion, than her chastity.°
   Pardon, my liege, I will not trust mine eyes: 140
   Women and devils will deceive the wise.

AMAGO [*to Claridiana*] The like, sir, is apparent on your side.
   [*He gives Claridiana a letter*]

CLARIDIANA Who, my wife chaste? Has your grace your sense? I'll
   sooner believe a conjuror may say his prayers with zeal, than her
   honesty. Had she been an hermaphrodite, I would scarce have given 145
   credit to you.
   Let him that hath drunk love-drugs trust a woman;
   By heaven, I think the air is not more common.°

AMAGO Then we impose a strict command upon you:
   On your allegiance, read what there is writ.   150

CLARIDIANA A writ of error, on my life, my liege.°

AMAGO You'll find it so, I fear.

CLARIDIANA [*looks at the letter*] What have we here, the art of
   brachygraphy?°

THAIS He's stung already,
   As if his eyes were turned on Perseus' shield:°   155
   Their motion is fixed like to the pool of Styx.

ABIGAIL Yonder's our flames, and from the hollow arches
   Of his quick eyes comes comet-trains of fire,
   Bursting like hidden furies from their caves.°

CLARIDIANA [*reads*] 'Yours till he sleep the sleep of all the world,° 160
   Mizaldus.'

MIZALDUS Marry, an that lethargy seize you, read again.

CLARIDIANA [*reads*] 'Thy servant so made by his stars, Mizaldus.'
   A fire on your wandering stars, Mizaldus!

MIZALDUS Satan, why hast thou tempted my wife?   165

CLARIDIANA Peace, seducer, I am branded in the forehead
   With your star-mark. May the stars drop upon thee°
   And with their sulphur vapours choke thee ere thou
   Come at the gallows.

MIZALDUS Stretch not my patience, Muhammad!°   170

CLARIDIANA Termagant, that will stretch thy patience!°

MIZALDUS Had I known this, I would have poisoned thee in the
chalice this morning when we received the sacrament.

CLARIDIANA [*showing the ring*] Slave, know'st thou this? 'Tis an
appendix to the letter; but the greater temptation is hidden   175
within. I will scour thy gorge° like a hawk: thou shalt swallow
thine own stone in this letter, sealed and delivered in the presence
of—
          Claridiana and Mizaldus bustle

AMAGO Keep them asunder! List to us, we command!

CLARIDIANA O violent villain, is not thy hand hereto,   180
And writ in blood to show thy raging lust?

THAIS Spice° of a new halter! When you go a-ranging thus like devils,
would you might burn for 't as they do.

MIZALDUS Thus 'tis to lie with another man's wife:
He shall be sure to hear on 't again.   185
[*To Thais*] But we are friends, sweet duck.
          He kisses her
And this shall be my maxim all my life:
Man never happy is till in a wife.

CLARIDIANA [*to Abigail*] Here sunk our hate lower than any
whirlpool,
And this chaste kiss I give thee for thy care,   190
Thou fame of women full as wise as fair.
          He kisses her

AMAGO [*to Abigail and Thais*] You have saved us a labour in your
love;
But, gentlemen, why stood you so prepost'rously?°
Would you have headlong run to infamy
In so defamed a death?   195

MIZALDUS O my liege, I had rather roar to death with Phalaris' bull°
than, Darius-like,° to have one of my wings extend to Atlas, the
other to Europa.
What is a cuckold learn of me.
Few can tell his pedigree,   200
Nor his subtle nature conster:
Born a man but dies a monster.
Yet great antiquaries say
They spring from our Methuselah,
Who after Noah's flood was found   205
To have his crest with branches crowned.°

God in Eden's happy shade
This same creature made.
Then, to cut off all mistaking,
Cuckolds are of women's making,   210
From whose snares, good lord, deliver us.

CLARIDIANA Amen, amen. Before I would prove a cuckold, I would
    endure a winter's pilgrimage in the frozen zone, go stark naked
    through Muscovia,° where the climate is nine degrees colder than
    ice. And thus much to all married men: 215
Now I see great reason why
Love should marry jealousy:°
Since man's best of life is fame,
He had need preserve the same.
When 'tis in a woman's keeping,   220
Let not Argus' eyes be sleeping.°
The box unto Pandora given°
By the better powers of heaven
That contains pure chastity
And each virgin sovereignty,   225
Wantonly she oped and lost,
Gift whereof a god might boast.
Therefore, shouldst thou Diana wed,
Yet be jealous of her bed.

AMAGO Night, like a masque, is entered heaven's great hall   230
With thousand torches ushering the way.°
To Risus will we consecrate this evening;
Like Mycerinus cheating of the dark°
We'll make this night the day. Fair joys befall
Us and our actions. Are you pleasèd all?   235
        Exeunt

73

THE MAID'S TRAGEDY

FRANCIS BEAUMONT *and* JOHN FLETCHER

THE PERSONS OF THE PLAY

The King of Rhodes
Lysippus, his brother
Two Gentlemen of the King's bedchamber

Amintor, a young courtier
Evadne, his wife
Dula, Evadne's lady-in-waiting
Amintor's Servant

Aspatia, Amintor's rejected love
Calianax,° an old, angry courtier, her father
Diagoras, his assistant
Antiphila ⎫
Olympias ⎭ Aspatia's servants

Melantius,° a noble soldier, Evadne's brother
Diphilus, his brother
A Lady, courted by Melantius

Cleon ⎫
Strato ⎭ gentlemen

Night ⎫
Cynthia ⎪
Neptune ⎪
Aeolus ⎪
Favonius ⎬ characters in the masque
The Winds ⎪
Proteus ⎪
The Sea-Gods ⎭

Lords and Ladies
Guards
Servants

1.1

Enter Cleon, Strato, Lysippus, and Diphilus

CLEON The rest are making ready, sir.

STRATO So let them; there's time enough.

DIPHILUS You are the brother to the King, my lord; we'll take your
word.°

LYSIPPUS Strato, thou hast some skill in poetry. 5
What think'st thou of a masque? Will it be well?°

STRATO As well as masques can be.

LYSIPPUS   As masques can be?

STRATO Yes, they must commend their King, and speak in praise
Of the assembly, bless the bride and groom,
In person of some god; they're tied to rules 10
Of flattery.

Enter Melantius

CLEON   See, good my lord, who is returned.

LYSIPPUS Noble Melantius,
The land by me welcomes thy virtues home to Rhodes,°
Thou that with blood abroad buyest us our peace.
The breath of kings is like the breath of gods: 15
My brother wished thee here, and thou art here.
He will be too kind, and weary thee
With often welcomes; but the time doth give thee
A welcome above his, or all the world's.

MELANTIUS My lord, my thanks; but these scratched limbs of mine 20
Have spoke my love and truth unto my friends
More than my tongue e'er could. My mind's the same
It ever was to you: where I find worth,
I love the keeper till he let it go,
And then I follow it.

DIPHILUS   Hail, worthy brother! 25
He that rejoices not at your return
In safety, is mine enemy forever.

MELANTIUS I thank thee, Diphilus; but thou art faulty.
I sent for thee to exercise thine arms
With me at Patria: thou cam'st not, Diphilus.° 30
'Twas ill.

DIPHILUS My noble brother, my excuse

Is my King's strict command, which you, my lord,
Can witness with me.
LYSIPPUS   'Tis true, Melantius:
  He might not come till the solemnities
  Of this great match were passed.
DIPHILUS   Have you heard of it?   35
MELANTIUS Yes, I have given cause to those that here
  Envy my deeds abroad, to call me gamesome;°
  I have no other business here at Rhodes.
LYSIPPUS We have a masque tonight,
  And you must tread a soldier's measure.   40
MELANTIUS These soft and silken wars are not for me:
  The music must be shrill and all confused
  That stirs my blood, and then I dance with arms.
  But is Amintor wed?
DIPHILUS   This day.
MELANTIUS All joys upon him, for he is my friend.   45
  Wonder not that I call a man so young my friend:
  His worth is great. Valiant he is and temperate,
  And one that never thinks his life his own
  If his friend need it. When he was a boy,
  As oft as I returned (as, without boast,   50
  I brought home conquest), he would gaze upon me
  And view me round, to find in what one limb
  The virtue lay to do those things he heard;°
  Then would he wish to see my sword, and feel
  The quickness of the edge, and in his hand   55
  Weigh it; he oft would make me smile at this.
  His youth did promise much, and his ripe years
  Will see it all performed.
        Enter Aspatia, passing by, attended [by Antiphila and
        Olympias]
                                  Hail, maid and wife!
  Thou fair Aspatia, may the holy knot°
  That thou hast tied today last till the hand   60
  Of age undo 't. May'st thou bring a race
  Unto Amintor that may fill the world
  Successively with soldiers.
ASPATIA   My hard fortunes
  Deserve not scorn, for I was never proud

When they were good.
    Exeunt Aspatia, [Antiphila, and Olympias]

MELANTIUS   How's this?°   65

LYSIPPUS You are mistaken, sir: she is not married.

MELANTIUS You said Amintor was.

DIPHILUS 'Tis true, but—

MELANTIUS   Pardon me, I did receive
  Letters at Patria from my Amintor
  That he should marry her.

DIPHILUS   And so it stood   70
  In all opinion long, but your arrival
  Made me imagine you had heard the change.

MELANTIUS Who hath he taken, then?

LYSIPPUS   A lady, sir,
  That bears the light about her, and strikes dead°
  With flashes of her eye: the fair Evadne,°   75
  Your virtuous sister.

MELANTIUS   Peace of heart betwixt them;
  But this is strange.

LYSIPPUS   The King my brother did it
  To honour you, and these solemnities
  Are at his charge.

MELANTIUS   'Tis royal, like himself;
  But I am sad my speech bears so unfortunate a sound   80
  To beautiful Aspatia. There is rage
  Hid in her father's breast, Calianax,
  Bent long against me, and he should not think,
  If I could call it back, that I would take°
  So base revenges as to scorn the state   85
  Of his neglected daughter. Holds he still
  His greatness with the King?

LYSIPPUS   Yes, but this lady
  Walks discontented, with her wat'ry eyes
  Bent on the earth. The unfrequented woods
  Are her delight, and when she sees a bank   90
  Stuck full of flowers, she with a sigh will tell°
  Her servants what a pretty place it were
  To bury lovers in, and make her maids
  Pluck 'em, and strew her over like a corpse.°
  She carries with her an infectious grief   95

That strikes all her beholders. She will sing°
The mournfull'st things that ever ear hath heard,
And sigh, and sing again; and when the rest
Of our young ladies in their wanton blood
Tell mirthful tales in course that fill the room°   100
With laughter, she will with so sad a look
Bring forth a story of the silent death
Of some forsaken virgin, which her grief
Will put in such a phrase that ere she end
She'll send 'em weeping one by one away.   105

MELANTIUS She has a brother under my command
Like her, a face as womanish as hers,
But with a spirit that hath much outgrown
The number of his years.
                Enter Amintor

CLEON   My lord the bridegroom.

MELANTIUS [*embracing Amintor*] I might run fiercely, not more
          hastily   110
Upon my foe. I love thee well, Amintor.
My mouth is much too narrow for my heart.°
I joy to look upon those eyes of thine.
Thou art my friend, but my disordered speech
Cuts off my love.

AMINTOR   Thou art Melantius: 115
All love is spoke in that. A sacrifice
To thank the gods Melantius is returned
In safety! Victory sits on his sword°
As she was wont; may she build there and dwell,°
And may thy armour be as it hath been,   120
Only thy valour and thine innocence.°
What endless treasures would our enemies give
That I might hold thee still thus!

MELANTIUS [*weeping*]   I am poor
In words; but, credit me, young man, thy mother
Could no more but weep for joy to see thee   125
After long absence. All the wounds I have
Fetched not so much away, nor all the cries°
Of widowed mothers. But this is peace
And that was war.

AMINTOR   Pardon, thou holy god
Of marriage bed, and frown not, I am forced,   130

In answer of such noble tears as those,
To weep upon my wedding day.

MELANTIUS I fear thou art grown too fickle, for I hear
A lady mourns for thee, men say to death,
Forsaken of thee, on what terms I know not.   135

AMINTOR She had my promise, but the King forbade it
And made me take this worthy 'change, thy sister,°
Accompanied with graces about her,
With whom I long to lose my lusty youth
And grow old in her arms.

MELANTIUS   Be prosperous.°   140

AMINTOR [to Lysippus] My lord, the masquers rage for you.°

LYSIPPUS We are gone. Cleon, Strato, Diphilus.°

  Exeunt Lysippus, attended by Cleon, Strato, Diphilus

AMINTOR We'll all attend you. [To Melantius] We shall trouble you
With our solemnities.

MELANTIUS   Not so, Amintor;
But if you laugh at my rude carriage°   145
In peace, I'll do as much for you in war
When you come thither. But I have a mistress°
To bring to your delights. Rough though I am,
I have a mistress and she has a heart,
She says; but trust me, it is stone, no better.   150
There is no place that I can challenge.°
But you stand still, and here my way lies.

      Exeunt

1.2

  *[Seats are set out for the masque.] Enter Calianax with
  Diagoras*

CALIANAX Diagoras, look to the doors° better, for shame. You let in
all the world, and anon the King will rail at me. Why, very well said!
By Jove, the King will have the show i' th' court.°

DIAGORAS Why do you swear so, my lord? You know he'll have it here.

CALIANAX By this light, if he be wise, he will not.   5

DIAGORAS And if he will not be wise, you are forsworn.

CALIANAX One may swear his heart out with swearing, and get thanks
on no side. I'll be gone. Look to 't who will.

DIAGORAS My lord, I shall never keep them out. Pray stay: your looks°
will terrify them.   10

CALIANAX My looks terrify them! You coxcombly ass, you, I'll be
judge by all the company whether thou hast not a worse face
than I!

DIAGORAS I mean because they know you, and your office.

CALIANAX Office! I would I could put it off. I am sure I sweat quite   15
through my office.° I might have made room° at my daughter's
wedding; they ha' near killed her amongst them. And now I must
do service for him that hath forsaken her. Serve that will!°
      Exit Calianax

DIAGORAS He's so humorous since his daughter was forsaken.
      There is knocking within
      Hark! Hark! There! There! So! So! Coads! Coads! [*Calls off stage*] 20
      What now?

MELANTIUS (*within*) Open the door.

DIAGORAS Who's there?

MELANTIUS (*within*) Melantius.

DIAGORAS [*opening the door*] I hope your lordship brings no troop° 25
with you, for if you do, I must return them.
      Enter Melantius with a Lady

MELANTIUS None but this lady, sir.

DIAGORAS The ladies are all placed above,° save those that come in
the King's troop. The best of Rhodes sit there, and there's room.°

MELANTIUS I thank you, sir. When I have seen you placed, madam, I   30
must attend the King; but, the masque done, I'll wait on you again.
      Exeunt Melantius and the Lady at another door

DIAGORAS [*calls off stage*] Stand back there! Room for my lord Melantius! Pray bear back: this is no place for such youths and their trulls!
Let the doors shut again! Ay, do your heads itch?° I'll scratch them
for you! [*He gets the door shut*] So, now, thrust and hang!°   35
      There is knocking within
      Again! Who is 't now? [*To himself*] I cannot blame my lord Calianax
for going away. Would he were here! He would run raging amongst
them, and break a dozen wiser heads than his own in the twinkling
of an eye! [*Calls off stage*] What's the news now?

VOICE [*within*] I pray you, can you help me to the speech of the master 40
cook?

DIAGORAS If I open the door I'll cook some of your calves' heads!°
Peace, rogues!
      There is knocking within

Again! Who is 't?

MELANTIUS (*within*) Melantius.   45
   Enter Calianax

CALIANAX Let him not in.

DIAGORAS O my lord, a° must.
   [*He opens the door and calls off stage*]
  Make room there for my lord!
   Enter Melantius
  [*To Melantius*] Is your lady placed?

MELANTIUS Yes, sir, I thank you. My lord Calianax, well met!   50
  Your causeless hate to me I hope is buried.

CALIANAX Yes, I do service for your sister here,
  That brings mine own poor child to timeless death.°
  She loves your friend Amintor, such another
  False-hearted lord as you.

MELANTIUS   You do me wrong,   55
  A most unmanly one, and I am slow
  In taking vengeance; but be well advised.

CALIANAX It may be so. [*To Diagoras*] Who placed the lady there
  So near the presence of the King?°

MELANTIUS I did.

CALIANAX   My lord, she must not sit there.

MELANTIUS   Why?   60

CALIANAX The place is kept for women of more worth.°

MELANTIUS More worth than she? It misbecomes your age
  And place to be thus womanish. Forbear.
  What you have spoke I am content to think
  The palsy shook your tongue to.

CALIANAX   Why, 'tis well°   65
  If I stand here to place men's wenches.

MELANTIUS I shall quite forget this place, thy age, my safety,
  And through all cut that poor sickly week
  Thou hast to live away from thee!

CALIANAX Nay, I know you can fight for your whore.   70

MELANTIUS Bate me the King, and be he flesh and blood,°
  A lies that says it! Thy mother at fifteen°
  Was black and sinful to her.

DIAGORAS [*to Melantius*] Good my lord!°

MELANTIUS Some god pluck threescore years from that fond man,
  That I may kill him and not stain mine honour!   75
  It is the curse of soldiers that in peace

They shall be braved by such ignoble men
As, if the land were troubled, would with tears°
And knees beg succour from 'em. Would that blood,
That sea of blood, that I have lost in fight   80
Were running in thy veins, that it might make thee
Apt to say less, or able to maintain,
Shouldst thou say more! [*To himself*] This Rhodes, I see, is
   nought°
But a place privileged to do men wrong.°
CALIANAX Ay, you may say your pleasure.
     Enter Amintor
AMINTOR   What vile injury°   85
Has stirred my worthy friend, who is as slow
To fight with words as he is quick of hand?
MELANTIUS That heap of age, which I should reverence
If it were temperate; but testy years
Are most contemptible.
AMINTOR   Good sir, forbear.   90
CALIANAX There is just such another as yourself.
AMINTOR [*to Melantius*] He will wrong you, or me, or any man,
And talk as if he had no life to lose
Since this our match. The King is coming in;
I would not for more wealth than I enjoy   95
He should perceive you raging. He did hear
You were at difference now, which hastened him.
CALIANAX [*calls off stage*] Make room there!
     Hautboys play within. Enter the King, Evadne, Aspatia, Lords
     and Ladies. [*They take their seats for the masque*]
KING Melantius, thou art welcome, and my love
Is with thee still; but this is not a place   100
To brabble in. Calianax, join hands.
CALIANAX He shall not have mine hand.
KING   This is no time
To force you to 't. I do love you both.
Calianax, you look well to your office;°
And you, Melantius, are welcome home.   105
Begin the masque.
MELANTIUS Sister, I joy to see you and your choice.
You looked with my eyes when you took that man;
Be happy in him.
     Recorders play°
EVADNE   O my dearest brother,

84

Your presence is more joyful than this day   110
Can be unto me.
      The masque begins
      Night rises° in mists
NIGHT *Our reign is come, for in the raging sea*
   The sun is drowned, and with him fell the day.
   Bright Cynthia, hear my voice: I am the night°
   For whom thou bear'st about thy borrowed light.   115
   Appear: no longer thy pale visage shroud,
   But strike thy silver horns quite through a cloud,°
   And send a beam upon my swarthy face
   By which I may discover all the place
   And persons, and how many longing eyes   120
   Are come to wait on our solemnities.
      Enter Cynthia
   How dull and black am I! I could not find
   This beauty without thee, I am so blind.
   Methinks they show like to those eastern streaks
   That warn us hence before the morning breaks.   125
   Back, my pale servant, for these eyes know how°
   To shoot far more and quicker rays than thou.
CYNTHIA *Great Queen, they be a troop for whom alone*
   One of my clearest moons I have put on,
   A troop that looks as if thyself and I   130
   Had plucked our reins in and our whips laid by°
   To gaze upon these mortals, that appear
   Brighter than we.
NIGHT   *Then let us keep 'em here*
   And never more our chariots drive away,
   But keep our places and outshine the day.   135
CYNTHIA *Great Queen of shadows, you are pleased to speak*
   Of more than may be done. We may not break
   The gods' decrees, but when our time is come
   Must drive away and give the day our room.°
NIGHT *Then shine at full, fair Queen, and by thy power*   140
   Produce a birth, to crown this happy hour,
   Of nymphs and shepherds; let their songs discover,
   Easy and sweet, who is a happy lover.
   Or, if thou wilt, then call thine own Endymion°
   From the sweet flow'ry bed he lies upon   145
   On Latmus' top: thy pale beams draw away
   And of this long night let him make the day.°

CYNTHIA   Thou dream'st, dark Queen: that fair boy was not mine,
Nor went I down to kiss him. Ease and wine
Have bred these bold tales: poets when they rage°   150
Turn gods to men and make an hour an age;
But I will give a greater state and glory
And raise to time a nobler memory°
Of what these lovers are. Rise, rise, I say,
Thou power of deeps, thy surges laid away,   155
Neptune, great King of waters, and by me
Be proud to be commanded.°
        Neptune rises°

NEPTUNE   Cynthia, see,
Thy word has fetched me hither. Let me know
Why I ascend.

CYNTHIA   Does this majestic show
Give thee no knowledge yet?

NEPTUNE   Yes, now I see   160
Something intended, Cynthia, worthy thee.
Go on, I'll be a helper.

CYNTHIA   Hie thee, then,°
And charge the wind-god from his rocky den°
Let loose his subjects; only Boreas,
Too foul for our intentions as he was,°   165
Still keep him fast chained. We must have none here
But vernal blasts and gentle winds appear,°
Such as blow flowers, and through the glad boughs sing°
Many soft welcomes to the lusty spring.
These are our music. Next, thy wat'ry race   170
Bring on in couples (we are pleased to grace
This noble night), each in their richest things
Your own deeps or the broken vessel brings.°
Be prodigal and I shall be as kind,
And shine at full upon you.
        Enter Aeolus out of a rock°

NEPTUNE   O, the wind—   175
Commanding Aeolus.

AEOLUS   Great Neptune.

NEPTUNE   He.

AEOLUS What is thy will?

NEPTUNE   We do command thee free
Favonius and thy milder winds to wait°

Upon our *Cynthia; but tie Boreas strait,*
He's too rebellious.
AEOLUS   *I shall do it.*
NEPTUNE   *Do.*   180
        [Exit Aeolus]
        [To Cynthia] *Great mistress of the flood and all below,*
        Thy full command has taken.
                [Enter Aeolus, with Favonius and the other Winds]
AEOLUS   *O! The main!*
    Neptune!
NEPTUNE *Here.*
AEOLUS   *Boreas has broke his chain*
    And, struggling with the rest, has got away.
NEPTUNE *Let him alone, I'll take him up at sea;*   185
    He will not long be thence. Go once again
    And call out of the bottoms of the main
    Blue Proteus and the rest; charge them put on
    The greatest pearls and the most sparkling stone
    The beaten rock breeds, till this night is done°   190
    By me a solemn honour to the moon.
    Fly like a full sail.
AEOLUS   *I am gone.*
        [Exit Aeolus]
CYNTHIA   *Dark night,*
    Strike a full silence, do a thorough right
    To this great chorus, that our music may
    Touch high as heaven, and make the east break day   195
    At midnight.
            [Enter Proteus and the Sea-Gods.] *Music plays*°
SEA-GODS [sing] *Cynthia, to thy power and thee,*
                        We obey.
                    Joy to this great company!
                        And no day   200
                    Come to steal this night away
                    Till the rites of love are ended
                    And the lusty bridegroom say,
                    'Welcome light, of all befriended.'°

                    Pace out, you watery powers below: 205
                        Let your feet
                    Like the galleys when they row
                        Even beat;°

87

> Let your unknown measures, set
> To the still winds, tell to all   210
> That gods are come, immortal, great,
> To honour this great nuptial.

[The Sea-Gods and the Winds dance a measure]

SEA-GODS [sing]   *Hold back thy hours, dark Night, till we have*
> *done;*
> *The day will come too soon.*
> *Young maids will curse thee if thou steal'st away*   215
> *And leav'st their blushes open to the day.*
> *Stay, stay, and hide*
> *The blushes of the bride.*

> *Stay, gentle Night, and with thy darkness cover*
> *The kisses of her lover.*   220
> *Stay and confound her tears and her shrill*
> *cryings,*
> *Her weak denials, vows, and often dyings.°*
> *Stay and hide all,*
> *But help not, though she call.°*

[Enter Aeolus]

AEOLUS   Ho, Neptune!

NEPTUNE   Aeolus.

AEOLUS   The sea goes high: 225
Boreas hath raised a storm. Go and apply
Thy trident; else, I prophesy, ere day°
Many a tall ship will be cast away.
Descend with all the gods and all their power
To strike a calm.

CYNTHIA   We thank you for this hour.   230

My favour to you all; to gratulate°
So great a service done at my desire,
Ye shall have many floods, fuller and higher
Than you have wished for; no ebb shall dare   235
To let the day see where your dwellings are.
Now back unto your government in haste°
Lest your proud charge should swell above the waste°
And win upon the island.

NEPTUNE   We obey.°

Neptune descends with the Sea-Gods. [Exeunt Aeolus,
Favonius, and the other Winds]

CYNTHIA *Hold up thy head, dead Night; see'st thou not day?*   240
   The East begins to lighten: I must down
   And give my brother place.
NIGHT   *O, I could frown°*
   To see the day, the day that flings his light
   Upon my kingdoms and contemns old Night.
   Let him go on, and flame; I hope to see   245
   Another wild-fire in his axle-tree,°
   And all fall drenched. But I forget. Speak, Queen.
   The day grows on: I must no more be seen.
CYNTHIA *Heave up thy drowsy head again and see*
   A greater light, a greater majesty°   250
   Between our sect and us. Whip up thy team.
   The day breaks here, and yon same flashing stream
   Shot from the south. Say, wilt thou go? Which way?°
NIGHT *I'll vanish into mists.*
CYNTHIA   *I into day.°*

     Exeunt Night and Cynthia
      The masque ends°

KING Take lights there! Ladies, get the bride to bed.   255
   We will not see you laid—goodnight, Amintor—°
   We'll ease you of that tedious ceremony.
   Were it my case I should think time run slow.
   If thou be'st noble, youth, get me a boy
   That may defend my kingdom from my foes.   260
AMINTOR All happiness to you.
KING   Goodnight, Melantius.°

     Exeunt. [The seats are removed°]

2.1

Enter Evadne, Aspatia, Dula, and other Ladies,° with lights

DULA Madam, shall we undress you for this fight?
　　The wars are nak'd that you must make tonight.°

EVADNE You are very merry, Dula.

DULA　　　　　　　　　　I should be
　　Far merrier, madam, if it were with me
　　As it is with you.

EVADNE　　　　How's that?

DULA　　　　　　　　　　That I might　　　　　　　5
　　Go to bed with him, with credit, that you do.°

EVADNE Why, how now, wench?

DULA　　　　　　　　　　Come, ladies, will you help?
　　　　　[They begin to undress Evadne]

EVADNE I am soon undone.

DULA　　　　　　　　　　And as soon done.°
　　Good store of clothes will trouble you at both.°

EVADNE Art thou drunk, Dula?

DULA　　　　　　　　　　Why, here's none but we.　　10

EVADNE Thou think'st belike there is no modesty
　　When we are alone.

DULA Ay, by my troth, you hit my thoughts aright.

EVADNE You prick me, lady.

FIRST LADY　　　　　　'Tis against my will.

DULA Anon you must endure more and lie still:°　　　15
　　You're best to practice.

EVADNE　　　　　　Sure this wench is mad.

DULA No, faith, this is a trick that I have had
　　Since I was fourteen.

EVADNE　　　　　　'Tis high time to leave it.

DULA Nay, now I'll keep it till the trick leave me.
　　A dozen wanton words put in your head　　　　　20
　　Will make you livelier in your husband's bed.

EVADNE Nay, faith, then, take it.

DULA　　　　　　　　Take it, madam, where?
　　We all, I hope, will take it that are here.°

EVADNE Nay, then, I'll give you o'er.

DULA　　　　　　　　So will I make°

The ablest man in Rhodes or his heart ache.°   25
EVADNE Wilt take my place tonight?
DULA   I'll hold your cards
  Against any two I know.
EVADNE   What wilt thou do?
DULA Madam, we'll do 't, and make 'em leave play too.
EVADNE Aspatia, take her part.
DULA   I will refuse it.
  She will pluck down a side, she does not use it.   30
EVADNE [to Aspatia] Why, do, I prithee.
DULA [to Evadne]   You will find the play
  Quickly, because your head lies well that way.°
EVADNE I thank thee, Dula. Would thou couldst instil
  Some of thy mirth into Aspatia:
  Nothing but sad thoughts in her breast do dwell.   35
  Methinks a mean betwixt you would do well.
DULA She is in love. Hang me if I were so,
  But I could run my country. I love too°
  To do those things that people in love do.
ASPATIA It were a timeless smile should prove my cheek.°   40
  It were a fitter hour for me to laugh
  When at the altar the religious priest
  Were pacifying the offended powers
  With sacrifice, than now. This should have been°
  My night, and all your hands have been employed°   45
  In giving me, a spotless offering,
  To young Amintor's bed, as we are now
  For you. Pardon, Evadne: would my worth
  Were great as yours, or that the King, or he,
  Or both, thought so. Perhaps he found me worthless;   50
  But till he did so, in these ears of mine,
  These credulous ears, he poured the sweetest words
  That art or love could frame. If he were false,
  Pardon it, heaven, and if I did want
  Virtue, you safely may forgive that too,   55
  For I have lost none that I had from you.
EVADNE Nay, leave this sad talk, madam.
ASPATIA Would I could, then I should leave the cause.
EVADNE See if you have not spoiled all Dula's mirth.
ASPATIA [to Dula] Thou think'st thy heart hard, but if thou be'st
    caught,
                                          60

Remember me; thou shalt perceive a fire
Shot suddenly into thee.

DULA   That's not so good.
Let 'em shoot anything but fire, I fear 'em not.

ASPATIA Well, wench, thou may'st be taken.

EVADNE Ladies, goodnight, I'll do the rest myself.   65

DULA Nay, let your lord do some.°

ASPATIA Madam, goodnight. May all the marriage joys
That longing maids imagine in their beds
Prove so unto you. May no discontent
Grow twixt your love and you; but if there do,   70
Inquire of me and I will guide your moan
And teach you an artificial way to grieve°
To keep your sorrow waking. Love your lord
No worse than I; but if you love so well,
Alas, you may displease him; so did I.   75
This is the last time you shall look on me.
Ladies, farewell; as soon as I am dead,
Come all and watch one night about my hearse;
Bring each a mournful story and a tear
To offer at it when I go to earth;   80
With flattering ivy clasp my coffin round;
Write on my brow my fortune; let my bier°
Be borne by virgins that shall sing by course°
The truth of maids, and perjuries of men.

EVADNE Alas, I pity thee.
            Exit Evadne

ALL   Madam, goodnight.   85

FIRST LADY Come, we'll let in the bridegroom.
            [*Dula goes to the door*°]

DULA [*calling off stage*]   Where's my lord?
            Enter Amintor

FIRST LADY Here, take this light.

DULA   You'll find her in the dark.

FIRST LADY Your lady's scarce abed yet; you must help her.

ASPATIA Go and be happy in your lady's love.
May all the wrongs that you have done to me   90
Be utterly forgotten in my death.
I'll trouble you no more; yet I will take
A parting kiss, and will not be denied.

[*She kisses Amintor*]

You'll come, my lord, and see the virgins weep
When I am laid in earth, though you yourself   95
Can know no pity. Thus I wind myself
Into this willow garland, and am prouder°
That I was once your love, though now refused,
Than to have had another true to me.
So with prayers I leave you, and must try   100
Some yet unpracticed way to grieve and die.
            Exit Aspatia

DULA   Come, ladies, will you go?

ALL   Goodnight, my lord.

AMINTOR   Much happiness unto you all.
            Exeunt Dula and Ladies

I did that lady wrong; methinks I feel
Her grief shoot suddenly through all my veins.   105
            [*He weeps*]
Mine eyes run: this is strange at such a time.
It was the King first moved me to 't, but he
Has not my will in keeping. Why do I
Perplex myself thus? Something whispers me,
'Go not to bed'. My guilt is not so great   110
As mine own conscience, too sensible,°
Would make me think: I only brake a promise,
And 'twas the King that forced me. Timorous flesh,
Why shak'st thou so? Away, my idle fears.
            Enter Evadne in her nightdress
Yonder she is, the lustre of whose eye   115
Can blot away the sad remembrance
Of all these things. O my Evadne, spare
That tender body, let it not take cold.
The vapours of the night will not fall here.°
To bed, my love. Hymen will punish us   120
For being slack performers of his rites.
Cam'st thou to call me?

EVADNE   No.

AMINTOR   Come, come, my love,
And let us lose ourselves to one another.
Why art thou up so long?

EVADNE   I am not well.

AMINTOR To bed then. Let me wind thee in these arms   125
  Till I have banished sickness.

EVADNE   Good my lord,
  I cannot sleep.

AMINTOR   Evadne, we'll watch;°
  I mean no sleeping.

EVADNE   I'll not go to bed.

AMINTOR I prithee do.

EVADNE   I will not for the world.

AMINTOR Why, my dear love?

EVADNE   Why? I have sworn I will not.   130

AMINTOR Sworn?

EVADNE Ay.

AMINTOR How? 'Sworn', Evadne?

EVADNE   Yes, sworn, Amintor,
  And will swear again if you will wish to hear me.

AMINTOR To whom have you sworn this?   135

EVADNE If I should name him the matter were not great.°

AMINTOR Come, this is but the coyness of a bride.

EVADNE 'The coyness of a bride'?

AMINTOR   How prettily
  That frown becomes thee.

EVADNE   Do you like it so?

AMINTOR Thou can'st not dress thy face in such a look   140
  But I shall like it.

EVADNE   What look likes you best?

AMINTOR Why do you ask?

EVADNE That I may show you one less pleasing to you.

AMINTOR How's that?

EVADNE That I may show you one less pleasing to you.   145

AMINTOR I prithee, put thy jests in milder looks,
  It shows as thou wert angry.

EVADNE   So perhaps I am indeed.

AMINTOR Why, who has done thee wrong?
  Name me the man, and by thy self I swear,
  Thy yet unconquered self, I will revenge thee.°   150

EVADNE Now I shall try thy truth. If thou dost love me,
  Thou weigh'st not anything compared with me.
  Life, honour, joys eternal, all delights
  This world can yield or hopeful people feign
  Are in the life to come, are light as air   155

To a true lover when his lady frowns
And bids him do this. Wilt thou kill this man?
Swear, my Amintor, and I'll kiss the sin
Off from thy lips.

AMINTOR   I wo' not swear, sweet love,
Till I do know the cause.

EVADNE   I would thou would'st.   160
Why, it is thou that wrong'st me. I hate thee.
Thou shouldst have killed thyself.

AMINTOR If I should know that, I should quickly kill
The man you hated.

EVADNE   Know it then, and do 't.

AMINTOR Oh no, what look soe'er thou shalt put on   165
To try my faith, I shall not think thee false.
I cannot find one blemish in thy face
Where falsehood should abide. Leave, and to bed.
If you have sworn to any of the virgins
That were your old companions to preserve   170
Your maidenhead a night, it may be done°
Without this means.

EVADNE A maidenhead, Amintor, at my years?

AMINTOR Sure she raves. This cannot be
Thy natural temper. Shall I call thy maids?   175
Either thy healthful sleep hath left thee long
Or else some fever rages in thy blood.

EVADNE Neither. Amintor, think you I am mad
Because I speak the truth?

AMINTOR   Is this the truth?
Will you not lie with me tonight?   180

EVADNE Tonight? You talk as if I would hereafter.

AMINTOR 'Hereafter'? Yes I do.

EVADNE   You are deceived.
Put off amazement, and with patience mark
What I shall utter, for the oracle°
Knows nothing truer: 'tis not for a night   185
Or two that I forbear thy bed, but ever.

AMINTOR I dream. Awake, Amintor.

EVADNE   You hear right.
I sooner will find out the beds of snakes
And with my youthful blood warm their cold flesh,
Letting them curl themselves about my limbs,   190

95

Than sleep one night with thee. This is not feigned,
Nor sounds it like 'the coyness of a bride'.

AMINTOR Is flesh so earthly to endure all this?
Are these the joys of marriage? Hymen, keep
This story, that will make succeeding youth   195
Neglect thy ceremonies, from all ears.°
Let it not rise up for thy shame and mine
To after ages. We will scorn thy laws
If thou no better bless them. Touch the heart
Of her that thou hast sent me, or the world   200
Shall know there's not an altar that will smoke
In praise of thee. We will adopt us sons;
Then virtue shall inherit, and not blood.
If we do lust, we'll take the next we meet,
Serving ourselves as other creatures do,   205
And never take note of the female more,
Nor of her issue. I do rage in vain:°
She can but jest. O pardon me, my love;
So dear the thoughts are that I hold of thee
That I must break forth. Satisfy my fear;°   210
It is a pain beyond the hand of death
To be in doubt. Confirm it with an oath
If this be true.

EVADNE   Do you invent the form:°
Let there be in it all the binding words
Devils and conjurors can put together,   215
And I will take it. I have sworn before,
And here by all things holy do again,
Never to be acquainted with thy bed.
Is your doubt over now?

AMINTOR I know too much; would I had doubted still.   220
Was ever such a marriage-night as this?
You powers above, if you did ever mean
Man should be used thus, you have thought a way
How he may bear himself and save his honour.
Instruct me in it, for to my dull eyes   225
There is no mean, no moderate course to run:
I must live scorned or be a murderer.
Is there a third? Why is this night so calm?
Why does not heaven speak in thunder to us
And drown her voice?

EVADNE   This rage will do no good.   230

96

AMINTOR Evadne, hear me: thou hast ta'en an oath,
    But such a rash one that to keep it were
    Worse than to swear it. Call it back to thee.
    Such vows as those never ascend the heaven;°
    A tear or two will wash it quite away.   235
    Have mercy on my youth, my hopeful youth,
    If thou be pitiful; for, without boast,
    This land was proud of me. What lady was there
    That men called fair and virtuous in this isle
    That would have shunned my love? It is in thee   240
    To make me hold this worth. O we vain men°
    That trust all our reputation
    To rest upon the weak and yielding hand
    Of feeble woman. But thou art not stone;
    Thy flesh is soft, and in thine eyes do dwell   245
    The spirit of love; thy heart cannot be hard.
    Come, lead me from the bottom of despair
    To all the joys thou hast (I know thou wilt),
    And make me careful lest the sudden change
    O'ercome my spirit.
EVADNE   When I call back this oath,   250
    The pains of hell environ me.
AMINTOR I sleep and am too temperate. Come to bed,
    Or by those hairs, which, if thou hast a soul
    Like to thy locks, were threads for kings to wear
    About their arms—
EVADNE   Why, so perhaps they are.°   255
AMINTOR —I'll drag thee to my bed, and make thy tongue
    Undo this wicked oath, or on thy flesh
    I'll print a thousand wounds to let out life.°
EVADNE I fear thee not; do what thou dar'st to me.
    Every ill-sounding word or threat'ning look   260
    Thou showest to me will be revenged at full.
AMINTOR It will not, sure, Evadne.
EVADNE Do not you hazard that.
AMINTOR   Ha' ye your champions?
EVADNE Alas, Amintor, think'st thou I forbear
    To sleep with thee because I have put on   265
    A maiden's strictness? Look upon these cheeks
    And thou shalt find the hot and rising blood
    Unapt for such a vow. No, in this heart
    There dwells as much desire and as much will

To put that wished act in practice, as ever yet   270
Was known to woman, and they have been shown
Both; but it was the folly of thy youth°
To think this beauty, to what land so e'er
It shall be called, shall stoop to any second.°
I do enjoy the best, and in that height   275
Have sworn to stand or die. You guess the man.

AMINTOR No, let me know the man that wrongs me so,
  That I may cut his body into motes
  And scatter it before the northern wind.°

EVADNE You dare not strike him.

AMINTOR   Do not wrong me so.   280
  Yes, if his body were a poisonous plant
  That it were death to touch, I have a soul
  Will throw me on him.

EVADNE   Why, 'tis the King.

AMINTOR The King!

EVADNE   What will you do now?

AMINTOR   'Tis not the King.

EVADNE What did he make this match for, dull Amintor?   285

AMINTOR O thou hast named a word that wipes away
  All thoughts revengeful. In that sacred name,
  The King, there lies a terror; what frail man
  Dares lift his hand against it? Let the gods
  Speak to him when they please, till when let us   290
  Suffer, and wait.°

EVADNE Why should you fill your self so full of heat
  And haste so to my bed? I am no virgin.°

AMINTOR What devil hath put it in thy fancy then
  To marry me?

EVADNE   Alas, I must have one   295
  To father children and to bear the name°
  Of husband to me, that my sin may be
  More honourable.

AMINTOR   What a strange thing am I!

EVADNE A miserable one, one that myself
  Am sorry for.

AMINTOR   Why, show it then in this: 300
  If thou hast pity, though thy love be none,
  Kill me, and all true lovers that shall live
  In after ages crossed in their desires

98

Shall bless thy memory and call thee good,
Because such mercy in thy heart was found   305
To rid a lingering wretch.°
EVADNE   I must have one
To fill thy room again if thou wert dead,
Else by this night I would. I pity thee.
AMINTOR These strange and sudden injuries have fall'n
So thick upon me that I lose all sense   310
Of what they are. Methinks I am not wronged,
Nor is it aught, if from the censuring world
I can but hide it. Reputation,
Thou art a word, no more, but thou hast shown
An impudence so high that to the world   315
I fear thou wilt betray or shame thyself.
EVADNE To cover shame I took thee; never fear
That I would blaze myself.
AMINTOR   Nor let the King°
Know I conceive he wrongs me; then mine honour
Will thrust me into action. That my flesh°   320
Could bear with patience, and it is some ease
To me in these extremes that I know this
Before I touched thee; else, had all the sins
Of mankind stood betwixt me and the King,
I had gone through 'em to his heart and thine.   325
I have lost one desire, 'tis not his crown
Shall buy me to thy bed. Now I resolve
He has dishonoured thee. Give me thy hand.
Be careful of thy credit, and sin close;°
'Tis all I wish. Upon thy chamber floor   330
I'll rest tonight, that morning visitors
May think we did as married people use;
And prithee smile upon me when they come
And seem to toy as if thou hadst been pleased
With what we did.
EVADNE   Fear not, I will do this.   335
AMINTOR Come, let us practice, and as wantonly°
As ever loving bride and bridegroom met,
Let's laugh and enter here.
EVADNE   I am content.
        [*He puts his arms around her*]
AMINTOR Down all the swellings of my troubled heart.

99

When we walk thus entwined, let all eyes see   340
If ever lovers better did agree.
    Exeunt

2.2

Enter Aspatia, followed by Antiphila and Olympias,
[carrying a sewing box°]

ASPATIA Away! You are not sad; force it no further.
  Good gods, how well you look! Such a full colour
  Young bashful brides put on. Sure you are new-married.
ANTIPHILA Yes, madam, to your grief.
ASPATIA   Alas, poor wenches!°
  Go learn to love first; learn to love yourselves;   5
  Learn to be flattered, and believe, and bless
  The double tongue that did it. Make a faith
  Out of the miracles of ancient lovers,°
  Such as spake truth and died in 't,
  And like me believe all faithful, and be miserable.   10
  Did you ne'er love yet, wenches? Speak, Olympias,
  Thou hast an easy temper, fit for stamp.°
OLYMPIAS Never.
ASPATIA   Nor you, Antiphila?
ANTIPHILA   Nor I.
ASPATIA Then, my good girls, be more than women, wise.
  At least, be more than I was.°   15
  Come, let's be sad, my girls.
  That downcast of thine eye, Olympias,
  Shows a fine sorrow; mark, Antiphila,
  Just such another was the nymph Oenone's
  When Paris brought home Helen. Now a tear,°   20
  And then thou art a piece expressing fully
  The Carthage Queen when from a cold sea rock,°
  Full with her sorrow, she tied fast her eyes
  To the fair Trojan ships, and, having lost them,
  Just as thine does, down stole a tear. Antiphila,   25
  What would this wench do if she were Aspatia?
  Here she would stand till some more pitying god
  Turned her to marble. 'Tis enough, my wench.°

Show me the piece of needlework you wrought.
ANTIPHILA Of Ariadne, madam?
ASPATIA   Yes, that piece.°   30
    [*Antiphila shows her a sampler*]
    This should be Theseus, he's a cozening face:°
    You meant him for a man.
ANTIPHILA   He was so, madam.
ASPATIA Why then, 'tis well enough. [*To the figure in the sampler*]
    Never look back!
    You have a full wind and a false heart, Theseus.
    [*To Antiphila*] Does not the story say his keel was split,   35
    Or his masts spent, or some kind rock or other°
    Met with his vessel?
ANTIPHILA   Not as I remember.
ASPATIA It should ha' been so. Could the gods know this
    And not of all their number raise a storm?
    But they are all as ill. This false smile was well expressed:°   40
    Just such another caught me. You shall not go so, Antiphila.°
    In this place work a quicksand,
    And over it a shallow smiling water,°
    And his ship ploughing it, and then a Fear.°
    Do that Fear to the life, wench.
ANTIPHILA   'Twill wrong the story.   45
ASPATIA 'Twill make the story, wronged by wanton poets,°
    Live long and be believed. But where's the lady?
ANTIPHILA There, madam.
ASPATIA   Fie, you have missed it here,
    Antiphila. You are much mistaken, wench.
    These colours are not dull and pale enough   50
    To show a soul so full of misery
    As this sad lady's was. Do it by me,°
    Do it again, by me, the lost Aspatia,
    And you shall find all true but the wild island.°
    Suppose I stand upon the sea beach now,   55
    Mine arms thus, and mine hair blown with the wind,
    Wild as that desert. And let all about me°
    Tell that I am forsaken. Do my face,
    If thou hadst ever feeling of a sorrow,
    Thus, thus, Antiphila; strive to make me look   60
    Like sorrow's monument. And the trees about me,°
    Let them be dry and leafless; let the rocks

Groan with continual surges; and behind me
Make all a desolation. Look, look, wenches,
A miserable life of this poor picture.°   65

OLYMPIAS Dear madam.

ASPATIA   I have done, sit down, and let us
Upon that point fix all our eyes, that point there.
    [*They sit on the ground*]
Make a dumb silence till you feel a sudden sadness
Give us new souls.
        Enter Calianax

CALIANAX The King may do this, and he may not do it.   70
My child is wronged, disgraced. Well, how now, hussies!
What, at your ease? Is this a time to sit still?
Up, you young lazy whores, up or I'll swinge you!

OLYMPIAS Nay, good my lord!

CALIANAX You'll lie down shortly. Get you in and work.   75
What, are you grown so resty? You want heats.
We shall have some of the court boys do that office.

ANTIPHILA My lord, we do no more than we are charged.
It is the lady's pleasure we be thus in grief;
She is forsaken.

CALIANAX   There's a rogue too,   80
A young dissembling slave. Well, get you in.
I'll have a bout with that boy. 'Tis high time
Now to be valiant; I confess my youth
Was never prone that way. What, made an ass?
A court stale? Well, I will be valiant,   85
And beat some dozen of these whelps, I will. And there's
Another of 'em, a trim, cheating soldier:
I'll maul that rascal. He's out-braved me twice,°
But now I thank the gods I am valiant.
Go, get you in. I'll take a course withal.°   90
        Exeunt

3.1

Enter Cleon, Strato, Diphilus

CLEON Your sister is not up yet.

DIPHILUS O, brides must take their morning's rest;
The night is troublesome.

STRATO   But not tedious.

DIPHILUS What odds he has not my sister's maidenhead tonight?

STRATO No, it's odds against any bridegroom living, he ne'er gets it   5
while he lives.°

DIPHILUS You're merry with my sister; you'll please to allow me the
same freedom with your mother.

STRATO She's at your service.°

DIPHILUS Then she's merry enough of herself, she needs no tickling.   10
Knock at the door.

STRATO We shall interrupt them.

DIPHILUS No matter, they have the year before them.
    [*Calls off stage*] Good morrow, sister, spare yourself today;
The night will come again.
    Enter Amintor

AMINTOR   Who's there? My brother?°   15
I am no readier yet; your sister is but now up.

DIPHILUS You look as you had lost your eyes tonight.°
I think you ha' not slept.

AMINTOR   I' faith I have not.

DIPHILUS You have done better, then.

AMINTOR We ventured for a boy. When he is twelve,°   20
A shall command against the foes of Rhodes.
Shall we be merry?

STRATO You cannot, you want sleep.

AMINTOR [*aside*]   'Tis true, but she,
As if she had drunk Lethe or had made°
Even with heaven, did fetch so still a sleep,°   25
So sweet and sound.

DIPHILUS   What's that?

AMINTOR   Your sister frets°
This morning, and does turn her eyes upon me
As people on their headsman. She does chafe°
And kiss and chafe again and clap my cheeks.°

She's in another world.   30
DIPHILUS Then I had lost. I was about to lay
    You had not got her maidenhead tonight.
AMINTOR [aside] Ha, does he not mock me? [Aloud] You'd lost
    indeed.
    I do not use to bungle.
CLEON   You do deserve her.
AMINTOR [aside] I laid my lips to hers, and that wild breath,   35
    That was so rude and rough to me last night,
    Was sweet as April. I'll be guilty too
    If these be the effects.°
        Enter Melantius
MELANTIUS Good day, Amintor—for to me the name
    Of brother is too distant. We are friends,   40
    And that is nearer.
        [*Amintor embraces him and looks intently at his face*]
AMINTOR   Dear Melantius,
    Let me behold thee. Is it possible?
MELANTIUS What sudden gaze is this?
AMINTOR   'Tis wondrous strange.
MELANTIUS Why does thine eye desire so strict a view
    Of that it knows so well? There's nothing here   45
    That is not thine.
AMINTOR   I wonder much, Melantius,
    To see those noble looks that make me think
    How virtuous thou art, and on the sudden
    'Tis strange to me thou shouldst have worth and honour,
    Or not be base and false and treacherous   50
    And every ill. But—
MELANTIUS   Stay, stay, my friend.
    I fear this sound will not become our loves.
    No more embrace me.
AMINTOR   O mistake me not.
    I know thee to be full of all those deeds
    That we frail men call good, but by the course   55
    Of nature thou shouldst be as quickly changed
    As are the winds, dissembling as the sea
    That now wears brows as smooth as virgins' be,
    Tempting the merchant to invade his face,
    And in an hour calls his billows up   60
    And shoots 'em at the sun, destroying all°
    A carries on him. [*Aside*] O how near am I°

To utter my sick thoughts.

MELANTIUS But why, my friend, should I be so by nature?

AMINTOR I have wed thy sister, who hath virtuous thoughts   65
　Enough for one whole family, and it is strange
　That you should feel no want.

MELANTIUS　　　　　　　　　　Believe me,
　This is compliment too cunning for me.°

DIPHILUS What should I be then by the course of nature,
　They having both robbed me of so much virtue?   70

STRATO O call the bride, my lord Amintor,
　That we may see her blush and turn her eyes down;
　It is the prettiest sport.

AMINTOR Evadne.

EVADNE [within] My lord.

AMINTOR　　　　　　　　Come forth, my love:
　Your brothers do attend to wish you joy.   75

EVADNE I am not ready yet.

AMINTOR　　　　　　　　Enough, enough.

EVADNE They'll mock me.

AMINTOR　　　　　　　　Faith, thou shalt come in.
　　　Enter Evadne

MELANTIUS Good morrow, sister. He that understands
　Whom you have wed need not to wish you joy:
　You have enough. Take heed you be not proud.   80

DIPHILUS O sister, what have you done?

EVADNE I, 'done'? Why, what have I done?

STRATO My lord Amintor swears you are no maid now.

EVADNE Push!

STRATO I' faith he does.

EVADNE　　　　　　　　I knew I should be mocked.   85

DIPHILUS With a truth.

EVADNE　　　　　　　　If 'twere to do again,
　In faith I would not marry.

AMINTOR [aside]　　　　Nor I, by heaven.

DIPHILUS Sister, Dula swears she heard you cry two rooms off.

EVADNE Fie, how you talk.

DIPHILUS Let's see you walk. By my troth, you're spoiled.°   90

MELANTIUS Amintor.

AMINTOR Ha?

MELANTIUS Thou art sad.

AMINTOR　　　　　　　Who I? I thank you for that.
　Shall Diphilus, thou, and I sing a catch?

MELANTIUS How?   95
AMINTOR Prithee, let's.
MELANTIUS Nay, that's too much the other way.
AMINTOR I am so lightened with my happiness.
   [*To Evadne*] How does thou, love? Kiss me.
EVADNE I cannot love you, you tell tales of me.   100
AMINTOR Nothing but what becomes us. Gentlemen,
   Would you had all such wives, and all the world,
   That I might be no wonder. You're all sad:
   What, do you envy me? I walk, methinks,
   On water and ne'er sink, I am so light.   105
MELANTIUS 'Tis well you are so.
AMINTOR Well? How can I be other when she looks thus?
   Is there no music there? Let's dance.
MELANTIUS Why, this is strange, Amintor.
AMINTOR   I do not know
   Myself, yet I could wish my joy were less.   110
DIPHILUS I'll marry too, if it will make one thus.°
EVADNE [*whispers*] Amintor, hark.
AMINTOR What says my love? I must obey.
     [*Evadne and Amintor talk apart*]
EVADNE You do it scurvily; 'twill be perceived.
    Enter the King and Lysippus
CLEON My lord the King is here.   115
AMINTOR Where?
STRATO   And his brother.
KING   Good morrow all.
   Amintor, joy on joy fall thick upon thee,
   And, madam, you are altered since I saw you.
   I must salute you, you are now another's.
   How liked you your night's rest?
EVADNE   Ill, sir.   120
AMINTOR Indeed she took but little.
LYSIPPUS You'll let her take more and thank her too, shortly.°
KING Amintor, wert thou truly honest° till thou wert married?
AMINTOR Yes, sir.
KING Tell me then, how shows the sport unto thee?   125
AMINTOR Why, well.
KING What did you do?
AMINTOR No more nor less than other couples use.
   You know what 'tis; it has but a coarse name.°

KING But prithee, I should think by her black eye   130
  And her red cheek she should be quick and stirring
  In this same business, ha?
AMINTOR   I cannot tell:
  I ne'er tried other, sir; but I perceive
  She is as quick as you delivered.°
KING Well, you'll trust me then, Amintor,   135
  To choose a wife for you again.
AMINTOR   No, never, sir.
KING Why, like you this so ill?
AMINTOR   So well I like her;
  For this I bow my knee in thanks to you
  And unto heaven will pay my grateful tribute
  Hourly, and do hope we shall draw out   140
  A long contented life together here
  And die both, full of grey hairs, in one day—
  For which the thanks is yours; but if the powers
  That rule us please to call her first away,
  Without pride spoke, this world holds not a wife   145
  Worthy to take her room.
KING [aside] I do not like this. [Aloud] All forbear the room
  But you, Amintor, and your lady.
     [Exeunt all but the King, Amintor, and Evadne]
  I have some speech with you that may concern
  Your after-living well.   150
AMINTOR [aside] A will not tell me that he lies with her.
  If he do, something heavenly stay my heart,
  For it is apt to thrust this arm of mine
  To acts unlawful.
KING   You will suffer me
  To talk with her, Amintor, and not have   155
  A jealous pang.
AMINTOR   Sir, I dare trust my wife
  With whom she dares to talk, and not be jealous.
     [The King and Evadne talk apart]
KING How do you like Amintor?
EVADNE   As I did, sir.
KING   How's that?
EVADNE As one that to fulfil your will and pleasure
  I have given leave to call me wife and love.   160
KING I see there is no lasting faith in sin.

107

They that break word with heaven will break again
With all the world, and so dost thou with me.

EVADNE How, sir?

KING   This subtle woman's ignorance   165
Will not excuse you. Thou hast taken oaths,
So great that methought they did misbecome
A woman's mouth, that thou wouldst ne'er enjoy
A man but me.

EVADNE   I never did swear so;
You do me wrong.

KING   Day and night have heard it.

EVADNE I swore indeed that I would never love   170
A man of lower place, but if your fortune
Should throw you from this height, I bade you trust
I would forsake you and would bend to him
That won your throne. I love with my ambition,
Not with my eyes. But if I ever yet   175
Touched any other, leprosy light here°
Upon my face, which for your royalty
I would not stain.

KING Why, thou dissemblest, and it is in me
To punish thee.

EVADNE   Why, it is in me, then,   180
Not to love you, which will more afflict
Your body than your punishment can mine.

KING But thou hast let Amintor lie with thee—

EVADNE I ha' not.

KING   Impudence, he says himself so.

EVADNE A lies.

KING   A does not.

EVADNE   By this light he does,   185
Strangely and basely, and I'll prove it so:
I did not only shun him for a night,
But told him I would never close with him.°

KING Speak lower. 'Tis false.

EVADNE   I am no man
To answer with a blow; or if I were,   190
You are the King; but urge not, 'tis most true.°

KING Do not I know the uncontrollèd thoughts
That youth brings with him when his blood is high
With expectation and desire of that

He long hath waited for? Is not his spirit,   195
Though he be temperate, of as valiant strain°
As this our age hath known? What could he do,
If such a sudden speech had met his blood,
But ruin thee forever, if he had not killed thee?°
He could not bear it thus: he is as we   200
Or any other wronged man.

EVADNE   It is dissembling.°
Amintor, thou hast an ingenious look°
And shouldst be virtuous. It amazeth me
That thou canst make such base, malicious lies.

AMINTOR What, my dear wife?

EVADNE   'Dear wife'? I do despise thee.   205
Why, nothing can be baser than to sow
Dissension amongst lovers.

AMINTOR   Lovers? Who?

EVADNE The King and me—

AMINTOR O God!°

EVADNE —Who should live long and love without distaste   210
Were it not for such pickthanks as thyself.
Did you lie with me? Swear now, and be punishèd
In hell for this.

AMINTOR   The faithless sin I made
To fair Aspatia is not yet revenged:
It follows me. [To the King] I will not loose a word   215
To this vile woman, but to you, my King,
The anguish of my soul thrusts out this truth:
You're a tyrant, and not so much to wrong
An honest man thus, as to take a pride
In talking with him of it.   220

EVADNE Now, sir, see how loud this fellow lied.

AMINTOR You, that can know to wrong, should know how
Men must right themselves. What punishment is due
From me to him that shall abuse my bed?
It is not death, nor can that satisfy,   225
Unless I send your lives through all the land
To show how nobly I have freed myself.°

KING Draw not thy sword. Thou know'st I cannot fear
A subject's hand, but thou shalt feel the weight
Of this if thou dost rage.

AMINTOR   The weight of that!°   230

If you have any worth, for heaven's sake think
I fear not swords, for as you are mere man
I dare as easily kill you for this deed
As you dare think to do it. But there is
Divinity about you, that strikes dead   235
My rising passions. As you are my king,
I fall before you and present my sword
To cut my own flesh if it be your will.
Alas! I am nothing but a multitude of
Waking griefs, yet, should I murder you,   240
I might before the world take the excuse
Of madness; for compare my injuries
And they will well appear too sad a weight
For reason to endure. But fall I first
Amongst my sorrows ere my treacherous hand   245
Touch holy things. But why? I know not what
I have to say. Why did you choose out me
To make thus wretched? There were thousands fools
Easy to work on and of state enough
Within the land.

EVADNE   I would not have a fool;   250
It were no credit for me.

AMINTOR   Worse and worse!
Thou that dar'st talk unto thy husband thus,
Profess thyself a whore and more than so,
Resolve to be so still: it is my fate
To bear and bow beneath a thousand griefs   255
To keep that little credit with the world.
But there were wise ones too: you might have ta'en
Another.

KING   No, for I believe thee honest,
As thou wert valiant.

AMINTOR   All the happiness
Bestowed upon me turns into disgrace.   260
Gods, take your honesty again, for I
Am loaden with it. Good my lord the King,
Be private in it.

KING   Thou may'st live, Amintor,°
Free as thy king, if thou wilt wink at this°
And be a means that we may meet in secret.   265

AMINTOR A bawd! Hold, hold my breast! A bitter curse

Seize me if I forget not all respects
That are religious, on another word
Sounded like that, and through a sea of sins
Will wade to my revenge, though I should call   270
Pains here and after life upon my soul.

KING Well, I am resolute: you lay not with her.
And so I leave you.

         Exit King

EVADNE   You must needs be prating,
And see what follows.

AMINTOR   Prithee vex me not.
Leave me; I am afraid some sudden start   275
Will pull a murder on me.

EVADNE   I am gone;°
I love my life well.

         Exit Evadne

AMINTOR   I hate mine as much.
This 'tis to break a troth. I should be glad
If all this tide of grief would make me mad.

         Exit

3.2

Enter Melantius

MELANTIUS I'll know the cause of all Amintor's griefs,
Or friendship shall be idle.

         Enter Calianax

CALIANAX   O Melantius,
My daughter will die.

MELANTIUS   Trust me, I am sorry;
Would thou hadst ta'en her room.

CALIANAX   Thou art a slave,
A cut-throat slave, a bloody, treacherous slave.

MELANTIUS Take heed, old man, thou wilt be heard to rave,   5
And lose thine offices.

CALIANAX   I am valiant grown,
At all these years, and thou art but a slave.

MELANTIUS Leave, company will come, and I respect
Thy years, not thee, so much that I could wish   10

To laugh at thee alone.
CALIANAX   I'll spoil your mirth:
  I mean to fight with thee.
        [*He removes his cloak and draws his sword*]
                              There lie, my cloak;
  This was my father's sword, and he durst fight.
  Are you prepared?
MELANTIUS   Why? Wilt thou dote thyself
  Out of thy life? Hence, get thee to bed,   15
  Have careful looking-to, and eat warm things,
  And trouble not me. My head is full of thoughts
  More weighty than thy life or death can be.
CALIANAX You have a name in war, where you stand safe°
  Amongst a multitude, but I will try   20
  What you dare do unto a weak old man
  In single fight. You'll give ground, I fear.
  Come, draw.
MELANTIUS I will not draw. Unless thou pull'st thy death
  Upon thee with a stroke, there's no one blow   25
  That thou canst give hath strength enough to kill me.
  Tempt me not so far then; the power of earth
  Shall not redeem thee.
CALIANAX [*aside*]   I must let him alone.
  He's stout and able, and, to say the truth,
  However I may set a face and talk,°   30
  I am not valiant. When I was a youth
  I kept my credit with a testy trick
  I had 'mongst cowards, but durst never fight.°
MELANTIUS I will not promise to preserve your life
  If you do stay.
CALIANAX [*aside*] I would give half my land   35
  That I durst fight with that proud man a little.
  If I had men to hold him, I would beat him
  Till he asked me mercy.
MELANTIUS   Sir, will you be gone?
CALIANAX [*aside*] I dare not stay, but I will go home and beat my ser-
  vants all over for this.   40
        Exit Calianax, [*retrieving his cloak as he goes*]
MELANTIUS This old fellow haunts me,
  But the distracted carriage of mine Amintor
  Takes deeply on me. I will find the cause.

I fear his conscience cries he wronged Aspatia.
        Enter Amintor
AMINTOR [*aside*] Men's eyes are not so subtle to perceive   45
My inward misery. I bear my grief
Hid from the world. How art thou wretched then?
For aught I know all husbands are like me,
And every one I talk with of his wife
Is but a well dissembler of his woes°   50
As I am. Would I knew it, for the rareness°
Afflicts me now.
MELANTIUS   Amintor, we have not enjoyed
Our friendship of late, for we were wont
To 'change our souls in talk.
AMINTOR   Melantius,°
I can tell thee a good jest of Strato   55
And a lady the last day.
MELANTIUS   How wast?
AMINTOR Why, such an odd one.
MELANTIUS   I have longed to speak
With you, not of an idle jest that's forced,°
But of matter you are bound to utter to me.
AMINTOR What is that, my friend?
MELANTIUS   I have observed, your words   60
Fall from your tongue wildly, and all your carriage
Like one that strove to show his merry mood,
When he were ill disposed. You were not wont
To put such scorn into your speech, or wear
Upon your face ridiculous jollity.   65
Some sadness sits here, which your cunning would
Cover o'er with smiles, and 'twill not be.
What is it?
AMINTOR   A sadness here? What cause
Can fate provide for me to make me so?
Am I not loved through all this isle? The King   70
Rains greatness on me. Have I not received
A lady to my bed that in her eye
Keeps mounting fire, and on her tender cheeks
Inevitable colour, in her heart
A prison for all virtue. Are not you—   75
Which is above all joys—my constant friend?
What sadness can I have? No, I am light,

And feel the courses of my blood more warm
And stirring than they were. Faith, marry too,
And you will feel so unexpressed a joy   80
In chaste embraces, that you will indeed°
Appear another.
MELANTIUS   You may shape, Amintor,°
Causes to cozen the whole world withal,°
And yourself too, but 'tis not like a friend
To hide your soul from me. 'Tis not your nature   85
To be thus idle: I have seen you stand°
As you were blasted, midst of all your mirth,°
Call thrice aloud, and then start, feigning joy
So coldly. World! What do I here? A friend
Is nothing. Heaven! I would ha' told that man°   90
My secret sins. I'll search an unknown land
And there plant friendship; all is withered here.
Come with a compliment! I would have fought
Or told my friend a lied ere soothed him so
Out of my bosom.°   95
AMINTOR But there is nothing.
MELANTIUS   Worse and worse! Farewell.
From this time have acquaintance, but no friend.
AMINTOR Melantius, stay; you shall know what that is.
MELANTIUS See how you played with friendship. Be advised°
How you give cause unto yourself to say   100
You ha' lost a friend.
AMINTOR   Forgive what I ha' done,
For I am so o'er-gone with injuries
Unheard of, that I lose consideration°
Of what I ought to do. O! O!
        [He weeps]
MELANTIUS Do not weep. What is 't? May I once but know the man   105
Hath turned my friend thus.
AMINTOR   I had spoke at first,
But that—
MELANTIUS But what?
AMINTOR   I held it most unfit
For you to know. Faith, do not know it yet.
MELANTIUS [weeping] Thou seest my love, that will keep company
With thee in tears; hide nothing then from me,   110
For when I know the cause of thy distemper,
With mine old armour I'll adorn myself,°

My resolution, and cut through thy foes
Unto thy quiet, till I place thy heart
As peaceable as spotless innocence. 115
What is it?

AMINTOR   Why, 'tis this—It is too big
To get out; let my tears make way awhile.°

MELANTIUS Punish me strangely, heaven, if he scape
Of life or fame, that brought this youth to this.°

AMINTOR Your sister—

MELANTIUS   Well said.

AMINTOR   You'll wish 't unknown 120
When you have heard it.

MELANTIUS   No.

AMINTOR   —is much to blame,
And to the King has given her honour up,
And lives in whoredom with him.

MELANTIUS   How's this?
Thou art run mad with injury indeed,
Thou couldst not utter this else. Speak again, 125
For I forgive it freely. Tell thy griefs.

AMINTOR She's wanton. I am loath to say 'a whore',
Though it be true.

MELANTIUS Speak yet again, before mine anger grow
Up beyond throwing down: what are thy griefs?° 130

AMINTOR By all our friendship, these.

MELANTIUS   What? Am I tame?
After mine actions, shall the name of friend
Blot all our family and strike the brand
Of whore upon my sister unrevenged?°
My shaking flesh, be thou a witness for me 135
With what unwillingness I go to scourge
This railer whom my folly had called friend.
        [He draws his sword]
I will not take thee basely: thy sword°
Hangs near thy hand; draw it, that I may whip
Thy rashness to repentance. Draw thy sword! 140

AMINTOR Not on thee, did thine anger go as high
As troubled waters. Thou shouldst do me ease,
Here and eternally, if thy noble hand°
Would cut me from my sorrows.

MELANTIUS   This is base
And fearful. They that use to utter lies 145

Provide not blows but words to qualify°
The men they wronged. Thou hast a guilty cause.

AMINTOR Thou pleasest me, for so much more like this
Will raise my anger up above my griefs,
Which is a passion easier to be borne,   150
And I shall then be happy.

MELANTIUS   Take then more,
To raise thine anger. 'Tis mere cowardice
Makes thee not draw, and I will leave thee dead
However; but if thou art so much pressed°
With guilt and fear as not to dare to fight,   155
I'll make thy memory loathed and fix a scandal
Upon thy name forever.

AMINTOR [drawing his sword] Then I draw
As justly as our magistrates their swords
To cut offenders off. I knew before°
'T would grate your ears, but it was base in you   160
To urge a weighty secret from your friend
And then rage at it. I shall be at ease
If I be killed, and if you fall by me,
I shall not long outlive you.

MELANTIUS   Stay awhile.°
The name of friend is more than family,   165
Or all the world besides. I was a fool.
Thou searching human nature, that didst wake°
To do me wrong, thou art inquisitive
And thrusts me upon questions that will take
My sleep away. Would I had died ere known   170
This sad dishonour. Pardon me, my friend.
        [He sheathes his sword]
If thou wilt strike, here is a faithful heart;
Pierce it, for I will never heave my hand
To thine. Behold the power thou hast in me:
I do believe my sister is a whore,   175
A leprous one. Put up thy sword, young man.

AMINTOR How should I bear it then, she being so?
I fear, my friend, that you will lose me shortly,
And I shall do a foul act on my self
Through these disgraces.

MELANTIUS   Better half the land   180
Were buried quick together. No, Amintor,

Thou shalt have ease. O, this adulterous King
That drew her to 't, where got he the spirit
To wrong me so?

AMINTOR   What is it then to me,
If it be wrong to you?

MELANTIUS   Why, not so much.   185
The credit of our house is thrown away;°
But from his iron den I'll waken Death
And hurl him on this King. My honesty
Shall steel my sword, and on my horrid point°
I'll wear my cause, that shall amaze the eyes   190
Of this proud man, and be too glittering
For him to look on.

AMINTOR   I have quite undone my fame.

MELANTIUS Dry up thy wat'ry eyes
And cast a manly look upon my face,
For nothing is so wild as I thy friend   195
Till I have freed thee. Still this swelling breast.°
I go thus from thee and will never cease
My vengeance till I find thy heart at peace.

AMINTOR It must not be so. Stay, mine eyes would tell
How loath I am to this, but love and tears   200
Leave me a while, for I have hazarded
All that this world calls happy. Thou hast wrought
A secret from me under name of friend
Which art could ne'er have found, nor torture wrung
From out my bosom. Give it me again,   205
For I will find it wheresoe'er it lies
Hid in the mortal'st part. Invent a way°
To give it back.

MELANTIUS   Why would you have it back?
I will to death pursue him with revenge.

AMINTOR Therefore I call it back from thee, for I know   210
Thy blood so high that thou wilt stir in this
And shame me to posterity. Take to thy weapon.

MELANTIUS Hear thy friend, that bears more years than thou.

AMINTOR I will not hear; but draw, or I—

MELANTIUS   Amintor!

AMINTOR Draw, then, for I am full as resolute   215
As fame and honour can enforce me be.
I cannot linger: draw!

MELANTIUS [*drawing his sword*] I do—but is not°
    My share of credit equal with thine
    If I do stir?
AMINTOR   No, for it will be called
    Honour in thee to spill thy sister's blood   220
    If she her birth abuse, and on the King°
    A brave revenge; but on me that have walked
    With patience in it, it will fix the name
    Of fearful cuckold. O, that word! Be quick.
MELANTIUS Then join with me.   225
AMINTOR I dare not do a sin, or else I would. Be speedy.
MELANTIUS Then dare not fight with me, for that's a sin.
    [*Aside*] His grief distracts him. [*To Amintor*] Call thy thoughts
      again,
    And to thyself pronounce the name of friend,
    And see what that will work. I will not fight.°   230
AMINTOR You must.
MELANTIUS   I will be killed first. Though my passions
    Offered the like to you, 'tis not this earth
    Shall buy my reason to it. Think a while,°
    For you are—I must weep when I speak that—
    Almost besides yourself.
AMINTOR   O my soft temper.   235
    So many sweet words from thy sister's mouth
    I am afraid would make me take her
    To embrace and pardon her. I am mad indeed,
    And know not what I do; yet have a care
    Of me in what thou dost.
MELANTIUS   Why, thinks my friend   240
    I will forget his honour, or, to save
    The bravery of our house, will lose his fame°
    And fear to touch the throne of majesty?
AMINTOR A curse will follow that; but rather live°
    And suffer with me.
MELANTIUS   I will do what worth   245
    Shall bid me, and no more.
AMINTOR   Faith, I am sick,
    And desperately, I hope; yet leaning thus
    I feel a kind of ease.
MELANTIUS   Come, take again°
    Your mirth about you.
AMINTOR   I shall never do 't.

MELANTIUS I warrant you, look up. We'll walk together;   250
    Put thine arm here. All shall be well again.
        [*They link arms*]
AMINTOR Thy love—O wretched I!—thy love, Melantius;
    Why, I have nothing else.
MELANTIUS   Be merry then.
     Exeunt Melantius and Amintor. Melantius returns
MELANTIUS This worthy young man may do violence
    Upon himself, but I have cherished him   255
    As well as I could, and sent him smiling from me
    To counterfeit again. Sword, hold thine edge;
    My heart will never fail me.
     Enter Diphilus
                      Diphilus,
    Thou com'st as sent.
DIPHILUS   Yonder has been such laughing.
MELANTIUS Betwixt whom?
DIPHILUS   Why, our sister and the King.   260
    I thought their spleens would break;°
    They laughed us all out of the room.
MELANTIUS They must weep, Diphilus.
DIPHILUS   Must they?
MELANTIUS   They must.
    Thou art my brother, and if I did believe
    Thou hadst a base thought, I would rip it out,   265
    Lie where it durst.
DIPHILUS   You should not; I would first
    Mangle myself and find it.
MELANTIUS   That was spoke
    According to our strain. Come, join thy hands to mine,
    And swear a firmness to what project I
    Shall lay before thee.
DIPHILUS   You do wrong us both.   270
    People hereafter shall not say there passed
    A bond more than our loves to tie our lives
    And deaths together.
MELANTIUS It is as nobly said as I would wish.
    Anon I'll tell you wonders. We are wronged.   275
DIPHILUS But I will tell you now, we'll right ourselves.
MELANTIUS Stay not, prepare the armour in my house,
    And what friends you can draw unto our side,
    Not knowing of the cause, make ready too.

Haste, Diphilus, the time requires it, haste.   280
    Exit Diphilus
I hope my cause is just. I know my blood
Tells me it is, and I will credit it.
To take revenge and lose myself withal
Were idle, and to scape, impossible
Without I had the fort, which—misery!—°   285
Remaining in the hands of my old enemy
Calianax—but I must have it.
    Enter Calianax
                See
Where he comes shaking by me. Good my lord,°
Forget your spleen to me. I never wronged you,
But would have peace with every man.

CALIANAX   'Tis well.   290
  If I durst fight, your tongue would lie at quiet.

MELANTIUS You're touchy without all cause.

CALIANAX   Do, mock me.

MELANTIUS By mine honour, I speak truth.

CALIANAX   Honour? Where is 't?

MELANTIUS See what starts you make into your hatred
  To my love and freedom to you. I come   295
  With resolution to obtain a suit
  Of you.

CALIANAX A suit of me? 'Tis very like
  It should be granted, sir.
    [*Calianax makes to leave*]

MELANTIUS   Nay, go not hence.
  'Tis this: you have the keeping of the fort,
  And I would wish you, by the love you ought   300
  To bear unto me, to deliver it
  Into my hands.

CALIANAX   I am in hope thou art mad,
  To talk to me thus.

MELANTIUS   But there is a reason
  To move you to it: I would kill the King,
  That wronged you and your daughter.

CALIANAX   Out, traitor!   305

MELANTIUS Nay, but stay. I cannot scape, the deed once done,
  Without I have this fort.

CALIANAX   And should I help thee?

Now thy treacherous mind betrays itself.
MELANTIUS Come, delay me not.
  Give me a sudden answer, or already   310
  Thy last is spoke; refuse not offered love
  When it comes clad in secrets.
CALIANAX [aside]   If I say
  I will not, he will kill me, I do see 't
  Writ in his looks; and should I say I will,
  He'll run and tell the King. [Aloud] I do not shun   315
  Your friendship, dear Melantius, but this cause
  Is weighty. Give me but an hour to think.
MELANTIUS Take it. [Aside] I know this goes unto the King,
  But I am armed.
     Exit Melantius
CALIANAX   Methinks I feel myself
  But twenty now again. This fighting fool   320
  Wants policy. I shall revenge my girl
  And make her red again. I pray my legs°
  Will last that pace that I will carry them;
  I shall want breath before I find the King.
     Exit

4.1

Enter Melantius, Evadne, and Ladies

MELANTIUS God save you.

EVADNE   Save you, sweet brother.

MELANTIUS In my blunt eye methinks you look, Evadne—

EVADNE [*interrupting*] Come, you would make me blush.

MELANTIUS I would, Evadne; I shall displease my ends else.°

EVADNE You shall if you commend me. I am bashful.   5
  Come, sir, how do I look?

MELANTIUS I would not have your women hear me
  Break into commendations of you; 'tis not seemly.

EVADNE [*to the Ladies*] Go, wait me in the gallery.

    Exeunt Ladies

                                Now speak.°

MELANTIUS I'll lock the door first.

EVADNE   Why?   10

MELANTIUS I will not have your gilded things that dance
  In visitation with their Milan skins°
  Choke up my business.

    [*He locks the door*]

EVADNE   You are strangely disposed, sir.°

MELANTIUS Good madam, not to make you merry.

EVADNE No, if you praise me 'twill make me sad.   15

MELANTIUS Such a sad commendation I have for you.

EVADNE Brother, the court has made you witty
  And learn to riddle.°

MELANTIUS I praise the court for 't. Has it learned you nothing?

EVADNE Me?   20

MELANTIUS Ay, Evadne, thou art young and handsome,
  A lady of a sweet complexion
  And such a flowing carriage that it cannot
  Choose but inflame a kingdom.

EVADNE   Gentle brother—

MELANTIUS 'Tis yet in thy repentance, foolish woman,   25
  To make me gentle.

EVADNE   How is this?

MELANTIUS   'Tis base,
  And I could blush at these years, through all°

My honoured scars, to come to such a parley.°
EVADNE I understand ye not.
MELANTIUS   You dare not, fool.
   They that commit thy faults fly the remembrance.   30
EVADNE My faults, sir? I would have you know I care not
   If they were written here, here in my forehead.°
MELANTIUS Thy body is too little for the story,
   The lusts of which would fill another woman,
   Though she had twins within her.
EVADNE   This is saucy!°   35
     [*She shows him the door*]
   Look you intrude no more. There's your way.
MELANTIUS Thou art my way, and I will tread upon thee
   Till I find truth out.
EVADNE   What truth is that you look for?
MELANTIUS Thy long lost honour. Would the gods had set me
   Rather to grapple with the plague, or stand   40
   One of their loudest bolts. Come, tell me quickly:
   Do it without enforcement, and take heed°
   You swell me not above my temper.°
EVADNE How, sir? Where got you this report?
MELANTIUS Where there was people in every place.   45
EVADNE They and the seconds of it are base people;°
   Believe them not; they lied.
MELANTIUS Do not play with mine anger, do not, wretch.
   I come to know that desperate fool that drew thee
   From thy fair life. Be wise, and lay him open.   50
     [*He seizes her*]
EVADNE Unhand me and learn manners. Such another
   Forgetfulness forfeits your life.°
MELANTIUS Quench me this mighty humour, and then tell me°
   Whose whore you are—for you are one, I know it.
   Let all mine honours perish but I'll find him,   55
   Though he lie locked up in thy blood. Be sudden,°
   There is no facing it, and be not flattered:
   The burnt air when the dog reigns is not fouler°
   Than thy contagious name, till thy repentance,
   If the gods grant thee any, purge thy sickness.   60
EVADNE Begone! You are my brother, that's your safety.
MELANTIUS I'll be a wolf first. 'Tis, to be thy brother,°
   An infamy below the sin of coward.

I am as far from being part of thee
As thou art from thy virtue. Seek a kindred   65
'Mongst sensual beasts, and make a goat thy brother;°
A goat is cooler. Will you tell me yet?°
EVADNE If you stay here and rail thus, I shall tell you,
I'll ha' you whipped. Get you to your command
And there preach to your sentinels, and tell them   70
What a brave man you are; I shall laugh at you.
MELANTIUS You're grown a glorious whore. Where be your
      fighters?°
What mortal fool durst raise thee to this daring,
And I alive? By my just sword, he'd safer
Bestride a billow when the angry north   75
Ploughs up the sea, or made heaven's fire his food.°
Work me no higher: will you discover yet?
EVADNE The fellow's mad. Sleep and speak sense.
MELANTIUS Force my swoll'n heart no further. I would save thee.
Your great maintainers are not here—they dare not!   80
Would they were all, and armed, I would speak loud;
Here's one should thunder to 'em. Will you tell me?
Thou hast no hope to scape. He that dares most,
And damns away his soul to do thee service,°
Will sooner snatch meat from a hungry lion   85
Than come to rescue thee. Thou hast death about thee:
He's undone thine honour, poisoned thy virtue,
And, of a lovely rose, left thee a canker.
EVADNE Let me consider.
MELANTIUS   Do: whose child thou wert,
Whose honour thou hast murdered, whose grave opened,   90
And so pulled on the gods that in their justice°
They must restore him flesh again and life
And raise his dry bones to revenge this scandal.
EVADNE The gods are not of my mind; they had better
Let 'em lie sweet still in the earth; they'll stink here.   95
MELANTIUS Do you raise mirth out of my easiness?
Forsake me then, all weaknesses of nature,
That make men women.
      [*He draws his sword*]
                              Speak, you whore, speak truth,°
Or by the dear soul of thy sleeping father

This sword shall be thy lover. Tell or I'll kill thee,°   100
And when thou hast told all, thou wilt deserve it.

EVADNE You will not murder me.

MELANTIUS No, 'tis a justice, and a noble one,
To put the light out of such base offenders.

EVADNE Help!   105

MELANTIUS By thy foul self, no human help shall help thee
If thou criest. When I have killed thee, as I have
Vowed to do if thou confess not, naked
As thou hast left thine honour will I leave thee,
That on thy branded flesh the world may read   110
Thy black shame and my justice. Wilt thou bend yet?

EVADNE Yes.

MELANTIUS Up, and begin your story.

EVADNE O, I am miserable.

MELANTIUS 'Tis true, thou art; speak truth still.°   115

EVADNE I have offended; noble sir, forgive me.

MELANTIUS With what secure slave?

EVADNE   Do not ask me, sir;
Mine own remembrance is a misery
Too mighty for me.

MELANTIUS   Do not fall back again;
My sword's unsheathèd yet.

EVADNE   What shall I do?   120

MELANTIUS Be true, and make your fault less.

EVADNE   I dare not tell.

MELANTIUS Tell, or I'll be this day a-killing thee.°

EVADNE Will you forgive me then?

MELANTIUS Stay, I must ask mine honour first.
I have too much foolish nature in me.

          [*He sheathes his sword*]
                                    Speak.   125

EVADNE Is there none else here?

MELANTIUS None but a fearful conscience; that's too many.
Who is't?

EVADNE   O hear me gently: it was the King.°

MELANTIUS No more. My worthy father's and my services
Are liberally rewarded. King, I thank thee: 130
For all my dangers and my wounds, thou hast paid me
In my own metal. These are soldier's thanks.

How long have you lived thus, Evadne?

EVADNE Too long. Too late I find it.

MELANTIUS   Can you be sorry?

EVADNE Would I were half as blameless.

MELANTIUS   Evadne,   135
Thou wilt to thy trade again.

EVADNE   First to my grave.

MELANTIUS Would gods thou hadst been so blessed.
Dost thou not hate this king now? Prithee hate him.
He's sunk thy fair soul. I command thee curse him,
Curse till the gods hear and deliver him   140
To thy just wishes. Yet I fear, Evadne,
You had rather play your game out.

EVADNE   No, I feel°
Too many sad confusions here to let in
Any loose flame hereafter.

MELANTIUS Dost thou not feel amongst all those one brave anger 145
That breaks out nobly, and directs thine arm
To kill this base king?

EVADNE   All the gods forbid it!

MELANTIUS No, all the gods require it:
They are dishonoured in him.

EVADNE   'Tis too fearful.

MELANTIUS You're valiant in his bed, and bold enough 150
To be a stale whore, and have your madam's name
Discourse for grooms and pages, and hereafter,
When his cool majesty hath laid you by,°
To be at pension with some needy sir
For meat and coarser clothes; thus far you knew no fear. 155
Come, you shall kill him.

EVADNE   Good sir!

MELANTIUS An 'twere to kiss him dead, thou'd'st smother him.°
Be wise and kill him. Canst thou live and know
What noble minds shall make thee see thyself,
Found out with every finger, made the shame°   160
Of all successions, and in this great ruin
Thy brother and thy noble husband broken?
Thou shalt not live thus. Kneel and swear to help me
When I shall call thee to it, or, by all
Holy in heaven and earth, thou shalt not live   165
To breathe a full hour longer, not a thought.

Come, 'tis a righteous oath. Give me thy hand,
And, both to heaven held up, swear by that wealth°
This lustful thief stole from thee, when I say it,
To let his foul soul out.

EVADNE   Here I swear it,   170
And all you spirits of abusèd ladies,
Help me in this performance.

MELANTIUS Enough. This must be known to none
But you and I, Evadne; not to your lord,
Though he be wise and noble, and a fellow   175
Dare step as far into a worthy action°
As the most daring, ay, as far as justice.
Ask me not why. Farewell.
          Exit Melantius

EVADNE Would I could say so to my black disgrace.
Gods, where have I been all this time? How friended,   180
That I should lose myself thus desperately,
And none for pity show me how I wandered?°
There is not in the compass of the light
A more unhappy creature. Sure I am monstrous,
For I have done those follies, those mad mischiefs   185
Would dare a woman. O my loaden soul,°
          Enter Amintor
Be not so cruel to me, choke not up
The way to my repentance. O, my lord.

AMINTOR How now?

EVADNE   My much abusèd lord.
          She kneels to him

AMINTOR   This cannot be.

EVADNE I do not kneel to live. I dare not hope it: 190
The wrongs I did are greater. Look upon me,
Though I appear with all my faults.

AMINTOR   Stand up.
This is a new way to beget more sorrows;
Heaven knows, I have too many.
          [*She prostrates herself*°]
                              Do not mock me:
Though I am tame and bred up with my wrongs,   195
Which are my foster-brothers, I may leap
Like a hand-wolf into my natural wildness
And do an outrage. Prithee, do not mock me.

EVADNE My whole life is so leprous it infects
        All my repentance. I would buy your pardon,   200
        Though at the highest set, even with my life.
        That slight contrition, that's no sacrifice
        For what I have committed.

AMINTOR   Sure I dazzle.°
        There cannot be a faith in that foul woman
        That knows no god more mighty than her mischiefs.   205
        Thou dost still worse, still number on thy faults
        To press my poor heart thus. Can I believe
        There's any seed of virtue in that woman
        Left to shoot up, that dares go on in sin,
        Known and so known as thine is? O Evadne,   210
        Would there were any safety in thy sex,
        That I might put a thousand sorrows off
        And credit thy repentance; but I must not.
        Thou hast brought me to that dull calamity,°
        To that strange misbelief of all the world   215
        And all things that are in it, that I fear
        I shall fall like a tree, and find my grave
        Only remembering that I grieve.

EVADNE   My lord,
        Give me your griefs. You are an innocent,
        A soul as white as heaven. Let not my sins   220
        Perish your noble youth. I do not fall here
        To shadow my dissembling with my tears,
        As all say women can, or to make less
        What my hot will hath done, which heaven and you
        Knows to be tougher than the hand of time   225
        Can cut from man's remembrance. No, I do not.
        I do appear the same, the same Evadne,
        Dressed in the shames I lived in, the same monster—
        But these are names of honour to what I am.
        I do present myself the foulest creature,   230
        Most poisonous, dangerous, and despised of men,
        Lerna e'er bred or Nilus. I am hell°
        Till you, my dear lord, shoot your light into me,
        The beams of your forgiveness. I am soul-sick,
        And wither with the fear of one condemned,   235
        Till I have got your pardon.

AMINTOR   Rise, Evadne.
        [She remains prostrate]

Those heavenly powers that put this good into thee
Grant a continuance of it. I forgive thee:
Make thyself worthy of it, and take heed,
Take heed, Evadne, this be serious.   240
Mock not the powers above, that can, and dare,
Give thee a great example of their justice
To all ensuing eyes, if thou play'st
With thy repentance, the best sacrifice.

EVADNE I have done nothing good to win belief,   245
My life hath been so faithless. All the creatures
Made for heaven's honours have their ends, and good ones—
All but the cozening crocodiles, false women.°
They reign here like those plagues, those killing sores
Men pray against, and when they die, like tales   250
Ill told and unbelieved, they pass away
And go to dust forgotten. But, my lord,
Those short days I shall number to my rest
(As many must not see me) shall, though too late,°
Though in my evening, yet perceive I will,   255
Since I can do no good because a woman,
Reach constantly at something that is near it.°
I will redeem one minute of my age,
Or like another Niobe I'll weep°
Till I am water.

AMINTOR   I am now dissolved;   260
My frozen soul melts. May each sin thou hast
Find a new mercy. Rise, I am at peace.
    [She rises]
Hadst thou been thus, thus excellently good
Before that devil King tempted thy frailty,
Sure thou hadst made a star. Give me thy hand.°   265
From this time I will know thee, and as far
As honour gives me leave, be thy Amintor.
When we meet next, I will salute thee fairly
And pray the gods to give thee happy days.
My charity shall go along with thee,   270
Though my embraces must be far from thee.
I should ha' killed thee, but this sweet repentance
Locks up my vengeance, for which,
    [He kisses her]
                              thus I kiss thee,
The last kiss we must take; and would to heaven

The holy priest that gave our hands together   275
Had given us equal virtues. Go, Evadne,
The gods thus part our bodies. Have a care
My honour falls no further; I am well then.
EVADNE All the dear joys here and above hereafter
Crown thy fair soul. Thus I take leave, my lord,   280
And never shall you see the foul Evadne
Till she have tried all the honoured means that may
Set her in rest and wash her stains away.
   Exeunt

4.2

  Hautboys play within. A banquet° is set out on a table. Enter
  the King and Calianax
KING I cannot tell how I should credit this
From you that are his enemy.
CALIANAX I am sure he said it to me, and I'll justify it
What way he dares oppose, but with my sword.
KING But did he break without all circumstance   5
To you, his foe, that he would have the fort
To kill me and then scape?
CALIANAX   If he deny it,
I'll make him blush.
KING   It sounds incredibly.
CALIANAX Ay, so does everything I say of late.
KING Not so, Calianax.
CALIANAX   Yes, I should sit   10
Mute whilst a rogue with strong arms cuts your throat.
KING Well, I will try him, and if this be true,
I'll pawn my life I'll find it; if 't be false,°
And that you clothe your hate in such a lie,
You shall hereafter dote in your own house,   15
Not in the court.
CALIANAX   Why, if it be a lie
Mine ears are false, for I'll be sworn I heard it.
Old men are good for nothing; you were best
Put me to death for hearing, and free him
For meaning it. You would ha' trusted me   20

130

Once, but the time is altered.

KING   And will still
Where I may do with justice to the world.
You have no witness.

CALIANAX   Yes, myself.

KING   No more,
I mean, there were that heard it.

CALIANAX   How 'no more'?
Would you have more? Why, am not I enough°   25
To hang a thousand rogues?

KING   But so you may
Hang honest men too, if you please.

CALIANAX   I may;
'Tis like I will do so. There are a hundred
Will swear it for a need too, if I say it.

KING Such witnesses we need not.

CALIANAX   And 'tis hard   30
If my word cannot hang a boisterous knave.

KING Enough. [*Calls off stage*] Where's Strato?
        Enter Strato

STRATO Sir.

KING Why, where's all the company? Call Amintor in,
Evadne. Where's my brother, and Melantius?   35
Bid him come too, and Diphilus. Call all
That are without there.
        Exit Strato
                        If he should desire
The combat of you, 'tis not in the power
Of all our laws to hinder it, unless
We mean to quit 'em.

CALIANAX   Why, if you do think   40
'Tis fit an old man, and a councillor,°
To fight for what he says, then you may grant it.
        *Enter Amintor, Evadne, Melantius, Diphilus, Lysippus, Cleon,
        and Strato*

KING Come, sirs. Amintor, thou art yet a bridegroom,°
And I will use thee so: thou shalt sit down.°
Evadne, sit, and you, Amintor, too: 45
This banquet is for you, sir.
        [*They all sit at the table*]
                        Who has brought

A merry tale about him, to raise laughter
Amongst our wine? Why, Strato, where art thou?
Thou wilt chop out with them unseasonably°
When I desire 'em not.   50

STRATO 'Tis my ill luck, sir, so to spend them then.°

KING Reach me a bowl of wine, Melantius.
  [*To Amintor*] Thou art sad.

AMINTOR   I should be, sir, the merriest here,
  But I ha' ne'er a story of mine own
  Worth telling at this time.

KING   Give me the wine.   55
        [*Melantius does so*]
  Melantius, I am now considering
  How easy 'twere for any man we trust
  To poison one of us in such a bowl.

MELANTIUS I think it were not hard, sir, for a knave.

CALIANAX Such as you are.°   60

KING I' faith, 'twere easy. It becomes us well
  To get plain-dealing men about ourselves
  Such as you all are here. Amintor, to thee,
  And to thy fair Evadne.
        [*He drinks*]

MELANTIUS [*aside to Calianax*] Have you thought
  Of this, Calianax?

CALIANAX [*aside to Melantius*] Yes, marry, have I.   65

MELANTIUS [*aside to Calianax*] And what's your resolution?

CALIANAX [*aside to Melantius*]   Ye shall have it—°
  [*Aside*] Soundly, I warrant you.

KING Reach to Amintor, Strato.
        [*Strato passes the King's bowl of wine to Amintor*°]

AMINTOR [*to Evadne*]   Here, my love;
  This wine will do thee wrong, for it will set
  Blushes upon thy cheeks, and till thou dost   70
  A fault, 'twere pity.

KING   Yet I wonder much
  Of the strange desperation of these men
  That dare attempt such acts here in our state;
  He could not scape that did it.

MELANTIUS   Were he known,
  Unpossible.

KING   It would be known, Melantius.   75

MELANTIUS It ought to be. If he got then away,
　　He must wear all our lives upon his sword:°
　　He need not fly the island, he must leave°
　　No-one alive.
KING　　　　　　No, I should think no man
　　Could kill me and scape clear, but that old man.　　　80
CALIANAX But I? Heaven bless me, I, should I, my liege?
KING I do not think thou wouldst, but yet thou might'st,
　　For thou hast in thy hands the means to scape
　　By keeping of the fort. He has, Melantius,
　　And he has kept it well.
MELANTIUS　　　　　From cobwebs, sir;　　　85
　　'Tis clean swept. I can find no other art
　　In keeping of it now: 'twas ne'er besieged
　　Since he commanded.
CALIANAX　　　　　　I shall be sure
　　Of your good word, but I have kept it safe
　　From such as you.
MELANTIUS　　　　Keep your ill temper in.　　　90
　　I speak no malice: had my brother kept it
　　I should ha' said as much.
KING　　　　　　　You are not merry.
　　Brother, drink wine. Sit you all still. Calianax.
　　[He and Calianax move away from the table; the other
　　　characters cannot hear them]
　　I cannot trust thus; I have thrown out words
　　That would have fetched warm blood upon the cheeks　　　95
　　Of guilty men, and he is never moved.
　　He knows no such thing.
CALIANAX　　　　　Impudence may scape
　　When feeble virtue is accused.
KING A must if he were guilty feel an alteration
　　At this our whisper, whilst we point at him.　　　100
　　You see he does not.
CALIANAX　　　　Let him hang himself;
　　What care I what he does, this he did say.
KING [aloud] Melantius, you can easily conceive
　　What I have meant, for men that are in fault
　　Can subtly apprehend when others aim　　　105
　　At what they do amiss; but I forgive
　　Freely before this man; heaven do so too.

I will not touch thee so much as with shame
Of telling it; let it be so no more.

CALIANAX Why, this is very fine.

MELANTIUS   I cannot tell   110
What 'tis you mean, but I am apt enough
Rudely to thrust into ignorant fault;
But let me know it, happily 'tis nought
But misconstruction, and where I am clear
I will not take forgiveness of the gods,   115
Much less of you.

KING   Nay, if you stand so stiff
I shall call back my mercy.

MELANTIUS   I want smoothness
To thank a man for pardoning of a crime
I never knew.

KING Not to instruct your knowledge, but to show you   120
My ears are everywhere, you meant to kill me,°
And get the fort to scape.

MELANTIUS   Pardon me, sir—
My bluntness will be pardoned—you preserve
A race of idle people here about you,
Eaters and talkers, to defame the worth   125
Of those that do things worthy. The man that uttered this
Had perished without food, be 't who it will,
But for this arm that fenced him from the foe.°
And if I thought you gave a faith to this,°
The plainness of my nature would speak more.   130
Give me a pardon—for you ought to do 't—°
To kill him that spake this.

CALIANAX [aside]   Ay, that will be
The end of all; then I am fairly paid
For all my care and service.

MELANTIUS   That old man,
Who calls me enemy, and of whom I,   135
Though I will never match my hate so low,
Have no good thought, would yet, I think, excuse me
And swear he thought me wronged in this.

CALIANAX   Who, I?
Thou shameless fellow, didst thou not speak to me
Of it thyself?

MELANTIUS   O, then it came from him.   140

134

CALIANAX From me? Who should it have come from but from me?

MELANTIUS Nay, I believe your malice is enough,
　　But I ha' lost my anger. Sir, I hope
　　You are well satisfied.

KING　　　　　　　　　　　Lysippus, cheer
　　Amintor and his lady; there's no sound　　　　　　　145
　　Comes from you. I will come and do 't myself.

AMINTOR You have done already, sir, for me, I thank you.

KING Melantius, I do credit this from him,
　　How slight so e'er you make it.

MELANTIUS　　　　　　　　　　'Tis strange you should.

CALIANAX 'Tis strange a should believe an old man's word,　　150
　　That never lied in 's life.

MELANTIUS　　　　　　I talk not to thee.
　　[To the King] Shall the wild words of this distempered man,
　　Frantic with age and sorrow, make a breach
　　Betwixt your majesty and me? 'Twas wrong
　　To hearken to him, but to credit him　　　　　　155
　　As much, at least, as I have power to bear.
　　But pardon me, whilst I speak only truth
　　I may commend myself. I have bestowed
　　My careless blood with you, and should be loath°
　　To think an action that would make me lose°　　160
　　That, and my thanks too. When I was a boy,
　　I thrust myself into my country's cause
　　And did a deed that plucked five years from time
　　And styled me man then, and for you, my King.°
　　Your subjects all have fed by virtue of my arm,°　　165
　　And you yourself have lived at home in ease.
　　So terrible I grew that without swords
　　My name hath fetched you conquest, and my heart°
　　And limbs are still the same, my will as great
　　To do you service. Let me not be paid　　　　170
　　With such a strange distrust.

KING　　　　　　　　　　　　Melantius,
　　I held it great injustice to believe
　　Thine enemy, and did not. If I did,
　　I do not: let that satisfy. [To the company] What, struck
　　With sadness all? More wine!

CALIANAX　　　　　　　　A few fine words　　　175
　　Have overthrown my truth. Ah, thou'rt a villain.

135

MELANTIUS [*whispers to Calianax*] Why, thou wert better let me
    have the fort.
  Dotard, I will disgrace thee thus forever;
  There shall no credit lie upon thy words.
  Think better and deliver it.

CALIANAX   My liege,   180
  He's at me now again to do it. [*To Melantius*] Speak,
  Deny it if thou canst. [*To the King*] Examine him
  Whilst he is hot, for if he cool again
  He will forswear it.

KING   This is lunacy,
  I hope, Melantius.

MELANTIUS   He hath lost himself   185
  Much since his daughter missed the happiness
  My sister gained; and though he call me foe,
  I pity him.

CALIANAX   A pity? A pox upon you!

MELANTIUS   Mark his disordered words, and at the masque,
  Diagoras knows, he raged and railed at me   190
  And called a lady 'whore', so innocent
  She understood him not; but it becomes
  Both you and me to forgive distraction.
  Pardon him as I do.

CALIANAX   I'll not speak for thee,
  For all thy cunning. [*To the King*] If you will be safe,   195
  Chop off his head, for there was never known
  So impudent a rascal.

KING   Some that love him,
  Get him to bed. Why, pity should not let age
  Make itself contemptible; we must be
  All old. Have him away.

MELANTIUS   Calianax,   200
  The King believes you. Come, you shall go home
  And rest; you ha' done well. [*Whispers to him*] You'll give it up
  When I have used you thus a month, I hope.

CALIANAX   Now, now, 'tis plain, sir, he does move me still.
  He says he knows I'll give him up the fort   205
  When he has used me thus a month. I am mad,
  Am I not, still?

ALL   Ha ha ha!

CALIANAX   I shall be mad indeed if you do thus.

Why should you trust a sturdy fellow there   210
    (That has no virtue in him, all's in his sword)
    Before me? Do but take his weapons from him
    And he's an ass, and I am a very fool
    Both with him and without him, as you use me.
ALL Ha ha ha!   215
KING 'Tis well, Calianax; but if you use
    This once again, I shall entreat some other
    To see your offices be well discharged.
    Be merry, gentlemen, it grows somewhat late.
    Amintor, thou wouldst be abed again.   220
AMINTOR Yes, sir.
KING   And you, Evadne. Let me take
    Thee in my arms, Melantius, and believe
    Thou art, as thou deserv'st to be, my friend
    Still and forever. Good Calianax,
    Sleep soundly: it will bring thee to thyself.   225
        Exeunt all but Melantius and Calianax
CALIANAX 'Sleep soundly'! I sleep soundly now, I hope,°
    I could not be thus else. How dar'st thou stay
    Alone with me, knowing how thou hast used me?
MELANTIUS You cannot blast me with your tongue,
    And that's the strongest part you have about you.   230
CALIANAX I do look for some great punishment for this,
    For I begin to forget all my hate,
    And take 't unkindly that mine enemy
    Should use me so extraordinarily scurvily.
MELANTIUS I shall melt too, if you begin to take   235
    Unkindnesses. I never meant you hurt.
CALIANAX Thou'lt anger me again. Thou wretched rogue,
    Meant me no hurt! Disgrace me with the King,
    Lose all my offices, this is no hurt,
    Is it? I prithee, what dost thou call hurt?   240
MELANTIUS To poison men because they love me not,
    To call the credit of men's wives in question,
    To murder children betwixt me and land:°
    This I call hurt.
CALIANAX   All this thou think'st is sport,
    For mine is worse; but use thy will with me,   245
    For betwixt grief and anger I could cry.
MELANTIUS Be wise then, and be safe; thou may'st revenge.

CALIANAX   Ay, o' th' King. I would revenge of thee.

MELANTIUS   That you must plot yourself.

CALIANAX   I am a fine plotter.

MELANTIUS   The short is, I will hold thee with the King   250
   In this perplexity, till peevishness
   And thy disgrace have laid thee in thy grave;
   But if thou wilt deliver up the fort
   I'll take thy trembling body in my arms
   And bear thee over dangers; thou shalt hold   255
   Thy wonted state.

CALIANAX   If I should tell the King,°
   Canst thou deny 't again?

MELANTIUS   Try and believe.

CALIANAX   Nay, then, thou canst bring anything about.
   Melantius, thou shalt have the fort.

MELANTIUS   Why, well. Here let our hate be buried, and   260
   This hand shall right us both. Give me thy agèd breast
   To compass.

          [He offers to embrace Calianax]

CALIANAX   Nay, I do not love thee yet;
   I cannot well endure to look on thee,
   And if I thought it were a courtesy,
   Thou shouldst not have it; but I am disgraced,   265
   My offices are to be ta'en away,
   And if I did but hold this fort a day
   I do believe the King would take it from me
   And give it thee, things are so strangely carried.
   Ne'er thank me for 't; but yet the King shall know   270
   There was some such thing in 't I told him of,
   And that I was an honest man.

MELANTIUS   He'll buy
   That knowledge very dearly.

        Enter Diphilus

                     Diphilus,
   What news with thee?

DIPHILUS   This were a night indeed
   To do it in: the King hath sent for her.   275

MELANTIUS   She shall perform it, then. Go, Diphilus,
   And take from this good man, my worthy friend,
   The fort; he'll give it thee.

DIPHILUS   Ha' you got that?

CALIANAX Art thou of the same breed? Canst thou deny
  This to the King too?
DIPHILUS   With a confidence   280
  As great as his.
CALIANAX   Faith, like enough.
MELANTIUS Away, and use him kindly.
      [Diphilus tries to take Calianax's arm]
CALIANAX   Touch not me;
  I hate the whole strain. If thou follow me
  A great way off, I'll give thee up the fort,
  And hang yourselves.
MELANTIUS   Begone.
DIPHILUS   He's finely wrought.°   285
      Exeunt Diphilus and Calianax
MELANTIUS This is a night, spite of astronomers,°
  To do the deed in. I will wash the stain
  That rests upon our house off with his blood.
      Enter Amintor
AMINTOR Melantius, now assist me if thou be'st
  That which thou say'st. Assist me: I have lost   290
  All my distempers, and have found a rage
  So pleasing. Help me.
MELANTIUS [aside]   Who can see him thus
  And not swear vengeance? [Aloud] What's the matter, friend?
AMINTOR Out with thy sword, and hand in hand with me
  Rush to the chamber of this hated king   295
  And sink him with the weight of all his sins
  To hell forever.
MELANTIUS   'Twere a rash attempt,
  Not to be done with safety. Let your reason
  Plot your revenge, and not your passion.
AMINTOR If thou refusest me in these extremes,   300
  Thou art no friend. He sent for her to me,
  By heaven, to me, myself, and I must tell ye
  I love her as a stranger. There is worth
  In that vile woman, worthy things, Melantius,
  And she repents. I'll do 't myself alone,   305
  Though I be slain. Farewell.
MELANTIUS [aside]   He'll overthrow
  My whole design with madness. [Aloud] Amintor,
  Think what thou dost. I dare as much as valour,

But 'tis the King, the King, the King, Amintor,
With whom thou fightest. [*Aside*] I know he's honest,   310
And this will work with him.

AMINTOR   I cannot tell
What thou hast said, but thou hast charmed my sword
Out of my hand, and left me shaking here
Defenceless.

MELANTIUS   I will take it up for thee.

AMINTOR What à wild beast is uncollected man!°   315
The thing that we call honour bears us all
Headlong unto sin, and yet itself is nothing.

MELANTIUS Alas, how variable are thy thoughts!

AMINTOR Just like my fortunes. I was run to that°
I purposed to have chid thee for. Some plot   320
I did distrust thou hadst against the King,
By that old fellow's carriage; but take heed
There's not the least limb growing to a king
But carries thunder in 't.

MELANTIUS   I have none°
Against him.

AMINTOR   Why, come, then, and still remember,   325
We may not think revenge.

MELANTIUS   I will remember.
      Exeunt. [*The table and banquet are removed*]

5.1

Enter Evadne and a Gentleman

EVADNE Sir, is the King abed?

GENTLEMAN   Madam, an hour ago.

EVADNE Give me the key, then, and let none be near.
    'Tis the King's pleasure.°

GENTLEMAN I understand you, madam: would 'twere mine.
    I must not wish good rest unto your ladyship.   5

EVADNE You talk, you talk.

GENTLEMAN 'Tis all I dare do, madam, but the King will
    Wake, and then—

EVADNE   Saving your imagination,
    Pray goodnight, sir.

GENTLEMAN   A good night be it, then,
    And a long one, madam. I am gone.   10

Exit Gentleman

EVADNE The night grows horrible, and all about me
    Like my black purpose. O, the conscience°
    Of a lost virgin, whither wilt thou pull me?
    To what things dismal, as the depth of hell,
    Wilt thou provoke me? Let no woman dare   15
    From this hour be disloyal. If her heart°
    Be flesh, if she have blood and can fear, 'tis a daring
    Above that desperate fool's that left his peace
    And went to sea to fight; 'tis so many sins°
    An age cannot prevent 'em, and so great   20
    The gods want mercy for; yet I must through 'em.°
    I have begun a slaughter on my honour,
    And I must end it there.

*[She draws the traverse curtain to reveal] the King [asleep] in
his bed*

                A sleeps. O God,°
    Why give you peace to this untemperate beast
    That hath so long transgressed you? I must kill him,   25
    And I will do 't bravely. The mere joy
    Tells me I merit in it. Yet I must not
    Thus tamely do it as he sleeps: that were
    To rock him to another world. My vengeance

Shall take him waking, and then lay before him   30
The number of his wrongs and punishments.
I'll shape his sins like Furies till I waken°
His evil angel, his sick conscience,
And then I'll strike him dead.

She ties his arms to the bed

                       King, by your leave,
I dare not trust your strength. Your grace and I   35
Must grapple upon even terms no more.
So. If he rail me not from my resolution,
As I believe a shall not, I shall fit him.°
My lord the King! My lord! A sleeps
As if he meant to wake no more. My lord!   40
Is he not dead already? Sir, my lord!

KING Who's that?

EVADNE   O you sleep soundly, sir.

KING   My dear Evadne,
I have been dreaming of thee. Come to bed.

EVADNE I am come at length, sir; but how welcome?

KING What pretty new device is this, Evadne?°   45
What, do you tie me to you by my love?
This is a quaint one. Come, my dear, and kiss me;
I'll be thy Mars. To bed, my Queen of Love,
Let us be caught together, that the gods may see
And envy our embraces.

EVADNE   Stay, sir, stay.°   50
You are too hot, and I have brought you physic
To temper your high veins.

KING Prithee to bed, then; let me take it warm.
There thou shalt know the state of my body better.

EVADNE I know you have a surfeited foul body,   55
And you must bleed.°

KING Bleed!

      [She draws a dagger]

EVADNE Ay, you shall bleed. Lie still, and, if the devil,
Your lust, will give you leave, repent. This steel
Comes to redeem the honour that you stole,
King, my fair name, which nothing but thy death   60
Can answer to the world.

KING   How's this, Evadne?

EVADNE I am not she, nor bear I in this breast
   So much cold spirit to be called a woman.
   I am a tiger, I am anything   65
   That knows not pity. Stir not. If thou dost,
   I'll take thee unprepared, thy fears upon thee°
   That make thy sins look double, and so send thee—
   By my revenge I will—to look those torments°
   Prepared for such black souls.   70
KING Thou dost not mean this; 'tis impossible;
   Thou art too sweet and gentle.
EVADNE   No, I am not,
   I am as foul as thou art, and can number
   As many such hells here. I was once fair,
   Once I was lovely, not a blowing rose   75
   More chastely sweet, till thou, thou, thou foul canker—
   Stir not!—didst poison me. I was a world of virtue
   Till your cursed court and you, hell bless you for 't,
   With your temptations on temptations
   Made me give up mine honour, for which, King,   80
   I am come to kill thee.
KING   No.
EVADNE   I am.
KING   Thou art not.
   I prithee speak not these things. Thou art gentle
   And wert not meant thus rugged.
EVADNE   Peace and hear me.
   Stir nothing but your tongue, and that for mercy
   To those above us, by whose lights I vow   85
   (Those blessèd fires that shot to see our sin),°
   If thy hot soul had substance with thy blood,
   I would kill that too, which, being past my steel,
   My tongue shall reach. Thou art a shameless villain,
   A thing out of the overcharge of nature,   90
   Sent like a thick cloud to disperse a plague
   Upon weak catching women; such a tyrant
   That for his lust would sell away his subjects,
   Ay, all his heaven hereafter.
KING   Hear, Evadne,
   Thou soul of sweetness, hear, I am thy King.   95
EVADNE Thou art my shame. Lie still; there's none about you

Within your cries; all promises of safety°
Are but deluding dreams. [*She stabs him*] Thus, thus, thou foul
   man,
Thus I begin my vengeance.

KING   Hold, Evadne,
I do command thee, hold.

EVADNE   I do not mean, sir,   100
To part so fairly with you. We must change
More of these love-tricks yet.

KING   What bloody villainy
Provoked thee to this murder?

EVADNE   Thou, thou monster.
      She stabs him

KING   O!

EVADNE Thou kept'st me brave at court and whored me, King,°
Then married me to a young noble gentleman   105
And whored me still.

KING   Evadne, pity me.

EVADNE Hell take me then. [*She stabs him*] This for my lord
   Amintor,
This for my noble brother, and this stroke
For the most wronged of women.

KING   O, I die.

EVADNE Die all our faults together; I forgive thee,   110
   [*Evadne draws the traverse curtain across the bed,*] *and exits.*°
   Enter two Gentlemen of the Bedchamber

FIRST GENTLEMAN Come now, she's gone. Let's enter. The King
expects it,° and will be angry.

SECOND GENTLEMAN 'Tis a fine wench. We'll have a snap at her one
of these nights as she goes from him.

FIRST GENTLEMAN Content. How quickly he had done with her. I see   115
kings can do no more that way than other mortal people.
   [*They draw the traverse curtain, revealing the King's dead
   body in bed*]

SECOND GENTLEMAN How fast he is! I cannot hear him breathe.

FIRST GENTLEMAN Either the tapers give a feeble light,
Or he looks very pale.

SECOND GENTLEMAN   And so he does;
Pray heaven he be well. Let's look. Alas,   120
He's stiff, wounded and dead. Treason, treason!

FIRST GENTLEMAN Run forth and call.

SECOND GENTLEMAN Treason, treason!
    Exit Second Gentleman
FIRST GENTLEMAN This will be laid on us. Who can believe
  A woman could do this?
    Enter Cleon and Lysippus
CLEON   How now? Where's the traitor?   125
FIRST GENTLEMAN Fled, fled away, but there her woeful act
  Lies still.
CLEON   Her act! A woman!
LYSIPPUS   Where's the body?
FIRST GENTLEMAN   There.
LYSIPPUS Farewell, thou worthy man; there were two bonds
  That tied our loves, a brother and a king,
  The least of which might fetch a flood of tears;   130
  But such the misery of greatness is,
  They have no time to mourn. Then pardon me.
    Enter Strato
  Sirs, which way went she?
STRATO   Never follow her,
  For she, alas, was but the instrument.
  News is now brought in that Melantius   135
  Has got the fort, and stands upon the wall
  And with a loud voice calls those few that pass
  At this dead time of night, delivering
  The innocence of this act.
LYSIPPUS   Gentlemen,
  I am your King.
STRATO   We do acknowledge it.   140
LYSIPPUS I would I were not. Follow all, for this
  Must have a sudden stop.°
    Exeunt

5.2

    Enter Melantius, Diphilus, and Calianax on the walls
MELANTIUS If the dull people can believe I am armed—
  Be constant, Diphilus. Now we have time
  Either to bring our banished honours home

Or to create new ones in our ends.
DIPHILUS   I fear not;°
  My spirit lies not that way. Courage, Calianax.   5
CALIANAX Would I had any; you should quickly know it.
MELANTIUS Speak to the people, thou art eloquent.
CALIANAX 'Tis a fine eloquence to come to the gallows.
  You were born to be my end, the devil take you.
  Now must I hang for company. 'Tis strange°   10
  I should be old and neither wise nor valiant.
          Enter King Lysippus, Diagoras, Cleon, Strato, and Guards
KING LYSIPPUS See where he stands, as boldly confident
  As if he had his full command about him.°
STRATO He looks as if he had the better cause, sir
  (Under your gracious pardon let me speak it);   15
  Though he be mighty-spirited and forward
  To all great things, to all things of that danger
  Worse men shake at the telling of, yet certainly
  I do believe him noble, and this action
  Rather pulled on than sought: his mind was ever   20
  As worthy as his hand.
KING LYSIPPUS   'Tis my fear too.
  Heaven forgive all. Summon him, lord Cleon.
CLEON Ho, from the walls there!
MELANTIUS   Worthy Cleon, welcome.
  We could ha' wished you here, lord: you are honest.
CALIANAX [aside] Well, thou art as flattering a knave, though I   25
  Dare not tell thee so.
KING LYSIPPUS   Melantius.
MELANTIUS   Sir.
KING LYSIPPUS I am sorry that we meet thus: our old love
  Never required such distance. Pray heaven
  You have not left yourself and sought this safety°
  More out of fear than honour. You have lost   30
  A noble master, which your faith, Melantius,
  Some think might have preserved. Yet you know best.°
MELANTIUS Royal young man, those tears look lovely on thee.
  Had they been shed for a deserving one,
  They had been lasting monuments. Thy brother,   35
  Whilst he was good, I called him King, and served him
  With that strong faith, that most unwearied valour,

Pulled people from the farthest sun to seek him
And buy his friendship. I was then his soldier,
But since his hot pride drew him to disgrace me   40
And brand my noble actions with his lust
(That never-cured dishonour of my sister,
Base stain of whore, and, which is worse,
The joy to make it still so) like myself
Thus I have flung him off with my allegiance   45
And stand here mine own justice to revenge°
What I have suffered in him, and this old man,
Wronged almost to lunacy.

CALIANAX Who, I? You would draw me in! I have had no wrong.
    I do disclaim ye all.

MELANTIUS   The short is this: 50
    'Tis no ambition to lift up myself
    Urgeth me thus. I do desire again
    To be a subject, so I may be free;
    If not, I know my strength, and will unbuild
    This goodly town. Be speedy, and be wise, in a reply.   55

STRATO [to Lysippus] Be sudden, sir, to tie all up again.
    What's done is past recall, and past you to revenge,
    And there are thousands that wait for such
    A troubled hour as this. Throw him the blank.°

KING LYSIPPUS Melantius, write in that thy choice;   60
    My seal is at it.
            [He throws up a document]

MELANTIUS It was our honours drew us to this act,
    No gain, and we will only work our pardons.

CALIANAX Put my name in too.

DIPHILUS   You disclaimed us all
    But now, Calianax.

CALIANAX   That's all one.   65
    I'll not be hanged hereafter by a trick,
    I'll have it in.

MELANTIUS   You shall, you shall.
    [To King Lysippus] Come to the back gate and we'll call you
        King
    And give you up the fort.

KING LYSIPPUS   Away, away.
            Exeunt

5.3

Enter Aspatia, dressed in man's apparel

ASPATIA This is my fatal hour. Heaven may forgive
My rash attempt, that causelessly hath laid
Griefs on me that will never let me rest,
And put a woman's heart into my breast.
It is more honour for you that I die,   5
For she that can endure the misery
That I have on me, and be patient too,
May live and laugh at all that you can do.
            Enter a Servant
God save you, sir.
SERVANT   And you, sir. What's your business?
ASPATIA With you, sir, now, to do me the fair office   10
To help me to your lord.
SERVANT   What, would you serve him?
ASPATIA I'll do him any service. But to haste,
For my affairs are earnest. I desire
To speak with him.
SERVANT Sir, because you are in such haste, I would be loath to delay 15
you longer: you cannot.
ASPATIA It shall become you, though, to tell your lord.
SERVANT Sir, he will speak with nobody; but in particular I have in
charge,° about no weighty matters.
ASPATIA This is most strange.   20
Art thou gold-proof? [*She gives him money*] There's for thee: help
me to him.
SERVANT Pray be not angry, sir; I'll do my best.
            Exit Servant
ASPATIA How stubbornly this fellow answered me!
There is a vile dishonest trick in man,
More than in women. All the men I meet   25
Appear thus to me: are harsh and rude,
And have a subtlety in everything,
Which love could never know; but we fond women
Harbour the easiest and the smoothest thoughts
And think all shall go so. It is unjust°   30
That men and women should be matched together.
            Enter Amintor and his Servant

148

AMINTOR Where is he?
SERVANT   There, my lord.
AMINTOR [to Aspatia]   What would you, sir?
ASPATIA Please it your lordship to command your man
    Out of the room; I shall deliver things
    Worthy your hearing.
AMINTOR [to Servant] Leave us.
        [Exit Servant]
ASPATIA (aside)   O that that shape   35
    Should bury falsehood in it!°
AMINTOR   Now, your will, sir.
ASPATIA When you know me, my lord, you needs must guess
    My business; and I am not hard to know,
    For till the chance of war marked this smooth face
    With these few blemishes, people would call me°   40
    My sister's picture, and her mine. In short,
    I am the brother to the wronged Aspatia.
AMINTOR 'The wronged Aspatia'. Would thou wert so too°
    Unto the wronged Amintor. Let me kiss
    That hand of thine in honour that I bear   45
    Unto the wronged Aspatia. Here I stand
    That did it; would I could not. Gentle youth,
    Leave me, for there is something in thy looks
    That calls my sins in a most hideous form
    Into my mind, and I have grief enough   50
    Without thy help.
ASPATIA   I would I could with credit.
    Since I was twelve years old I had not seen
    My sister till this hour I now arrived
    (She sent for me to see her marriage),
    A woeful one; but they that are above   55
    Have ends in everything. She used few words,
    But yet enough to make me understand
    The baseness of the injuries you did her.
    That little training I have had is war:
    I may behave myself rudely in peace;   60
    I would not, though. I shall not need to tell you
    I am but young, and would be loath to lose
    Honour, that is not easily gained again.
    Fairly I mean to deal. The age is strict
    For single combats, and we shall be stopped°   65

149

If it be published. If you like your sword,
Use it; if mine appear a better to you,
Change; for the ground is this, and this the time
To end our difference.

AMINTOR   Charitable youth,
If thou be'st such, think not I will maintain   70
So strange a wrong, and for thy sister's sake
Know that I could not think that desperate thing
I durst not do. Yet to enjoy this world
I would not see her, for beholding thee
I am I know not what. If I have ought°   75
That may content thee, take it and begone,
For death is not so terrible as thou:
Thine eyes shoot guilt into me.

ASPATIA   Thus she swore
Thou wouldst behave thyself, and give me words
That would fetch tears into my eyes, and so   80
Thou dost indeed; but yet she bade me watch
Lest I were cozened, and be sure to fight
Ere I returned.

AMINTOR   That must not be with me.
For her I'll die directly, but against her
Will never hazard it.

ASPATIA   You must be urged.   85
I do not deal uncivilly with those
That dare to fight, but such a one as you
Must be used thus.
        She strikes him°

AMINTOR   I prithee, youth, take heed:
Thy sister is a thing to me so much
Above mine honour that I can endure   90
All this. Good gods, a blow I can endure,
But stay not, lest thou draw a timeless death
Upon thyself.

ASPATIA   Thou art some prating fellow,
One that has studied out a trick to talk
And move soft-hearted people. To be kicked,   95
Thus to be kicked—
        She kicks him
                        (*Aside*) Why should he be so slow
In giving me my death?

AMINTOR   A man can bear

No more and keep his flesh. Forgive me, then,°
I would endure yet if I could. Now show
The spirit thou pretendest, and understand 100
Thou hast no hour to live.

They fight. [Aspatia is wounded, and falls to the ground]

What dost thou mean? Thou canst not fight.
The blows thou mak'st at me are quite besides,°
And those I offer at thee, thou spread'st thine arms
And tak'st upon thy breast, alas, defenceless. 105

ASPATIA I have got enough, and my desire.
There is no place so fit for me to die as here.

Enter Evadne, with bloody hands, carrying a knife

EVADNE Amintor, I am loaden with events
That fly to make thee happy. I have joys
That in a moment can call back thy wrongs 110
And settle thee in thy free state again.
It is Evadne still that follows thee,
But not her mischiefs.

AMINTOR Thou canst not fool me to believe again;
But thou hast looks and things so full of news 115
That I am stayed.

EVADNE Noble Amintor, put off thy amaze,
Let thine eyes loose, and speak. Am I not fair?
Looks not Evadne beauteous with these rites now?
Were those hours half so lovely in thine eyes 120
When our hands met before the holy man?
I was too foul within to look fair then,
Since I knew ill I was not free till now.°

AMINTOR There is presage of some important thing
About thee, which it seems thy tongue hath lost. 125
Thy hands are bloody, and thou hast a knife.

EVADNE In this consists thy happiness and mine.
Joy to Amintor, for the King is dead.

AMINTOR Those have most power to hurt us that we love:
We lay our sleeping lives within their arms. 130
Why, thou hast raised up mischief to his height
And found one to out-name thy other faults.
Thou hast no intermission of thy sins,
But all thy life is a continued ill.
Black is thy colour now, disease thy nature. 135
'Joy to Amintor'? Thou hast touched a life
The very name of which had power to chain

151

> Up all my rage and calm my wildest wrongs.

EVADNE 'Tis done, and since I could not find a way
 To meet thy love so clear as through his life,   140
 I cannot now repent it.

AMINTOR Couldst thou procure the gods to speak to me,
 To bid me love this woman and forgive,
 I think I should fall out with them. Behold,
 Here lies a youth whose wounds bleed in my breast,   145
 Sent by his violent fate to fetch his death
 From my slow hand; and to augment my woe°
 You are now present, stained with a king's blood
 Violently shed. This keeps night here,
 And throws an unknown wilderness about me.   150

ASPATIA O, O, O!°

> [*Amintor makes to leave; Evadne stops him*]

AMINTOR No more, pursue me not.

EVADNE   Forgive me then,
 And take me to thy bed. We may not part.

AMINTOR Forbear, be wise, and let my rage go this way.

EVADNE 'Tis you that I would stay, not it.

AMINTOR   Take heed,   155
 It will return with me.

EVADNE   If it must be,
 I shall not fear to meet it. Take me home.

AMINTOR Thou monster of cruelty, forbear.

EVADNE [*kneeling*] For heaven's sake look more calm; thine eyes are
      sharper
 Than thou canst make thy sword.

AMINTOR   Away, away,   160
 Thy knees are more to me than violence.
 I am worse than sick to see knees follow me
 For that I must not grant. For God's sake, stand.

EVADNE Receive me, then.

AMINTOR   I dare not stay. Thy language!
 In midst of all my anger and my grief,   165
 Thou dost awake something that troubles me
 And says I loved thee once. I dare not stay.
 There is no end of woman's reasoning.
      He leaves her

EVADNE Amintor, thou shalt love me now again.
 Go, I am calm. Farewell, and peace forever.   170

Evadne whom thou hat'st will die for thee.
        She stabs herself
AMINTOR (*returning*) I have a little humane nature yet
    That's left for thee, that bids me stay thy hand.
EVADNE Thy hand was welcome, but it came too late.
    O, I am lost; the heavy sleep makes haste.   175
        She dies
ASPATIA O, O, O!
AMINTOR This earth of mine doth tremble, and I feel
    A stark affrighted motion in my blood.
    My soul grows weary of her house, and I°
    All over am a trouble to myself.   180
    There is some hidden power in these dead things
    That calls my flesh into 'em. I am cold.
    Be resolute, and bear 'em company.
    There's something yet which I am loath to leave.
    There's man enough in me to meet the fears   185
    That death can bring, and yet would it were done.
    I can find nothing in the whole discourse
    Of death I durst not meet the boldest way;
    Yet still, betwixt the reason and the act,
    The wrong I to Aspatia did stands up.   190
    I have not such another fault to answer.
    Though she may justly arm herself with scorn
    And hate of me, my soul will part less troubled
    When I have paid to her in tears my sorrow.
    I will not leave this act unsatisfied°   195
    If all that's left in me can answer it.
ASPATIA Was it a dream? There stands Amintor still,
    Or I dream still.
AMINTOR How dost thou? Speak, receive my love and help.
    Thy blood climbs up to his old place again;   200
    There's hope of thy recovery.
ASPATIA Did you not name Aspatia?
AMINTOR   I did.
ASPATIA And talked of tears and sorrow unto her?
AMINTOR 'Tis true, and till these happy signs in thee
    Stayed my course, it was thither I was going.   205
ASPATIA Thou art there already, and these wounds are hers.
    Those threats I brought with me sought not revenge
    But came to fetch this blessing from thy hand.

I am Aspatia yet.

AMINTOR   Dare my soul ever look abroad again?°   210

ASPATIA   I shall sure live, Amintor, I am well:
A kind of healthful joy wanders within me.

AMINTOR   The world wants loveliness to excuse thy loss.°
Come, let me bear thee to some place of help.

ASPATIA   Amintor, thou must stay. I must rest here: 215
My strength begins to disobey my will.
How dost thou, my best soul? I would fain live
Now, if I could; wouldst thou have loved me then?°

AMINTOR   Alas, all that I am's not worth a hair from thee.

ASPATIA   Give me thine hand. Mine hands grope up and down   220
And cannot find thee. I am wondrous sick.
Have I thy hand, Amintor?

AMINTOR   Thou greatest blessing of the world, thou hast.

ASPATIA   I do believe thee better than my sense.
O, I must go. Farewell.   225
          [She dies]

AMINTOR   She swoons. Aspatia! Help, for God's sake! Water,
Such as may chain life ever to this frame!
Aspatia, speak! What, no help? Yet I fool.
I'll chafe her temples, yet there nothing stirs.
Some hidden power tell her Amintor calls   230
And let her answer me. Aspatia, speak.
I have heard, if there be any life, but bow°
The body thus and it will show itself.
O, she is gone. I will not leave her yet.
Since out of justice we must challenge nothing,°   235
I'll call it mercy if you'll pity me,
You heavenly powers, and lend forth some few years
The blessed soul to this fair seat again.
No comfort comes: the gods deny me too.
I'll bow the body once again. Aspatia!   240
The soul is fled forever, and I wrong
Myself so long to lose her company.
Must I talk now? Here's to be with thee, love.
          He stabs himself. Enter Servant

SERVANT   This is a great grace to my lord, to have the new King come
to him. I must tell him he is entering. [He sees the bodies] O God,   245
help help!
          Enter King Lysippus, Melantius, Calianax, Cleon, Diphilus,
          and Strato

KING LYSIPPUS Where's Amintor?

STRATO O there, there!

KING LYSIPPUS How strange is this!

CALIANAX What should we do here?   250

MELANTIUS These deaths are such acquainted things with me
    That yet my heart dissolves not. May I stand
    Stiff here forever. Eyes, call up your tears,
    This is Amintor. Heart, he was my friend:
    Melt. [*He weeps*] Now it flows. Amintor, give a word   255
    To call me to thee.

AMINTOR   O!

MELANTIUS   Melantius
    Calls his friend Amintor. O, thy arms
    Are kinder to me than thy tongue. Speak, speak!

AMINTOR What?

MELANTIUS   That little word was worth all the sounds
    That ever I shall hear again.

DIPHILUS   O brother,   260
    Here lies your sister slain. You lose yourself
    In sorrow there.

MELANTIUS   Why, Diphilus, it is
    A thing to laugh at in respect of this.
    Here was my sister, father, brother, son,
    All that I had. [*To Amintor*] Speak once again:°   265
    What youth lies slain there by thee?

AMINTOR   'Tis Aspatia.
    My last is said. Let me give up my soul
    Into thy bosom.
       [*He dies*]

CALIANAX   What's that? What's that? Aspatia?

MELANTIUS I never did repent the greatness of
    My heart till now: it will not burst at need.   270

CALIANAX My daughter dead here too, and you have all fine new tricks
    to grieve, but I ne'er knew any but direct crying.

MELANTIUS I am a prattler, but no more.
     [*He draws his sword and makes to stab himself*]

DIPHILUS   Hold, brother!

KING LYSIPPUS Stop him.
     [*The courtiers disarm Melantius*]

DIPHILUS Fie, how unmanly was this offer in you.   275
    Does this become our strain?

CALIANAX I know not what the matter is, but I am grown very kind,

and am friends with you all now. You have given me that among you
will kill me quickly, but I'll go home and live as long as I can.
  Exit Calianax

MELANTIUS His spirit is but poor that can be kept   280
  From death for want of weapons.
  Is not my hands a weapon sharp enough
  To stop my breath? Or if you tie down those,
  I vow, Amintor, I will never eat,°
  Or drink, or sleep, or have to do with that   285
  That may preserve life. This I swear to keep.

KING LYSIPPUS Look to him, though, and bear those bodies in.
  May this a fair example be to me
  To rule with temper; for on lustful kings°
  Unlooked-for sudden deaths from God are sent;   290
  But cursed is he that is their instrument.
    Exeunt with the bodies

ADDITIONAL PASSAGES

The following five passages of four or more lines appear only in Q2 (1622) and do not seem to be censorship cuts. It is likely that some were cut from the text before the first performance, while others were added in a revision, possibly by Francis Beaumont, working from the authors' pre-theatrical draft. Material in pointed brackets indicates the context in the main text.

A. *After 1.2.139*

〈CYNTHIA *We may not break*
    The gods' decrees, but when our time is come
    Must drive away and give the day our room.〉
    Yet while our reign lasts, let us stretch our power
    To give our servants one contented hour   5
    With such unwonted solemn grace and state
    As may for ever after force them hate
    Our brother's glorious beams, and wish the night,
    Crowned with a thousand stars and our cold light;
    For almost all the world their service bend   10
    To Phoebus, and in vain my light I lend,°
    Gazed on unto my setting from my rise
    Almost of none but of unquiet eyes.°

B. *After 1.2.224*

NEPTUNE [to Cynthia] *Great Queen of us and heaven, hear what*
    I bring°
    To make this hour a full one.
CYNTHIA   *Speak, seas' king.*
NEPTUNE *The tunes my Amphitrite joys to have*°
    When she will dance upon the rising wave
    And court me as the sails. My Tritons, play°   5
    Music to lead a storm. I'll lead the way.
        [*Another measure is danced, led by Neptune*]
SEA-GODS [*sing*] *To bed, to bed! Come, Hymen, lead the bride,*
               And lay her by her husband's side;
               Bring in the virgins every one
               That grieve to lie alone,   10

That they may kiss, while they may say a maid;°
Tomorrow 'twill be other kissed and said.°
Hesperus be long a-shining
Whilst these lovers are a-twining.

C. *After 2.1.66*

ASPATIA [*sings*] Lay a garland on my hearse of the dismal yew.°

EVADNE That's one of your sad songs, madam.

ASPATIA Believe me, 'tis a very pretty one.

EVADNE How is it, madam?

ASPATIA [*sings*] *Lay a garland on my hearse*   5
            Of the dismal yew;
            Maidens, willow branches bear;°
            Say I dièd true.
            My love was false, but I was firm
            From my hour of birth;   10
            Upon my buried body lay
            Lightly, gentle earth.

EVADNE Fie on't, madam, the words are so strange they are able to
    make one dream of hobgoblins. 'I could never have the power,' sing
    that, Dula.   15

DULA [*sings*] *I could never have the power*
            To love one above an hour,
            But my heart would prompt mine eye
            On some other man to fly.
            Venus, fix mine eyes fast,   20
            Or if not, give me all that I shall see at last.

EVADNE So, leave me now.

DULA Nay, we must see you laid.°

D. *After 2.2.15*

⟨ASPATIA Then, my good girls, be more than women, wise.
    At least, be more than I was⟩, and be sure
    You credit anything the light gives life to
    Before a man; rather believe the sea
    Weeps for the ruined merchant when he roars,   5
    Rather the wind courts but the pregnant sails°
    When the strong cordage cracks, rather the sun
    Comes but to kiss the fruit in wealthy autumn
    When all falls blasted. If you needs must love,°
    Forced by ill fate, take to your maiden bosoms   10

Two dead, cold aspics, and of them make lovers:
They cannot flatter nor forswear; one kiss
Makes a long peace for all. But man, O that beast man—

E.° After 3.1.201

KING Take him. Farewell. Henceforth I am thy foe,
  And what disgraces I can blot thee with, look for.
EVADNE Stay, sir.—Amintor!—You shall hear.—Amintor!
AMINTOR What, my love?

THE MAIDEN'S TRAGEDY

THOMAS MIDDLETON

THE PERSONS OF THE PLAY

Govianus,° the deposed King
The Lady, betrothed to him
Govianus' Servant
Govianus' Page

The usurping Tyrant
Helvetius, the Lady's father
Memphonius° ⎫
Sophonirus° ⎬ courtiers
Noblemen of the court ⎭
Court Attendants
Soldiers of the Tyrant's Guard
Singers

Anselmus, Govianus' brother
His Wife
Votarius, his resident friend°
Leonella, waiting-woman to Anselmus' wife
Bellarius, her lover, and Votarius' enemy
Anselmus' Servants

1.1

[*The throne is set out.*] *A sennet is played. Enter the new usurping Tyrant, with the Nobles of his faction, including Memphonius, Sophonirus, Helvetius, and others; followed by Govianus, the right heir deposed.* [*The Tyrant ascends the throne*]

TYRANT Thus high, my lords, your powers and constant loves
Have fixed our glories like unmovèd stars°
That know not what it is to fall or err.
We're now the kingdom's love, and he that was
Flattered awhile so, stands before us now,   5
Readier for doom than dignity.

GOVIANUS   So much
Can the adulterate friendship of mankind,
False fortune's sister, bring to pass on kings
And lay usurpers sunning in their glories°
Like adders in warm beams.

TYRANT   There was but one°   10
In whom my heart took pleasure amongst women,
One in the whole creation, and in her
You dared to be my rival! Was 't not bold?
Now we are King, she'll leave the lower path
And find the way to us. Helvetius!°   15
It is thy daughter. Happier than a king,
And far above him, for she kneels to thee
Whom we have kneeled to, richer in one smile°
That came from her than she in all thy blessings;
If thou be'st proud thou art to be forgiven,   20
'Tis no deadly sin in thee. While she lives,
High lust is not more natural to youth
Than that to thee. Be not afraid to die in 't:°
'Tis but the sin of joy. There is no gladness
But has a pride it lives by—that's the oil   25
That feeds it into flames. Let her be sent for,
And honourably attended as beseems
Her that we make our Queen. My lords Memphonius
And Sophonirus, take into your care
The royal business of my heart. Conduct her   30

With a respect equal with that to us.
If more, it shall be pardoned: so still err.
You honour us, but ourself honours her.
MEMPHONIUS [aside] Strange fortune, does he make his Queen of
    her?
    Exit Memphonius
SOPHONIRUS [aside] I have a wife; would she were so preferred.   35
I could be but her subject. So I'm now.
I allow her her own friend to stop her mouth°
And keep her quiet, gi' him his table free,°
And the huge feeding of his great stone-horse°
On which he rides in pomp about the city,   40
Only to speak to gallants in bay-windows.
Marry, his lodging he pays dearly for:
He gets me all my children, there I save by 't;
Beside, I draw my life out by the bargain
Some twelve years longer than the time's appointed,   45
When my young, prodigal gallant kicks up's heels
At one-and-thirty, and lies dead and rotten°
Some five-and-forty years before I'm coffined.
'Tis the right way to keep a woman honest:
One friend is barricado to a hundred   50
And keeps 'em out. Nay, more, a husband's sure
To have his children all of one man's getting,
And he that performs best can have no better.
I'm e'en as happy, then, that save a labour.
    Exit Sophonirus
TYRANT [to Helvetius] Thy honours with thy daughter's love shall
    rise;   55
I shall read thy deservings in her eyes.
HELVETIUS O may they be eternal books of pleasure
    To show you all delight.
    [*The Tyrant consults with his Nobles*°]
GOVIANUS [aside] The loss of her sits closer to my heart
Than that of kingdom, or the whorish pomp   60
Of this world's title that with flattery swells us
And makes us die like beasts fat for destruction.
O she's a woman, and her eye will stand
Upon advancement, never weary yonder;°
But when she turns her head by chance and sees   65
The fortunes that are my companions,

She'll snatch her eyes off and repent the looking.

TYRANT [*to the Nobles*] 'Tis well advised.—We doom thee, Govianus,
  To banishment forever from our kingdom.

GOVIANUS What could be worse to one whose heart is locked   70
  Up in another's bosom? Banishment?
  And why not death? Is that too easy for me?

TYRANT But that the world would call our way to dignity
  A path of blood, it should be the first act in all our reign.

GOVIANUS She's lost forever. [*To the Nobles*] Farewell, virtuous men,   75
  Too honest for your greatness. Now you're mightier
  Than when we knew the kingdom, your styles heavier;
  Then, ponderous nobility, farewell.

FIRST NOBLEMAN How's that, sir?

GOVIANUS Weighty and serious. O, sir, is it you?°   80
  I knew you one-and-twenty and a lord
  When your discretion sucked; is 't come from nurse yet?°
  You scorn to be a scholar: you were born better,
  You have good lands—that's the best grounds of learning.
  If you can construe but your doctor's bill,   85
  Pierce your wife's waiting-women, and decline your tenants°
  Till they're all beggars with new fines and rackings,°
  You're scholar good enough for a lady's son
  That's born to living. If you list to read,°
  Ride but to th' city and bestow your looks   90
  On the court library, the mercers' books;°
  They'll quickly furnish you. Do but entertain
  A tailor for your tutor, to expound
  All the hard stuff to you, by what name and title°
  Soever they be called.

FIRST NOBLEMAN   I thank you, sir.   95

GOVIANUS 'Tis happy you have learnt so much manners,
  Since you have so little wit. Fare you well, sir.
    [*He begins to go*]

TYRANT Let him be stayed a while.

SECOND NOBLEMAN   Stay!

FIRST NOBLEMAN   You must stay, sir.

GOVIANUS [*aside*] He's not so honest, sure, to change his mind,
  Revoke his doom: hell has more hope on him.°   100

TYRANT We have not ended yet: the worst part's coming.

The banishment were gentle, were that all;
But to afflict thy soul, before thou goest
Thou shalt behold the heav'n that thou must lose
In her that must be mine.   105
Then to be banished, then to be deprived,
Shows the full torment we provide for thee.

GOVIANUS   Here's a right tyrant now: he will not bate me
Th' affliction of my soul; he'll have all parts
Suffer together.

    *Enter Memphonius and Sophonirus with the Lady, clad in
    black*

                   Now I see my loss   110
I never shall recover 't: my mind's beggared.

TYRANT   Whence rose that cloud? Can such a thing be seen°
In honour's glorious day, the sky so clear?
Why mourns the kingdom's mistress? Does she come
To meet advancement in a funeral garment?   115
Back! She forgot herself; 'twas too much joy°
That bred this error, and we heartily pardon it.
[*To Helvetius*°] Go, bring me her hither like an illustrious bride
With her best beams about her. Let her jewels
Be worth ten cities: that beseems our mistress,   120
And not a widow's case, a suit to weep in.

LADY   I am not to be altered.

TYRANT   How?

LADY   I have a mind
That must be shifted ere I cast off these
Or I shall wear strange colours. 'Tis not titles
Nor all the bastard honours of this frame°   125
That I am taken with. I come not hither
To please the eye of glory, but of goodness,
And that concerns not you, sir: you're for greatness.

    [*She goes to stand with Govianus*]

I dare not deal with you: I have found my match,
And I will never lose him.

GOVIANUS   If there be man   130
Above a king in fortunes, read my story
And you shall find him there. Farewell, poor kingdom!
[*To the Tyrant*] Take it to help thee; thou hast need on 't now.
I see thee in distress, more miserable
Than some thou lay'st taxations on, poor subjects.   135

Thou'rt all beset with storms, more overcast
Than ever any man that brightness flattered.
'Tis only wretchedness to be there with thee,
And happiness to be here.
TYRANT   Sure some dream crowned me.°
If it were possible to be less than nothing,   140
I wake the man you seek for. There's the kingdom
Within yon valley fixed, while I stand here,
Kissing false hopes upon a frozen mountain
Without the confines. I am he that's banished:
The King walks yonder, chose by her affection,   145
Which is the surer side; for where she goes
Her eye removes the court. What is he here°
Can spare a look? They're all employed on her!°
Helvetius, thou art not worth the waking neither:
I lose but time in thee. Go, sleep again.   150
Like an old man, thou canst do nothing;
Thou tak'st no pains at all to earn thine honours.
Which way shall we be able to pay thee
To thy content, when we receive not ours?
The master of the work must needs decay   155
When he wants means and sees his servant play.°
HELVETIUS [to the Lady] Have I bestowed so many blessings on thee,
And do they all return to me in curses?
Is that the use I ha' for 'em? Be not to me°
A burden ten times heavier than my years.   160
Thou'd'st wont to be kind to me and observe
What I thought pleasing. Go, entreat the King.
LADY I will do more for you, sir: you're my father.
I'll kiss him too.
          [She embraces and kisses Govianus]
HELVETIUS   How am I dealt withal!
LADY Why that's the usurper, sir; this is the King.   165
I happened righter than you thought I had,
And were all kingdoms of the earth his own,
As sure as this is not, and this dear gentleman
As poor as virtue, and almost as friendless,
I would not change this misery for that sceptre,   170
Wherein I had part with him. Sir, be cheerful.
'Tis not the reeling fortune of great state
Or low condition that I cast mine eye at:

167

It is the man I seek; the rest I loose°
As things unworthy to be kept or noted.   175
Fortunes are but the outsides of true worth:
It is the mind that sets his master forth.°

TYRANT Has there so many bodies been hewn down,
Like trees in progress, to cut out a way°
That was ne'er known, for us and our affections,   180
And is our game so crossed? There stands the first°
Of all her kind that ever refused greatness.°

HELVETIUS 'Tis in your power, my lord, to force her to you
And pluck her from his arms.

TYRANT   Thou talk'st unkindly.°
That had been done before thy thought begot it   185
If my affection could be so hard-hearted
To stand upon such payment. It must come
Gently and kindly like a debt of love,
Or 'tis not worth receiving.

GOVIANUS   Now, usurper,
I wish no happier freedom than the banishment   190
That thou hast laid upon me.

TYRANT [aside]   O he kills me
At mine own weapon. 'Tis I that live in exile
Should she forsake the land. I'll feign some cause
Far from the grief itself, to call it back.
[Aloud] That doom of banishment was but lent to thee   195
To make a trial of thy factious spirit,
Which flames in thy desire. Thou wouldst be gone:
There is some combination betwixt thee°
And foreign plots; thou hast some powers to raise—
Which to prevent, thy banishment we revoke,   200
Confine thee to thy house nearest our court,
And place a guard about thee. Lord Memphonius,
See it effected.

MEMPHONIUS   With best care, my lord.

GOVIANUS Confine me? Here's my liberty in mine arms.°
I wish no better to bring me content: 205
Lovers' best freedom is close prisonment.

         Exeunt the Lady and Govianus, [with Memphonius°]

TYRANT Methinks the day e'en darkens at her absence.
I stand as in a shade, when a great cloud

Muffles the sun, whose beams shine afar off
On towers and mountains; but I keep the valleys,   210
The place that is last served.

HELVETIUS   My lord.
TYRANT   Your reason, sir.
HELVETIUS Your grace is mild to all but your own bosom:
  They should have both been sent to several prisons
  And not committed to each other's arms.
  There's a hot durance: he'll ne'er wish more freedom.   215
TYRANT 'Tis true. Let 'em both be forced back.
    [*Some Noblemen make to leave*]
  Stay! We command you!°
  [*To Helvetius*] Thou talk'st not like a statesman. Had my wrath
  Took hold of such extremity at first
  They'd lived suspectful still, warned by their fears,   220
  Where now that liberty makes 'em more secure.
  I'll take 'em at my pleasure: it gives thee
  Freer access to play the father for us
  And ply her to our will.
HELVETIUS   Mass, so it does.
  Let a man think on 't twice, your grace hath happened   225
  Upon a strange way, yet it proves the nearest.
TYRANT Nay, more, to vex his soul, give command straight
  They be divided into several rooms
  Where he may only have a sight of her,
  To his mind's torment, but his arms and lips,   230
  Locked up like felons, from her.
HELVETIUS   Now you win me.
  I like that cruelty passing well, my lord.
TYRANT Give order with all speed.
HELVETIUS   Though I be old
  I need no spur, my lord: honour pricks me.°
  I do beseech your grace, look cheerfully: 235
  You shall not want content. If it be locked
  In any blood of mine, the key's your own,
  You shall command the wards.
TYRANT   Say'st thou so, sir?°
  I were ingrateful, then, should I see thee
  Want honour, that provides content for me.   240
    Exeunt. A flourish is played. [*The throne is removed*]

1.2

*Enter Lord Anselmus, the deposed King's brother, with his
friend Votarius*

VOTARIUS Pray, sir, confine your thoughts and excuse me:°
  Methinks the deposed king your brother's sorrow
  Should find you business enough.

ANSELMUS   How, Votarius,
  Sorrow for him? Weak ignorance talks not like thee:
  Why, he was never happier.

VOTARIUS   Pray prove that, sir.   5

ANSELMUS He's lost the kingdom, but his mind's restored.
  Which is the larger empire, prithee tell me?
  Dominions have their limits; the whole earth
  Is but a prisoner, nor the sea her jailer
  That with a silver hoop locks in her body;   10
  They're fellow-prisoners, though the sea look bigger
  Because he is in office, and pride swells him.°
  But the unbounded kingdom of the mind
  Is as unlimitable as heaven,
  That glorious court of spirits, all honest courtiers.°   15
  Sir, if thou lov'st me, turn thine eye to me
  And look not after him that needs thee not.
  My brother's well attended: peace and pleasure
  Are never from his sight. He has his mistress:
  She brought those servants and bestowed them on him;   20
  But who brings mine?

VOTARIUS   Had you not both long since
  By a kind, worthy lady, your chaste wife?

ANSELMUS That's it that I take pains with thee to be sure of.
  What true report can I send to my soul
  Of that, I know not. We must only think°   25
  Our ladies are good people, and so live with 'em,
  A fine security for them. Our own thoughts
  Make the best fools of us; next to them, our wives.°
  But say she's all chaste yet, is that her goodness?
  What labour is 't for woman to keep constant   30
  That's never tried or tempted? Where's her fight?
  The war's within her breast, her honest anger
  Against the impudence of flesh and hell.

So let me know the lady of my rest°
Or I shall never sleep well; give not me   35
The thing that is thought good but what's approved so.°
So wise men choose. O what a lazy virtue
Is chastity in a woman if no sin
Should lay temptation to 't! Prithee set to her
And bring my peace along with thee.

VOTARIUS   You put to me   40
A business that will do my words more shame
Than ever they got honour among women.
Lascivious courtings among sinful mistresses
Come ever seasonably, please best;
But let the boldest ruffian touch the ear   45
Of modest ladies with adulterous sounds,
Their very looks confound him and force grace
Into that cheek where impudence sets her seal.
That work is never undertook with courage
That makes his master blush. However, sir,   50
What profit can return to you by knowing
That which you do already, with more toil?
Must a man needs, in having a rich diamond,
Put it between a hammer and an anvil
And, not believing the true worth and value,   55
Break it in pieces to find out the goodness,
And in the finding lose it? Good sir, think on 't.
Nor does it taste of wit to try their strengths
That are created sickly, nor of manhood.
We ought not to put blocks in women's ways,   60
For some too often fall upon plain ground.
Let me dissuade you, sir.

ANSELMUS   Have I a friend,
And has my love so little interest in him°
That I must trust some stranger with my heart,
And go to seek him out?

VOTARIUS   Nay, hark you, sir,   65
I am so jealous of your weaknesses
That rather than you should lie prostituted°
Before a stranger's triumph, I would venture
A whole hour's shaming for you.

ANSELMUS   Be worth thy word, then.
    Enter Anselmus' Wife

Yonder she comes. [*Aside*] I'll have an ear to you both: 70
I love to have such things at the first hand.
    [*He conceals himself*]
VOTARIUS [*aside*] I'll put him off with somewhat: guile in this
    Falls in with honest dealing. O, who could move°
    Adultery to yon face? So rude a sin
    May not come near the meekness of her eye.   75
    My client's cause looks so dishonestly
    I'll ne'er be seen to plead in 't.
WIFE   What, Votarius!
VOTARIUS Good morrow, virtuous madam.
WIFE   Was my lord
    Seen lately here?
VOTARIUS   He's newly walked forth, lady.
WIFE How was he attended?
VOTARIUS   Faith, I think with none, madam.   80
WIFE That sorrow for the King his brother's fortune
    Prevails too much with him, and leads him strangely
    From company and delight.
VOTARIUS [*aside*]   How she's beguiled in him!
    There's no such natural touch, search all his bosom.°
    [*Aloud*] That grief's too bold with him indeed, sweet madam,   85
    And draws him from the pleasure of his time;
    But 'tis a business of affection
    That must be done. We owe a pity, madam,
    To all men's misery, but especially
    To those afflictions that claim kindred of us: 90
    We're forced to feel 'em; all compassion else
    Is but a work of charity, this of nature,
    And ties our pity in a bond of blood.
WIFE Yet, sir, there is a date set to all sorrows:
    Nothing is everlasting in this world.   95
    Your counsel will prevail: persuade him, good sir,
    To fall into life's happiness again
    And leave the desolate path. I want his company.
    He walks at midnight in thick shady woods
    Where scarce the moon is starlight. I have watched him°   100
    In silver nights when all the earth was dressed
    Up like a virgin in white innocent beams;
    Stood in my window, cold and thinly clad,
    T' observe him through the bounty of the moon

That liberally bestowed her graces on me;   105
And when the morning dew began to fall,
Then was my time to weep. He's lost his kindness,
Forgot the way of wedlock, and become
A stranger to the joys and rites of love;
He's not so good as a lord ought to be.   110
Pray tell him so from me, sir.

VOTARIUS   That will I, madam.
    Exit Wife
    Now must I dress a strange dish for his humour.

ANSELMUS [*aside*] Call you this courting? Life, not one word near it!
There was no syllable but was twelve score off!
My faith, hot temptation! Woman's chastity   115
In such a conflict had great need of one
To keep the bridge. 'Twas dangerous for the time.°
Why, what fantastic faiths are in these days
Made without substance! Whom should a man trust
In matters about love?
    [*He crosses to Votarius*]

VOTARIUS   Mass, here he comes too.   120

ANSELMUS How now, Votarius? What's the news for us?

VOTARIUS You set me a task, sir, that will find
Ten ages work enough, and then unfinished.°
Bring sin before her, why, it stands more quaking
Than if a judge should frown on 't. Three such fits°   125
Would shake it into goodness, and quite beggar
The under-kingdom. Not the art of man,°
Woman, or devil—

ANSELMUS   O peace, man, prithee peace!

VOTARIUS —can make her fit for lust.

ANSELMUS   Yet again, sir!
Where lives that mistress of thine, Votarius,   130
That taught thee to dissemble? I'd fain learn.
She makes good scholars.

VOTARIUS   How, my lord?

ANSELMUS Thou art the son of falsehood; prithee leave me.
How truly constant, charitable, and helpful
Is woman unto woman in affairs   135
That touch affection and the peace of spirit;
But man to man how crookèd and unkind!
I thank my jealousy I heard thee all,

173

For I heard nothing. Now thou'rt sure I did.°

VOTARIUS Now, by this light, then wipe but off this score,°   140
　　Since you're so bent; and if I ever run
　　In debt again to falsehood and dissemblance
　　For want of better means, tear the remembrance of me
　　From your best thoughts.

ANSELMUS　　　　　For thy vow's sake I pardon thee.
　　Thy oath is now sufficient watch itself   145
　　Over thy actions. I discharge my jealousy;
　　I ha' no more use for 't now. To give thee way,°
　　I'll have an absence made purposely for thee°
　　And presently take horse; I'll leave behind me
　　An opportunity that shall fear no starting.°   150
　　Let but thy pains deserve it.

VOTARIUS　　　　　　　I am bound to 't.

ANSELMUS For a small time farewell, then. Hark thee——

VOTARIUS　　　　　　　　　　O good sir,
　　It will do wondrous well.
　　　　　　Exit Anselmus
　　　　　　　　　What a wild seed
　　Suspicion sows in him, and takes small ground for 't.°
　　How happy were this lord if he would leave   155
　　To tempt his fate and be resolved he were so:
　　He would be but too rich.
　　Man has some enemy still that keeps him back
　　In all his fortunes, and his mind is his,°
　　And that's a mighty adversary. I had rather   160
　　Have twenty kings my enemies than that part;
　　For let me be at war with earth and hell
　　So that be friends with me. I ha' sworn to make
　　A trial of her faith. I must put on
　　A courtier's face and do 't: mine own will shame me.   165
　　　　　　Enter Anselmus' Wife

WIFE This is most strange of all! How one distraction
　　Seconds another!

VOTARIUS　　　　　What's the news, sweet madam?

WIFE He's took his horse, but left his leave untaken.°
　　What should I think on 't, sir? Did ever lord
　　Depart so rudely from his lady's presence?   170

VOTARIUS Did he forget your lip?

WIFE　　　　　　　　He forgot all°

That nobleness remembers.
VOTARIUS   I'm ashamed on him.
Let me help, madam, to repair his manners
And mend that unkind fault.
     [*He makes to kiss her*]
WIFE   Sir, pray forbear.
You forget worse than he.
VOTARIUS [*aside*]   So virtue save me,   175
I have enough already.
WIFE   'Tis himself
Must make amends, good sir, for his own faults.
VOTARIUS [*aside*] I would he'd do 't, then, and ne'er trouble me
    in 't.
[*Aloud*] But madam, you perceive he takes the course
To be far off from that. He's rode from home,   180
But his unkindness stays and keeps with you.
Let whose will please his wife, he rides his horse:°
That's all the care he takes. I pity you, madam.
You've an unpleasing lord. Would 'twere not so.
I should rejoice with you.   185
You're younger: the very spring's upon you now;
The roses on your cheeks are but new blown.
Take you together, you're a pleasant garden°
Where all the sweetness of man's comfort breathes.
But what is it to be a work of beauty   190
And want the heart that should delight in you?
You still retain your goodness in yourselves,
But then you lose your glory, which is all.°
The grace of every benefit is the use,°
And is 't not pity you should want your grace?   195
Look you like one whose lord should walk in groves
About the peace of midnight? Alas, madam,
'Tis to me wondrous how you should spare the day
From amorous clips, much less the general season
When all the world's a gamester.°   200
That face deserves a friend of heart and spirit,
Discourse and motion; indeed such a one
That should observe you, madam, without ceasing,°
And not a weary lord.
WIFE   Sure I was married, sir,
In a dear year of love, when scarcity°   205

175

And famine of affection vexed poor ladies,
Which makes my heart so needy. It ne'er knew
Plenty of comfort yet.
VOTARIUS   Why, that's your folly,
  To keep your mind so miserably, madam.
  Change into better times: I'll lead you to 'em.   210
  What bounty shall your friend expect for his!
  O you that can be hard to your own heart,
  How would you use your friend's? If I thought kindly,
  I'd be the man myself should serve your pleasure.
WIFE How, sir!   215
VOTARIUS Nay, and ne'er miss you too. I'd not come sneaking
  Like a retainer once a week or so°
  To show myself before you for my livery.
  I'd follow business like a household servant,
  Carry on my work before me and dispatch°   220
  Before my lord be up, and make no words on 't—°
  The sign of a good servant.
WIFE   'Tis not friendly done, sir,
  To take a lady at advantage thus,
  Set all her wrongs before her and then tempt her.
VOTARIUS [aside] Heart, I grow fond myself! 'Twas well she waked
    me°   225
  Before the dead sleep of adultery took me:
  'Twas stealing on me. Up, you honest thoughts,
  And keep watch for your master. I must hence.
  I do not like my health: it's a strange relish.°
  Pray heav'n I plucked mine eyes back time enough.°   230
  I'll never see her more. I praised the garden,
  But little thought a bed of snakes lay hid in 't.
WIFE [aside] I know not how I am! I'll call my woman.
  Stay, for I fear thou'rt too far gone already.°
VOTARIUS [aside] I'll see her but once more. Do thy worst, Love: 235
  Thou art too young, fond boy, to master me.°
  [Aloud] I come to tell you, madam, and that plainly,
  I'll see your face no more. Take 't how you please!
WIFE You will not offer violence to me, sir,
  In my lord's absence? What does that touch you   240
  If I want comfort?
VOTARIUS   Will you take your answer?
WIFE It is not honest in you to tempt woman

When her distresses take away her strength:
How is she able to withstand her enemy?

VOTARIUS I would fain leave your sight an I could possibly.   245

WIFE What is 't to you, good sir, if I be pleased
  To weep myself away and run thus violently
  Into the arms of death, and kiss destruction?
  Does this concern you now?

VOTARIUS   Ay, marry, does it.
  What serve these arms for but to pluck you back,   250
  These lips but to prevent all other tasters
  And keep that cup of nectar for themselves?
      [*He kisses her*]
  [*Aside*] Heart, I'm beguiled again! Forgive me, heaven.
  My lips have been naught with her.°
  I will be master once and whip the boy°   255
  Home to his mother's lap. Face, fare thee well.°
      Exit Votarius

WIFE Votarius? Sir? My friend? Thanks heaven, he's gone,
  And he shall never come so near again.
  I'll have my frailty watched ever: henceforward
  I'll no more trust it single; it betrays me   260
  Into the hands of folly. Where's my woman?
  [*Calls*] My trusty Leonella!
      Enter Leonella

LEONELLA   Call you, madam?

WIFE Call I! I want attendance! Where are you?

LEONELLA Never far from you, madam.

WIFE   Pray be nearer,
  Or there is some that will, and thank you too;   265
  Nay, perhaps bribe you to be absent from me.

LEONELLA How, madam?

WIFE   Is that strange to a lady's woman?
  There are such things i' th' world, many such buyers
  And sellers of a woman's name and honour,
  Though you be young in bribes and never came   270
  To the flesh-market yet. Beshrew your heart
  For keeping so long from me!

LEONELLA   What ail you, madam?

WIFE Somewhat commands me, and takes all the power
  Of myself from me!

LEONELLA   What should that be, lady?

WIFE When did you see Votarius?

LEONELLA [aside]   Is that next?   275
  Nay, then I have your ladyship in the wind.°
  [Aloud] I saw him lately, madam.

WIFE   Whom didst see?

LEONELLA Votarius!

WIFE   What have I to do with him
  More than another man? [To herself] Say he be fair
  And has parts proper both of mind and body,   280
  You praise him but in vain in telling me so.°

LEONELLA [aside] Yea, madam, are you prattling in your sleep?
  'Tis well my lord and you lie in two beds.

WIFE [aside] I was ne'er so ill. [Aloud] I thank you, Leonella,
  My negligent woman: here you showed your service.   285

LEONELLA [aside] Life, have I power or means to stop a sluice
  At a high water? What would she've me do in 't?°

WIFE I charge thee, while thou liv'st with me, henceforward
  Use not an hour's absence from my sight.
        Exit Wife

LEONELLA By my faith, madam, you shall pardon me.   290
  I have a love of mine own to look to,
  And he must have his breakfast. [Calls off stage] Pist! Bellarius!
        Enter Bellarius, muffled in his cloak

BELLARIUS Leonella!

LEONELLA Come forth and show yourself a gentleman—
  Although most commonly they hide their heads,°   295
  As you do there, methinks. And why a taffety muffler?
  Show your face, man, I'm not ashamed on you.

BELLARIUS I fear the servants.

LEONELLA And they fear their mistress, and ne'er think on you.
  Their thoughts are upon dinner and great dishes.   300
  If one thing hap—impossible to fail, too,°
  I can see so far in 't—you shall walk boldly, sir,
  And openly in view through every room
  About the house; and let the proudest meet thee,
  I charge you give no way to 'em.

BELLARIUS   How thou talk'st!°   305

LEONELLA I can avoid the 'fool', and give you reason for 't.°

BELLARIUS 'Tis more than I should do, if I asked more on thee.
  I prithee tell me how.

LEONELLA   With ease, i' faith, sir.

My lady's heart is wondrous busy, sir,
About the entertainment of a friend, too,   310
And she and I must bear with one another°
Or we shall make but a madhouse betwixt us.
BELLARIUS I'm bold to throw my cloak off at this news,
Which I ne'er durst before, and kiss thee freelier.
What is he, sirrah?
LEONELLA   'Faith, an indifferent fellow   315
With good long legs. A near friend of my lord's.
BELLARIUS 'A near friend of my lady's,' you would say.
His name, I prithee.
LEONELLA   One Votarius, sir.
BELLARIUS What sayest thou?
LEONELLA   He walks under the same title.
BELLARIUS The only enemy that my life can show me.   320
LEONELLA Your enemy! Let my spleen then alone with him.
Stay you your anger: I'll confound him for you.
BELLARIUS As how, I prithee?
LEONELLA   I'll prevent his venery:
He shall ne'er lie with my lady.
BELLARIUS   Troth, I thank you!
Life, that's the way to save him. Art thou mad?   325
Whereas the other way he confounds himself
And lies more naked to revenge and mischief.
LEONELLA Then let him lie with her, and the devil go with him.
He shall have all my furtherance.
BELLARIUS Why now you pray heartily, and speak to purpose.   330
        Exeunt

2.1

Enter the Lady with a Servant

LADY Who is 't would speak with us?

SERVANT   My lord your father.

LADY My father? Pray make haste, he waits too long.
    Entreat him hither.

    [*Exit Servant*]
                         In despite of all
    The Tyrant's cruelties, we have got that friendship
    E'en of the guard that he has placed about us,   5
    My lord and I have free access together,
    As much as I would ask of liberty.
    They'll trust us largely now, and keep sometimes
    Three hours from us, a rare courtesy
    In jailers' children.

        Enter Helvetius

                    Some mild news I hope°   10
    Comes with my father. No, his looks are sad:
    There is some further tyranny. Let it fall:
    Our constant suff'rings shall amaze it.

        [*She kneels to Helvetius*]

HELVETIUS   Rise.°
    I will not bless thee: thy obedience
    Is after custom, as most rich men pray,   15
    Whose saint is only Fashion and Vainglory.
    So 'tis with thee in thy dissembled duty:
    There is no religion in 't, no reverent love,
    Only for fashion and the praise of men.

LADY Why should you think so, sir?

HELVETIUS   Think? I know 't and see 't.°   20
    I'll sooner give my blessing to a drunkard
    Whom the ridiculous power of wine makes humble,
    As foolish use makes thee. Base-spirited girl,
    That canst not think above disgrace and beggary
    When glory is set for thee and thy seed,   25
    Advancement for thy father, beside joy
    Able to make a latter spring in me
    In this my fourscore summer, and renew me

With a reversion yet of heat and youth!°
But the dejection of thy mind and spirit°
Makes me thy father guilty of a fault
That draws thy birth in question, and e'en wrongs°
Thy mother in her ashes, being at peace
With heav'n and man. Had not her life and virtues
Been seals unto her faith, I should think thee now
The work of some hired servant, some house-tailor,
And no one part of my endeavour in thee.
Had I neglected greatness, or not rather
Pursued almost to my eternal hazard,°
Thou'd'st ne'er been a lord's daughter.

LADY   Had I been
A shepherd's, I'd been happier and more peaceful.

HELVETIUS Thy very seed will curse thee in thy age
When they shall hear the story of thy weakness:
How in thy youth thy fortunes tendered thee
A kingdom for thy servant, which thou left'st
Basely to serve thyself. What dost thou in this°
But merely cozen thy posterity
Of royalty and succession, and thyself
Of dignity present?

LADY   Sir, your king did well
'Mongst all his nobles to pick out yourself
And send you with these words. His politic grace
Knew what he did, for well he might imagine
None else should have been heard: they'd had their answer
Before the question had been halfway through.
But, dearest sir, I owe to you a reverence,
A debt which both begins and ends with life—
Never till then discharged, 'tis so long-lasting.
Yet could you be more precious than a father,
Which, next a husband, is the richest treasure°
Mortality can show us, you should pardon me
(And yet confess too that you found me kind)
To hear your words, though I withstood your mind.

HELVETIUS Say you so, daughter? Troth, I thank you kindly.
I am in hope to rise well by your means,
Or you to raise yourself: we're both beholding to you!
Well, since I cannot win you, I commend you,
I praise your constancy and pardon you.

Take Govianus to you, make the most of him.
Pick out your husband there, so you'll but grant me
One light request that follows.

LADY   Heaven forbid else, sir.°   70

HELVETIUS Give me the choosing of your friend, that's all.°

LADY How, sir? My friend? A light request indeed,
Somewhat too light, sir, either for my wearing
Or your own gravity, an you look on 't well.

HELVETIUS Push, talk like a courtier, girl, not like a fool.°   75
Thou know'st the end of greatness, and hast wit
Above the flight of twenty feathered mistresses°
That glister in the sun of princes' favours.
Thou hast discourse in thee fit for a king's fellowship,
A princely carriage and astonishing presence.   80
What should a husband do with all this goodness?
Alas, one end on 't is too much for him,°
Nor is it fit a subject should be master
Of such a jewel. 'Tis in the King's power
To take it for the forfeit, but I come   85
To bear thee gently to his bed of honours,
All force forgotten. The King commends him to thee
With more than the humility of a servant,
That since thou wilt not yield to be his Queen,
Be yet his mistress. He shall be content   90
With that or nothing. He shall ask no more,
And with what easiness that is performed
Most of your women know. Having a husband,
That kindness costs thee nothing: you've that in
All over and above to your first bargain,°   95
And that's a brave advantage for a woman
If she be wise, as I suspect not thee.°
And having youth, and beauty, and a husband,
Thou'st all the wish of woman: take thy time, then,
Make thy best market.

LADY   Can you assure me, sir,°   100
Whether my father spake this, or some spirit
Of evil-wishing that has for a time
Hired his voice of him to beguile me that way,
Presuming on his power and my obedience?
I'd gladly know, that I might frame my answer   105

According to the speaker.

HELVETIUS   How now, baggage?
  Am I in question with thee? Does thy scorn cast
  So thick an ignorance before thine eyes
  That I am forgotten too? Who is 't speaks to thee
  But I, thy father?
     Enter Govianus, discharging a pistol

GOVIANUS   The more monstrous he!   110
     [*Helvetius falls to the ground*]
  Art down but with the bare voice of my fury?
  Up, ancient sinner! Thou'rt but mocked with death:
  I missed thee purposely. Thank this dear creature:
  O hadst thou been anything beside her father,
  I'd made a fearful separation on thee;   115
  I would have sent thy soul to a darker prison
  Than any made of clay, and thy dead body
  As a token to the lustful King thy master.
  Art thou struck down so soon with the short sound
  Of this small earthen instrument, and dost thou   120
  So little fear th' eternal noise of hell?
  What's she? Does she not bear thy daughter's name?
  How stirs thy blood, sir? Is there a dead feeling°
  Of all things fatherly and honest in thee?
  Say thou couldst be content for greatness' sake   125
  To end the last act of thy life in panderism
  (As you perhaps will say your betters do),
  Must it needs follow that unmanly sin
  Can work upon the weakness of no woman
  But hers, whose name and honour natural love   130
  Bids thee preserve more charily than eyesight,
  Health or thy senses? Can promotion's thirst
  Make such a father? Turn a grave old lord
  To a white-headed squire? Make him so base°
  To buy his honours with his daughter's soul   135
  And the perpetual shaming of his blood?
  Hast thou the leisure, thou forgetful man,
  To think upon advancement at these years?
  What wouldst thou do with greatness? Dost thou hope
  To fray death with 't, or hast thou that conceit   140
  That honour will restore thy youth again?

Thou art but mocked, old fellow: 'tis not so;
Thy hopes abuse thee. Follow thine own business
And list not to the Sirens of the world.°
Alas, thou hadst more need kneel at an altar   145
Than to a chair of state,
And search thy conscience for thy sins of youth.
That's work enough for age; it needs no greater.
Thou'rt called within: thy very eyes look inward°
To teach thy thoughts the way, and thy affections.   150
But miserable notes that conscience sings
That cannot truly pray, for flattering kings.°

HELVETIUS This was well searched indeed, and without
        favouring.°
    Blessing reward thee. Such a wound as mine
    Did need a pitiless surgeon. Smart on, soul: 155
    Thou'lt feel the less hereafter. Sir, I thank you.
    I ever saw my life in a false glass
    Until this friendly hour: with what fair faces
    My sins would look on me! But now truth shows 'em.
    How loathsome and how monstrous are their forms!   160
    Be you my King and master still: henceforward
    My knee shall know no other earthly lord.
    Well may I spend this life to do you service
    That sets my soul in her eternal path.

GOVIANUS Rise, rise, Helvetius.

HELVETIUS   I'll see both your hands°   165
    Set to my pardon first.

GOVIANUS   Mine shall bring hers.

LADY Now, sir, I honour you for your goodness chiefly.
    You're my most worthy father: you speak like him;
    The first voice was not his. My joy and reverence
    Strive which should be most seen. Let our hands, sir,   170
    Raise you from the earth thus high,
        [*She and Govianus help Helvetius to his feet.*]
                                and may it prove
    The first ascent of your immortal rising,
    Never to fall again.

HELVETIUS   A spring of blessings
    Keep ever with thee, and the fruit thy lord's.

GOVIANUS I have lost an enemy and have found a father.   175
        Exeunt

2.2

Enter Votarius sadly

VOTARIUS All's gone. There's nothing but the prodigal left.°
I have played away my soul at one short game
Where e'en the winner loses.
Pursuing sin, how often did I shun thee!°
How swift art thou afoot, beyond man's goodness,   5
Which has a lazy pace: so was I catched.
A curse upon the cause! Man in these days
Is not content to have his lady honest
And so rest pleased with her without more toil,
But he must have her tried forsooth, and tempted,   10
And when she proves a quean, then he lies quiet:
Like one that has a watch of curious making,
Thinking to be more cunning than the workman,
Never gives over tamp'ring with the wheels
Till either spring be weakened, balance bowed,°   15
Or some wrong pin put in, and so spoils all.
How I could curse myself! Most business else
Delight in the dispatch (that's the best grace to 't);°
Only this work of blind, repented lust
Hangs shame and sadness on his master's cheek.   20
Yet wise men take no warning—
    Enter Anselmus' Wife
                              nor can I now.
Her very sight strikes my repentance backward:
It cannot stand against her. Chamber thoughts
And words that have sport in 'em, they're for ladies.
WIFE My best and dearest servant.
VOTARIUS   Worthiest mistress.   25
    Enter Leonella
LEONELLA Madam.
WIFE   Who's that? My woman. She's myself.°
Proceed, sir.
LEONELLA   Not if you love your honour, madam:
I came to give you warning my lord's come.
VOTARIUS How?
WIFE My lord!   30
LEONELLA [*aside*] Alas, poor vessels, how this tempest tosses 'em!

They're driven both asunder in a twinkling.°
Down goes the sails here, and the mainmast yonder.°
Here rides a bark with better fortune yet:
I fear no tossing, come what weather will;°   35
I have a trick to hold out water still.°

VOTARIUS [*aside*] His very name shoots like a fever through me,
Now hot, now cold. Which cheek shall I turn toward him
For fear he should read guiltiness in my looks?
I would he would keep from home like a wise man: 40
'Tis no place for him now. I would not see him
Of any friend alive! It is not fit
We two should come together. We have abused
Each other mightily: he used me ill
To employ me thus, and I ha' used him worse.   45
I'm too much even with him.

    Enter Anselmus

                        Yonder's a sight on him.

WIFE My loved and honoured lord. Most welcome, sir.

    [*Anselmus kisses his Wife*]

LEONELLA [*aside*] O, there's a kiss. Methinks my lord might taste
Dissimulation rank in 't, if he had wit:
He takes but the breath of his friend's lip.   50
A second kiss is hers, but that she keeps
For her first friend. We women have no cunning.°

WIFE You parted strangely from me.

ANSELMUS   That's forgotten!°
Votarius! I make speed to be in thine arms.

    [*He and Votarius embrace, and talk apart*]

VOTARIUS You never come too soon, sir.

ANSELMUS   How goes business?   55

VOTARIUS Pray think upon some other subject, sir.
What news at court?

ANSELMUS   Pish, answer me.

VOTARIUS Alas, sir, would you have me work by wonders
To strike fire out of ice? You're a strange lord, sir.
Put me to possible things and find 'em finished   60
At your return to me. I can say no more.

ANSELMUS I see by this thou didst not try her throughly.

VOTARIUS How, sir, 'not throughly'? By this light, he lives not
That could make trial of a woman better.

ANSELMUS I fear thou wast too slack.

VOTARIUS   Good faith, you wrong me, sir.°   65

She never found it so.

ANSELMUS   Then I've a jewel,
And nothing shall be thought too precious for her.
I may advance my forehead and boast purely.°
Methinks I see her worth with clear eyes now.
O when a man's opinion is at peace   70
'Tis a fine life to marry! No state's like it!
[To his Wife] My worthy lady, freely I confess
To thy wronged heart, my passion had o' late
Put rudeness on me, which I now put off.
I will no more seem so unfashionable   75
For pleasure and the chamber of a lady.

WIFE I'm glad you're changed so well, sir.

VOTARIUS [aside]   Thank himself for 't.
        Exeunt Anselmus and his Wife

LEONELLA [aside] This comes like physic when the party's dead.°
Flows kindness now when 'tis so ill-deserved?
This is the fortune still. Well, for this trick   80
I'll save my husband and his friend a labour:
I'll never marry as long as I'm honest,
For commonly queans have the kindest husbands.
        Exit Leonella

VOTARIUS I do not like his company now; 'tis irksome;
His eye offends me. Methinks 'tis not kindly   85
We two should live together in one house,
And 'tis impossible to remove me hence.°
I must not give way first: she is my mistress,
And that's a degree kinder than a wife.°
Women are always better to their friends   90
Than to their husbands, and more true to them.
Then let the worst give place, whom she's least need on,
He that can best be spared, and that's her husband.
I do not like his overboldness with her:
He's too familiar with the face I love.   95
I fear the sickness of affection,
I feel a grudging on 't: I shall grow jealous
E'en of that pleasure which she has by law,
I shall go so near with her.
        Enter Bellarius, [muffled;] he passes over the stage and exits
                    Ha, what's he?°
Life, 'tis Bellarius, my rank enemy!   100
Mine eye snatched so much sight of him. What's his business,

His face half-darkened, stealing through the house
With a whoremaster's pace? I like it not.
This lady will be served like a great woman,
With more attendants, I perceive, than one.   105
She has her shift of friends. My enemy one?°
Do we both shun each other's company
In all assemblies public, at all meetings,
And drink to one another in one mistress?°
My very thought's my poison: 'tis high time   110
To seek for help. Where is our head physician,°
A doctor of my making and that lecher's?
O woman, when thou once leav'st to be good,
Thou car'st not who stands next thee. Every sin°
Is a companion for thee, for thy once-cracked honesty   115
Is like the breaking of whole money:°
It never comes to good but wastes away.
        Enter Anselmus
ANSELMUS Votarius.
VOTARIUS   Ha?
ANSELMUS   We miss you, sir, within.
VOTARIUS I missed you more without. Would you had come sooner,
    sir!
ANSELMUS Why, what's the business?
VOTARIUS   You should ha' seen a fellow,   120
    A common bawdy-house ferret, one Bellarius,
    Steal through this room, his whorish barren face
    Three-quarters muffled. He is somewhere hid
    About the house, sir.
ANSELMUS   Which way took the villain,
    That marriage felon, one that robs the mind   125
    Twenty times worse than any highway striker?
    Speak, which way took he?
VOTARIUS   Marry, my lord, I think—
    Let me see, which way was 't now? Up yon stairs.
ANSELMUS The way to chamb'ring! Did I not say still
    All thy temptations were too faint and lazy?   130
    Thou didst not play 'em home.
VOTARIUS   To tell you true, sir,°
    I found her yielding ere I left her last,
    And wavering in her faith.
ANSELMUS   Did not I think so?

VOTARIUS That makes me suspect him.

ANSELMUS   Why, partial man?
  Couldst thou hide this from me, so dearly sought for,   135
  And rather waste thy pity upon her?
  Thou'rt not so kind as my heart praised thee to me.
     [Footsteps are heard off stage, above]
  Hark!

VOTARIUS 'Tis his footing, certain.

ANSELMUS   Are you chambered?
  I'll fetch you from aloft.
     Exit Anselmus

VOTARIUS   He takes my work°   140
  And toils to bring me ease. This use I'll make on him:
  His care shall watch to keep all strange thieves out,
  Whiles I familiarly go in and rob him
  Like one that knows the house.
  But how has rashness and my jealousy used me?   145
  Out of my vengeance to mine enemy,
  Confessed her yielding! I have locked myself°
  From mine own liberty with that key. Revenge
  Does no man good but to his greater harm.°
  Suspect and malice like a mingled cup°   150
  Made me soon drunk: I knew not what I spoke,
  And that may get me pardon.
     Enter Anselmus, a dagger in his hand, with Leonella.
     [He throws her to the ground]

LEONELLA   Why, my lord!

ANSELMUS Confess, thou mystical panderess! Run, Votarius,
  To the back gate. The guilty slave leapt out
  And scaped me so. This strumpet locked him up   155
  In her own chamber.
     Exit Votarius

LEONELLA   Hold, my lord! I might.
  He is my husband, sir.

ANSELMUS   O soul of cunning,
  Came that arch-subtlety from thy lady's counsel
  Or thine own sudden craft? Confess to me
  How oft thou hast been a bawd to their close actions,   160
  Or all thy light goes out.

LEONELLA   My lord, believe me,
  In troth I love a man too well myself

To bring him to my mistress.
ANSELMUS   Leave thy sporting,
  Or my next offer makes thy heart weep blood.°
LEONELLA O spare that strength, my lord, and I'll reveal   165
  A secret that concerns you, for this does not.
ANSELMUS Back, back my fury then,
  It shall not touch thy breast. Speak freely: what is 't?
LEONELLA Votarius and my lady are false gamesters:
  They use foul play, my lord.
ANSELMUS   Thou liest.
LEONELLA   Reward me then   170
  For all together; if it prove not so,
  I'll never bestow time to ask your pity.
ANSELMUS Votarius and thy lady! 'Twill ask days
  Ere it be settled in belief. So, rise.
      [*He releases her and she stands up*]
  Go get thee to thy chamber.
      Exit Anselmus
LEONELLA   A pox on you!   175
  You hindered me of better business: thank you.°
  He's frayed a secret from me: would he were whipped.
  'Faith, from a woman a thing's quickly slipped.
      Exit

2.3

A flourish is played. Enter the Tyrant, with Sophonirus,
Memphonius, and other Nobles

TYRANT My joys have all false hearts. There's nothing true to me
  That's either kind or pleasant. I'm hardly dealt withal.
  I must not miss her. I want her sight too long.°
  Where's this old fellow?
SOPHONIRUS Here's one, my lord, of threescore and seventeen.
TYRANT Push! That old limber ass puts in his head still.   5
  Helvetius: where is he?
      Enter Helvetius
MEMPHONIUS Not yet returned, my lord.
TYRANT   Your lordship lies:°
  Here comes the kingdom's father. Who amongst you

Dares say this worthy man has not made speed;   10
I would fain hear that fellow.

SOPHONIRUS [*aside*]   I'll not be he.
I like the standing of my head too well
To have it mended.

TYRANT [*to Helvetius*] Thy sight quickens me.°
I find a better health when thou art present
Than all times else can bring me. Is the answer   15
As pleasing as thyself?

HELVETIUS   Of what, my lord?

TYRANT 'Of what?' Fie, no! He did not say so! Did he?

SOPHONIRUS Oh no, my lord, not he, spoke no such word.
[*Aside*] I'll say as he would ha't, for I'd be loath
To have my body used like butchers' meat.   20

TYRANT When comes she to our bed?

HELVETIUS   Who, my lord?

TYRANT   Hark!
You heard that plain amongst you?

SOPHONIRUS   O my lord,
As plain as my wife's tongue: that drowns a sance bell.°
[*Aside*] Let me alone to lay about for honour;
I'll shift for one.

TYRANT   When comes the lady, sir,°   25
That Govianus keeps?

HELVETIUS   Why, that's my daughter.

TYRANT Oh, is it so? Have you unlocked your memory?
What says she to us?

HELVETIUS   Nothing.

TYRANT   How thou tempt'st us!°
What didst thou say to her, being sent from us?

HELVETIUS More than was honest, yet it was but little.   30

TYRANT How cruelly thou work'st upon our patience,
Having advantage 'cause thou art her father.
But be not bold too far: if duty leave thee,
Respect will fall from us.

HELVETIUS   Have I kept life
So long, till it looks white upon my head,   35
Been threescore years a courtier, and a flatterer
Not above threescore hours (which time's repented°
Amongst my greatest follies), and am I at these days
Fit for no place but bawd to mine own flesh?

You'll prefer all your old courtiers to good services° 40
If your lust keep but hot some twenty winters:
We are like to have a virtuous world of wives,
Daughters, and sisters, besides kinswomen
And cousin-germans removed up and down
Where'er you please to have 'em. Are white hairs 45
A colour fit for panders and flesh-brokers,
Which are the honoured ornaments of age
To which e'en kings owe reverence, as they're men
And greater in their goodness than their greatness?
And must I take my pay all in base money? 50
I was a lord born, set by all court grace,°
And am I thrust now to a squire's place?°
TYRANT How comes the moon to change so in this man,
That was at full but now in all performance
And swifter than our wishes? I beshrew that virtue 55
That busied herself with him. Now his art fails him,°
What makes the man at court? This is no place
For fellows of no parts; he lives not here°
That puts himself from action when we need him.
[To Helvetius] I take off all thy honours and bestow 'em 60
On any of this rank that will deserve 'em.
SOPHONIRUS My lord, that's I. Trouble your grace no further:
I'll undertake to bring her to your bed
With some ten words—marry, they're special charms,
No lady can withstand 'em; a witch taught me 'em. 65
If you doubt me, I'll leave my wife in pawn
For my true loyalty, and your majesty
May pass away the time till I return.°
I have a care in all things.
TYRANT   That may thrive best
Which the least hope looks after; but however,° 70
Force shall help nature; I'll be too sure now.°
Thy willingness may be fortunate, we employ thee.
SOPHONIRUS Then I'll go fetch my wife, and take my journey.
TYRANT Stay, we require no pledge; we think thee honest.
SOPHONIRUS [aside] Troth, the worse luck for me: we had both
been made by 't; 75
It was the way to make my wife great too.°
TYRANT [to Helvetius] I'll teach thee to be wide and strange to me:°

I'll not leave thee a title to put on
But the bare name that men must call thee by,
And know thee miserable.°   80
HELVETIUS 'Tis miserable, King, to be of thy making,
  And leave a better workman. If thy honours°
  Only keep life in baseness, take 'em to thee
  And give 'em to the hungry. [*Points to Sophonirus*] There's one
    gapes.
SOPHONIRUS One that will swallow you, sir, for that jest,   85
  And all your titles after.
HELVETIUS   The devil follow 'em,
  There's room enough for him too. Leave me, thou king,
  As poor as Truth, the mistress I now serve,
  And never will forsake her for her plainness;
  That shall not alter me.
TYRANT   No? [*Calls*] Our guard, within there!   90
      Enter Guard
GUARD My lord?
TYRANT Bear that old fellow to our castle prisoner;
  Give charge he be kept close.
HELVETIUS   Close prisoner?°
  Why, my heart thanks thee; I shall have more time
  And liberty to virtue in one hour   95
  Than all those threescore years I was a courtier.
  So by imprisonment I sustain great loss;
  Heaven opens to that man the world keeps close.
      Exit Helvetius guarded
SOPHONIRUS [*aside*] But I'll not go to prison to try that:
  Give me the open world, there's a good air.   100
TYRANT [*aside*] I would fain send death after him, but I dare not.
  He knows I dare not: that would give just cause
  Of her unkindness everlasting to me.
  His life may thank his daughter. [*Aloud*] Sophonirus!
  Here take this jewel. Bear it as a token   105
  To our heart's saint; 'twill do thy words no harm.
  Speech may do much, but wealth's a greater charm
  Than any made of words; and to be sure,
  If one or both should fail, I provide farther.
  Call forth those resolute fellows whom our clemency   110
  Saved from a death of shame in time of war
  For field offences. Give 'em charge from us

They arm themselves with speed, beset the house
Of Govianus round, that if thou fail'st
Or stay'st beyond the time thou leav'st with them,   115
They may with violence break in themselves
And seize her for our use.
        Exeunt all but Sophonirus
SOPHONIRUS   They're not so saucy
To seize her for their own, I hope—
As there are many knaves will begin first
And bring their lords the bottom. I have been served so°   120
A hundred times myself, by a scurvy page
That I kept once; but my wife loved him,
And I could not help it.
        A flourish is played.° Exit

3.1

Enter Govianus with his Lady and a Servant

GOVIANUS What is he?

SERVANT   An old lord come from the court.

GOVIANUS He should be wise by 's years; he will not dare
   To come about such business; 'tis not man's work.
   Art sure he desired conference with thy lady?

SERVANT Sure, sir.

GOVIANUS   Faith, thou'rt mistook: 'tis with me, certain.   5
   Let's do the man no wrong. Go, know it truly, sir.

SERVANT This° a strange humour; we must now know things
   twice.

      Exit Servant

GOVIANUS There's no man is so dull but he will weigh
   The work he undertakes, and set about it   10
   E'en in the best sobriety of his judgement
   With all his senses watchful; then his guilt
   Does equal his for whom 'tis undertaken.

      Enter Servant

   What says he now?

SERVANT   E'en as he said at first, sir:
   He's business to my lady from the King.   15

GOVIANUS Still from the King. He will not come near, will he?

SERVANT Yes, when he knows he shall, sir.

GOVIANUS   I cannot think it.°
   Let him be tried.

SERVANT Small trial will serve him, I warrant you, sir.

      [*Exit Servant*]

GOVIANUS Sure, honesty has left man. Has fear forsook him?   20
   Yes, faith, there is no fear when there's no grace.

LADY What way shall I devise to gi' 'm his answer?°
   Denial is not strong enough to serve, sir.

GOVIANUS No, 't must have other helps.

      Enter Sophonirus, [with a jewel]

                              I see he dares.
   O patience, I shall lose a friend of thee!   25

SOPHONIRUS I bring thee, precious lady, this dear stone
   And commendations from the King my master.

GOVIANUS [*drawing his sword*] I set before thee, panderous lord, this
    steel,
  And much good do 't thy heart. Fall to and spare not!°
    [*He stabs Sophonirus*]
LADY 'Las, what have you done, my lord?
GOVIANUS   Why, sent a bawd   30
  Home to his lodging; nothing else, sweetheart.°
SOPHONIRUS Well, you have killed me, sir, and there's an end;
  But you'll get nothing by the hand, my lord,
  When all your cards are counted. There be gamesters
  Not far off, will set upon the winner   35
  And make a poor lord on you ere they've left you.
  I'm fetched in like a fool to pay the reckoning,
  Yet you'll save nothing by 't.
GOVIANUS   What riddle's this?
SOPHONIRUS There she stands by thee now, who yet ere midnight
  Must lie by the King's side.
GOVIANUS   Who speaks that lie?   40
SOPHONIRUS One hour will make it true. She cannot scape
  No more than I from death. You've a great gain on 't
  An you look well about you, that's my comfort:
  The house is round beset with armèd men
  That know their time when to break in and seize her.   45
LADY My lord!
GOVIANUS   'Tis boldly done to trouble me
  When I've such business to despatch. [*Calls*] Within there!
    Enter Servant
SERVANT My lord?
GOVIANUS   Look out, and tell me what thou seest.
    Exit Servant
SOPHONIRUS How quickly now my death will be revenged,
  Before the King's first sleep. I depart laughing   50
  To think upon the deed.
    [*He dies*]
GOVIANUS   'Tis thy banquet.°
  Down, villain, to thy everlasting weeping,
  That canst rejoice so in the rape of virtue
  And sing light tunes in tempests when near shipwrecked,
  And have no plank to save us.
    Enter Servant
                  Now, sir, quickly.   55

SERVANT Which way soe'er I cast mine eye, my lord,
   Out of all parts o' th' house, I may see fellows
   Gathered in companies and all whispering
   Like men for treachery busy—
LADY   'Tis confirmed.
SERVANT —Their eyes still fixed upon the doors and windows.°   60
GOVIANUS I think thou'st never done, thou lov'st to talk on 't;
   'Tis fine discourse. Prithee find other business.
SERVANT Nay, I am gone; I'm a man quickly sneaped.
    Exit Servant
GOVIANUS He's flattered me with safety for this hour!
LADY Have you leisure to stand idle? Why, my lord,   65
   It is for me they come.
GOVIANUS   For thee, my glory,
   The riches of my youth, it is for thee.
LADY Then is your care so cold? Will you be robbed
   And have such warning of the thieves? Come on, sir,
   Fall to your business, lay your hands about you;   70
   Do not think scorn to work. A resolute captain°
   Will rather fling the treasure of his bark
   Into whales' throats than pirates should be gorged with 't.
   Be not less man than he: thou art master yet,°
   And all's at thy disposing. Take thy time,   75
   Prevent mine enemy, away with me:°
   Let me no more be seen. I'm like that treasure
   Dangerous to him that keeps it: rid thy hands on 't.
GOVIANUS I cannot lose thee so.
LADY   Shall I be taken
   And lost the cruellest way? Then wouldst thou curse   80
   That love that sent forth pity to my life:
   Too late thou wouldst.
GOVIANUS   O this extremity!
   Hast thou no way to scape 'em but in soul?°
   Must I meet peace in thy destruction,
   Or will it ne'er come at me?°   85
   'Tis a most miserable way to get it;
   I had rather be content to live without it
   Than pay so dear for 't, and yet lose it too.
LADY Sir, you do nothing: there's no valour in you.
   You're the worst friend to a lady in affliction   90
   That ever love made his companion.

For honour's sake despatch me! Thy own thoughts
Should stir thee to this act more than my weakness;
The sufferer should not do 't. I speak thy part,°
Dull and forgetful man, and all to help thee.   95
Is it thy mind to have me seized upon
And borne with violence to the Tyrant's bed,
There forced unto the lust of all his days?

GOVIANUS O no, thou liv'st no longer now I think on 't.
I take thee at all hazard!

    [*He raises his sword to strike*]

LADY   O stay! Hold, sir!   100

GOVIANUS Lady, what had you made me done now?
You never cease till you prepare me cruel 'gainst my heart,
And then you turn 't upon my hand and mock me.

LADY Cowardly flesh,
Thou show'st thy faintness still: I felt thee shake,   105
E'en when the storm came near thee. [*To Govianus*] Thou'rt the same,
But 'twas not for thy fear I put death by.
I had forgot a chief and worthy business
Whose strange neglect would have made me forgotten
Where I desire to be remembered most.°   110
I will be ready straight, sir.

    [*She kneels in prayer*]

GOVIANUS   O poor lady!
Why might not she expire now in that prayer,
Since she must die, and never try worse ways?
'Tis not so happy, for we often see
Condemned men sick to death, yet 'tis their fortune   115
To recover to their execution
And rise again in health to set in shame!°
What if I steal a death unseen of her now,
And close up all my miseries with mine eyes? O fie,
And leave her here alone! That were unmanly.   120

LADY [*rising*] My lord, be now as sudden as you please, sir:
I am ready to your hand.

GOVIANUS   But that's not ready.
'Tis the hardest work that ever man was put to:
I know not which way to begin to come to 't.
Believe me, I shall never kill thee well: 125
I shall but shame myself. It were but folly,

Dear soul, to boast of more than I can perform:
I shall not have the power to do thee right in 't.
Thou deserv'st death with speed, a quick despatch,
The pain but of a twinkling, and so sleep;   130
If I do 't, I shall make thee live too long
And so spoil all that way. I prithee excuse me.

LADY I should not be disturbed, an you did well, sir.
I have prepared myself for rest and silence
And took my leave of words. I am like one   135
Removing from her house, that locks up all
And, rather than she would displace her goods,
Makes shift with anything for the time she stays.
Then look not for more speech, th' extremity speaks
Enough to serve us both, had we no tongues.

    Knocking is heard within

                            Hark!   140

FELLOW [*within*] Lord Sophonirus?
GOVIANUS   Which hand shall I take?
LADY Art thou yet ignorant? There is no way
But through my bosom.
GOVIANUS   Must I lose thee then?
LADY They're but enemies that tell thee so.
His lust may part me from thee, but death never.   145
Thou canst not lose me there, for, dying thine,°
Thou dost enjoy me still: kings cannot rob thee.

    Knocking is heard within

FELLOW [*within*] Do you hear, my lord?
LADY   Is it yet time or no?
Honour remember thee.
GOVIANUS   I must. Come, prepare thyself.
LADY Never more dearly welcome.

    Govianus runs at her [with his sword], and falls by the way in
    a swoon

                       Alas, sir!   150
My lord, my love! O thou poor-spirited man!
He's gone before me. Did I trust to thee,°
And hast thou served me so? Left all the work
Upon my hand, and stole away so smoothly?
There was not equal suffering shown in this,   155
And yet I cannot blame thee. Every man
Would seek his rest: eternal peace sleep with thee.

[*She picks up his sword*]
Thou art my servant now. Come, thou hast lost°
A fearful master, but art now preferred°
Unto the service of a resolute lady,   160
One that knows how to employ thee, and scorns death
As much as great men fear it. Where's hell's ministers,
The Tyrant's watch and guard? 'Tis of much worth
When with this key the prisoner can slip forth.
        Knocking is heard within. She kills herself
GOVIANUS [*recovering*] How now? What noise is this? I heard doors
        beaten.   165
Where are my servants? Let men knock so loud
Their master cannot sleep?
        A great knocking again
FELLOW [*within*]   The time's expired,
And we'll break in, my lord.
GOVIANUS   Ha! Where's my sword?
I had forgot my business! [*Sees the Lady's dead body*] O, 'tis done,
And never was beholding to my hand.   170
Was I so hard to thee? So respectless of thee°
To put all this to thee? Why, it was more
Than I was able to perform myself
With all the courage that I could take to me.
It tired me—I was fain to fall and rest—   175
And hast thou, valiant woman, overcome
Thy honour's enemies with thine own white hand,
Where virgin victory sits, all without help?
Eternal praise go with thee!—Spare not now,°
Make all the haste you can.—I'll plant this bawd   180
Against the door, the fittest place for him
That, when with ungoverned weapons they rush in,
Blinded with fury, they may take his death
Into the purple number of their deeds°
And wipe it off from mine.
        [*He places the body of Sophonirus against the door.*] *Knocking
        is heard within*

                    [*Calls off stage*] How now, forbear!   185
My lord's at hand.
FELLOW [*within*]   My lord, and ten lords more,°
I hope the King's officers are above 'em all.
        [*They force the door from within. Sophonirus' body is hurled to
        the ground*]

        200

GOVIANUS Life, what do you do? Take heed!
   Enter the Fellows, well-weaponed, [pushing past Sophonirus'
   body]
           Bless the old man!
 My lord All-Ass! My lord! He's gone.
SECOND FELLOW   Heart, farewell he, then.°
 We have no eyes to pierce thorough inch-boards.°   190
 'Twas his own folly. The King must be served,
 And shall. The best is, we shall ne'er be hanged for 't,
 There's such a number guilty.
FIRST FELLOW   Poor my lord!
 He went some twice ambassador, and behaved himself
 So wittily in all his actions.   195
SECOND FELLOW [*seeing the Lady*] My lord! What's she?
GOVIANUS   Let me see!
 What should she be? Now I remember her.
 O she was a worthy creature
 Before destruction grew so inward with her.°
FIRST FELLOW Well, for her worthiness, that's no work of ours. 200
 You have a lady, sir; the King commands her°
 To court with speed, and we must force her thither.
GOVIANUS Alas, she'll never strive with you; she was born
 E'en with the spirit of meekness. Is 't for the King?
FIRST FELLOW For his own royal and most gracious lust, 205
 Or let me ne'er be trusted.
GOVIANUS   Take her, then.
SECOND FELLOW Spoke like an honest subject, by my troth.
 I'd do the like myself to serve my prince.
 Where is she, sir?
GOVIANUS   Look but upon yon face,
 Then do but tell me where you think she is.   210
SECOND FELLOW Life, she's not here!
GOVIANUS   She's yonder.
FIRST FELLOW   Faith, she's gone°
 Where we shall ne'er come at her, I see that.
GOVIANUS No, nor thy master neither. Now I praise
 Her resolution; 'tis a triumph to me
 When I see those about her.
SECOND FELLOW   How came this, sir?   215
 The King must know.
GOVIANUS   From yon old fellow's prattling:
 All your intents he revealed largely to her,

And she was troubled with a foolish pride
To stand upon her honour, and so died.
'Twas a strange trick of her. Few of your ladies   220
In ordinary will believe it: they abhor it.°
They'll sooner kill themselves with lust than for it.°
FIRST FELLOW We have done the King good service to kill him,°
More than we were aware on; but this news
Will make a mad court. 'Twill be a hard office   225
To be a flatterer now: his grace will run
Into so many moods there'll be no finding on him.
As good seek a hare without a hound now.
[_To Sophonirus' body_] A vengeance of your babbling! These old
    fellows°
Will hearken after secrets as their lives,   230
But keep 'em in e'en as they keep their wives.°
FELLOWS We have watched fairly.
       Exeunt the Fellows [_with Sophonirus' body_]
GOVIANUS   What a comfort 'tis
To see 'em gone without her.°
      [_He picks up the Lady's body_]
Come, thou delicious treasure of mankind.
To him that knows what virtuous woman is   235
And can discreetly love her, the whole world°
Yields not a jewel like her, ransack rocks
And caves beneath the deep. O thou fair spring°
Of honest and religious desires,
Fountain of weeping honour, I will kiss thee   240
After death's marble lip. [_He kisses the body_] Thou'rt cold enough
To lie entombed now by my father's side.
Without offence in kindred there I'll place thee,°
With one I loved the dearest next to thee.
Help me to mourn, all that love chastity.   245
      Exit, [_carrying the body_]

4.1

Enter Votarius, with Anselmus' Wife

VOTARIUS Prithee forgive me, madam; come, thou shalt.

WIFE I' faith, 'twas strangely done, sir.

VOTARIUS   I confess it.

WIFE Is that enough to help it, sir? 'Tis easy
  To draw a lady's honour in suspicion,
  But not so soon recovered and confirmed   5
  To the first faith again from whence you brought it.
  Your wit was fetched out about other business
  Or such forgetfulness had never seized you.

VOTARIUS 'Twas but an overflowing, a spring tide°
  In my affection, raised by too much love;
  And that's the worst words you can give it, madam.   10

WIFE Jealous of me?

VOTARIUS   Life, you'd ha' sworn yourself, madam,
  Had you been in my body and changed cases.
  To see a fellow with a guilty pace
  Glide through the room, his face three-quarters nighted 15
  As if a deed of darkness had hung on him—

WIFE I tell you twice, 'twas my bold woman's friend.°
  Hell take her impudence!

VOTARIUS   Why, I have done, madam.

WIFE You've done too late, sir. Who shall do the rest now?
  Confessed me yielding! Was thy way too free?°   20
  Why, didst thou long to be restrained? Pray speak, sir.

VOTARIUS A man cannot cozen you of the sin of weakness
  Or borrow it of a woman for one hour,
  But how he's wondered at! Where, search your lives,°
  We shall ne'er find it from you. We can suffer you°   25
  To play away your days in idleness
  And hide your imperfections with our loves,
  Or the most part of you would appear strange creatures;
  And now 'tis but our chance to make an offer
  And snatch at folly, running, yet to see   30
  How earnest you're against us, as if we had robbed you
  Of the best gift your natural mother left you!°

WIFE 'Tis worth a kiss, i' faith, and thou shalt ha' 't,

Were there not one more left for my lord's supper.
    [They kiss]
And now, sir, I've bethought myself—

VOTARIUS   That's happy!   35

WIFE You say we're weak, but the best wits on you all
  Are glad of our advice for aught I see,
  And hardly thrive without us.

VOTARIUS   I'll say so too,
  To give you encouragement and advance your virtues;
  'Tis not good always to keep down a woman.   40

WIFE Well, sir, since you've begun to make my lord
  A doubtful man of me, keep on that course
  And ply his faith still with that poor belief
  That I'm inclining unto wantonness.
  Take heed you pass no further now.

VOTARIUS   Why, dost think   45
  I'll be twice mad together in one moon?°
  That were too much for any freeman's son
  After his father's funeral.

WIFE   Well, then, thus, sir:°
  Upholding still the same, as being emboldened
  By some loose glance of mine, you shall attempt,   50
  After you've placed my lord in some near closet,
  To thrust yourself into my chamber rudely,
  As if the game went forward to your thinking.
  Then leave the rest to me: I'll so reward thee
  With bitterness of words, but prithee pardon 'em.   55
  My lord shall swear me into honesty
  Enough to serve his mind all his life after.
  Nay, for a need I'll draw some rapier forth
  That shall come near my hand as 'twere by chance
  And set a lively face upon my rage.°   60
  But fear thou nothing: I too dearly love thee
  To let harm touch thee.

VOTARIUS   O, it likes me rarely!
  I'll choose a precious time for 't.
    Exit Votarius

WIFE Go thy ways, I'm glad I had it for thee.°
    Enter Leonella

LEONELLA Madam, my lord entreats your company.   65

WIFE Pshaw ye!

LEONELLA Pshaw ye! My lord entreats your company.°
WIFE What now?
  Are ye so short-heeled?
LEONELLA   I am as my betters are, then.
WIFE How came you by such impudence o' late, minion?   70
  You're not content to entertain your playfellow
  In your own chamber closely, which I think
  Is large allowance for a lady's woman.
  There's many a good knight's daughter is in service°
  And cannot get such favour of her mistress   75
  But what she has by stealth; she and the chambermaid
  Are glad of one between 'em; and must you
  Give such bold freedom to your long-nosed fellow°
  That every room must take a taste of him?
LEONELLA Does that offend your ladyship?
WIFE   How think you, forsooth?   80
LEONELLA Then he shall do 't again!
WIFE   What?
LEONELLA   And again, madam,
  So often till it please your ladyship,
  And when you like it he shall do 't no more.
WIFE What's this?
LEONELLA   I know no difference, virtuous madam,
  But in love all have privilege alike.   85
WIFE You're a bold quean.
LEONELLA   And are not you my mistress?
WIFE This' well, i' faith!
LEONELLA You spare not your own flesh no more than I;
  Hell take me an I spare you!
WIFE [aside]   O the wrongs
  That ladies do their honours when they make   90
  Their slaves familiar with their weaknesses!
  They're ever thus rewarded for that deed:
  They stand in fear e'en of the grooms they feed!
  I must be forced to speak my woman fair now
  And be first friends with her—nay, all too little:°   95
  She may undo me at her pleasure else.
  She knows the way so well, myself not better;
  My wanton folly made a key for her
  To all the private treasure of my heart;
  She may do what she list. [Aloud] Come, Leonélla,   100

I am not angry with thee.

LEONELLA Pish!

WIFE Faith, I am not.

LEONELLA   Why, what care I an you be?

WIFE Prithee forgive me.

LEONELLA   I have nothing to say to you.

WIFE Come, thou shalt wear this jewel for my sake.   105
    A kiss, and friends, we'll never quarrel more.

LEONELLA Nay, choose you, faith. The best is, an you do,
    You know who'll have the worst on 't.

WIFE   True: myself.

LEONELLA [aside] Little thinks she I have set her forth already:°
    I please my lord, yet keep her in awe too.   110

WIFE One thing I had forgot: I prithee, wench,
    Steal to Votarius closely and remember him
    To wear some privy armour then about him,°
    That I may feign a fury without fear.

LEONELLA Armour? When, madam?

WIFE   See, now, I chide thee   115
    When I least thought upon thee; thou'rt my best hand,
    I cannot be without thee. Thus, then, sirrah:
    To beat away suspicion from the thoughts
    Of ruder list'ning servants about house,
    I have advised Votarius at fit time   120
    Boldly to force his way into my chamber,
    The admittance being denied him, and the passage
    Kept strict by thee, my necessary woman—
    La, there I should have missed thy help again!—
    At which attempt I'll take occasion   125
    To dissemble such an anger that the world
    Shall ever after swear us to their thoughts
    As clear and free from any fleshly knowledge
    As nearest kindred are, or ought to be,
    Or what can more express it, if that failed.   130

LEONELLA You know I'm always at your service, madam;
    But why some privy armour?

WIFE   Marry, sweetheart,
    The best is yet forgotten: thou shalt hang
    A weapon in some corner of the chamber,
    Yonder, or there—

LEONELLA   Or anywhere. Why, i' faith, madam,   135

Do you think I'm to learn now to hang a weapon?°
As much as I'm uncapable of what follows!°
I've all your mind without book: think it done, madam.°

WIFE Thanks, my good wench—I'll never call thee worse.
    Exit Wife

LEONELLA Faith, you're like to ha' 't again an you do, madam.°   140
    Enter Bellarius

BELLARIUS What, art alone?

LEONELLA   Cuds me, what make you here, sir?
You're a bold, long-nosed fellow!

BELLARIUS   How!

LEONELLA   So my lady says.
Faith, she and I have had a bout for you, sir,
But she got nothing by 't.

BELLARIUS   Did I not say still
Thou wouldst be too adventurous?

LEONELLA   Ne'er a whit, sir!   145
I made her glad to seek my friendship first.

BELLARIUS By my faith, that showed well. If you come off
So brave a conqueress, to 't again and spare not;
I know not which way you should get more honour.

LEONELLA She trusts me now to cast a mist, forsooth,   150
Before the servants' eyes. I must remember
Votarius to come at once with privy armour
Into her chamber, when, with a feigned fury
And rapier drawn (which I must lay o' purpose
Ready for her dissemblance), she will seem   155
T' act wonders for her juggling honesty.

BELLARIUS I wish no riper vengeance! Canst conceive me?
Votarius is my enemy.

LEONELLA   That's stale news, sir.

BELLARIUS Mark what I say to thee: forget of purpose
That privy armour; do not bless his soul   160
With so much warning, nor his hated body
With such sure safety. Here express thy love:
Lay some empoisoned weapon next her hand,
That in that play he may be lost forever.°
I'd have him kept no longer: away with him!   165
One touch would set him flying: let him go!

LEONELLA Bribe me but with a kiss, it shall be so.
    Exeunt

4.2

Enter the Tyrant wondrous discontentedly; the Nobles,
including Memphonius, follow afar off

FIRST NOBLE My lord——

TYRANT   Begone or never see life more!
 I'll send thee far enough from court.
    [*Exit First Noble*]

                                              Memphonius!
 Where's he now?

MEMPHONIUS   Ever at your highness' service.

TYRANT How dar'st thou be so near, when we have threatened
 Death to thy fellow? Have we lost our power?   5
 Or thou thy fear? Leave us in time of grace:°
 'Twill be too late anon.

MEMPHONIUS [*aside, going*] I think 'tis so
 With thee already.

TYRANT   Dead! And I so healthful!
 There's no equality in this. [*To Memphonius*] Stay!

MEMPHONIUS   Sir?°

TYRANT Where is that fellow brought the first report to us?   10

MEMPHONIUS He waits without.

TYRANT   I charge thee, give command
 That he be executed speedily,
 As thou'lt stand firm thyself.

MEMPHONIUS [*aside*]   Now, by my faith,
 His tongue has helped his neck to a sweet bargain.
    Exit Memphonius

TYRANT Her own fair hand so cruel? Did she choose   15
 Destruction before me? Was I no better?
 How much am I exalted to my face,°
 And, where I would be graced, how little worthy!
 There's few kings know how rich they are in goodness
 Or what estate they have in grace and virtue: 20
 There is so much deceit in glozers' tongues
 The truth is taken from us; we know nothing
 But what is for their purpose; that's our stint,°
 We are allowed no more. O wretched greatness!
 I'll cause a sessions for my flatterers   25
 And have 'em all hanged up. 'Tis done too late.

O she's destroyed, married to death and silence,
Which nothing can divorce: riches, nor laws,
Nor all the violence that this frame can raise.
I've lost the comfort of her sight forever.   30
I cannot call this 'life' that flames within me,
But everlasting torment lighted up
To show my soul her beggary! —A new joy
Is come to visit me in spite of death:
It takes me of that sudden, I'm ashamed°   35
Of my provision, but a friend will bear.°
[*Calls*] Within there!
     Enter Soldiers

FIRST SOLDIER   Sir.
SECOND SOLDIER   My lord.
TYRANT   The men I wished for
  For secrecy and employment.
  Go, give order that Govianus be released.
FOURTH SOLDIER Released, sir?   40
TYRANT Set free!
     [*Exit a Soldier*]
               And then I trust he will fly the kingdom
  And never know my purpose. [*To First Soldier*] Run, sir, you,°
  Bring me the keys of the cathedral.
FIRST SOLDIER [*aside*] Are you so holy now? Do you curse all day
  And go to pray at midnight?   45
     Exit First Soldier
TYRANT Provide you, sirs, close lanterns and a pickaxe.°
  Away, be speedy.
SECOND SOLDIER Lanterns and a pickaxe?
  Life, does he mean to bury himself alive, trow?
     [*Exeunt Soldiers*]
TYRANT Death nor the marble prison my love sleeps in
  Shall keep her body locked up from mine arms.   50
  I must not be so cozened! Though her life
  Was like a widow's 'state made o'er in policy°
  To defeat me and my too confident heart,
  'Twas a most cruel wisdom to herself,
  As much to me that loved her.
     Enter First Soldier
                       What, returned?   55
FIRST SOLDIER Here be the keys, my lord.

TYRANT   I thank thy speed.
      [*Enter Soldiers with pickaxes and dark lanterns*]
   Here comes the rest full-furnished. Follow me
   And wealth shall follow you.
            Exit Tyrant
FIRST SOLDIER   Wealth! By this light,
   We go to rob a church. I hold my life,°
   The money will ne'er thrive. That's a sure saw: 60
   'What's got from grace is ever spent in law.'°
            Exeunt

   4.3°

   [*Enter Memphonius*]
MEMPHONIUS What strange fits grow upon him! Here o' late
   His soul has got a very dreadful leader.°
   What should he make in the cathedral now,
   The hour so deep in night? All his intents
   Are contrary to man: in spirit or blood   5
   He waxes heavy in his noble minds;
   His moods are such they cannot bear the weight,
   Nor will not long, if there be truth in whispers!
   The honourable father of the state,
   Noble Helvetius, all the lords agree   10
   By some close policy shortly to set free.
            [*Exit*]

   4.4

   *Enter the Tyrant [with the Soldiers] at a different door, which
   opened brings him to the tomb where the Lady lies buried. The
   tomb is here discovered,° richly set forth*
TYRANT Softly, softly.
   Let's give this place the peace that it requires.
   The vaults e'en chide our steps with murmuring sounds
   For making bold so late. [*Aside*] It must be done.
FIRST SOLDIER I fear nothing but the whorish ghost of a quean I kept   5
   once. She swore she would so haunt me I should never pray in quiet

for her, and I have kept myself from church this fifteen year to
prevent her.

TYRANT The monument woos me: I must run and kiss it.°
　　Now trust me if the tears do not e'en stand　　　　　　　10
　　Upon the marble. What slow springs have I!°
　　'Twas weeping to itself before I came.
　　How pity strikes e'en through insensible things
　　And makes them shame our dullness.°
　　Thou house of silence and the calms of rest　　　　　　　15
　　After tempestuous life, I claim of thee
　　A mistress, one of the most beauteous sleepers
　　That ever lay so cold; not yet due to thee
　　By natural death, but cruelly forced hither
　　Many a year before the world could spare her.　　　　　　20
　　We miss her 'mongst the glories of our court
　　When they be numbered up. All thy still strength,
　　Thou grey-eyed monument, shall not keep her from us.
　　[To the Second Soldier] Strike, villain, though the echo rail us all
　　Into ridiculous deafness! Pierce the jaws　　　　　　　　25
　　Of this cold ponderous creature.

SECOND SOLDIER　　　　　　　Sir!
TYRANT　　　　　　　　　　　Why strik'st thou not?
SECOND SOLDIER I shall not hold the axe fast: I'm afraid, sir.
TYRANT O shame of men, a soldier and so fearful?
SECOND SOLDIER 'Tis out of my element to be in a church, sir.°
　　Give me the open field and turn me loose, sir.°　　　　　30
TYRANT True, then thou hast room enough to run away.
　　[To the First Soldier] Take thou the axe from him.
FIRST SOLDIER　　　　　　　　I beseech your grace,
　　'Twill come to a worse hand: you'll find us all°
　　Of one mind for the church, I can assure you, sir.
TYRANT [to the Third Soldier] Nor thou?
THIRD SOLDIER　　　　　　　I love not to disquiet ghosts　　35
　　Of any people living.°
TYRANT O slaves of one opinion, give me 't from thee,
　　Thou man made out of fear.
　　　　[He takes the pickaxe from the Second Soldier]
SECOND SOLDIER　　　　　By my faith,
　　I'm glad I'm rid on 't. I that was ne'er before in cathedral,
　　And have the battering of a lady's tomb　　　　　　　　40

Lie hard upon my conscience at first coming?
I should get much by that. It shall be a warning to me:
I'll ne'er come here again.

    [*The Tyrant strikes at the tomb*]

TYRANT   No, wilt not yield?
Art thou so loath to part from her?

FIRST SOLDIER   Life, what means he?
Has he no feeling with him? By this light, if I be not afraid to stay   45
any longer, I'm a villain. Very fear will go nigh to turn me of some
religion or other, and so make me forfeit my lieutenantship.°

    [*The Tyrant loosens the tombstone*]

TYRANT O, have we got the mastery? Help, you vassals!
Freeze you in idleness and can see us sweat?

SECOND SOLDIER We sweat with fear as much as work can make us.   50

TYRANT Remove the stone that I may see my mistress.
Set to your hands, you villains, and that nimbly,
Or the same axe shall make you all fly open!

SOLDIERS O, good my lord!

TYRANT   I must not be delayed.

    [*The Soldiers remove the tombstone*]

FIRST SOLDIER This is ten thousand times worse than entering upon   55
a breach.°
'Tis the first stone that ever I took off°
From any lady. Marry, I have brought 'em many:
Fair diamonds, sapphires, rubies.

TYRANT   O blessed object!
I never shall be weary to behold thee.   60
I could eternally stand thus and see thee.°
Why, 'tis not possible death should look so fair:
Life is not more illustrious when health smiles on 't.
She's only pale, the colour of the court
And most attractive; mistresses most strive for 't,   65
And their lascivious servants best affect it.°

    [*To the Soldiers*] Lay to your hands again!

SOLDIERS   My lord?

TYRANT Take up her body.

FIRST SOLDIER   How, my lord?

TYRANT   Her body!

FIRST SOLDIER She's dead, my lord!

TYRANT   True: if she were alive,
Such slaves as you should not come near to touch her.   70

Do 't, and with all best reverence place her here.°
FIRST SOLDIER Not only, sir, with reverence, but with fear.
    You shall have more than your own asking once.
    I am afraid of nothing but she'll rise
    At the first jog and save us all a labour.   75
SECOND SOLDIER Then we were best take her up and never touch
    her!
FIRST SOLDIER Life, how can that be? Does fear make thee mad?
    I've took up many a woman in my days,°
    But never with less pleasure, I protest!   80
    [*They lift the Lady's body out of the tomb*]
TYRANT O, the moon rises! What reflection°
    Is thrown about this sanctified building
    E'en in a twinkling. How the monuments glister,
    As if Death's palaces were all massy silver
    And scorned the name of marble. [*To the body*] Art thou cold? 85
    I have no faith in 't, yet I believe none.
    Madam! 'Tis I, sweet lady, prithee speak.
    'Tis thy love calls on thee, thy King, thy servant.
    No? Not a word. All prisoners to pale silence.
    I'll prove a kiss.
    [*He embraces the body*]
FIRST SOLDIER   Here's a fine chill venery:°   90
    'Twould make a pander's heels ache. I'll be sworn°
    All my teeth chatter in my head to see 't.
TYRANT By th' mass, thou'rt cold indeed, beshrew thee for 't.
    Unkind to thine own blood? Hard-hearted lady,
    What injury hast thou offered to the youth   95
    And pleasure of thy days! Refuse the court
    And steal to this hard lodging: was that wisdom?
    O, I could chide thee with mine eye brim-full,
    And weep out my forgiveness when I ha' done.
    Nothing hurt thee but want of woman's counsel: 100
    Hadst thou but asked the opinion of most ladies,
    Thou'd'st never come to this! They would have told thee
    How dear a treasure life and youth had been.
    'Tis that they fear to lose: the very name
    Can make more gaudy tremblers in a minute   105
    Than heaven or sin or hell; those are last thought on.
    And where got'st thou such boldness, from the rest°
    Of all thy timorous sex, to do a deed here

Upon thyself, would plunge the world's best soldier
And make him twice bethink him, and again,   110
And yet give over? Since thy life has left me,
I'll clasp the body for the spirit that dwelt in 't
And love the house still for the mistress' sake.°
Thou art mine now, spite of destruction
And Govianus, and I will possess thee.   115
I once read of a Herod whose affection°
Pursued a virgin's love, as I did thine,
Who for the hate she owed him killed herself,
As thou too rashly didst, without all pity;
Yet he preserved her body dead in honey   120
And kept her long after her funeral;
But I'll unlock the treasure-house of art
With keys of gold and bestow all on thee.
Here, slaves, receive her humbly from our arms.
Upon your knees, you villains! All's too little   125
If you should sweep the pavement with your lips!°

FIRST SOLDIER [aside] What strange brooms he invents.
        [The Soldiers take the body]
TYRANT   So, reverently
Bear her before us gently to our palace.
[To the First Soldier] Place you the stone again where first we
    found it.
        [Exeunt the Soldiers, carrying the body, followed by the
        Tyrant; the First Soldier remains and replaces the tombstone°]
FIRST SOLDIER Life, must this on now to deceive all comers   130
And cover emptiness? 'Tis for all the world
Like a great city pie brought to a table
Where there be many hands that lay about:
The lid's shut close when all the meat's picked out,
Yet stands to make a show and cozen people.°   135
        Exit

4.5

        Enter a Page carrying a torch, followed by Govianus in black,
        a book in his hand
GOVIANUS Already mine eye melts. The monument

No sooner stood before it but a tear
Ran swiftly from me to express her duty.
Temple of honour, I salute thee early,
The time that my griefs rise. Chamber of peace,   5
Where wounded virtue sleeps, locked from the world,
I bring to be acquainted with thy silence
Sorrows that love no noise. They dwell all inward,
Where truth and love in every man should dwell.
Be ready, boy, give me the strain again—   10
'Twill show well here—whilst in my grief's devotion
At every rest mine eye lets forth a bead°
To keep the number perfect.

    Govianus kneels at the tomb, wondrous passionately

PAGE [*sings*]   *If ever pity were well placed*
        On true desert and virtuous honour,   15
        It could ne'er be better graced:
        Freely then bestow 't upon her.

        Never lady earned her fame
        In virtue's war with greater strife;
        To preserve her constant name   20
        She gave up beauty, youth, and life.
        There she sleeps
        And here he weeps,
        The lord unto so rare a wife.

        Weep, weep, and mourn lament,   25
        You virgins that pass by her,
        For if praise come by death again,
        I doubt few will lie nigh her.

GOVIANUS Thou art an honest boy. 'Tis done like one
That has a feeling of his master's passions   30
And the unmatched worth of thy dead mistress.
Thy better years shall find me good to thee
When understanding ripens in thy soul,
Which truly makes the man, and not long time.
Prithee withdraw a little and attend me   35
At cloister door.

PAGE   It shall be done, my lord.

    [*Exit Page*]

GOVIANUS Eternal maid of honour, whose chaste body
Lies here like virtue's close and hidden seed
To spring forth glorious to eternity

At the everlasting harvest—

LADY'S VOICE [*within*]   I am not here.°   40

GOVIANUS What's that? Who is not here? I'm forced to question it.
    Some idle sounds the beaten vaults send forth.
            On a sudden, in a kind of noise like a wind, the doors°
            clattering, the tombstone flies open and a great light appears in
            the midst of the tomb. Enter the Ghost of the Lady, as she was
            last seen, standing just before him° all in white, stuck° with
            jewels, and with a great crucifix on her breast
    Mercy, look to me! Faith, I fly to thee!
    Keep a strong watch about me. Now, thy friendship!
    O never came astonishment and fear   45
    So pleasing to mankind. I take delight
    To have my breast shake and my hair stand stiff.
    If this be horror, let it never die.
    Came all the pains of hell in that shape to me,
    I should endure 'em smiling! [*To the Ghost*] Keep me still   50
    In terror, I beseech thee; I'd not change
    This fever for felicity of man
    Or all the pleasures of ten thousand ages.

LADY'S GHOST Dear lord, I come to tell you all my wrongs.

GOVIANUS Welcome. Who wrongs the spirit of my love?   55
    Thou art above the injuries of blood:
    They cannot reach thee now. What dares offend thee?
    No life that has the weight of flesh upon 't
    And treads as I do can now wrong my mistress!°

LADY'S GHOST The peace that death allows me is not mine.   60
    The monument is robbed: behold, I'm gone,
    My body taken up.

GOVIANUS [*looking into the tomb*] 'Tis gone indeed.
    What villain dares so fearfully run in debt
    To black eternity?°

LADY'S GHOST   He that dares do more:
    The Tyrant.

GOVIANUS   All the miseries below°   65
    Reward his boldness.

LADY'S GHOST   I am now at court
    In his own private chamber. There he woos me
    And plies his suit to me with as serious pains
    As if the short flame of mortality
    Were lighted up again in my cold breast,   70

Folds me within his arms and often sets
A sinful kiss upon my senseless lip,
Weeps when he sees the paleness of my cheek,
And will send privately for a hand of art°
That may dissemble life upon my face   75
To please his lustful eye.

GOVIANUS   O piteous wrongs,
Inhuman injuries without grace or mercy.

LADY'S GHOST I leave 'em to thy thought, dearest of men.
My rest is lost; thou must restore 't again.°

GOVIANUS O fly me not so soon!

LADY'S GHOST   Farewell, true lord.   80
    Exit the Lady's Ghost°

GOVIANUS I cannot spare thee yet. I'll make myself
Over to death too, and we'll walk together
Like loving spirits. I prithee, let's do so.
She's snatched away by fate and I talk sickly.
I must despatch this business upon earth   85
Before I take that journey.
I'll to my brother for his aid or counsel.
So wronged! O heav'n, put armour on my spirit.
Her body I will place in her first rest,°
Or in th' attempt lock death into my breast.   90
    Exit. [The curtain is drawn over the tomb]

5.1

Enter Votarius with Anselmus the husband

VOTARIUS You shall stand here, my lord, unseen, and hear all.
    Do I deal now like a right friend with you?

ANSELMUS   Like a most faithful.

VOTARIUS You shall have her mind, e'en as it comes to me,
    Though I undo her by 't. Your friendship, sir,
    Is the sweet mistress that I only serve.   5
    I prize the roughness of a man's embrace
    Before the soft lips of a hundred ladies.

ANSELMUS And that's an honest mind of thee.

VOTARIUS   Lock yourself, sir,
    Into that closet, and be sure none see you.
    Trust not a creature: we'll have all run clear   10
    E'en as the heart affords it.

ANSELMUS   'Tis a match, sir.
    Exit Anselmus

VOTARIUS Troth, he says true there: 'tis a match indeed.
    He does not know the strength of his own words,
    For if he did there were no mast'ring on him!
    He's cleft the pin in two with a blind man's eyes: 15
    Though I shoot wide, I'll cozen him of the game.°
    Exit Votarius. [As he goes,] enter Leonella above in a gallery
    with her love Bellarius

LEONELLA Dost thou see thine enemy walk?

BELLARIUS   I would I did not.

LEONELLA Prithee rest quiet, man, I have fee'd one for him,
    A trusty catchpole, too, that will be sure on him.
    Thou know'st this gallery well: 'tis at thy use now;   20
    It's been at mine full often. Thou may'st sit
    Like a most private gallant in yon corner,°
    See all the play and ne'er be seen thyself.

BELLARIUS Therefore I chose it.

LEONELLA   Thou shalt see my lady
    Play her part naturally, more to the life   25
    Than she's aware on.

BELLARIUS   There must I be pleased.

Thou'rt one of the actors: thou'lt be missed anon.

LEONELLA Alas, a woman's action's always ready;°
Yet I'll down now I think on 't.

BELLARIUS   Do: 'tis time, i' faith.

Leonella exits and descends

ANSELMUS [*at one door*] I know not yet where I should plant belief, 30
I am so strangely tossed between two tales.
I'm told by my wife's woman the deed's done,
And in Votarius' tongue 'tis yet to come,
The castle is but upon yielding yet,
'Tis not delivered up. Well, we shall find° 35
The mystery shortly; I will entertain
The patience of a prisoner i' th' meantime.

He locks himself in the closet.° Enter Anselmus' Wife with
Leonella [carrying a sword, which she hangs up]

WIFE [*aside to Leonella*] Is all set ready, wench?

LEONELLA [*aside to Wife*]   Push, madam, all.

WIFE [*aloud*] Tell me not so, she lives not for a lady°
That has less peace than I.

LEONELLA   Nay, good sweet madam, 40
You would not think how much this passion alters you:
It drinks up all the beauty of your cheek.
I promise you, madam, you have lost much blood.

WIFE Let it draw death upon me, for till then
I shall be mistress of no true content. 45
Who could endure hourly temptation
And bear it as I do?

LEONELLA   Nay, that's most certain,
Unless it were myself again. I can do 't:
I suffer the like daily. You should complain, madam.

WIFE Which way? Were that wisdom? Prithee wench, to whom? 50

LEONELLA To him that makes all whole again, my lord:
To one that, if he be a kind, good husband,
Will let you bear no more than you are able.°

WIFE Thou know'st not what thou speak'st. Why, my lord's he
That gives him the house-freedom, all his boldness; 55
Keeps him o' purpose here to war with me.

LEONELLA Now, I hold wiser of my lord than so:
He knows the world, he would not be so idle.°

WIFE I speak sad truth to thee. I am not private°
In mine own chamber, such his impudence is. 60

Nay, my repenting time is scarce blessed from him:
He will offend my prayers.

LEONELLA   Out upon him!
I believe, madam, he's of no religion.°

WIFE He serves my lord, and that's enough for him,
And preys upon poor ladies like myself: 65
There's all the gentleman's devotion!

LEONELLA Marry, the devil of hell give him his blessing!

WIFE Pray watch the door, and suffer none to trouble us,
Unless it be my lord.

LEONELLA [aside]   'Twas finely spoke, that:
My lord indeed is the most trouble to her.   70
Now must I show a piece of service here.
How do I spend my days! Life, shall I never
Get higher than a lady's door-keeper?
I must be married as my lady is first,
And then my maid may do as much for me.   75

WIFE O miserable time! Except my lord
Do wake in honourable pity to me
And rid this vicious gamester from his house,
Whom I have checked so often, here I vow
I'll imitate my noble sister's fate,   80
Late mistress to the worthy Govianus,
And cast away my life as she did hers.

        Votarius comes to the door within, and opens it°

LEONELLA Back! You're too forward, sir; there's no coming for
you.°

VOTARIUS How, mistress Len, my lady's smock-woman,
Am I no farther in your duty yet?°   85

LEONELLA Duty! Look for 't of them you keep under, sir.°

VOTARIUS You'll let me in.

LEONELLA   Who would you speak withal?

VOTARIUS With the best lady you make curtsy to.

LEONELLA She will not speak with you.

VOTARIUS   Have you her mind?
I scorn to take her answer of her broker.   90

LEONELLA Madam!

WIFE What's there? How now, sir, what's your business?
We see your boldness plain.

VOTARIUS   I came to see you, madam.

WIFE Farewell, then—though 'twas impudence too much

When I was private.

VOTARIUS   Madam—

WIFE   Life, he was born   95
  To beggar all my patience!

VOTARIUS   I'm bold
  Still to prefer my love. Your woman hears me not.°

WIFE Where's modesty and honour? Have I not thrice
  Answered thy lust?

LEONELLA [aside]   By 'r lady, I think oftener.

WIFE And dar'st thou yet look with temptation on us?   100
  Since nothing will prevail, come death, come vengeance!
  I will forget the weakness of my kind
  And force thee from my chamber.
     [She takes up the sword and attacks Votarius]

VOTARIUS   How now, lady?
  Uds life, you prick me, madam!

WIFE [aside to Votarius]   Prithee, peace,
  I will not hurt thee. [Aloud] Will you yet begone, sir?   105

LEONELLA He's upon going, I think.°

VOTARIUS Madam! Heart, you deal false with me. O, I feel it!
  You're a most treacherous lady! This thy glory?
  My breast is all afire! O!
     [He dies]

LEONELLA   Ha ha ha!°
     [Enter Anselmus]

ANSELMUS Ha? I believe her constancy too late,   110
  Confirmed e'en in the blood of my best friend!
     [He takes the sword from his Wife] and kills Leonella.
     [Exit Bellarius from the gallery°]
  Take thou my vengeance, thou bold, perjurous strumpet,
  That dost accuse thy virtuous lady falsely!
     Enter Bellarius

BELLARIUS O deadly poison after a sweet banquet!
  What make I here? I had forgot my heart.   115
  I am an actor too, and never thought on 't.
  The blackness of this season cannot miss me.
  [To Anselmus] Sirrah! You, lord!

WIFE   Is he there? Welcome, ruin!

BELLARIUS There is a life due to me in that bosom
  For this poor gentlewoman.

ANSELMUS   And art thou then receiver?   120

I'll pay thee largely, slave, for thy last scape.

Bellarius and Anselmus make a dangerous pass at one another with their swords. The Wife purposely runs between them, and is killed by them both

WIFE I come, Votarius!

[*She dies*]

ANSELMUS [*to Bellarius*] Hold, if manhood guide thee!°
O what has fury done?

[*He kneels by his Wife's body*]

BELLARIUS   What has it done now?
Why, killed an honourable whore, that's all.

ANSELMUS Villain, I'll seal that lie upon thy heart: 125
A constant lady.

BELLARIUS   To the devil as could be.
Heart, must I prick you forward? Either up
Or, sir, I'll take my chance. Thou couldst kill her,
Without repenting, that deserved more pity,
And spend'st thy time and tears upon a quean—   130

ANSELMUS [*rising*] Slave!

BELLARIUS —That was deceived once in her own deceit?

[*Anselmus attacks Bellarius, and they are both wounded in the pass*°]

—As I am now. The poison I prepared
Upon that weapon for mine enemy's bosom
Is bold to take acquaintance of my blood too,   135
And serves us both to make up death withal.°

ANSELMUS I ask no more of destiny but to fall
Close by the chaste side of my virtuous mistress.

[*He drags himself towards his Wife's body*]

If all the treasure of my weeping strength
Be left so wealthy but to purchase that,   140
I have the dear wish of a great man's spirit.
Yet favour me, O yet!

[*He reaches the body*]

                        I thank thee, fate,
I expire cheerfully and give death a smile.
He collapses

BELLARIUS O rage! I pity now mine enemy's flesh.°

Enter Govianus with Servants

GOVIANUS Where should he be?

FIRST SERVANT   My lady, sir, will tell you: 145

She's in her chamber here.

SECOND SERVANT   O my lord!

GOVIANUS   Peace!
My honourable brother, madam, all:
So many dreadful deeds and not one tongue
Left to proclaim 'em?

BELLARIUS   Yes, here, if a voice
Some minute long may satisfy your ear,   150
I've that time allowed it.

GOVIANUS   'Tis enough.
Bestow it quickly ere death snatch it from thee.

BELLARIUS That lord, your brother, made his friend Votarius
To tempt his lady. She was won to lust;
The act revealed here by her serving-woman;   155
But that wise, close adulteress, stored with art,
To prey upon the weakness of that lord,
Dissembled a great rage upon her love
And indeed killed him, which so won her husband,
He slew this right discoverer in his fury;   160
Who being my mistress, I was moved in heart
To take some pains with him, and he's paid me for 't.
As for the cunning lady, I commend her.°
She performed that which never woman tried:
She ran upon our weapons and so died.°   165
Now you have all, I hope I shall sleep quiet.
                    He dies

ANSELMUS O thunder that awakes me e'en from death
And makes me curse my confidence with cold lips.
I feel his words in flames about my soul:
He's more than killed me.

GOVIANUS   Brother.

ANSELMUS   I repent the smile   170
That I bestowed on destiny! A whore!
          [*He pushes away his Wife's body*]
I fling thee thus from my believing breast
With all the strength I have. My rage is great,
Although my veins grow beggars. Now I sue°
To die far from thee; may we never meet!   175
Were my soul bid to joy's eternal banquet
And were assured to find thee there a guest,°
I'd sup with torments and refuse that feast!

O thou beguiler of man's easy trust.
The serpent's wisdom is in women's lust.°   180
        He dies

GOVIANUS Brother, I came for thy advice, but I
        Find thee so ill a counsellor to thyself
        That I repent my pains and depart sighing.
        The body of my love is still at court.
        I am not well to think on 't: the poor spirit   185
        Was with me once again about it, troth,
        And I can put it off no more for shame,
        Though I desire to have it haunt me still
        And never to give o'er, 'tis so pleasing.
        I must to court; I've plighted my faith to 't.   190
        It's opened me the way to the revenge,
        And I must thorough.°
        Tyrant, I'll run thee on a dangerous shelf°
        Though I be forced to flee the land myself.
                Exeunt with the bodies

5.2

        [The throne is set out.] Enter the Tyrant with Attendants°
TYRANT In vain my spirit wrestles with my blood.
        Affection will be mistress here on earth:
        The house is hers, the soul is but a tenant.°
        I ha' tasked myself but with the abstinence
        Of one poor hour, yet cannot conquer that.   5
        I cannot keep from sight of her so long.
        I starve mine eye too much. Go, bring her forth
        As we have caused her body to be decked
        In all the glorious riches of our palace.
                [Exit Attendants]
        Our mind has felt a famine for the time: 10
        All comfort has been dear and scarce with us.
        The times are altered since. Strike on, sweet harmony!
                Music plays
        A braver world comes toward us.
                Enter Soldiers, who bring in the body of the Lady in a chair,
                dressed up in black velvet (which sets out° *the paleness of her*

hands and face), and a fair chain of pearl across her breast,
and the crucifix above it. The Tyrant stands silent awhile,
letting the music play, beckoning the Soldiers that bring her in
to make obeisance to her, and he himself makes a low honour to
the body and kisses the hand

SINGERS (*sing within, in voices°*)

      O what is beauty that's so much adorèd?
      A flatt'ring glass that cozens her beholders.   15
      One night of death makes it look pale and horrid;
      The dainty preserved flesh, how soon it moulders.
      To love it living it bewitcheth many,
      But after life is seldom heard of any.

FIRST SOLDIER [*aside*] By this hand, mere idolatry! I make curtsy   20
  To my damnation—I have learnt so much,
  Though I could never know the meaning yet
  Of all my Latin prayers, nor ne'er sought for 't.°

TYRANT [*to the Lady's body*] How pleasing art thou to us even in
      death!
  I love thee yet, above all women living.°   25
  I can see nothing to be 'mended in thee
  But the too-constant paleness of thy cheek.
  I'd give the kingdom but to purchase there
  The breadth of a red rose in natural colour;°
  But fate is my hinderer,   30
  And I must only rest content with art,
  And that I'll have in spite on 't! [*To the Second Soldier*] Is he
      come, sir?

SECOND SOLDIER Who, my lord?

TYRANT   Dull! The fellow that we sent
  For a court schoolmaster, a picture-drawer,
  A lady's forenoon tutor. Is he come, sir?°   35

FIRST SOLDIER Not yet returned, my lord.

TYRANT   The fool belike
  Makes his choice carefully, for so we charged him.°
  Where is he?

      Enter the Third Soldier with Govianus [disguised as a painter]

SECOND SOLDIER He's come, my lord.

TYRANT   Depart, then.
      [*Exeunt the Soldiers and Attendants; the Third Soldier*
      remains]
                          Is that he?

THIRD SOLDIER The privat'st I could get, my lord.°   40
GOVIANUS [*aside*] O heaven, marry patience to my spirit;
  Give me a sober fury, I beseech thee,
  A rage that may not overcharge my blood
  And do myself most hurt! 'Tis strange to me
  To see thee here at court, and gone from hence.   45
  Didst thou make haste to leave the world for this?
  And kept in the worst corner!
  O who dares play with destiny but he
  That wears security so thick upon him,°
  The thought of death and hell cannot pierce through.   50
TYRANT [*to the Third Soldier*] 'Twas circumspectly carried. Leave
  us, go.
      [*Exit the Third Soldier*]
  Be nearer, sir. Thou'rt much commended to us.
GOVIANUS It is the hand, my lord, commends the workman.
TYRANT Thou speak'st both modesty and truth in that.
  We need the art that thou art master of.   55
GOVIANUS My King is master both of that and me.
TYRANT Look on yon face and tell me what it wants.
GOVIANUS Which, that, sir?
TYRANT   That! What wants it?
GOVIANUS   Troth, my lord,
  Some thousand years' sleep, and a marble pillow.°
TYRANT What's that? Observe it still. All the best arts   60
  Hath the most fools and drunkards to their masters;°
  Thy apprehension has too gross a film°
  To be employed at court! What colour wants she?
GOVIANUS By my troth, all, sir. I see none she has,
  Nor none she cares for.
TYRANT   I am overmatched here.°   65
GOVIANUS A lower chamber with less noise were kinder°
  For her, poor woman, whatsoe'er she was.
TYRANT But how if we be pleased to have it thus,
  And thou well hired to do what we command?°
  Is not your work for money?
GOVIANUS   Yes, my lord,   70
  I would not trust at court an I could choose.°
TYRANT Let but thy art hide death upon her face,
  That now looks fearfully on us, and but strive
  To give our eye delight in that pale part
  Which draws so many pities from these springs,   75

And thy reward for 't shall outlast thy end
And reach to thy friend's fortunes, and his friend.°
GOVIANUS Say you so, my lord? I'll work out my heart, then,
    But I'll show art enough.
TYRANT   About it, then.
    I never wished so seriously for health   80
    After long sickness.
        [*Govianus paints the face of the corpse*]
GOVIANUS [*aside*] A religious trembling shakes me by the hand
    And bids me put by such unhallowed business;
    But revenge calls for 't, and it must go forward.
    'Tis time the spirit of my love took rest;   85
    Poor soul, 'tis weary, much abused and toiled.
TYRANT Could I now send for one to renew heat
    Within her bosom, that were a fine workman!
    I should but too much love him. But alas,
    'Tis as unpossible for living fire   90
    To take hold there as for dead ashes to burn back again
    Into those hard, tough bodies whence they fell.
    Life is removed from her now, as the warmth
    Of the bright sun from us when it makes winter
    And kills with unkind coldness. So is 't yonder: 95
    An everlasting frost hangs now upon her,
    And as in such a season men will force
    A heat into their bloods with exercise
    In spite of extreme weather, so shall we
    By art force beauty on yon lady's face,   100
    Though death sit frowning on 't, a storm of hail,
    To beat it off. Our pleasure shall prevail.
GOVIANUS My lord.
TYRANT   Hast done so soon?
GOVIANUS   That's as your grace
    Gives approbation.
TYRANT   O, she lives again!°
    She'll presently speak to me. Keep her up,   105
    I'll have her swoon no more: there's treachery in 't.
    Does she not feel warm to thee?
GOVIANUS   Very little, sir.
TYRANT The heat wants cherishing, then. Our arms and lips
    Shall labour life into her. Wake, sweet mistress!
    'Tis I that call thee at the door of life!   110
        [*He embraces and kisses the body*]

Ha!
I talk so long to death, I'm sick myself;
Methinks an evil scent still follows me.

GOVIANUS   Maybe 'tis nothing but the colour, sir,
That I laid on.

TYRANT   Is that so strong?

GOVIANUS   Yes, faith, sir: 115
'Twas the best poison I could get for money.
    [*He removes his disguise*]

TYRANT Govianus!

GOVIANUS   O thou sacrilegious villain,°
Thou thief of rest, robber of monuments!
Cannot the body after funeral
Sleep in the grave for thee? Must it be raised   120
Only to please the wickedness of thine eye?
Does all things end with death and not thy lust?
Hast thou devised a new way to damnation
More dreadful than the soul of any sin
Did ever pass yet between earth and hell?   125
Dost strive to be particularly plagued
Above all ghosts beside? Is thy pride such°
Thou scorn'st a partner in thy torments too?

TYRANT What fury gave thee boldness to attempt
This deed, for which I'll doom thee with a death   130
Beyond the Frenchmen's tortures.

GOVIANUS   I smile at thee.°
Draw all the death that ever mankind suffered
Unto one head to help thine own invention°
And make my end as rare as this thy sin
And full as fearful to the eyes of women,   135
My spirit shall fly singing to his lodging°
In midst of that rough weather. Doom me, Tyrant.°
Had I feared death, I'd never appeared, noble,°
To seal this act upon me, which e'en honours me
Unto my mistress' spirit: it loves me for 't.°   140
I told my heart 'twould prove destruction to 't,
Who, hearing 'twas for her, charged me to do 't.

TYRANT Thy glories shall be shortened. Who's within, there?
        Enter the Ghost° of the Lady, dressed in the same form as her
        body in the chair
I called not thee, thou enemy to firmness,

228

Mortality's earthquake.

GOVIANUS   Welcome to mine eyes!   145
As is the day-spring from the morning's womb
Unto that wretch whose nights are tedious,
As liberty to captives, health to labourers,
And life still to old people (never weary on 't),
So welcome art thou to me. The deed's done,   150
Thou queen of spirits: he has his end upon him.
Thy body shall return to rise again,°
For thy abuser falls, and has no power
To vex thee farther.

LADY'S GHOST   My truest love,
Live ever honoured here, and blessed above.   155
          [Exit the Lady's Ghost]

TYRANT O if there be a hell for flesh and spirit,
'Tis built within this bosom! My lords, treason!°
          Enter the Nobles, including Memphonius

GOVIANUS Now, death, I'm for thee, welcome.

TYRANT   Your King's poisoned!°

MEMPHONIUS The King of Heaven be praised for 't.

TYRANT   Lay hold on him,
On Govianus.

MEMPHONIUS   E'en with the best loves   160
And truest hearts that ever subjects owed.

TYRANT How's that? I charge you all, lay hands on him!°

MEMPHONIUS Look you, my lord, your will shall be obeyed.
          [The Nobles lead Govianus to the throne.°] Enter Helvetius
Here comes another, we'll have his hand too.

HELVETIUS You shall have both mine if that work go forward,°   165
Beside my voice and knee.

TYRANT   Helvetius!
Then my destruction was confirmed amongst 'em;
Premeditation wrought it. O my torments!

ALL Live Govianus long our virtuous King!
          A flourish is played

TYRANT That thunder strikes me dead.
          [He dies]

GOVIANUS   I cannot better°   170
Reward my joys than with astonished silence,
For all the wealth of words is not of power
To make up thanks for you, my honoured lords.

    I'm like a man plucked up from many waters
    That never looked for help, and am here placed   175
    Upon this cheerful mountain where prosperity°
    Shoots forth her richest beam.

MEMPHONIUS   Long-injured lord,
    The tyranny of his actions grew so weighty,
    His life so vicious—

HELVETIUS   To which this is witness,
    Monster in sin, this, the disquieted body   180
    Of my too resolute child in honour's war.

MEMPHONIUS —That he became as hateful to our minds
    As death's unwelcome to a house of riches,
    Or what can more express it.

GOVIANUS   Well, he's gone,
    And all the kingdom's evils perish with him;   185
    And since the body of that virtuous lady
    Is taken from her rest, in memory
    Of her admirèd mistress, 'tis our will°
    It receive honour dead as it took part
    With us in all affections when it lived.   190
    Here place it in this throne, crown her our Queen,
    The first and last that ever we make ours:
    Her constancy strikes so much firmness in us.
       [*The Lady's body is placed on the throne and crowned*]
    That honour done, let her be solemnly borne
    Unto the house of peace from whence she came   195
    As queen of silence.
       The Lady's spirit enters again and stays to go out with the
       body, as it were attending it
                  O welcome blessed spirit!
    Thou needst not mistrust me. I have a care
    As jealous as thine own. We'll see it done
    And not believe report, our zeal is such.
    We cannot reverence chastity too much.   200
    Lead on. I would those ladies that fill honour's rooms°
    Might all be borne so virtuous to their tombs.
       Exeunt° [*with the Lady's body*]. *Recorders*° *or other solemn*
       music plays them out

ADDITIONAL PASSAGES

The following five passages of four or more lines were cut from the author's draft text in the process of revision for the theatre, and do not appear to be censorship cuts. Material in pointed brackets indicates the context in the main text.

A. Following 1.1.182

⟨TYRANT⟩
>   A woman to set light by sovereignty!°
>   What age can bring her forth, and hide that book?°
>   'Tis their desire most commonly to rule
>   More than their part comes to—sometimes their husbands.

B. Following 2.3.56

⟨TYRANT   I beshrew that virtue*
>   That busied herself with him⟩: she might have found
>   Some other work; the man was fit for me
>   Before she spoiled him. She has wronged my heart in 't
>   And marred me a good workman.   5

C. Following 3.1.233

⟨GOVIANUS⟩   Faith, she told me
>   Her everlasting sleep would bring me joy,
>   Yet I was still unwilling to believe her,
>   Her life was so sweet to me. Like some man
>   In time of sickness that would rather wish,   5
>   To please his fearful flesh, his former health
>   Restored to him than death; when, after trial,
>   If it were possible, ten thousand worlds
>   Could not entice him to return again
>   And walk upon the earth from whence he flew:°   10
>   So stood my wish, joyed in her life and breath
>   Now gone. There is no heav'n but after death.

D. Following 5.1.166 (and replaced by ll. 167–80)

GOVIANUS Is death so long a-coming to mankind
>   It must be met half-ways? 'Las, the full time°
>   Is to eternity but a minute, a [*blank*]°

Was that so long to stay? O cruel speed!
There's few men pay their debts before their day;   5
If they be ready at their time, 'tis well,
And but a few that are so. What strange haste
Was made among these people! My heart weeps for 't.
[*To Servants*] Go, bear those bodies to a place more comely.

E. Following 5.2.37

⟨TYRANT   The fool belike
Makes his choice carefully, for so we charged him,⟩
To fit our close deeds with some private hand.°
[*To the Lady's body*] It is no shame for thee, most silent mistress,
To stand in need of art, when youth   5
And all thy warm friends has forsook thee.
Women alive are glad to seek her friendship°
To make up the fair number of their graces,
Or else the reckoning would fall short sometimes,°
And servants would look out for better wages.°   10

THE TRAGEDY OF VALENTINIAN

JOHN FLETCHER

THE PERSONS OF THE PLAY

Valentinian, Emperor of Rome
Eudoxa, the Empress

Lucina, a chaste Roman lady
Maximus, her husband, a great soldier
Claudia⎱
Marcellina⎰ Lucina's waiting women

Aëtius,° a veteran general
Phidias⎱
Aretus⎰ eunuchs, formerly his servants, now members of Valentinian's court
Pontius, a captain in the army
Affranius, a high-ranking army officer

Chilax, a Greek freedman of Valentinian's court
Balbus⎱
Proculus⎰ Roman freedmen°
Lycinius
Lycias, a Mantuan eunuch
Ardelia⎱
Phorba⎰ old panderesses

Fulvius⎱
Lucius⎰ Senators
Sempronius

Paulus, a poet
Lycippus, a gentleman of the court
A Boy, who appears as a Grace in the masque
A Chorus of Singers in the masque

Maximus' Servant
Valentinian's Servant
A Boy Singer
Three Men
Physicians
Attendants
A Messenger
Soldiers
Gentlemen of Rome
Lictors

Epilogue

234

1.1

Enter Balbus, Proculus, Chilax, and Lycinius

BALBUS I never saw the like. She's no more stirred—
No more another woman, no more altered
With any hopes or promises laid to her,
Let 'em be ne'er so weighty, ne'er so winning—
Than I am with the motion of my own legs.   5

PROCULUS Chilax,
You are a stranger yet in these designs,
At least in Rome. Tell me, and tell me truth,
Did you e'er know in all your course of practice,°
In all the ways of woman you have run through   10
(For I presume you have been brought up, Chilax,
As we, to fetch and carry)—

CHILAX   True, I have so.°

PROCULUS Did you, I say again, in all this progress
Ever discover such a piece of beauty,
Ever so rare a creature (and no doubt   15
One that must know her worth too, and affect it,°
Ay, and be flattered, else 'tis none) and honest?°
Honest against the tide of all temptations,
Honest to one man, to her husband only,
And yet not eighteen, not of age to know   20
Why she is honest?

CHILAX   I confess it freely:
I never saw her fellow, nor e'er shall,
For all our Grecian dames, all I have tried°
(And sure I have tried a hundred; if I say two
I speak within my compass); all these beauties,°   25
And all the constancy of all these faces,
Maids, widows, wives, of what degree or calling°
(So they be Greeks, and fat, for there's my cunning),°
I would undertake (and not sweat for 't, Proculus),°
Were they to try again (say twice as many),°   30
Under a thousand pound to lay 'em bedrid;°
But this wench staggers me.

LYCINIUS   Do you see these jewels?°
You would think these pretty baits. Now, I'll assure ye

235

Here's half the wealth of Asia.

BALBUS   These are nothing°
To the full honours I propounded to her.   35
I bid her think and be (and presently)
Whatever her ambition, what the counsel
Of others would add to her, what her dreams
Could more enlarge, what any precedent
Of any woman rising up to glory   40
And standing certain there (and in the highest)
Could give her more—nay, to be Empress.

PROCULUS And cold at all these offers?

BALBUS   Cold as crystal,
Never to be thawed again.

CHILAX   I tried her further,°
And so far that I think she is no woman,   45
At least as women go now.

LYCINIUS   Why, what did you?

CHILAX I offered that that, had she been but mistress
Of as much spleen as doves have, I had reached her:°
A safe revenge of all that ever hates her,°
The crying-down forever all beauties   50
That may be thought come near her.

PROCULUS   That was pretty.°

CHILAX I never knew that way fail; yet I'll tell ye,
I offered her a gift beyond all yours,
That that had made a saint start, well considered:
The law to be her creature, she to make it,   55
Her mouth to give it, every creature living
From her aspect to draw their good or evil
Fixed in 'em spite of fortune. A new nature
She should be called, and mother of all ages.°
Time should be hers, and what she did, lame virtue   60
Should bless to all posterities. Her air
Should give us life, her earth and water feed us.
And last, to none but to the Emperor
(And then but when she pleased to have it so)
She should be held for mortal.

LYCINIUS   And she heard you?°   65

CHILAX Yes, as a sick man hears a noise, or he
That stands condemned his judgement. Let me perish,
But if there can be virtue, if that name

236

Be anything but name and empty title,
If it be so as fools have been pleased to feign it,   70
A power that can preserve us after ashes°
And make the names of men out-reckon ages,
This woman has a god of virtue in her.

BALBUS I would the Emperor were that god.

CHILAX   She has in her°
All the contempt of glory and vain seeming   75
Of the Stoics, all the truth of Christians,°
And all their constancy. Modesty was made
When she was first intended. When she blushes,°
It is the holiest thing to look upon,
The purest temple of her sect, that ever   80
Made nature a blessed founder.

PROCULUS   Is there no way
To take this Phoenix?

LYCINIUS   None but in her ashes.°

CHILAX If she were fat, or any way inclining
To ease or pleasure, or affected glory,
Proud to be seen and worshipped, 'twere a venture;   85
But on my soul she is chaster than cold camphor.

BALBUS I think so too, for all the ways of woman
Like a full sail she bears against. I ask her,°
After my many offers, walking with her,
And her as many down denials: how   90
If the Emperor, grown mad with love, should force her?
She pointed to a Lucrece that hung by,°
And with an angry look that from her eyes
Shot vestal fire against me, she departed.°

PROCULUS This is the first wench I was ever posed in,°   95
Yet have I brought young loving things together
This two-and-thirty year.

CHILAX   I find by this wench
The calling of a bawd to be a strange,
A wise, and subtle calling, and for none
But staid, discreet, and understanding people.   100
And as the tutor to great Alexander°
Would say a young man should not dare to read
His moral books till after five-and-twenty,
So must that he or she that will be bawdy
(I mean discreetly bawdy), and be trusted: 105

237

    If they will rise and gain experience,
    Well-steeped in years and discipline begin it.
    I take it 'tis no boys' play.
BALBUS   Well, what's thought of?
PROCULUS The Emperor must know it.
LYCINIUS   If the women
    Should chance to fail too?
CHILAX   As 'tis ten to one.   110
PROCULUS Why, what remains but new nets for the purchase?°
CHILAX Let's go consider, then, and if all fail,
    This is the first quick eel that saved her tail.°
       Exeunt

1.2

    Enter Lucina, Ardelia, and Phorba
ARDELIA [*to Lucina*] You still insist upon that idol, honour.
    Can it renew your youth? Can it add wealth,
    That takes off wrinkles? Can it draw men's eyes
    To gaze upon you in your age? Can honour
    (That truly is a saint to none but soldiers,°   5
    And, looked into, bears no reward but danger)
    Leave you the most respected person living?
    Or can the common kisses of a husband
    (Which to a sprightly lady is a labour)
    Make ye almost immortal? Ye are cozened: 10
    The honour of a woman is her praises,
    The way to get these, to be seen and sought to,
    And not to bury such a happy sweetness
    Under a smoky roof—
LUCINA   I'll hear no more.°
PHORBA That white, that red, and all that blessèd beauty,°   15
    Kept from the eyes that make it so, is nothing:°
    Then you are rarely fair when men proclaim it.
    The Phoenix, were she never seen, were doubted.
    That most unvalued horn the unicorn°
    Bears to oppose the huntsman, were it nothing   20
    But tale and mere tradition, would help no man.
    But when the virtue's known, the honour's doubled.

Virtue is either lame or not at all,
And love a sacrilege and not a saint,
When it bars up the way to men's petitions.   25
ARDELIA Nay, ye shall love your husband too: we come not
　　To make a monster of ye.
LUCINA   Are ye women?
ARDELIA You'll find us so, and women you shall thank, too,
　　If you have grace to make your use.
LUCINA   Fie on ye!
PHORBA Alas, poor bashful lady, by my soul,   30
　　Had ye no other virtue but your blushes,
　　And I a man, I should run mad for those.°
　　How daintily they set her off, how sweetly!
ARDELIA Come, goddess, come, you move too near the earth.
　　It must not be, a better orb stays for you.°   35
　　　　[She offers Lucina jewels]
　　Here. Be a maid, and take 'em.
LUCINA   Pray, leave me.°
PHORBA That were a sin, sweet lady, and a way
　　To make us guilty of your melancholy.°
　　You must not be alone: in conversation
　　Doubts are resolved, and what sticks near the conscience   40
　　Made easy and allowable.
LUCINA   Ye are devils.
ARDELIA That you may one day bless for your damnation.
LUCINA I charge ye in the name of chastity,
　　Tempt me no more. How ugly ye seem to me!
　　There is no wonder men defame our sex   45
　　And lay the vices of all ages on us,
　　When such as you shall bear the names of women.
　　If ye had eyes to see yourselves, or sense
　　Above the base rewards ye play the bawds for,
　　If ever in your lives ye heard of goodness   50
　　(Though many regions off, as men hear thunder),
　　If ever ye had mothers, and they souls,
　　If ever fathers, and not such as you are,
　　If ever anything were constant in you
　　Beside your sins, or coming but your curses,°   55
　　If ever any of your ancestors
　　Died worth a noble deed that would be cherished,
　　Soul-frighted with this black infection

You would run from one another to repentance,
And from your guilty eyes drop out those sins   60
That made ye blind, and beasts.

PHORBA   Ye speak well, lady:
A sign of fruitful education,
If your religious zeal had wisdom with it.

ARDELIA [to Phorba] This lady was ordained to bless the empire,
And we may all give thanks for 't.

PHORBA   I believe ye.   65

ARDELIA And if anything redeem the Emperor
From his wild, flying courses, this is she.
She can instruct him if ye mark: she is wise, too.

PHORBA Exceeding wise, which is a wonder in her,
And so religious that I well believe   70
Though she would sin, she cannot.

ARDELIA   And, besides,
She has the empire's cause in hand, not love's:
There lies the main consideration
For which she is chiefly born.

PHORBA   She finds that point
Stronger than we can tell her; and, believe it,   75
I look by her means for a reformation,
And such a one, and such a rare way carried,
That all the world shall wonder at.

ARDELIA   'Tis true.
I never thought the Emperor had wisdom,
Pity, or fair affection to his country,   80
Till he professed this love. Gods give 'em children
Such as her virtues merit, and his zeal.
I look to see a Numa from this lady,
Or greater than Octavius.

PHORBA   Do you mark, too°
(Which is a noble virtue) how she blushes,   85
And what a flowing modesty runs through her
When we but name the Emperor?

ARDELIA   But mark it,
Yes, and admire it too, for she considers,
Though she be as fair as heaven and virtuous
As holy truth, yet to the Emperor   90
She is a kind of nothing but her service,°
Which she is bound to offer; and she'll do it,

And, when her country's cause commands affection,
She knows obedience is the key of virtues.
Then fly the blushes out like Cupid's arrows,   95
And though the tie of marriage to her lord
Would fain cry, 'Stay, Lucina,' yet the cause
And general wisdom of the Prince's love
Makes her find surer ends and happier,
And if the first were chaste, this is twice doubled.   100

PHORBA   Her tartness unto us, too.

ARDELIA   That's a wise one.

PHORBA   I rarely like: it shows a rising wisdom,°
That chides all common fools as dare enquire
What princes would have private.

ARDELIA   What a lady
Shall we be blessed to serve!

LUCINA   Go, get ye from me!   105
Ye are your purses' agents, not the Prince's.
Is this the virtuous lure ye trained me out to?
Am I a woman fit to imp your vices?°
But that I had a mother, and a woman
Whose ever-living fame turns all it touches   110
Into the good itself is, I should now°
Even doubt myself, I have been searched so near
The very soul of honour. Why should you two,
That happily have been as chaste as I am,°
Fairer, I think, by much (for yet your faces,   115
Like ancient, well-built piles, show worthy ruins),°
After that angel age turn mortal devils?
For shame, for womanhood, for what ye have been
(For rotten cedars have borne goodly branches),
If ye have hope of any heaven but court   120
(Which like a dream you'll find hereafter vanish,
Or at the best but subject to repentance),
Study no more to be ill spoken of.
Let women live themselves; if they must fall,
Their own destruction find 'em, not your fevers'.°   125

ARDELIA   Madam, ye are so excellent in all,
And I must tell it you with admiration:
So true a joy ye have, so sweet a fear,
And when ye come to anger, 'tis so noble,
That for mine own part, I could still offend   130

To hear you angry. Women that want that,
And your way guided (else I count it nothing),
Are either fools or cowards.

PHORBA She were a mistress for no private greatness,
    Could she not frown a ravished kiss from anger,°   135
    And such an anger as this lady learns us,
    Stuck with such pleasing dangers. Gods, I ask ye,
    Which of ye all could hold from?

LUCINA   I perceive ye:°
    Your own dark sins dwell with ye, and that price
    You sell the chastity of modest wives at   140
    Runs to diseases with your bones. I scorn ye,°
    And all the nets ye have pitched to catch my virtues
    Like spiders' webs I sweep away before me.
    Go tell the Emperor ye have met a woman
    That neither his own person, which is god-like,   145
    The world he rules, nor what that world can purchase,
    Nor all the glories subject to a Caesar,
    The honours that he offers for my body,
    The hopes, gifts, everlasting flatteries,
    Nor anything that's his, and apt to tempt me,·   150
    No, not to be the mother of the empire
    And queen of all the holy fires he worships,
    Can make a whore of.

ARDELIA   You mistake us, lady.

LUCINA Yet tell him this: he's thus much weakened me
    That I have here his knaves and you his matrons°   155
    (Fit nurses for his sins), which gods forgive me;
    But ever to be leaning to his folly,
    Or to be brought to love his lust, assure him,
    And from her mouth whose life shall make it certain,
    I never can. I have a noble husband   160
    (Pray tell him that too), yet a noble name,
    A noble family, and, last, a conscience.
    Thus much for your answer. For yourselves,
    Ye have lived the shame of women; die the better.
       Exit Lucina

PHORBA What's now to do?

ARDELIA   Ev'n as she said, to die;   165
    For there's no living here, and women thus,°

    I am sure, for us two.

PHORBA   Nothing stick upon her?

ARDELIA   We have lost a mass of money. Well, Dame Virtue,
    Yet ye may halt, if good luck serve.

PHORBA   Worms take her!°
    She has almost spoiled our trade.

ARDELIA   So godly!   170
    This is ill breeding, Phorba.

PHORBA   If the women
    Should have a longing now to see this monster,
    And she convert 'em all!

ARDELIA   That may be, Phorba,
    But if it be, I'll have the young men gelded.
    Come, let's go think. She must not scape us thus.   175
    There is a certain season, if we hit,
    That women may be rid without a bit.°

       Exeunt

1.3

    Enter Maximus and Aëtius

MAXIMUS   I cannot blame the nations, noble friend,°
    That they fall off so fast from this wild man,
    When (under our allegiance be it spoken,
    And the most happy tie of our affections)
    The world's weight groans beneath him. Where lives virtue,   5
    Honour, discretion, wisdom? Who are called
    And chosen to the steering of the empire
    But bawds and singing-girls? O my Aëtius,
    The glory of a soldier and the truth
    Of men made up for goodness' sake, like shells°   10
    Grow to the raggèd walls for want of action.°
    Only your happy self and I that love ye,
    Which is a larger means for me than favour—°

AËTIUS   No more, my worthy friend. Though these be truths,
    And though these truths would ask a reformation,   15
    (At least a little squaring), yet remember
    We are but subjects, Maximus. Obedience

To what is done and grief for what is ill done
Is all we can call ours. The hearts of princes°
Are like the temples of the gods: pure incense   20
(Until unhallowed hands defile those off'rings),
Burns ever there. We must not put 'em out,
Because the priests that touch those sweets are wicked.
We dare not, dearest friend, nay, more, we cannot
(While we consider why we are, and how,°   25
To what laws bound, much more to what law-giver;
Whilst majesty is made to be obeyed,
And not inquired into; whilst gods and angels
Make but a rule as we do, though a stricter),°
Like desperate and unseasoned fools, let fly   30
Our killing angers and forsake our honours.
MAXIMUS My noble friend (from whose instructions
    I never yet took surfeit), weigh but thus much,°
    Nor think I speak it with ambition,
    For by the gods I do not: why, Aëtius,   35
    Why are we thus, or how become thus wretched?—
AËTIUS You'll fall again into your fit.
MAXIMUS   I will not.—
    Or are we now no more the sons of Romans,
    No more the followers of their happy fortunes,
    But conquered Gauls, or quivers for the Parthians?° 40
    Why is this Emperor, this man we honour,
    This god that ought to be?—
AËTIUS   You are too curious.°
MAXIMUS Good, give me leave.—Why is this author of us—
AËTIUS [interrupting] I dare not hear ye speak thus.
MAXIMUS   I'll be modest.—
    Thus led away, thus vainly led away,   45
    And we beholders? Misconceive me not,
    I sow no danger in my words; but wherefore°
    And to what end are we the sons of fathers
    Famous and fast to Rome? Why are their virtues
    Stamped in the dangers of a thousand battles   50
    For goodness' sake, their honours time out-daring?°
    I think for our example.
AËTIUS   Ye speak nobly.
MAXIMUS Why are we seeds of these, then, to shake hands
    With bawds and base informers, kiss Discredit

And court her like a mistress? Pray, your leave yet.   55
You'll say the Emperor is young and apt
To take impression rather from his pleasures
Than any constant worthiness. It may be.°
But why do these the people call his pleasures°
Exceed the moderation of a man?   60
Nay, to say justly, friend, why are they vices,
And such as shake our worths with foreign nations?

AËTIUS You search the sore too deep, and I must tell ye,
In any other man this had been boldness,
And so rewarded. Pray depress your spirit,°   65
For, though I constantly believe ye honest
(Ye were no friend for me else) and what now
Ye freely spake but good ye owe to th' empire,
Yet take heed, worthy Maximus, all ears
Hear not with that distinction mine do: few   70
You'll find admonishers, but urgers of your actions,
And to the heaviest, friend. And pray consider,°
We are but shadows: motions others give us,
And though our pities may become the times,
Justly our powers cannot. Make me worthy   75
To be your ever friend in fair allegiance,
But not in force, for durst mine own soul urge me
(And by that 'soul' I speak my just affections)
To turn my hand from truth, which is obedience,
And give the helm my virtue holds to anger,   80
Though I had both the blessings of the Brutii°
And both their instigations, though my cause
Carried a race of justice beyond theirs,
And as I am a servant to my fortunes,
That daring soul that first taught disobedience   85
Should feel the first example. Say the Prince,°
As I may well believe, seems vicious,
Who justly knows 'tis not to try our honours?
Or say he be an ill prince, are we therefore
Fit fires to purge him? No, my dearest friend,   90
The elephant is never won with anger,°
Nor must that man that would reclaim a lion
Take him by th' teeth.

MAXIMUS   I pray mistake me not.

AËTIUS Our honest actions, and the light that breaks

245

Like morning from our service, chaste and blushing,   95
Is that that pulls a prince back. Then he sees,°
And not till then truly repents his errors,
When subjects' crystal souls are glasses to him.

MAXIMUS My ever-honoured friend, I'll take your counsel.

    Enter the Emperor Valentinian and Chilax [at one door]

The Emperor appears. I'll leave ye to him,   100
And as we both affect him may he flourish.°

    Exit Maximus [at another door]

VALENTINIAN Is that the best news?

CHILAX   Yet the best we know, sir.

VALENTINIAN Bid Maximus come to me, and be gone then.
    [*Exit Chilax*]
Mine own head be my helper; these are fools.
How now, Aëtius, are the soldiers quiet?   105

AËTIUS Better, I hope, sir, than they were.

VALENTINIAN   They are pleased, I hear,
To censure me extremely for my pleasures.
Shortly they'll fight against me.

AËTIUS   Gods defend, sir.°
And, for their censures, they are such shrewd judgers.°
A donative of ten sesterces,   110
I'll undertake, shall make 'em ring your praises
More than they sang your pleasures.

VALENTINIAN   I believe thee.
Art thou in love, Aëtius, yet?

AËTIUS   Oh, no, sir.
I am too coarse for ladies. My embraces,
That only am acquainted with alarums,   115
Would break their tender bodies.

VALENTINIAN   Never fear it,
They are stronger than ye think, they'll hold the hammer.°
My Empress swears thou art a lusty soldier.°
A good one I believe thee.

AËTIUS   All that goodness
Is but your grace's creature.

VALENTINIAN   Tell me truly,   120
For thou dar'st tell me—

AËTIUS   Anything concerns ye
That's fit for me to speak and you to pardon.

VALENTINIAN What say the soldiers of me? And the same words,

Mince 'em not, good Aëtius, but deliver
The very forms and tongues they talk withal.   125

AËTIUS I'll tell your grace, but with this caution:
You be not stirred, for should the gods live with us,
Even those we certainly believe are righteous,
Give 'em but drink, they would censure them too.

VALENTINIAN Forward.   130

AËTIUS Then, to begin, they say you sleep too much,
By which they judge your majesty too sensual,
Apt to decline your strength to ease and pleasures.
And when you do not sleep, you drink too much,
From which they fear suspicions first, then ruins.°   135
And when ye neither drink nor sleep, ye wench much,
Which they affirm first breaks your understanding,
Then takes the edge off honour, makes us seem,
That are the ribs and rampires of the empire,
Fencers and beaten fools, and so regarded.°   140
But I believe 'em not, for were these truths
Your virtue can correct them.

VALENTINIAN   They speak plainly.

AËTIUS They say moreover (since your grace will have it—
For they will talk their freedoms, though the sword
Were in their throat) that of late time, like Nero,°   145
And with the same forgetfulness of glory,
You have got a vein of fiddling—so they term it.

VALENTINIAN Some drunken dreams, Aëtius.

AËTIUS   So I hope, sir.—
And that you rather study cruelty
And to be feared for blood than loved for bounty,   150
Which makes the nations, as they say, despise ye,
Telling your years and actions by their deaths
Whose truth and strength of duty made you Caesar.
They say besides you nourish strange devourers
Fed with the fat o' th' empire, they call 'bawds':   155
Lazy and lustful creatures that abuse ye,
A people, as they term 'em, made of paper
In which the secret sins of each man's moneys
Are sealed and sent a-working.

VALENTINIAN   What sin's next?°
For I perceive they have no mind to spare me.   160

AËTIUS Nor hurt ye, o' my soul, sir, but such people

(Nor can the power of man restrain it)
When they are full of meat and ease must prattle.
VALENTINIAN Forward.
AËTIUS I have spoken too much, sir.
VALENTINIAN   I'll have all.
AËTIUS   It fits not   165
Your ears should hear their vanities. No profit
Can justly rise to you from their behaviour,
Unless ye were guilty of those crimes.
VALENTINIAN   It may be
I am so; therefore forward.
AËTIUS   I have ever
Learned to obey, nor shall my life resist it.   170
VALENTINIAN No more apologies.
AËTIUS   They grieve besides, sir,
To see the nations, whom our ancient virtue
With many a weary march and hunger conquered,
With loss of many a daring life subdued,
Fall from their fair obedience, and even murmur   175
To see the warlike eagles mew their honours°
In obscure towns, that wont to prey on princes.°
They cry for enemies, and tell the captains,
'The fruits of Italy are luscious: give us Egypt
Or sandy Afric to display our valours,   180
There where our swords may make us meat, and danger
Digest our well-got viands. Here our weapons
And bodies that were made for shining brass°
Are both unedged and old with ease and women.'
And then they cry again, 'Where are the Germans?   185
Lined with hot Spain or Gallia bring 'em on,°
And let the son of war, steeled Mithridates,
Lead up his wingèd Parthians like a storm,
Hiding the face of heaven with show'rs of arrows,°
Yet we dare fight like Romans.' Then as soldiers   190
Tired with a weary march they tell their wounds,
Even weeping ripe they were no more nor deeper,
And glory in those scars that make 'em lovely,°
And, sitting where a camp was, like sad pilgrims
They reckon up the times and living labours   195
Of Julius or Germanicus, and wonder
That Rome, whose turrets once were topped with honours,

Can now forget the custom of her conquests.
And then they blame your grace, and say, 'Who leads us?
Shall we stand here like statues? Were our fathers   200
The sons of lazy Moors, our princes Persians,
Nothing but silks and softness? Curses on 'em
That first taught Nero wantonness and blood,
Tiberius doubts, Caligula all vices,°
For from the spring of these, succeeding princes . . .'   205
Thus they talk, sir.

VALENTINIAN Well,
Why do you hear these things?

AËTIUS   Why do you do 'em?
I take the gods to witness, with more sorrow
And more vexation do I hear these taintures   210
Than were my life dropped from me through an hour-glass.

VALENTINIAN Belike then you believe 'em, or at least
Are glad they should be so. Take heed, you were better
Build your own tomb and run into it living
Than dare a prince's anger.

AËTIUS   I am old, sir,   215
And ten years' more addition is but nothing.
Now if my life be pleasing to ye, take it.
        [He kneels]
Upon my knees, if ever any service
(As, let me brag, some have been worthy notice),
If ever any worth or trust ye gave me   220
Deserved a fair respect, if all my actions,
The hazards of my youth, colds, burnings, wants,
For you and for the empire be not vices,
By that style ye have stamped upon me, 'soldier',°
Let me not fall into the hands of wretches.   225

VALENTINIAN I understand ye not.

AËTIUS   Let not this body
That has looked bravely in his blood for Caesar,°
And covetous of wounds, and for your safety,
After the scape of swords, spears, slings, and arrows°
(Gainst which my beaten body was mine armour),   230
The seas and thirsty deserts, now be purchase°
For slaves and base informers. I see anger
And death look through your eyes: I am marked for slaughter,
And know the telling of this truth has made me

A man clean lost to this world. I embrace it.   235
Only my last petition, sacred Caesar,
Is, I may die a Roman.
VALENTINIAN   Rise my friend still,°
    [*Aëtius rises*]
And worthy of my love. Reclaim the soldier.°
I'll study to do so upon myself too.
Go, keep your command, and prosper.
AËTIUS   Life to Caesar.   240
    Exit Aëtius. Enter Chilax
CHILAX   Lord Maximus attends your grace.
VALENTINIAN   Go tell him
I'll meet him in the gallery.
    [*Exit Chilax*]
                      The honesty of this Aëtius,
Who is indeed the bulwark of the empire,
Has dived so deep into me that of all
The sins I covet, but this woman's beauty,°   245
With much repentance now could I be quit of.
But she is such a pleasure, being good,
That though I were a god, she would fire my blood.
    Exit

2.1

[A table is set out.] Enter the Emperor Valentinian, Maximus,
Lycinius, Proculus, Chilax, playing dice

VALENTINIAN Nay, ye shall set my hand out. 'Tis not just°
  I should neglect my fortune, now 'tis prosperous.
LYCINIUS If I have anything to set, your grace,
  But clothes or good conditions, let me perish.°
  You have all my money, sir.
PROCULUS   And mine.
CHILAX   And mine too.   5
MAXIMUS Unless your grace will credit us—
VALENTINIAN   No bare-board.
LYCINIUS Then at my garden-house.
VALENTINIAN   The orchard too.°
LYCINIUS An't please your grace.
VALENTINIAN   Have at 'em.
    [He rolls the dice]
PROCULUS   They are lost.
LYCINIUS Why, farewell, fig-trees.
VALENTINIAN   Who sets more?
CHILAX   At my horse, sir.
VALENTINIAN The dappled Spaniard?
CHILAX   He.
    [Valentinian rolls the dice]
VALENTINIAN   He's mine.
CHILAX   He is so.°   10
MAXIMUS Your short horse is soon curried.
CHILAX   So it seems, sir.
  So may your mare be too, if luck serve.
MAXIMUS   Ha?
CHILAX Nothing, my lord, but grieving at my fortune.
VALENTINIAN Come, Maximus, you were not wont to flinch thus.
MAXIMUS By heaven, sir, I have lost all.
VALENTINIAN   There's a ring yet.   15
MAXIMUS This was not made to lose, sir.
VALENTINIAN   Some love token.
  Set it, I say.
MAXIMUS   I do beseech your grace,

Rather name any house I have.

VALENTINIAN   How strange
And curious you are grown of toys! Redeem 't,
If so I win it, when you please, tomorrow   20
Or next day as ye will, I care not;
But only for my luck's sake. 'Tis not rings°
Can make me richer.

MAXIMUS   Will you throw, sir?
    [*He lays down his ring*]
                                        There 'tis.

VALENTINIAN Why, then, have at it fairly.
    [*He rolls the dice*]
                            Mine.

MAXIMUS   Your grace
Is only ever fortunate. Tomorrow,   25
An't be your pleasure, sir, I'll pay the price on 't.

VALENTINIAN Tomorrow you shall have it without price, sir,
But this day 'tis my victory. Good Maximus,
Now I bethink myself, go to Aëtius
And bid him muster all the cohorts presently   30
(They mutiny for pay, I hear), and be you
Assistant to him. When you know their numbers,
Ye shall have moneys for 'em, and above,°
Something to stop their tongues withal.

MAXIMUS   I will, sir,
And gods preserve you in this mind still.   35

VALENTINIAN Shortly I'll see 'em march myself.

MAXIMUS   Gods ever keep ye.
    Exit Maximus

VALENTINIAN To what end do you think this ring shall serve now?
For you are fellows only know by rote,
As birds record their lessons.

CHILAX   For the lady.°

VALENTINIAN But how for her?

CHILAX   That I confess I know not.   40

VALENTINIAN Then pray for him that does. Fetch me an eunuch
That never saw her yet.
    Exit Chilax
                            And you two see
The court made like a paradise—

LYCINIUS   We will, sir.

VALENTINIAN —Full of fair shows and musics. All your arts,
　As I shall give instructions, screw to th' highest, 45
　For my main piece is now a-doing. And for fear
　You should not take, I'll have another engine,°
　Such as, if virtue be not only in her,
　She shall not choose but lean to: let the women
　Put on a graver show of welcome.
PROCULUS　　　　　　　　　Well, sir. 50
VALENTINIAN They are a thought too eager.
　　　　Enter Chilax and Lycias the Eunuch
CHILAX　　　　　　　　　Here's the eunuch.°
LYCIAS Long life to Caesar.
VALENTINIAN　　　　　I must use you, Lycias.
　Come, let's walk in, and then I'll show ye all.
　If women may be frail, this wench shall fall.
　　　　Exeunt. [The table is removed]

2.2

Enter Claudia and Marcellina

CLAUDIA Sirrah, what ails my lady, that of late
　She never cares for company?
MARCELLINA　　　　　　I know not,
　Unless it be that company causes cuckolds.
CLAUDIA That were a childish fear.
MARCELLINA　　　　　　What were those ladies
　Came to her lately? From the court?
CLAUDIA　　　　　　　The same, wench. 5
　Some grave instructors, on my life. They look
　For all the world like old hatched hilts.
MARCELLINA　　　　　　'Tis true, wench,°
　For here and there (and yet they painted well too)°
　One might discover, where the gold was worn,
　Their iron ages.
CLAUDIA　　　If my judgement fail not,° 10
　They have been sheathed like rotten ships.
MARCELLINA　　　　　　It may be.°
CLAUDIA For if ye mark their rudders, they hang weakly.
MARCELLINA They have passed the line, belike. Wouldst live,
　　Claudia,°

Till thou wert such as they are?

CLAUDIA   Chimney-pieces.
Now heaven have mercy on me, and young men,   15
I had rather make a drollery till thirty,°
While I were able to endure a tempest,
And bear my fights out bravely, till my tackle
Whistled i' th' wind, and held against all weathers,
While I were able to bear with my tires,   20
And so discharge 'em; I would willingly
Live, Marcellina, not till barnacles
Bred in my sides.

MARCELLINA   Thou art i' th' right, wench.
For who would live (whom pleasures had forsaken),
To stand at mark and cry, 'A bow short, signor'?°   25
Were there not men came hither too?

CLAUDIA   Brave fellows.
I fear me, bawds of five i' th' pound.

MARCELLINA   How know you?°

CLAUDIA They gave me great lights to it.

MARCELLINA   Take heed, Claudia.°

CLAUDIA Let them take heed, the spring comes on.

MARCELLINA   To me, now,°
They seemed as noble visitants.

CLAUDIA   To me, now,   30
Nothing less, Marcellina, for I mark 'em,
(And by this honest light, for yet 'tis morning),
Saving the reverence of their gilded doublets°
And Milan skins.

MARCELLINA   Thou art a strange wench, Claudia.°

CLAUDIA Ye are deceived, they showed to me directly°   35
Court crabs that creep a side way for their living.
I know 'em by the breeches that they begged last—°
        *Enter Lucina [holding Maximus' ring], and Lycias the
        Eunuch*

MARCELLINA Peace, my lady comes. [*Seeing Lycias*] What may
    that be?

CLAUDIA   A sumner
That cites her to appear.

MARCELLINA   No more of that, wench.

LYCIAS Madam, what answer to your lord?

LUCINA   Pray tell him   40

I am subject to his will.

LYCIAS   Why weep you, madam?
Excellent lady, there are none will hurt you.

LUCINA I do beseech you tell me, sir—

LYCIAS   What, lady?

LUCINA Serve ye the Emperor?

LYCIAS   I do.

LUCINA   In what place?

LYCIAS In 's chamber, madam.

LUCINA   Do ye serve his will, too?°   45

LYCIAS In fair and just commands.

LUCINA   Are ye a Roman?°

LYCIAS Yes, noble lady, and a Mantuan.°

LUCINA What office bore your parents?

LYCIAS   One was praetor.°

LUCINA Take heed then how you stain his reputation.

LYCIAS Why, worthy lady?

LUCINA   If ye know, I charge ye,   50
Aught in this message but what honesty,
The trust and fair obedience of a servant
May well deliver, yet take heed, and help me.

LYCIAS Madam, I am no broker—

CLAUDIA [aside]   I'll be hanged then.

LYCIAS Nor base procurer of men's lusts. Your husband   55
Prayed me to do this office. I have done it.
It rests in you to come or no.

LUCINA   I will, sir.

LYCIAS If ye mistrust me, do not.

LUCINA   Ye appear so worthy,
And to all my sense so honest, and this
Is such a certain sign ye have brought me   60
That I believe.

LYCIAS   Why should I cozen you?
Or, were I bribed to do this villainy,
Can money prosper, or the fool that takes it,
When such a virtue falls?

LUCINA   Ye speak well, sir.
Would all the rest that serve the Emperor   65
Had but your way.

CLAUDIA [aside]   And so they have, ad unguem.°

LUCINA Pray tell my lord I have received his token

And will not fail to meet him. Yet, good sir,
Thus much before you go I do beseech ye to:
As little notice as ye can, deliver°   70
Of my appearance there.

LYCIAS   It shall be, madam,
And so I wish you happiness.

LUCINA   I thank you.
    Exeunt

2.3

    Tumult and noise within. Enter Aëtius, pursuing Pontius the
    Captain, followed by Maximus

MAXIMUS Temper yourself, Aëtius.

PONTIUS   Hold, my lord.
  I am a Roman, and a soldier.

MAXIMUS   Pray, sir—
    [*He stands between Aëtius and Pontius*]

AËTIUS [*to Pontius*] Thou art a lying villain and a traitor!
  [*To Maximus*] Give me myself, or by the gods, my friend,°
  You'll make me dangerous. [*To Pontius*] How dar'st thou pluck   5
  The soldiers to sedition, and I living,°
  And sow rebellion in 'em, and even then
  When I am drawing out to action?

PONTIUS   Hear me—°

MAXIMUS [*to Aëtius*] Are ye a man?

AËTIUS   I am a true-hearted, Maximus,
  And if the villain live, we are dishonoured.   10

MAXIMUS But hear him what he can say.

AËTIUS   That's the way
  To pardon him. I am so easy natured
  That if he speak but humbly, I forgive him.

PONTIUS I do beseech ye, noble general—

AËTIUS He's found the way already. [*To Maximus*] Give me room—   15
  One stroke, and if he scape me then he's mercy.°

PONTIUS I do not call ye noble that I fear ye.°
  I never cared for death: if ye will kill me,
  Consider first for what, not what you can do.°
  'Tis true, I know ye for my general,   20

And by that great prerogative may kill.°
But do it justly, then.

AËTIUS   He argues with me.
By heaven, a made-up rebel!

MAXIMUS   Pray consider
What certain grounds ye have for this.

AËTIUS   What grounds?
Did I not take him preaching to the soldiers   25
How lazily they lived, and what dishonours
It was 'to serve a prince so full of woman':
Those were his very words, friend.

MAXIMUS   These, Aëtius,
Though they were rashly spoke, which was an error—
A great one, Pontius—yet, from him that hungers   30
For wars and brave employment, might be pardoned.
The heart and harboured thoughts of ill make traitors,
Not spleeny speeches.

AËTIUS   Why should you protect him?
Go to, it shows not honest.

MAXIMUS   Taint me not,
For that shows worse, Aëtius. All your friendship   35
And that pretended love ye lay upon me
(Hold back, my honesty) is like a favour°
You do your slave today, tomorrow hang him.
Was I your bosom piece for this?

AËTIUS   Forgive me.°
The nature of my zeal, and for my country,   40
Makes me sometimes forget myself. For know,
Though I most strive to be without my passions,
I am no god. [*To Pontius*] For you, sir, whose infection
Has spread itself like poison through the army
And cast a killing fog on fair allegiance,   45
First, thank this noble gentleman: ye'd died else.°
Next, from your place, and honour of a soldier,
I here seclude you—

PONTIUS   May I speak yet?

MAXIMUS [*to Aëtius*]   Hear him.°

AËTIUS And while Aëtius holds a reputation,
At least command, ye bear no arms for Rome, sir.   50

PONTIUS Against her shall I never. The condemned man
Has yet that privilege to speak, my lord:

Law were not equal else.
MAXIMUS   Pray hear, Aëtius;
   For happily the fault he has committed,
   Though I believe it mighty, yet, considered   55
   (If mercy may be thought upon), will prove
   Rather a hasty sin than heinous.
AËTIUS [to Pontius]   Speak.
PONTIUS 'Tis true, my lord, ye took me tired with peace,
   My words, almost as raggèd with my fortunes.°
   'Tis true I told the soldier whom we served,   60
   And then bewailed we had an emperor
   Led from us by the flourishes of fencers.
   I blamed him too for women.
AËTIUS   To the rest, sir.
PONTIUS And like enough I blessed him then as soldiers
   Will do sometimes. 'Tis true I told 'em too   65
   We lay at home to show our country
   We durst go naked, durst want meat and money,
   And, when the slave drinks wine, we durst be thirsty.
   I told 'em this, too: that the trees and roots°
   Were our best paymasters, the charity   70
   Of longing women that had bought our bodies,
   Our beds, fires, tailors, nurses. Nay, I told 'em°
   (For you shall hear the greatest sin I said, sir)
   By that time there be wars again, our bodies,
   Laden with scars and aches and ill lodgings,   75
   Heats and perpetual wants, were fitter prayers°
   And certain graves than cope the foe on crutches.
   'Tis likely too, I counselled 'em to turn
   Their warlike pikes to plough-shares, their sure targets
   And swords, hatched with the blood of many nations,°   80
   To spades and pruning-knives (for those get money),
   Their warlike eagles into daws or starlings,°
   To give an 'Ave, Caesar' as he passes,
   And be rewarded with a thousand drachmas,
   For thus we get but years and beets.
AËTIUS [to Maximus]   What think you?°   85
   Were these words to be spoken by a captain,
   One that should give example?
MAXIMUS   'Tis too much.
PONTIUS My lord, I did not woo 'em from the empire,
   Nor bid 'em turn their daring steel 'gainst Caesar.

The gods forever hate me if that motion 90
Were part of me. Give me but employment, sir,
And way to live, and where you hold me vicious,
Bred up in mutiny, my sword shall tell ye
(And if you please, that place I held, maintain it
'Gainst the most daring foes of Rome) I am honest,° 95
A lover of my country, one that holds
His life no longer his than kept for Caesar.
    [*He kneels*]
Weigh not (I thus low on my knee beseech you)
What my rude tongue discovered. 'Twas my want,°
No other part of Pontius. You have seen me, 100
And you, my lord, do something for my country,
And both beheld the wounds I gave and took,
Not like a backward traitor.

AËTIUS   All this language°
Makes but against you, Pontius. You are cast,°
And, by mine honour, and my love to Caesar, 105
By me shall never be restored. In my camp
I will not have a tongue, though to himself,
Dare talk but near sedition. As I govern,°
All shall obey, and when they want, their duty
And ready service shall redress their needs, 110
Not prating what they would be.

PONTIUS   Thus I leave ye,
Yet shall my prayers still, although my fortunes
Must follow you no more, be still about ye.
Gods give ye where ye fight the victory.
Ye cannot cast my wishes.
    [*Exit Pontius*]

AËTIUS [*to Maximus*]   Come, my lord, 115
Now to the field again.

MAXIMUS   Alas, poor Pontius.
    Exeunt

2.4

    Enter Chilax at one door, Lycinius and Balbus at another
LYCINIUS How now?
CHILAX   She's come.
BALBUS   Then I'll to the Emperor.

CHILAX Do.
    Exit Balbus
        Is the music placed well?
LYCINIUS   Excellent.
CHILAX Lycinius, you and Proculus receive her
  In the great chamber. At her entrance
  Let me alone, and—do you hear, Lycinius?—   5
  Pray let the ladies ply her further off
  And with much more discretion. One word more—
LYCINIUS Well?
CHILAX   Are the jewels and those ropes of pearl
  Laid in the way she passes?
LYCINIUS   Take no care, man.°
    Exit Lycinius. Enter the Emperor Valentinian, Balbus, and
    Proculus
VALENTINIAN What, is she come?
CHILAX   She is, sir. But 'twere best 10
  Your grace were seen last to her.
VALENTINIAN   So I mean.
  Keep the court empty, Proculus.
PROCULUS   'Tis done, sir.
VALENTINIAN Be not too sudden to her.
CHILAX   Good your grace,
  Retire and man yourself. Let us alone,°
  We are no children this way. Do you hear, sir?   15
  'Tis necessary that her waiting-women
  Be cut off in the lobby by some ladies.°
  They'd break the business else.
VALENTINIAN   'Tis true, they shall.
CHILAX Remember your place, Proculus.
PROCULUS   I warrant ye.
    Exit Valentinian, Balbus, and Proculus. Enter Lucina,
    Claudia, and Marcellina
CHILAX [*aside*] She enters. [*Aloud*] Who are waiters there? The
  Emperor°   20
  Calls for his horse to air himself.
LUCINA [*aside*]   I am glad
  I come so happily to take him absent.
  This takes away a little fear. [*Seeing Chilax*] I know him.
  Now I begin to fear again. O honour,
  If ever thou hadst temple in weak woman,   25

And sacrifice of modesty burnt to thee,
Hold me fast now, and help me.
CHILAX   Noble madam,
  Ye are welcome to the court, most nobly welcome.
  Ye are a stranger, lady.
LUCINA   I desire so.
CHILAX A wondrous stranger here, nothing so strange,   30
  And therefore need a guide, I think.
LUCINA   I do, sir,
  And that a good one, too.
CHILAX   My service, lady,
  Shall be your guard in this place. But pray ye tell me,
  Are ye resolved a courtier?
LUCINA   No, I hope, sir.°
CLAUDIA You are, sir?
CHILAX   Yes, my fair one.
CLAUDIA   So it seems,   35
  You are so ready to bestow yourself.
  Pray, what might cost those breeches?
CHILAX   Would you wear 'em?
  Madam, ye have a witty woman.
MARCELLINA   Two, sir,
  Or else ye underbuy us.
LUCINA [to her women]   Leave your talking.
  [To Chilax] But is my lord here, I beseech ye, sir?   40
CHILAX He is, sweet lady, and must take this kindly,
  Exceeding kindly of ye, wondrous kindly,
  Ye come so far to visit him. I'll guide ye.
LUCINA Whither?
CHILAX   Why, to your lord.
LUCINA   Is it so hard, sir,
  To find him in this place without a guide?   45
  For I would willingly not trouble you.
CHILAX It will be so for you that are a stranger.
  Nor can it be a trouble to do service
  To such a worthy beauty, and besides—
MARCELLINA [to Claudia] I see he will go with us.
CLAUDIA [to Marcellina]   Let him amble.°   50
CHILAX It fits not that a lady of your reckoning
  Should pass without attendants.
LUCINA   I have two, sir.

CHILAX I mean without a man. You'll see the Emperor?
LUCINA Alas, I am not fit, sir.
CHILAX   You are well enough.
  He'll take it wondrous kindly. Hark—
    [*He whispers to her*]
LUCINA   Ye flatter.   55
  Good sir, no more of that.
CHILAX   Well, but I tell ye—
LUCINA Will ye go forward? Since I must be manned,
  Pray take your place.
CLAUDIA   Cannot ye man us too, sir?°
CHILAX Give me but time.
MARCELLINA   And you'll try all things?
CHILAX   No,
  I'll make ye no such rash promise.
CLAUDIA   If ye do, sir,   60
  Take heed ye stand to 't.
CHILAX   Wondrous merry, ladies.°
LUCINA The wenches are disposed. Pray, keep your way, sir.
    Exeunt

2.5

    Enter Lycinius with° *Proculus and Balbus*
LYCINIUS She is coming up the stairs. Now the music,
  And as that stirs her, let's set on. Perfumes there.
PROCULUS Discover all the jewels.
LYCINIUS Peace!°
    Music is played
  [*sings*]   *Now the lusty spring is seen:*
                      Green, yellow, gaudy blue,°   5
                      Daintily invite the view
                      On every bush, on every green.°
                      Roses blushing as they blow,
                      And enticing men to pull,°   10
                      Lilies whiter than the snow,
                      Woodbines of sweet honey full:
                      All love's emblems, and all cry,
                      'Ladies, if not plucked, we die.'

Yet the lusty spring hath stayed, 15
Blushing red and purest white,
Daintily to love invite
Every woman, every maid:
Cherries kissing as they grow,
And inviting men to taste, 20
Apples even ripe below,
Winding gently to the waste:
All love's emblems, and all cry,
'Ladies, if not plucked, we die.'

[*A second air is played*]
Hear ye, ladies that despise,
What the mighty love has done. 25
Fear examples and be wise:
Fair Callisto was a nun;
Leda sailing on the stream
To deceive the hopes of men,
Love accounting but a dream, 30
Doted on a silver swan;
Danaë in a brazen tower
Where no love was, loved a shower.°

Hear ye, ladies that are coy, 35
What the mighty love can do.
Fear the fierceness of the boy:°
The chaste moon he makes to woo;
Vesta, kindling holy fires,
Circled round about with spies, 40
Never dreaming loose desires,
Doting at the altar dies.°
Ilion in a short hour higher°
He can once more build, and once more fire.

Enter Chilax, Lucina,° Claudia, and Marcellina

LUCINA [*aside*] Pray heaven my lord be here, for now I fear it. 45
Well, ring, if thou be'st counterfeit or stol'n
(As by this preparation I suspect it),
Thou hast betrayed thy mistress. [*To Chilax*] Pray, sir, forward,
I would fain see my lord.

CHILAX   But tell me, madam,

How do ye like the song?

LUCINA   I like the air well,   50
But for the words, they are lascivious,
And over-light for ladies.

CHILAX   All ours love 'em.

LUCINA 'Tis like enough, for yours are loving ladies.

LYCINIUS Madam, ye are welcome to the court. [*Calls*]
     Who waits?
Attendants for this lady!

LUCINA   You mistake, sir: 55
I bring no triumph with me.

LYCINIUS   But much honour.°

PROCULUS Why, this was nobly done, and like a neighbour,
So freely of yourself to be a visitant.
The Emperor shall give ye thanks for this.

LUCINA   Oh no, sir,
There's nothing to deserve 'em.

PROCULUS   Yes, your presence.   60

LUCINA Good gentlemen, be patient, and believe
I come to see my husband, on command, too.
I were no courtier else.

LYCINIUS   That's all one, lady.
Now ye are here, you're welcome, and the Emperor,
Who loves ye but too well—

LUCINA   No more of that, sir.   65
I came not to be catechized.

PROCULUS [*to Lycinius*]   Ah, sirrah!
[*To Lucina*] And have we got you here? Faith, noble lady,
We'll keep you one month courtier.

LUCINA   Gods defend, sir.
I never liked a trade worse.

PROCULUS   Hark ye.
          [*He whispers to her*]

LUCINA   No, sir!

PROCULUS Ye are grown the strangest lady.

LUCINA   How?

PROCULUS   By heaven,   70
'Tis true I tell ye, and you'll find it.

LUCINA   I?
I'll rather find my grave, and so inform him.°

PROCULUS Is it not pity, gentlemen, this lady

264

(Nay, I'll deal roughly with ye, yet not hurt ye)
Should live alone, and give such heavenly beauty   75
Only to walls and hangings?

LUCINA   Good sir, patience.
I am no wonder, neither come to that end.
Ye do my lord an injury to stay me,
Who, though ye are the Prince's, yet dare tell ye
He keeps no wife for your ways.

BALBUS   Well, well, lady.   80
However you are pleased to think of us,
Ye are welcome, and ye shall be welcome.

LUCINA   Show it
In that I come for, then: in leading me
Where my loved lord is, not in flattery.

        Curtains are opened to show a display of jewels in the
        discovery space

Nay, you may draw the curtain, I have seen 'em,   85
But none worth half my honesty.

        [*Lucina and Lycinius talk apart*]

CLAUDIA   Are these, sir,
Laid here to take?

PROCULUS   Yes, for your lady, gentlewoman.

MARCELLINA We had been doing else.

BALBUS   Meaner jewels
Would fit your worths.

CLAUDIA   And meaner clothes your bodies.

LUCINA The gods shall kill me first.

LYCINIUS   There's better dying°   90
I' th' Emperor's arms. Go to, but be not angry.
These are but talks, sweet lady.

        Enter Phorba and Ardelia

PHORBA Where is this stranger? [*To Claudia and Marcellina*]
    Rushes, ladies, rushes,°
Rushes as green as summer for this stranger.

        [*Exeunt Claudia and Marcellina*]

PROCULUS [*going*] Here's ladies come to see you.

LUCINA   You are gone, then?   95
I take it 'tis your cue.

PROCULUS   Or rather manners:
You are better fitted, madam, we but tire ye,°
Therefore we'll leave you for an hour, and bring

Your much loved lord unto you.

Exeunt Chilax, Lycinius, Proculus, and Balbus

LUCINA   Then I'll thank ye.

[*Aside*] I am betrayed for certain. Well, Lucina,   100
If thou dost fall from virtue, may the earth
That after death should shoot up gardens of thee,
Spreading thy living goodness into branches,
Fly from thee, and the hot sun find thy vices.°

PHORBA   You are a welcome woman.

ARDELIA   Bless me, heaven,   105
How did you find the way to court?

LUCINA   I know not.
Would I had never trod it.

PHORBA   Prithee tell me,
Good noble lady (and, good sweetheart, love us,
For we love thee extremely), is not this place
A paradise to live in?

LUCINA   To those people   110
That know no other paradise but pleasure.
That little I enjoy contents me better.°

ARDELIA   What, heard ye any music yet?

LUCINA   Too much.

PHORBA   You must not be thus froward. What, this gown
Is one o' th' prettiest, by my troth, Ardelia,   115
I ever saw yet: 'twas not to frown in, lady,
Ye put this gown on when ye came.

ARDELIA   How do ye?

[*She takes Lucina's hand*]
Alas, poor wretch, how cold it is!

LUCINA   Content ye.°
I am as well as may be, and as temperate,
If ye will let me be so. Where's my lord?   120
For there's the business that I came for, ladies.

PHORBA   We'll lead ye to him. He's i' th' gallery.

ARDELIA   We'll show ye all the court, too.

LUCINA   Show me him
And you have showed me all I come to look on.

PHORBA   Come on, we'll be your guides, and as ye go,   125
We have some pretty tales to tell ye, lady,
Shall make ye merry too. Ye come not here

To be a sad Lucina.

LUCINA   Would I might not.
    Exeunt

2.6

Enter Chilax and Balbus

CHILAX Now the soft music: Balbus, run.
BALBUS   I fly, boy.
    Exit Balbus
CHILAX The women by this time are worming of her.°
  If she can hold out them, the Emperor
  Takes her to task.
    Music plays
          He has her: hark, the music.
    [*Exit Chilax. Enter the Emperor Valentinian and Lucina*]
LUCINA Good your grace,   5
  Where are my women, sir?
VALENTINIAN   They are wise, beholding
  What you think scorn to look upon, the court's bravery.
  Would you have run away so slyly, lady,
  And not have seen me?
LUCINA   I beseech your majesty,
  Consider what I am, and whose.
VALENTINIAN   I do so.   10
LUCINA Believe me, I shall never make a whore, sir.
VALENTINIAN A friend ye may, and to that man that loves ye
  More than you love your virtue.
LUCINA [*kneeling*]   Sacred Caesar—
VALENTINIAN You shall not kneel to me, sweet.
LUCINA   Look upon me,
  And if ye be so cruel to abuse me,   15
  Think how the gods will take it. Does this beauty
  Afflict your soul? I'll hide it from you ever;
  Nay, more, I will become so leprous°
  That ye shall curse me from ye. My dear lord
  Has served ye ever truly, fought your battles   20
  As if he daily longed to die for Caesar,

Was never traitor, sir, nor never tainted
In all the actions of his life.

VALENTINIAN   I know it.

LUCINA His fame and family have grown together
And spread together like two sailing cedars°   25
Over the Roman diadem. O let not
(As ye have any flesh that's human in you),
The having of a modest wife decline him;
Let not my virtue be the wedge to break him.
I do not think ye are lascivious: 30
These wanton men belie ye. You are Caesar,
Which is the father of the Empire's honour:
Ye are too near the nature of the gods
To wrong the weakest of all creatures, women.

VALENTINIAN [aside] I dare not do it here. [Aloud] Rise, fair Lucina.   35
I did but try your temper: ye are honest,
And, with the commendations wait on that,
I'll lead ye to your lord, and ye to him.°
Wipe your fair eyes. [Aside] He that endeavours ill
May well delay, but never quench his hell.   40
        Exeunt

3.1

Enter Chilax, Lycinius, Proculus, and Balbus

CHILAX 'Tis done, Lycinius.

LYCINIAS   Ha?

CHILAX   I shame to tell it.
  If there be any justice, we are villains
  And must be so rewarded.

BALBUS   If it be done,
  I take it 'tis no time now to repent it.
  Let's make the best o' th' trade.

PROCULUS   Now vengeance take it,   5
  Why should not he have settled on a beauty
  Whose honesty stuck in a piece of tissue,°
  Or one a ring might rule, or such a one
  That had an itching husband to be honourable,
  And ground to get it. If he must have women,°   10
  And no allay without 'em, why not those
  That know the mystery, and are best able
  To play again with judgement? Such as she is,°
  Grant they be won with long siege, endless travail,
  And brought to opportunity with millions;   15
  Yet, when they come to motion, their cold virtue°
  Keeps 'em like cakes of ice. I'll melt a crystal
  And make a dead flint fire himself ere they
  Give greater heat than now-departing embers
  Gives to old men that watch 'em.

LYCINIUS   A good whore   20
  Had saved all this, and happily as wholesome,°
  Ay, and the thing once done, too, as well thought of.
  But this same chastity, forsooth——

PROCULUS   A pox on 't,
  Why should not women be as free as we are?
  They are (but not in open) and far freer;   25
  And the more bold ye bear yourself, more welcome;
  And there is nothing you dare say (but truth),
  But they dare hear.

    Enter the Emperor Valentinian and Lucina

CHILAX   The Emperor! Away,

And if we can repent, let's home and pray.
  / *Exeunt Chilax, Lycinius, Proculus, and Balbus*
VALENTINIAN Your only virtue now is patience.   30
  Take heed, and save your honour. If you talk—
LUCINA As long as there is motion in my body
  And life to give me words, I'll cry for justice.
VALENTINIAN Justice shall never hear ye: I am justice.
LUCINA Wilt thou not kill me? Monster, ravisher,   35
  Thou bitter bane o' th' empire, look upon me,
  And if thy guilty eyes dare see these ruins
  Thy wild lust have laid level with dishonour,
  The sacrilegious razing of this temple
  The mother of thy black sins would have blushed at,   40
  Behold, and curse thyself. The gods will find thee—
  That's all my refuge now—for they are righteous.
  Vengeance and horror circle thee! The empire,
  In which thou liv'st a strong, continued surfeit,
  Like poison will disgorge thee; good men raze thee   45
  For ever being read again but vicious;°
  Women and fearful maids make vows against thee.
  Thy own slaves, if they hear of this, shall hate thee,
  And those thou hast corrupted first fall from thee,
  And, if thou let'st me live, the soldier,   50
  Tired with thy tyrannies, break through obedience
  And shake his strong steel at thee.
VALENTINIAN   This prevails not,
  Nor any agony ye utter, lady.
  If I have done a sin, curse her that drew me.
  Curse the first cause, the witchcraft that abused me.   55
  Curse those fair eyes, and curse that heavenly beauty,
  And curse your being good too.
LUCINA   Glorious thief,
  What restitution canst thou make to save me?
VALENTINIAN I'll ever love and honour you.
LUCINA   Thou canst not,
  For that which was mine honour, thou hast murdered,   60
  And can there be a love in violence?
VALENTINIAN You shall be only mine.
LUCINA   Yet I like better
  Thy villainy than flattery: that's thine own,
  The other, basely counterfeit. Fly from me,

Or, for thy safety sake and wisdom, kill me,   65
For I am worse than thou art: thou may'st pray,
And so recover grace, I am lost forever,
And if thou let'st me live, thou'rt lost thyself too.

VALENTINIAN I fear no loss but love; I stand above it.

LUCINA Call in your lady bawds and gilded panders°   70
And let them triumph too, and sing to Caesar,
'Lucina's fall'n, the chaste Lucina's conquered'.
Gods, what a wretched thing has this man made me!
For I am now no wife for Maximus,
No company for women that are virtuous.   75
No family I now can claim, nor country,
Nor name, but 'Caesar's whore'. O sacred Caesar
(For that should be your title), was your empire,
Your rods and axes that are types of justice,°
Those fires that ever burn to beg you blessings,   80
The people's adoration, fear of nations,
What victory can bring ye home, what else
The useful elements can make your servants,
Even light itself, and sons of light—truth, justice,
Mercy, and starlike piety—sent to you   85
(And from the gods themselves) to ravish women?
The curses that I owe to enemies
(Even those the Sabines sent, when Romulus,
As thou hast me, ravished their noble maids),°
Made more and heavier, light on thee.

VALENTINIAN   This helps not.   90

LUCINA The sins of Tarquin be remembered in thee,
And, where there has a chaste wife been abused,
Let it be thine: the shame thine, thine the slaughter,
And, last, forever thine the feared example.
Where shall poor virtue live, now I am fallen?   95
What can your honours now, and empire, make me,
But a more glorious whore?

VALENTINIAN   A better woman;
But if ye will be blind, and scorn it, who can help it?
Come, leave these lamentations: they do nothing
But make a noise. I am the same man still.   100
Were it to do again (therefore be wiser),°
By all this holy light, I should attempt it.
Ye are so excellent and made to ravish,

271

(There were no pleasure in ye else)—

LUCINA   Oh villain!

VALENTINIAN —So bred for man's amazement that my reason   105
　　And every help to hold me right has lost me.
　　The god of love himself had been before me,
　　Had he but power to see ye. Tell me justly,
　　How can I choose but err, then? If ye dare,
　　Be mine, and only mine, for ye are so precious   110
　　I envy any other should enjoy ye,
　　Almost look on ye. And your daring husband
　　Shall know he's kept an offering from the empire
　　Too holy for his altars. Be the mightiest:
　　More than myself I'll make it. If ye will not,°   115
　　Sit down with this, and silence; for which wisdom
　　Ye shall have use of me, and much honour ever,°
　　And be the same you were. If ye divulge it,
　　Know I am far above the faults I do,
　　And those I do I am able to forgive too;   120
　　And where your credit in the knowledge of it
　　May be with gloss enough suspected, mine
　　Is as mine own command shall make it.°
　　Princes, though they be sometime subject to loose whispers,
　　Yet wear they two-edged swords for open censures.   125
　　Your husband cannot help ye, nor the soldier.
　　Your husband is my creature, they my weapons,
　　And only where I bid 'em strike. I feed 'em,
　　Nor can the gods be angry at this action,
　　For as they make me most, they mean me happiest,°   130
　　Which I had never been without this pleasure.
　　Consider, and farewell. You'll find your women
　　At home before ye. They have had some sport too,
　　But are more thankful for it.

　　　　　　　Exit Valentinian

LUCINA   Destruction find thee!
　　Now which way must I go? My honest house   135
　　Will shake to shelter me, my husband fly me;
　　My family, because they are honest and desire to be so,
　　Must not endure me, not a neighbour know me.
　　What woman now dare see me without blushes,
　　And, pointing as I pass, 'There, there, behold her,   140
　　Look on her, little children, that is she,

272

That handsome lady, mark'? O my sad fortunes!
Is this the end of goodness, this the prize°
Of all my early prayers to protect me?
Why, then, I see there is no god but power,   145
Nor virtue now alive that cares for us,
But what is either lame or sensual.
How had I been thus wretched else?
     [*She sits on the ground and weeps.*] *Enter Maximus and*
      Aëtius

AËTIUS   Let Titius
Command the company that Pontius lost,
And see the fosses deeper.

MAXIMUS   How now, sweetheart?   150
What make you here, and thus?

AËTIUS   Lucina weeping?
This must be much offence.

MAXIMUS   Look up and tell me,
Why are you thus? My ring? O friend, I have found it.
Ye were at court, sweet.

LUCINA [*showing the ring*] Yes, this brought me thither.

MAXIMUS Rise, and go home. I have my fears, Aëtius.   155
O my best friend, I am ruined. Go, Lucina,
Already in thy tears I have read thy wrongs,
Already found a Caesar. Go, thou lily,
Thou sweetly drooping flower. Go, silver swan,
And sing thine own sad requiem. Go, Lucina,°   160
And if thou dar'st, outlive this wrong.

LUCINA   I dare not.

AËTIUS [*to Maximus*] Is that the ring ye lost?

MAXIMUS   That, that, Aëtius,
That cursed ring, myself, and all my fortunes.
'T has pleased the Emperor, my noble master,
For all my services and dangers for him,   165
To make me mine own pander. Was this justice?
O my Aëtius, have I lived to bear this?

LUCINA Farewell forever, sir.

MAXIMUS   That's a sad saying,
But such a one becomes ye well, Lucina.
And yet methinks we should not part so lightly.   170
Our loves have been of longer growth, more rooted
Than the sharp word of one farewell can scatter.

Kiss me.
> [*She kisses him on the mouth*]
>> I find no Caesar here. These lips
Taste not of ravisher in my opinion.
Was it not so?
LUCINA   O yes.
MAXIMUS   I dare believe thee,   175
For thou wert ever truth itself, and sweetness.
Indeed she was, Aëtius.
AËTIUS   So she is still.
MAXIMUS Once more.
> [*He and Lucina kiss again*]
>> O my Lucina, O my comfort,
The blessing of my youth, the life of my life.
AËTIUS I have seen enough to stagger my obedience.°   180
Hold me, ye equal gods; this is too sinful.
MAXIMUS Why wert thou chosen out to make a whore of?
To me thou wert too chaste. Fall crystal fountains
And ever feed your streams, you rising sorrows,
Till you have dropped your mistress into marble.°   185
Now go forever from me.
LUCINA   Long farewell, sir.
And as I have been loyal, gods think on me.
MAXIMUS Stay, let me once more bid farewell, Lucina.
> [*He kisses her*]
Farewell, thou excellent example of us.
Thou starry virtue, fare thee well. Seek heaven,   190
And there by Cassiopeia shine in glory.°
We are too base and dirty to preserve thee.
AËTIUS Nay, I must kiss too. Such a kiss again,
And from a woman of so ripe a virtue,
Aëtius must not take.
> [*He kisses her*]
>> Farewell, thou phoenix,°   195
If thou wilt die, Lucina (which, well weighed,
If you can cease a while from these strange thoughts,
I wish were rather altered)—
LUCINA   No.
AËTIUS   Mistake not.
I would not stain your honour for the empire,
Nor any way decline you to discredit: 200

274

'Tis not my fair profession but a villain's.
I find and feel your loss as deep as you do,
And am the same Aëtius, still as honest,
The same life I have still for Maximus,
The same sword wear for you, where justice wills me,   205
And 'tis no dull one. Therefore misconceive not.
Only I would have you live a little longer,
But a short year.

MAXIMUS   She must not.
LUCINA   Why so long, sir?
    Am I not grey enough with grief already?

AËTIUS To draw from that wild man a sweet repentance,   210
    And goodness in his days to come.

MAXIMUS   They are so,
    And will be ever coming, my Aëtius.

AËTIUS For who knows but the sight of you (presenting
    His swoll'n sins at the full) and your fair virtues,
    May like a fearful vision fright his follies,   215
    And once more bend him right again; which blessing
    (If your dark wrongs would give you leave to read)
    Is more than death, and the reward more glorious.
    Death only eases you, this the whole empire.
    Besides, compelled and forced with violence   220
    To what ye have done, the deed is none of yours;
    No, nor the justice neither. Ye may live,°
    And still a worthier woman, still more honoured.
    For are those trees the worse we tear the fruits from?
    Or should the eternal gods desire to perish   225
    Because we daily violate their truths,
    Which is the chastity of heaven? No, lady,
    If ye dare live, ye may; and, as our sins
    Makes them more full of equity and justice,°
    So this compulsive wrong makes you more perfect.   230
    The empire too will bless ye.

MAXIMUS   Noble sir,
    If she were anything to me but honour,
    (And that that's wedded to me too, laid in,°
    Not to be worn away without my being),
    Or could the wrong be hers alone, or mine,   235
    Or both our wrongs, not tied to after issues,°
    Not born anew in all our names and kindreds,

I would desire her live; nay, more, compel her.
But since it was not youth, but malice, did it,
And not her own, nor mine, but both our losses   240
(Nor stays it there but that our names must find it,
Even those to come; and when they read she lived,
Must they not ask how often she was ravished,
And make a doubt she loved that more than wedlock?),
Therefore she must not live.
AËTIUS   Therefore she must live,   245
  To teach the world such deaths are superstitious.
LUCINA The tongues of angels cannot alter me;
  For could the world again restore my credit
  As fair and absolute as first I bred it,
  That world I should not trust again. The empire   250
  By my life can get nothing but my story,
  Which, whilst I breathe, must be but his abuses.
  And where ye counsel me to live that Caesar
  May see his errors and repent, I'll tell ye
  His penitence is but increase of pleasures,   255
  His prayers never said but to deceive us,
  And when he weeps, as you think for his vices,
  'Tis but as killing drops from baleful yew trees
  That rot their honest neighbour. If he can grieve°
  As one that yet desires his free conversion   260
  And almost glories in his penitence,
  I'll leave him robes to mourn in, my sad ashes.
AËTIUS The farewells then of happy souls be with thee,
  And to thy memory be ever sung
  The praises of a just and constant lady.   265
  This sad day whilst I live, a soldier's tears°
  I'll offer on thy monument, and bring,
  Full of thy noble self with tears untold yet,°
  Many a worthy wife to weep thy ruin.
MAXIMUS All that is chaste, upon thy tomb shall flourish, 270
  All living epitaphs be thine. Time, story,
  And what is left behind to piece our lives°
  Shall be no more abused with tales and trifles,
  But, full of thee, stand to eternity.°
AËTIUS Once more farewell. Go, find Elysium,°   275
  There where the happy souls are crowned with blessings,
  There where 'tis ever spring, and ever summer.

MAXIMUS There where no bedrid justice comes: Truth, Honour,°
　　　Are keepers of that blessed place. Go thither,
　　　For here thou liv'st chaste fire in rotten timber.   280
AËTIUS And so our last farewells.
MAXIMUS   Gods give thee justice.
　　　Exit Lucina
AËTIUS [*aside*] His thoughts begin to work. I fear him, yet°
　　　He ever was a noble Roman. But
　　　I know not what to think on 't. He hath suffered
　　　Beyond a man, if he stand this.
MAXIMUS   Aëtius,°   285
　　　Am I alive, or has a dead sleep seized me?
　　　It was my wife the Emperor abused thus,
　　　And I must say I am glad I had her for him,°
　　　Must I not, my Aëtius?
AËTIUS   I am stricken
　　　With such a stiff amazement that no answer   290
　　　Can readily come from me, nor no comfort.
　　　Will ye go home, or go to my house?
MAXIMUS   Neither.
　　　I have no home, and you are mad, Aëtius,
　　　To keep me company. I am a fellow
　　　My own sword would forsake, not tied unto me.°   295
　　　A pander is a prince to what I am fall'n.°
　　　By heaven I dare do nothing.
AËTIUS   Ye do better.
MAXIMUS I am made a branded slave, Aëtius,
　　　And yet I bless the maker.
　　　Death o' my soul, must I endure this tamely?   300
　　　Must Maximus be mentioned for his tales?°
　　　I am a child too. What should I do railing?
　　　I cannot mend myself: 'tis Caesar did it,
　　　And what am I to him?
AËTIUS   'Tis well considered.
　　　However you are tainted, be no traitor: 305
　　　Time may outwear the first, the last lives ever.
MAXIMUS O that thou wert not living and my friend!
AËTIUS [*aside*] I'll bear a wary eye upon your actions.
　　　I fear ye, Maximus, nor can I blame thee
　　　If thou break'st out, for, by the gods, thy wrong   310
　　　Deserves a general ruin. Do ye love me?°

MAXIMUS That's all I have to live on.
AËTIUS   Then go with me.
  Ye shall not to your own house.
MAXIMUS   Nor to any.
  My griefs are greater far than walls can compass,
  And yet I wonder how it happens with me   315
  I am not dangerous, and, o' my conscience,
  Should I now see the Emperor i' th' heat on 't,°
  I should not chide him for 't. An awe runs through me:
  I feel it sensibly, that binds me to it.
  'Tis at my heart now: there it sits and rules,   320
  And methinks 'tis a pleasure to obey it.
AËTIUS [aside] This is a mask to cozen me. I know ye,
  And how far ye dare do (no Roman farther,
  Nor with more fearless valour); and I'll watch ye.
  [Aloud] Keep that obedience still.
MAXIMUS   Is a wife's loss   325
  (For her abuse much good may do his grace:°
  I'll make as bold with his wife, if I can)
  More than the fading of a few fresh colours,
  More than a lusty spring lost?
AËTIUS   No more, Maximus,°
  To one that truly lives.
MAXIMUS   Why, then, I care not.   330
  I can live well enough, Aëtius.
  For (look you, friend), for virtue and those trifles,
  They may be bought, they say.
AËTIUS [aside]   He's crazed a little.
  His grief has made him talk things from his nature.°
MAXIMUS But chastity is not a thing (I take it),   335
  To get in Rome, unless it be bespoken
  A hundred year before (is it, Aëtius?),
  By'r lady, and well-handled too i' th' breeding.°
AËTIUS Will ye go any way?
MAXIMUS   I'll tell thee, friend,
  If my wife for all this should be a whore now,   340
  A kind of kicker-out of sheets, 'twould vex me,
  For I am not angry yet. The Emperor
  Is young and handsome, and the woman flesh,°
  And may not these two couple without scratching?

AËTIUS Alas, my noble friend.

MAXIMUS   'Alas' not me: 345
  I am not wretched, for there's no man miserable
  But he that makes himself so.

AËTIUS   Will ye walk yet?

MAXIMUS Come, come, she dare not die, friend: that's the truth
    on 't.
  She knows the enticing sweets and delicacies
  Of a young prince's pleasures, and I thank her   350
  She has made a way for Maximus to rise by.
  Will 't not become me bravely? Why do you think
  She wept and said she was ravished? Keep it here°
  And I'll discover to you.

AËTIUS   Well?

MAXIMUS   She knows
  I love no bitten flesh, and out of that hope°   355
  She might be from me, she contrived this knavery.°
  Was it not monstrous, friend?

AËTIUS [aside]   Does he but seem so,
  Or is he mad indeed?

MAXIMUS   O gods, my heart!

AËTIUS Would it would fairly break.

MAXIMUS Methinks I am somewhat wilder than I was,   360
  And yet I thank the gods I know my duty.
      Enter Claudia

CLAUDIA Nay, ye may spare your tears. She's dead. She is so.

MAXIMUS Why, so it should be. How?

CLAUDIA   When first she entered
  Into her house, after a world of weeping
  And blushing like the sunset, as we saw her,   365
  'Dare I,' said she, 'defile this house with "whore"
  In which his noble family has flourished?'
  At which she fell, and stirred no more. We rubbed her—

MAXIMUS No more of that. Begone.
      Exit Claudia

                Now, my Aëtius,
  If thou wilt do me pleasure, weep a little.   370
  I am so parched I cannot.
      [Aëtius weeps. Then Maximus weeps]
            Your example

Has brought the rain down now. Now lead me, friend,
And as we walk together let's pray together truly
I may not fall from faith.

AËTIUS   That's nobly spoken.

MAXIMUS Was I not wild, Aëtius?

AËTIUS   Somewhat troubled.   375

MAXIMUS I felt no sorrow then. Now I'll go with ye;
But do not name the woman. Fie, what fool
Am I to weep thus! Gods, Lucina, take thee,
For thou wert even the best and worthiest lady.

AËTIUS Good sir, no more; I shall be melted with it.°   380

MAXIMUS I have done; and, good sir, comfort me.
Would there were wars now.

AËTIUS Settle your thoughts, come.

MAXIMUS   So I have now, friend.
Of my deep lamentations here's an end.

          Exeunt

3.2

Enter Pontius, Phidias, and Aretus

PHIDIAS By my faith, Captain Pontius, besides pity
Of your fall'n fortunes, what to say I know not,
For 'tis too true the Emperor desires not,
But my best master, any soldier near him.°

ARETUS And when he understands he cast your fortunes°   5
For disobedience, how can we incline him
(That are but under-persons to his favours),
To any fair opinion? Can ye sing?

PONTIUS Not to please him, Aretus, for my songs
Go not to th' lute or viol but to th' trumpet,   10
My time kept on a target, and my subject°
The well-struck wounds of men, not love or women.

PHIDIAS And those he understands not.

PONTIUS   He should, Phidias.°

ARETUS Could you not leave this killing way a little?
You must, if here you would plant yourself, and rather   15
Learn, as we do, to like what those affect
That are above us; wear their actions

And think they keep us warm too; what they say,
Though oftentimes they speak a little foolishly,
Not stay to construe but prepare to execute,° 20
And think, however the end falls, the business
Cannot run empty-handed.
PHIDIAS   Can ye flatter,°
And, if it were put to you, lie a little?
PONTIUS Yes, if it be a living.
ARETUS   That's well said, then.
PONTIUS But must these lies and flatteries be believed, then? 25
PHIDIAS Oh yes, by any means.
PONTIUS   By any means, then,
I cannot lie nor flatter.
ARETUS   Ye must swear, too,
If ye be there.
PONTIUS   I can swear, if they move me.
PHIDIAS Cannot ye forswear too?
PONTIUS   The court forever,
If it be grown so wicked. 30
ARETUS You should procure a little too.
PONTIUS   What's that?
Men's honest sayings for my truth?
ARETUS   Oh no, sir,°
But women's honest actions for your trial.°
PONTIUS Do you do all these things?
PHIDIAS   Do you not like 'em?
PONTIUS Do ye ask me seriously or trifle with me? 35
I am not so low yet, to be your mirth.
ARETUS You do mistake us, Captain, for sincerely
We ask you how you like 'em.
PONTIUS   Then sincerely
I tell ye I abhor 'em. They are ill ways,
And I will starve before I fall into 'em; 40
The doers of 'em wretches, their base hungers
Cares not whose bread they eat, nor how they get it.
ARETUS What then, sir?
PONTIUS   If you profess this wickedness,
Because ye have been soldiers and borne arms,
The servants of the brave Aëtius 45
And by him put to th' Emperor, give me leave
(Or I must take it else), to say ye are villains,

For all your golden coats; debauched, base villains.
Yet I do wear a sword to tell ye so.
Is this the way you mark out for a soldier,   50
A man that has commanded for the empire
And borne the reputation of a man?
Are there not lazy things enough called fools and cowards,
And poor enough to be preferred for panders,
But wanting soldiers must be knaves too? Ha!   55
This the trim course of life? Were ye not born bawds,°
And so inherit but your rights? I am poor,
And may expect a worse, yet digging, pruning,°
Mending of broken ways, carrying of water,°
Planting of worts and onions, anything   60
That's honest, and a man's, I'll rather choose;
Ay, and live better on it, which is juster;
Drink my well-gotten water with more pleasure,
When my endeavour's done and wages paid me,
Than you do wine; eat my coarse bread not cursed,   65
And mend upon 't (your diets are diseases);°
And sleep as soundly, when my labour bids me,
As any forward pander of ye all,
And rise a great deal honester. My garments,
Though not as yours, the soft sins of the empire,   70
Yet may be warm, and keep the biting wind out,
When every single breath of poor opinion
Finds you through all your velvets.

ARETUS   You have hit it,°
    Nor are we those we seem. The lord Aëtius
    Put us good men to th' Emperor; so we have served him,°   75
    Though much neglected for it, so dare be still:
    Your curses are not ours. We have seen your fortune,
    But yet know no way to redeem it. Means,
    Such as we have, ye shall not want, brave Pontius;
    But pray be temperate. If we can wipe out   80
    The way of your offences, we are yours sir,
    And you shall live at court an honest man too.°

PHIDIAS That little meat and means we have, we'll share it.
    Fear not to be as we are: what we told ye
    Were but mere trials of your truth. You're worthy,   85
    And so we'll ever hold ye. Suffer better,

And then ye are a right man, Pontius.
If my good master be not ever angry,°
Ye shall command again.

PONTIUS I have found two good men. Use my life,   90
For it is yours, and all I have to thank ye.

    Exeunt

3.3

Enter Maximus

MAXIMUS There's no way else to do it: he must die.
This friend must die, this soul of Maximus,
Without whom I am nothing but my shame;
This perfectness that keeps me from opinion°
Must die, or I must live thus branded ever.   5
A hard choice, and a fatal. Gods, ye have given me
A way to credit, but the ground to go on
Ye have levelled with that precious life I love most.
Yet I must on, and through, for if I offer
To take my way without him, like a sea   10
He bears his high command twixt me and vengeance,
And in my own road sinks me. He is honest,°
Of a most constant loyalty to Caesar,
And when he shall but doubt, I dare attempt him.
But make a question of this ill, but say,°   15
'What is a Caesar, that he dare do this?',
Dead sure he cuts me off. Aëtius dies,
Or I have lost myself! Why should I kill him?
Why should I kill myself? For 'tis my killing:
Aëtius is my root, and wither him,°   20
Like a decaying branch I fall to nothing.
Is he not more to me than wife, than Caesar,
Though I had now my safe revenge upon him?
Is he not more than rumour, and his friendship°
Sweeter than the love of women? What is honour   25
We all so strangely are bewitched withal?
Can it relieve me if I want? He has.
Can honour, twixt the incensèd prince and envy,

Bear up the lives of worthy men? He has.°
Can honour pull the wings off fearful cowards   30
And make 'em turn again like tigers? He has,°
And I have lived to see this, and preservèd so.°
Why should this empty word incite me then
To what is ill and cruel? Let her perish.
A friend is more than all the world, than honour.   35
She is a woman and her loss the less,
And with her go my griefs. But hark ye, Maximus,
Was she not yours? Did she not die to tell ye
She was a ravished woman? Did not justice
Nobly begin with her, that not deserved it,   40
And shall he live that did it? Stay a little,
Can this abuse die here? Shall not men's tongues
Dispute it afterward, and say I gave
(Affecting dull obedience and tame duty,
And led away with fondness of a friendship)°
The only virtue of the world to slander?   45
Is not this certain: was not she a chaste one,
And such a one that no compeer dwelt with her,
One of so sweet a virtue that Aëtius
(Even he himself, this friend that holds me from it),   50
Out of his worthy love to me and justice°
(Had it not been on Caesar) had revenged her?
By heaven, he told me so. What shall I do then?
          Enter a Servant°
Can other men affect it, and I cold?°
I fear he must not live.
SERVANT   My lord, the general   55
Is come to seek ye.
MAXIMUS   Go, entreat him to enter.
     [*Exit Servant*]
O brave Aëtius, I could wish thee now
As far from friendship to me as from fears,
That I might cut thee off like that I weighed not.
Is there no way without him to come near it?   60
For out of honesty he must destroy me
If I attempt it. He must die as others,°
And I must loose him: 'tis necessity,°
Only the time and means is all the difference.°
But yet I would not make a murder of him,   65

284

Take him directly for my doubts. He shall die:°
I have found a way to do it, and a safe one.
It shall be honour to him too. I know not
What to determine certain, I am so troubled,
And such a deal of conscience presses me.   70
    Enter Aëtius
Would I were dead myself.

AËTIUS   You run away well.
How got you from me, friend?

MAXIMUS   That that leads madmen,
A strong imagination, made me wander.

AËTIUS I thought ye had been more settled.

MAXIMUS   I am well,
But you must give me leave a little sometimes   75
To have a buzzing in my brains.

AËTIUS [*aside*]   Ye are dangerous,
But I'll prevent it if I can. [*Aloud*] Ye told me
You would go to th' army.

MAXIMUS   Why, to have my throat cut?
Must he not be the bravest man, Aëtius,
That strikes me first?

AËTIUS   You promised me a freedom   80
From all these thoughts. And why should any strike you?°

MAXIMUS I am an enemy, a wicked one,
Worse than the foes of Rome. I am a coward,
A cuckold and a coward: that's two causes
Why everyone should beat me.

AËTIUS   Ye are neither,   85
And durst another tell me so, he died for it;
For thus far on mine honour I'll assure you
No man more loved than you, and, for your valour,
And what ye may be, fair, no man more followed.°

MAXIMUS A doughty man indeed, but that's all one.   90
The Emperor, nor all the princes living,
Shall find a flaw in my coat. I have suffered,
And can yet. Let them find inflictions,
I'll find a body for 'em, or I'll break it.
'Tis not a wife can thrust me out. Some looked for it,   95
But let 'em look till they are blind with looking;
They are but fools. Yet there is anger in me
That I would fain disperse. And now I think on 't,

You told me, friend, the provinces are stirring:
We shall have sport, I hope, then, and what's dangerous   100
A battle shall beat from me.

AËTIUS   Why do ye eye me
With such a settled look?

MAXIMUS   Pray tell me this:
Do we not love extremely? I love you so.

AËTIUS If I should say I loved not you as truly,
I should do that I never durst do, lie.   105

MAXIMUS If I should die, would it not grieve you much?

AËTIUS Without all doubt.

MAXIMUS   And could you live without me?

AËTIUS It would much trouble me to live without ye:
Our loves and loving souls have been so used
Both to one household in us. But to die   110
Because I could not make you live were woman,
Far much too weak. Were it to save your worth,
Or to redeem your name from rooting out,
To quit you bravely fighting from the foe,
Or fetch ye off where honour had engaged ye,°   115
I ought and would die for ye.

MAXIMUS   Truly spoken.
[*Aside*] What beast but I, that must, could hurt this man now?
Would he had ravished me, I would have paid him,°
I would have taught him such a trick his eunuchs
Nor all his black-eyed boys e'er dreamt of yet.°   120
By all the gods, I am mad now. Now were Caesar
Within my reach, and on his glorious top
The pile of all the world, he went to nothing.°
The destinies nor all the dames of hell,°
Were I once grappled with him, should relieve him;   125
No, not the hope of mankind more: all perished.°
But this is words, and weakness.

AËTIUS   Ye look strangely.

MAXIMUS I look but as I am: I am a stranger.

AËTIUS   To me?

MAXIMUS To everyone: I am no Roman,°
Nor what I am do I know.

AËTIUS   Then I'll leave ye.   130

MAXIMUS I find I am best so. If ye meet with Maximus,°

Pray bid him be an honest man for my sake.
You may do much upon him. For his shadow,°
Let me alone.
AËTIUS   Ye were not wont to talk thus,
And to your friend. Ye have some danger in you   135
That willingly would run to action.
Take heed, by all our love, take heed.
MAXIMUS   I, 'danger'?
I, willing to do anything? Ay, die!
Has not my wife been dead two days already?
Are not my mournings by this time moth-eaten?   140
Are not her sins dispersed to other women,
And many one ravished to relieve her?
Have I shed tears these twelve hours?
AËTIUS   Now ye weep.
MAXIMUS Some lazy drops that stayed behind.
AËTIUS   I'll tell ye,
And I must tell ye truth, were it not hazard   145
And almost certain loss of all the empire,
I would join with ye. Were it any man's
But his life that is life of us, he lost it°
For doing of this mischief: I would take it,
And to your rest give ye a brave revenge.   150
But as the rule now stands, and as he rules,
And as the nations hold in disobedience°
(One pillar falling, all must fall), I dare not,
Nor is it just you should be suffered in it.
Therefore again take heed: on foreign foes   155
We are our own revengers, but at home,
On princes that are eminent and ours,°
'Tis fit the gods should judge us. Be not rash,
Nor let your angry steel cut those ye know not;
For by this fatal blow (if ye dare strike it,   160
As I see great aims in ye) those unborn yet
And those to come of them, and those succeeding,
Shall bleed the wrath of Maximus. For me,
As ye now bear yourself I am your friend still.
If ye fall off, I will not flatter ye,   165
And in my hands, were ye my soul, you perished.
Once more be careful, stand, and still be worthy.

I'll leave ye for this hour.
MAXIMUS   Pray do.
        Exit Aëtius

                              'Tis done.
And, friendship, since thou canst not hold in dangers,
Give me a certain ruin, I must through it.°   170
        Exit

4.1

Enter the Emperor Valentinian, Lycinius, Chilax, and Balbus

VALENTINIAN Dead?

CHILAX   So 'tis thought, sir.

VALENTINIAN   How?

LYCINIUS   Grief and disgrace,
    As people say.

VALENTINIAN   No more, I have too much on 't;
    Too much by you, you whetters of my follies,
    Ye angel formers of my sins, but devils.
    Where is your cunning now? You would work wonders;   5
    There was no chastity above your practice;
    You would undertake to make her love her wrongs
    And dote upon her rape. Mark what I tell ye,
    If she be dead—

CHILAX   Alas, sir!

VALENTINIAN   Hang ye, rascals!
    Ye blasters of my youth, if she be gone,   10
    'Twere better ye had been your fathers' camels,
    Groaned under daily weights of wood and water—
    Am I not Caesar?

LYCINIUS   Mighty and our maker.°

VALENTINIAN —Than thus have given my pleasures to destruction.
    Look she be living, slaves.

LYCINIUS   We are no gods, sir,   15
    If she be dead, to make her new again.

VALENTINIAN She cannot die, she must not die. Are those
    I plant my love upon but common livers,
    Their hours as others', told 'em? Can they be ashes?°
    Why do ye flatter a belief into me   20
    That I am all that is, the world's my creature,
    The trees bring forth their fruit when I say 'Summer',
    The wind, that knows no limit but his wildness,
    At my command moves not a leaf, the sea
    With his proud mountain waters envying heaven,   25
    When I say 'Still', run into crystal mirrors?
    Can I do this, and she die? Why, ye bubbles
    That with my least breath break, no more remembered,

Ye moths that fly about my flame and perish,
Ye golden cankerworms that eat my honours,   30
Living no longer than my spring of favour,
Why do ye make me God that can do nothing?
Is she not dead?
CHILAX   All women are not with her.
VALENTINIAN A common whore serves you and far above ye;
   The pleasures of a body lamed with lewdness,   35
   A mere perpetual motion makes ye happy.
   Am I a man to traffic with diseases?
   Can any but a chastity serve Caesar,
   And such a one the gods would kneel to purchase?
   You think because you have bred me up to pleasures   40
   And almost run me over all the rare ones,°
   Your wives will serve the turn. I care not for 'em:
   Your wives are fencers' whores, and shall be footmen's.°
   Though sometimes my nice will, or rather anger,°
   Have made ye cuckolds for variety,   45
   I would not have ye hope nor dream, ye poor ones,
   Always so great a blessing from me. Go,
   Get your own infamy hereafter, rascals.
   I have done too nobly for ye: ye enjoy
   Each one an heir, the royal seed of Caesar,   50
   And I may curse ye for 't. Your wanton jennets,
   That are so proud the wind gets 'em with fillies,°
   Taught me this foul intemperance. Thou, Lycinius,
   Hast such a Messalina, such a Lais,°
   The backs of bulls cannot content, nor stallions;°   55
   The sweat of fifty men a night does nothing.
LYCINIUS Your grace but jests, I hope.
VALENTINIAN   'Tis oracle.°
   The sins of other women put by hers°
   Show off like sanctities. Thine's a fool, Chilax,
   Yet she can tell to twenty, and all lovers,   60
   And all lain with her too, and all as she is,
   Rotten, and ready for an hospital.°
   Yours is a holy whore, friend Balbus.
BALBUS   Well, sir.
VALENTINIAN One that can pray away the sins she suffers,
   But not the punishments. She has had ten bastards   65

(Five of 'em now are lictors)—yet she prays.
She has been the song of Rome and common Pasquil.°
Since I durst see a wench, she was camp mistress,°
And mustered all the cohorts, paid 'em too
(They have it yet to show)—and yet she prays.° 70
She is now to enter old men that are children
And have forgot their rudiments. Am I
Left for these withered vices? And but one,
But one of all the world that could content me,
And snatched away in showing? If your wives 75
Be not yet witches, or yourselves, now be so
And save your lives: raise me this noble beauty
As when I forced her, full of constancy,
Or by the gods—
LYCINIUS   Most sacred Caesar—
VALENTINIAN   Slaves!
    Enter Proculus, [with a letter]
LYCINIUS Good Proculus.
PROCULUS *[to someone off stage]* By heaven, you shall not see it! 80
    It may concern the empire.
VALENTINIAN   Ha? What said'st thou?
    Is she not dead?
PROCULUS   Not anyone I know, sir.
    I come to bring your grace a letter, here,
    Scattered belike i' th' court.
        [He gives Valentinian the letter]
                    'Tis sent to Maximus,
    And bearing danger in it.
VALENTINIAN   Danger? Where? 85
    Double our guard.
PROCULUS   Nay, nowhere but i' th' letter.
VALENTINIAN What an afflicted conscience do I live with,
    And what a beast I am grown! I had forgotten
    To ask heaven mercy for my fault, and was now
    Even ravishing again her memory. 90
    I find there must be danger in this deed.
    Why do I stand disputing, then, and whining?
    For what is not the gods' to give? They cannot,
    Though they would link their powers in one, do mischief.
    This letter may betray me. Get ye gone 95

And wait me in the garden: guard the house well,
And keep this from the Empress.
    Exeunt Lycinius, Chilax, Balbus, and Proculus
                    The name Maximus
Runs through me like a fever. This may be
Some private letter upon private business,
Nothing concerning me. Why should I open 't?   100
I have done him wrong enough already. Yet
It may concern me too, the time so tells me.
The wicked deed I have done assures me 'tis so.
Be what it will, I'll see it. If that be not
Part of my fears, among my other sins°   105
I'll purge it out in prayers.
    [*He opens the letter*]
                    How? What's this?
(*Reads*) 'Lord Maximus, you love Aëtius
And are his noble friend too. Bid him be less;
I mean less with the people. Times are dangerous:
The army's his, the Emperor in doubts,   110
And, as some will not stick to say, declining.
You stand a constant man in either fortune.
Persuade him, he is lost else. Though ambition
Be the last sin he touches at, or never,
Yet what the people, mad with loving him,   115
And, as they willingly desire another,°
May tempt him to, or rather force his goodness,
Is to be doubted mainly. He is all,
As he stands now, but the mere name of Caesar,
And should the Emperor enforce him lesser,   120
Not coming from himself, it were more dangerous.°
He is honest, and will hear you. Doubts are scattered,
And almost come to growth in every household.
Yet (in my foolish judgement) were this mastered,
The people that are now but rage and his   125
Might again be obedience. You shall know me
When Rome is fair again; till when I love you.'
No name! This may be cunning, yet it seems not,
For there is nothing in it but is certain,
Besides my safety. Had not good Germanicus,°   130
That was as loyal and as straight as he is,
If not prevented by Tiberius,

Been by the soldiers forced their emperor?
He had, and 'tis my wisdom to remember it.
And was not Corbulo (even that Corbulo,°   135
That ever fortunate and living Roman
That broke the heart-strings of the Parthians
And brought Arsaces' line upon their knees°
Chained to the awe of Rome), because he was thought
(And but in wine once) fit to make a Caesar,   140
Cut off by Nero? I must seek my safety,
For 'tis the same again, if not beyond it.
I know the soldier loves him more than heaven,
And will adventure all his gods to raise him.°
Me he hates more than peace. What this may breed,   145
If dull security and confidence
Let him grow up, a fool may find, and laughed at.°
But why lord Maximus I injured so
Should be the man to counsel him, I know not,
More than he has been friend and loved allegiance.   150
What now he is I fear; for his abuses,
Without the people, dare draw blood. [*Calls*] Who waits there?
        Enter a Servant
SERVANT Your grace.
VALENTINIAN   Call Phidias and Aretus hither.
        [*Exit Servant*]
I'll find a day for him, too. 'Times are dangerous:
The army his, the Emperor in doubts.'   155
I find it is too true. Did he not tell me,
As if he had intent to make me odious,
And to my face, and by a way of terror,
What vices I was grounded in, and almost
Proclaimed the soldier's hate against me? Is not   160
The sacred name and dignity of Caesar
(Were this Aëtius more than man) sufficient
To shake off all his honesty? He's dangerous,
Though he be good; and though a friend, a feared one,
And such I must not sleep by. [*Calls*] Are they come yet? 165
I do believe this fellow, and I thank him.°
'Twas time to look about. If I must perish,°
Yet shall my fears go foremost.
        Enter Phidias and Aretus
PHIDIAS   Life to Caesar.

VALENTINIAN Is Lord Aëtius waiting?
PHIDIAS   Not this morning.
  I rather think he's with the army.
VALENTINIAN [*aside*]   'Army'?   170
  I do not like that 'army'. [*Aloud*] Go unto him
  And bid him straight attend me, and, do ye hear,
  Come private without any. I have business
  Only for him.
PHIDIAS   Your grace's pleasure.
VALENTINIAN   Go.
    Exit Phidias
  What soldier is the same (I have seen him often)   175
  That keeps you company, Aretus?
ARETUS Me, sir?
VALENTINIAN Ay, you, sir.
ARETUS   One they call Pontius.
  An 't please your grace.
VALENTINIAN   A captain?
ARETUS   Yes, he was so,
  But speaking something roughly in his want,
  Especially of wars, the noble general,   180
  Out of a strict allegiance, cast his fortunes.
VALENTINIAN He's been a valiant fellow?
ARETUS   So he's still.
VALENTINIAN Alas, the general might have pardoned follies.
  Soldiers will talk sometimes.
ARETUS [*aside*]   I am glad of this.
VALENTINIAN He wants preferment, as I take it.
ARETUS   Yes, sir,   185
  And for that noble grace his life shall serve.
VALENTINIAN I have a service for him.
  I shame a soldier should become a beggar.
  I like the man, Aretus.
ARETUS   Gods protect ye.
VALENTINIAN Bid him repair to Proculus, and there   190
  He shall receive the business, and reward for 't.
  I'll see him settled too, and as a soldier.
  We shall want such.
ARETUS   The sweets of heaven still crown ye.
VALENTINIAN [*aside*] I have a fearful darkness in my soul,
  And till I be delivered, still am dying.   195
    Exeunt

4.2

Enter Maximus

MAXIMUS My way has taken: all the court's in guard,
And business everywhere, and every corner
Full of strange whispers. I am least in rumour,
Enter Aëtius [with his arm injured,] and Phidias
And so I'll keep myself. Here comes Aëtius.
I see the bait is swallowed. If he be lost,   5
He is my martyr, and my way stands open,
And, honour, on thy head his blood is reckoned.

AËTIUS Why, how now, friend, what make ye here unarmed?
Are ye turned merchant?

MAXIMUS   By your fair persuasions,
And such a merchant traffics without danger.   10
I have forgotten all, Aëtius,
And, which is more, forgiven.

AËTIUS   Now I love ye,
Truly I do, ye are a worthy Roman.

MAXIMUS The fair repentance of my prince to me
Is more than sacrifice of blood and vengeance.   15
No eyes shall weep her ruins but mine own.

AËTIUS Still ye take more love from me. Virtuous friend,
The gods make poor Aëtius worthy of thee.

MAXIMUS Only in me you're poor, sir, and I worthy
Only in being yours. But why your arm thus?   20
Have ye been hurt, Aëtius?

AËTIUS   Bruised a little.
My horse fell with me, friend, which till this morning
I never knew him do.

MAXIMUS   Pray gods it bode well.
And, now I think on 't better, ye shall back.
Let my persuasions rule ye.

AËTIUS   Back? Why, Maximus?   25
The Emperor commands me come.

MAXIMUS   I like not
At this time his command.

AËTIUS   I do at all times,
And all times will obey it. Why not now, then?

MAXIMUS I'll tell ye why, and as I have been governed,
Be you so, noble friend. The court's in guard,   30

Armed strongly; for what purpose, let me fear.
I do not like your going.

AËTIUS   Were it fire,
And that fire certain to consume this body,
If Caesar sent, I would go. Never fear, man,
If he take me, he takes his arms away.   35
I am too plain and true to be suspected.

MAXIMUS [aside] Then I have dealt unwisely.

AËTIUS   If the Emperor,
Because he merely may, will have my life
(That's all he has to work on, and all shall have),
Let him. A loves me better: here I wither,°   40
And happily may live till ignorantly
I run into a fault worth death, nay, more, dishonour.
Now all my sins, I dare say those of duty,
Are printed here, and if I fall so happy°
I bless the grave I lie in, and the gods   45
Equal, as dying on the enemy,°
Must take me up a sacrifice.

MAXIMUS   Go on, then,
And I'll go with ye.

AËTIUS   No, ye may not, friend.

MAXIMUS He cannot be a friend bars me, Aëtius.
Shall I forsake ye in my doubts?

AËTIUS   Ye must.   50

MAXIMUS I must not, nor I will not. Have I lived
Only to be a carpet-friend for pleasure?
I can endure a death as well as Cato.°

AËTIUS There is no death nor danger in my going,
Nor none must go along.

MAXIMUS   I have a sword too,   55
And once I could have used it for my friend.

AËTIUS I need no sword nor friend in this. Pray leave me,
And as ye love me, do not overlove me.
I am commanded none shall come. At supper
I'll meet ye, and we'll drink a cup or two.   60
Ye need good wine; ye have been sad. Farewell.

MAXIMUS Farewell, my noble friend. Let me embrace ye
Ere ye depart. It may be one of us
Shall never do the like again.

AËTIUS   Yes, often.

296

[*They embrace*]

MAXIMUS Farewell, good, dear Aëtius.

AËTIUS   Farewell, Maximus,   65
Till night. Indeed you doubt too much.

Exeunt Aëtius [and Phidias]

MAXIMUS   I do not.
Go, worthy innocent, and make the number
Of Caesar's sins so great, heaven may want mercy.
I'll hover hereabout to know what passes,
And if he be so devilish to destroy thee,   70
In thy blood shall begin his tragedy.

Exit

4.3

Enter Proculus and Pontius

PROCULUS Besides this, if you do it, you enjoy
The noble name patrician. More than that, too,
'The friend of Caesar' ye are styled. There's nothing
Within the hopes of Rome or present being
But you may safely say is yours.

PONTIUS   Pray stay, sir.   5
What has Aëtius done to be destroyed?
At least I would have a colour.

PROCULUS   Ye have more,
Nay, all that may be given: he is a traitor,
One any man would strike that were a subject.

PONTIUS Is he so foul?

PROCULUS   Yes, a most fearful traitor.   10

PONTIUS A fearful plague upon thee, for thou liest.
I ever thought the soldier would undo him
With his too much affection.

PROCULUS   Ye have hit it:°
They have brought him to ambition.

PONTIUS   Then he is gone.

PROCULUS The Emperor, out of a foolish pity,   15
Would save him yet.

PONTIUS   Is he so mad?

PROCULUS   He's madder!

Would go to th' army to him.

PONTIUS   Would a so?

PROCULUS Yes, Pontius, but we consider—

PONTIUS   Wisely.

PROCULUS How else, man?—that the state lies in it.

PONTIUS And your lives too.

PROCULUS   And every man's.

PONTIUS   He did me   20
    All the disgrace he could.

PROCULUS   And scurvily.

PONTIUS Out of a mischief merely. Did you mark it?°

PROCULUS Yes, well enough. Now ye have means to quit it.
    The deed done, take his place.

PONTIUS   Pray let me think on 't.
    'Tis ten to one I do it.

PROCULUS   Do, and be happy.   25
        Exit Proculus

PONTIUS The Emperor is made of nought but mischief.
    Sure, Murder was his mother. None to lop
    But the main link he had? Upon my conscience,°
    The man is truly honest, and that kills him,
    For to live here and study to be true   30
    Is all one to be traitors. Why should he die?°
    Have they not slaves and rascals for their offerings
    In full abundance, bawds more than beasts for slaughter?
    Have they not singing whores enough, and knaves too,
    And millions of such martyrs to sink Charon,°   35
    But the best sons of Rome must sail too? I will show him,
    Since he must die, a way to do it truly,
    And though he bears me hard, yet shall he know
    I am born to make him bless me for a blow.
        Exit

4.4

Enter Phidias, Aretus, and Aëtius

PHIDIAS Yet ye may scape to the camp. We'll hazard with ye.

ARETUS Lose not your life so basely, sir. Ye are armed,
    And many, when they see your sword out and know why,

Must follow your adventure.

AËTIUS   Get ye from me.
Is not the doom of Caesar on this body?   5
Do not I bear my last hour here now sent me?
Am I not old Aëtius, ever dying?
You think this tenderness and love you bring me;
'Tis treason and the strength of disobedience,
And if ye tempt me further, ye shall feel it.   10
I, seek the camp for safety, when my death,
Ten times more glorious than my life, and lasting,
Bids me be happy? Let the fool fear dying,
Or he that weds a woman for his humour,°
Dreaming no other life to come but kisses.   15
Aëtius is not now to learn to suffer.
If ye dare show a just affection, kill me;
I stay but those who must. Why do ye weep?°
Am I so wretched to deserve men's pities?
Go, give your tears to those that lose their worths: 20
Bewail their miseries; for me wear garlands,
Drink wine, and much. Sing paeans to my praise:
I am to triumph, friends, and more than Caesar,
For Caesar fears to die; I love to die.

PHIDIAS O my dear lord!

AËTIUS   No more. Go, go I say.   25
Show me not the signs of sorrow: I deserve none.
Dare any man lament I should die nobly?
Am I grown old to have such enemies?
When I am dead, speak honourably of me,
That is, preserve my memory from dying.   30
Then if you needs must weep your ruined master
A tear or two will seem well. This I charge ye,
Because ye say you yet love old Aëtius,
See my poor body burnt, and some to sing
About my pile, and what I have done and suffered,   35
If Caesar kill not that too. At your banquets
When I am gone, if any chance to number
The times that have been sad and dangerous,
Say how I fell, and 'tis sufficient.
No more, I say. He that laments my end   40
By all the gods dishonours me. Begone,
And suddenly, and wisely from my dangers.

299

My death is catching else.

PHIDIAS   We fear not dying.

AËTIUS Yet fear a wilful death: the just gods hate it.°
　I need no company to that that children   45
　Dare do alone and slaves are proud to purchase.
　Live till your honesties, as mine has done,
　Make this corrupted age sick of your virtues,
　Then die a sacrifice, and then ye know
　The noble use of dying well and Roman.   50

ARETUS And must we leave ye, sir?

AËTIUS   We must all die,
　All leave ourselves. It matters not where, when,
　Nor how, so we die well; and can that man that does so
　Need lamentation for him? Children weep
　Because they have offended, or for fear,   55
　Women for want of will, and anger. Is there°
　In noble man, that truly feels both poises°
　Of life and death, so much of this wet weakness
　To drown a glorious death in child and woman?
　I am ashamed to see ye. Yet ye move me,   60
　And were it not my manhood would accuse me
　For covetise to live, I should weep with ye.

PHIDIAS O we shall never see you more.

AËTIUS   'Tis true,
　Nor I the miseries that Rome shall suffer,
　Which is a benefit life cannot reckon.   65
　But what I have been, which is just and faithful,°
　One that grew old for Rome, when Rome forgot him,
　And for he was an honest man durst die,°
　Ye shall have daily with ye. Could that die too,
　And I return no traffic of my travails,°   70
　No pay to have been soldier but this silver,°
　No annals of Aëtius but 'He lived',
　My friends, ye had cause to weep, and bitterly;
　The common overflows of tender women
　And children new-born crying were too little   75
　To show me then most wretch'd. If tears must be,
　I should in justice weep 'em, and for you:
　You are to live and yet behold those slaughters
　The dry and withered bones of death would bleed at.
　But sooner than I have time to think what must be   80
　I fear you'll find what shall be. If ye love me,

Let that word serve for all. Begone and leave me.
I have some little practice with my soul,
And then the sharpest sword is welcom'st. Go,
Pray begone. Ye have obeyed me living;   85
Be not for shame now stubborn. So I thank ye,
And fare ye well. A better fortune guide ye.
    Exeunt Phidias and Aretus
I am a little thirsty, not for fear;
And yet it is a kind of fear I say so.°
Is it to be a just man now again,   90
And leave my flesh unthought of? 'Tis departed.
I hear 'em come. Who strikes first? I stay for ye.
    Enter Balbus, Chilax, and Lycinius, [armed. They hang back
    from Aëtius]
Yet I will die a soldier, my sword drawn,
But against none. Why do ye fear? Come forward.

BALBUS You were a soldier, Chilax.

CHILAX   Yes, I mustered,   95
But never saw the enemy.

LYCINIUS   He's drawn.
By heaven, I dare not do it.

AËTIUS   Why do ye tremble?
I am to die. Come ye not now from Caesar
To that end? Speak.

BALBUS   We do, and we must kill ye.
'Tis Caesar's will.

CHILAX   I charge you put your sword up,   100
That we may do it handsomely.

AËTIUS   Ha ha ha!
My sword up? 'Handsomely'? Where were ye bred?
Ye are the merriest murderers, my masters,°
I ever met withal. Come forward, fools.
Why do ye stare? Upon mine honour, bawds,   105
I will not strike ye.

LYCINIUS   I'll not be first.

BALBUS   Nor I.

CHILAX You had best die quietly. The Emperor
Sees how you bear yourself.

AËTIUS   I would die, rascals,
If you would kill me quietly.

BALBUS   Pox of Proculus,
He promised us to bring a captain hither   110

That has been used to kill.

AËTIUS   I'll call the guard°
Unless you will kill me quickly, and proclaim
What beastly, base, and cowardly companions
The Emperor has trusted with his safety.
Nay, I'll give out ye fell of my side, villains.°   115
Strike home, ye bawdy slaves!

CHILAX   By heaven, he will kill us!
I marked his hand, he waits but time to reach us.°
Now do you offer.

AËTIUS   If ye do mangle me
And kill me not at two blows, or at three,
Or not so stagger me my senses fail me,   120
Look to yourselves.

CHILAX   I told ye.

AËTIUS   Strike me manly,
And take a thousand strokes.
        Enter Pontius, [armed]

BALBUS   Here's Pontius.

PONTIUS Not killed him yet?
Is this the love ye bear the Emperor?
Nay, then, I see ye are traitors all. Have at ye!   125
        [*He attacks and wounds Chilax and Balbus.*] *Exit Lycinius,*
        running away

CHILAX O, I am hurt.

BALBUS   And I am killed.
        Exeunt Chilax and Balbus

PONTIUS   Die, bawds,
As ye have lived and flourished.

AËTIUS   Wretched fellow,
What hast thou done?

PONTIUS   Killed them that durst not kill,
And you are next.

AËTIUS   Art thou not Pontius?

PONTIUS I am the same you cast, Aëtius,   130
And in the face of all the camp disgraced.

AËTIUS Then so much nobler, as thou wert a soldier,
Shall my death be. Is it revenge provoked thee,
Or art thou hired to kill me?

PONTIUS   Both.

AËTIUS   Then do it.

302

PONTIUS Is that all?
AËTIUS   Yes.
PONTIUS   Would you not live?
AËTIUS   Why should I?   135
  To thank thee for my life?
PONTIUS   Yes, if I spare it.
AËTIUS Be not deceived: I was not made to thank
  For any courtesy but killing me,°
  A fellow of thy fortune. Do thy duty.°
PONTIUS Do not you fear me?
AËTIUS   No.
PONTIUS   Nor love me for it?   140
AËTIUS That's as thou dost thy business.
PONTIUS   When you are dead,
  Your place is mine, Aëtius.
AËTIUS   Now I fear thee,
  And not alone thee, Pontius, but the empire.
PONTIUS Why, I can govern, sir.
AËTIUS   I would thou couldst,
  And first, thyself. Thou canst fight well and bravely;   145
  Thou canst endure all dangers, heats, colds, hungers;
  Heaven's angry flashes are not suddener°
  Than I have seen thee execute, nor more mortal;
  The wingèd feet of flying enemies
  I have stood and viewed thee mow away like rushes,   150
  And still kill the killer. Were thy mind
  But half so sweet in peace as rough in dangers,
  I died to leave a happy heir behind me.
  Come, strike, and be a general.
PONTIUS   Prepare, then.
  And for I see your honour cannot lessen,   155
  And 'twere a shame for me to strike a dead man,
  Fight your short span out.
AËTIUS   No, thou know'st I must not.
  I dare not give thee so much vantage of me
  As disobedience.
PONTIUS   Dare ye not defend ye
  Against your enemy?
AËTIUS   Not sent from Caesar.   160
  I have no power to make such enemies.
  For as I am condemned, my naked sword

Stands but a hatchment by me, only held°
To show I was a soldier. Had not Caesar
Chained all defence in this doom (let him die°   165
Old as I am, and quenched with scars and sorrows),
Yet would I make this withered arm do wonders
And open in an enemy such wounds
Mercy would weep to look on.

PONTIUS   Then have at ye,
And look upon me, and be sure ye fear not.   170
Remember who you are, and why you live,
And what I have been to you. Cry not 'Hold',
Nor think it base injustice I should kill ye.

AËTIUS I am prepared for all.

PONTIUS   For now, Aëtius,
Thou shalt behold I was no traitor,   175
And as I do it, bless me. Die as I do.
        He stabs himself

AËTIUS Thou hast deceived me, Pontius, and I thank thee.
By all my hopes in heaven, thou art a Roman.

PONTIUS To show you what you ought to do this is not,
For slander's self would shame to find you coward,   180
Or willing to outlive your honesty.
But, noble sir, ye have been jealous of me,
And held me in the ranks of dangerous persons,
And I must dying say it was but justice
Ye cast me from my credit. Yet believe me   185
(For there is nothing now but truth to save me,
And your forgiveness), though ye held me heinous
And of a troubled spirit that, like fire,
Turns all to flames it meets with, ye mistook me.
If I were foe to anything, 'twas ease,   190
Want of the soldier's due, the enemy,
The nakedness we found at home, and scorn
(Children of peace and pleasures), no regard
Or comfort for our scars but how we got 'em;°
To rusty time, that ate our bodies up,   195
And even began to prey upon our honours;
To wants at home, and, more than wants, abuses;
To them that, when the enemy invaded,
Made us their saints, but now the sores of Rome;
To silken flattery, and pride plumed over,   200

304

Forgetting with what wind their feathers sail,
And under whose protection their soft pleasures
Grow full and numberless. To this I am foe,
Not to the state or any point of duty,
And (let me speak but what a soldier may)   205
Truly I ought to be so. Yet I erred,
Because a far more noble sufferer°
Showed me the way to patience, and I lost it.
This is the end I die, sir. To live basely°
And not the follower of him that bred me,   210
In full account and virtue Pontius dare not,
Much less to outlive what is good, and flatter.

AËTIUS I want a name to give thy virtue, soldier,
For only 'good' is far below thee, Pontius.
The gods shall find thee one. Thou hast fashioned death°   215
In such an excellent and beauteous manner
I wonder men can live. Canst thou speak once more,
For thy words are such harmony a soul
Would choose to fly to heaven in.

PONTIUS   A farewell.
Good, noble general, your hand. Forgive me,   220
And think, whatever was displeasing you
Was none of mine. Ye cannot live.

AËTIUS   I will not.
Yet one word more.

PONTIUS   Die nobly. Rome, farewell,
And Valentinian fall: thou hast broke thy basis.
In joy ye have given me a quiet death.   225
I would strike more wounds if I had more breath.
    He dies

AËTIUS Is there an hour of goodness beyond this,
Or any man would outlive such a dying?°
Would Caesar double all my honours on me
And stick me o'er with favours like a mistress,°   230
Yet would I grow to this man. I have loved,
But never doted on a face till now.
O death, thou art more than beauty, and thy pleasure
Beyond posterity. Come friends and kill me.
Caesar be kind, and send a thousand swords.   235
The more, the greater is my fall. Why stay ye?
Come, and I'll kiss your weapons. Fear me not.

By all the gods, I'll honour ye for killing.
Appear, or through the court and world I'll search ye.
    [He throws his sword away]
My sword is gone. Ye are traitors if ye spare me,   240
And Caesar must consume ye. All base cowards?
I'll follow ye, and ere I die proclaim ye
The weeds of Italy, the dross of nature.
    Exit Aëtius°
[Within] Where are ye, villains, traitors, slaves?
    Enter Proculus and three Men,° running over the stage
PROCULUS I knew he'd killed the captain.
FIRST MAN   Here's his sword.   245
PROCULUS Let it alone, 'twill fight itself else. Friends,
    An hundred men are not enough to do it.
    I'll to the Emperor, and get more aid.
AËTIUS *[within]* None strike a poor condemnèd man?
PROCULUS   He is mad.
    Shift for yourselves, my masters.
    Exeunt Proculus and the three Men. Enter Aëtius
AËTIUS   Then, Aëtius,°   250
    See what thou dar'st thyself.
    [He picks up his sword]
                        Hold, my good sword,
    Thou hast been kept from blood too long. I'll kiss thee,
    For thou art more than friend now. My preserver,
    Show me the way to happiness, I seek it.
    And all you great ones that have fall'n, as I do,   255
    To keep your memories and honours living,
    Be present in your virtues and assist me,
    That, like strong Cato, I may put away
    All promises but what shall crown my ashes.
    Rome, fare thee well. Stand long, and know to conquer   260
    Whilst there is people and ambition.
    Now for a stroke shall turn me to a star.
    I come, ye blessèd spirits, make me room
    To live forever in Elysium.
    [He stabs himself]
    Do men fear this? O that posterity   265
    Could learn from him but this (that loves his wound):
    There is no pain in dying well,
    Nor none are lost but those that make their hell.
    He dies

FIRST MAN (*within*) He's dead. Draw in the guard again.
     Enter Proculus and two of the Men
PROCULUS   He's dead indeed,
  And I am glad he's gone. He was a devil.   270
  His body, if his eunuchs come, is theirs.°
  The Emperor, out of his love to virtue,
  Has given 'em that. Let no man stop their entrance.
       Exeunt Proculus and the two Men [with Pontius' body.°] Enter
       Phidias and Aretus; [they find Aëtius' body]
PHIDIAS O my most noble lord. Look here, Aretus,
  Here's a sad sight.
ARETUS   O cruelty! O Caesar!   275
  O times that bring forth nothing but destruction
  And overflows of blood. Why wast thou killed?
  Is it to be a just man now again,
  As when Tiberius and wild Nero reigned,
  Only assurance of his overthrow?°   280
PHIDIAS It is, Aretus. He that would live now
  Must, like the toad, feed only on corruptions°
  And grow with those to greatness. Honest virtue
  And the true Roman honour, faith, and valour
  That have been all the riches of the empire,   285
  Now like the fearful tokens of the plague°
  Are mere forerunners of their ends that owe 'em.°
ARETUS Never-enough-lamented lord, dear master,
     Enter Maximus [unseen]
  Of whom now shall we learn to live like men,
  From whom draw out our actions just and worthy?   290
  O thou art gone, and gone with thee all goodness!
  The great example of all equity!
  O thou alone a Roman, thou art perished,
  Faith, fortitude, and constant nobleness!
  Weep, Rome, weep, Italy, weep, all that knew him,   295
  And you that feared him as a noble foe,
  If enemies have honourable tears,
  Weep this decayed Aëtius, fall'n and scattered
     [Maximus comes forward]
  By foul and base suggestion.
PHIDIAS   O lord Maximus,
  This was your worthy friend.
MAXIMUS [*aside*]   The gods forgive me.   300
  [*Aloud*] Think not the worse, my friends, I shed not tears.

Great griefs lament within. [*Aside*] Yet now I have found 'em.
Would I had never known the world, nor women,
Nor what that cursèd name of honour was,
So this were once again Aëtius;   305
But I am destined to a mighty action,
And beg my pardon, friend. My vengeance taken,
I will not be long from thee. [*Aloud*] Ye have a great loss,
But bear it patiently. [*Aside*] Yet to say truth,
In justice 'tis not sufferable. I am next,   310
And were it now, I would be glad on 't. [*Aloud*] Friends,
Who shall preserve you now?

ARETUS   Nay, we are lost too.

MAXIMUS I fear ye are, for likely such as love
  The man that's fall'n and have been nourished by him
  Do not stay long behind. 'Tis held no wisdom.   315
  I know what I must do. O my Aëtius,
  Canst thou thus perish, plucked up by the roots,
  And no man feel thy worthiness? From boys
  He bred you both, I think.

PHIDIAS   And from the poorest.

MAXIMUS And loved ye as his own.

ARETUS   We found it, sir.   320

MAXIMUS Is not this a loss, then?

PHIDIAS   O, a loss of losses.
  Our lives, and ruins of our families,
  The utter being nothing of our names°
  Were nothing near it.

MAXIMUS   As I take it, too,
  He put ye to the Emperor.

ARETUS   He did so.   325

MAXIMUS And kept ye still in credit.

PHIDIAS   'Tis most true, sir.

MAXIMUS He fed your fathers, too, and made them means;°
  Your sisters he preferred to noble wedlocks,
  Did he not, friends?

ARETUS   O yes, sir.

MAXIMUS   As I take it,
  This worthy man would not be now forgotten.   330
  I tell ye, to my grief, he was basely murdered,
  And something would be done by those that loved him.°
  And something may be. Pray stand off a little.

Let me bewail him private. [*To Aëtius' body*] O my dearest.
    [*Phidias and Aretus talk apart*]

PHIDIAS Aretus, if we be not sudden, he outdoes us.   335
  I know he points at vengeance. We are cold,°
  And base ungrateful wretches, if we shun it.
  Are we to hope for more rewards, or greatness,
  Or anything but death, now he is dead?
  Dar'st thou resolve?

ARETUS   I am perfect.

PHIDIAS   Then like flowers   340
  That grew together all, we'll fall together,
  And with us he that bore us. When 'tis done,
  The world shall style us two deserving servants.
  I fear he will be before us.

ARETUS   This night, Phidias.

PHIDIAS   Done bravely.   No more.

MAXIMUS Now, worthy friends, I have done my mournings.   345
  Let's burn this noble body. Sweets as many
  As sunburnt Meroe breeds, I'll make a flame of,°
  Shall reach his soul in heaven. He that shall live
  Ten ages hence, but to rehearse this story,
  Shall with the sad discourse on 't darken heaven   350
  And force the painful burdens from the wombs
  Conceived anew with sorrow. Even the grave°
  Where mighty Scylla sleeps shall rend asunder°
  And give her shadow up to come and groan
  About our piles, which will be more and greater   355
  Than green Olympus, Ida, or old Latmus°
  Can feed with cedar, or the east with gums,°
  Greece with her wines or Thessaly with flowers,°
  Or willing heaven can weep for in her showers.
       Exeunt with the body

5.1

Enter Phidias with his dagger in him, and Aretus poisoned°

ARETUS He has his last.

PHIDIAS   Then come, the worst of danger.
Aëtius, to thy soul we give a Caesar.
How long is 't since ye gave it him?

ARETUS   An hour,
Mine own two hours before him. How it boils me!

PHIDIAS It was not to be cured, I hope.

ARETUS   No, Phidias,   5
I dealt above his antidotes. Physicians
May find the cause, but where the cure?

PHIDIAS   Done bravely.
We are got before his tyranny, Aretus.

ARETUS We had lost our worthiest end else, Phidias.

PHIDIAS Canst thou hold out a while?

ARETUS   To torture him,   10
Anger would give me leave to live an age yet.
That man is poorly spirited whose life
Runs in his blood alone, and not in 's wishes.
And yet I swell, I burn like flaming Etna.
A thousand new-found fires are kindled in me,   15
But yet I must not die this four hours, Phidias.

PHIDIAS Remember who dies with thee and despise death.

ARETUS I need no exhortation. The joy in me
Of what I have done, and why, makes poison pleasure
And my most killing torments mistresses.   20
For how can he have time to die, or pleasure,°
That falls, as fools, unsatisfied and simple?°

PHIDIAS This that consumes my life yet keeps it in me,°
Nor do I feel the danger of a dying,
And if I but endure to hear the curses   25
Of this fell tyrant dead, I have half my heaven.

ARETUS Hold thy soul fast but four hours, Phidias,
And thou shalt see to wishes beyond ours,
Nay, more, beyond our meanings.

PHIDIAS   Thou hast steeled me.
Farewell, Aretus; and the souls of good men,   30

That, as ours do, have left their Roman bodies
In brave revenge for virtue, guide our shadows.
I would not faint yet.

ARETUS   Farewell, Phidias,
And as we have done nobly, gods look on us.
        Exeunt severally

5.2

        Enter Lycias and Proculus

LYCIAS Sicker and sicker, Proculus?

PROCULUS   Oh Lycias,
What shall become of us? Would we had died
With happy Chilax, or, with Balbus, bedrid°
And made too lame for justice.
        Enter Lycinius

LYCINIUS [*speaking to someone off stage*] The soft music.
And let one sing to fasten sleep upon him.
O friends, the Emperor.   5

PROCULUS   What say the doctors?

LYCINIUS For us a most sad saying: he is poisoned,
Beyond all cure, too.

LYCIAS   Who?

LYCINIUS   The wretch Aretus,
That most unhappy villain.

LYCIAS   How do you know it?

LYCINIUS He gave him drink last. Let's disperse and find him,   10
And since he has opened misery to all,
Let it begin with him first. Softly, he slumbers.
        [*Exeunt Lycias, Proculus, and Lycinius.*] *Valentinian is carried*
        on, sick in a chair, followed by Eudoxa the Empress,
        Physicians, Attendants, [and a Boy.] Music is played

BOY [*sings*] *Care-charming sleep, thou easer of all woes,°*
            Brother to death, sweetly thyself dispose
            On this afflicted prince. Fall like a cloud   15
            In gentle showers. Give nothing that is loud
            Or painful to his slumbers. Easy, light,
            And as a purling stream, thou son of night,
            Pass by his troubled senses. Sing his pain

311

        Like hollow murmuring wind or silver rain.　　20
        Into this prince gently, O gently, O gently slide°
        And kiss him into slumbers like a bride.
    [*Exit Boy*]

VALENTINIAN O gods, gods! Drink, drink, colder, colder
  Than snow on Scythian mountains! O my heart-strings!°

EUDOXA How does your grace?

PHYSICIAN　　　　　　　　The Empress speaks, sir.

VALENTINIAN　　　　　　　　　　　Dying,　　25
  Dying, Eudoxa, dying.

PHYSICIAN　　　　　Good sir, patience.

EUDOXA What have ye given him?

PHYSICIAN　　　　　　　　Precious things, dear lady,
  We hope shall comfort him.

VALENTINIAN　　　　　　　O flattered fool,
  See what thy godhead's come to. O Eudoxa.

EUDOXA O patience, patience, sir.

VALENTINIAN　　　　　　Danubius　　30
  I'll have brought through my body—

EUDOXA　　　　　　　　Gods give comfort.

VALENTINIAN —And Volga, on whose face the north wind freezes.
  I am an hundred hells, an hundred piles
  Already to my funerals are flaming.
  Shall I not drink?

PHYSICIAN　　　You must not, sir.

VALENTINIAN　　　　　　　By heaven,　　35
  I'll let my breath out, that shall burn ye all,
  If ye deny me longer. Tempests, blow me,
  And inundations that have drunk up kingdoms,
  Flow over me and quench me. Where's the villain?
  Am I immortal now, ye slaves? By Numa,°　　40
  If he do scape—O, O!

EUDOXA　　　Dear sir.

VALENTINIAN　　　　Like Nero,
  But far more terrible and full of slaughter,
  I' th' midst of my flames I'll fire the empire.°
  A thousand fans, a thousand fans to cool me!
  Invite the gentle winds, Eudoxa.

EUDOXA　　　　　　Sir.　　45

VALENTINIAN O do not flatter me. I am but flesh,
  A man, a mortal man. [*To the Physicians*] Drink, drink, ye dunces.

What can your doses now do, and your scrapings,
Your oils and mithridates? If I do die,°
You only words of health and names of sickness,°   50
Finding no true disease in man but money,
That talk yourselves into revenues—O!—
And ere ye kill your patients beggar 'em,
I'll have ye flayed and dried.

    Enter Proculus and Lycinius, with Aretus

PROCULUS   The villain, sir,
  The most accursèd wretch.

VALENTINIAN   Begone, my queen,   55
  This is no sight for thee. Go to the Vestals,
  Cast holy incense in the fire, and offer
  One powerful sacrifice to free thy Caesar.

PROCULUS Go, go and be happy.

    Exit Eudoxa

ARETUS   Go, but give no ease.
  The gods have set thy last hour, Valentinian.   60
  Thou art but man, a bad man too, a beast,
  And like a sensual bloody thing thou diest.

PROCULUS O damnèd traitor.

ARETUS   Curse yourselves, ye flatterers,
  And howl your miseries to come, ye wretches.
  You taught him to be poisoned.

VALENTINIAN   Yet no comfort?°   65

ARETUS Be not abused with priests nor 'pothecaries,
  They cannot help thee. Thou hast now to live
  A short half-hour, no more, and I ten minutes.
  I gave thee poison for Aëtius' sake,
  Such a destroying poison would kill nature,°   70
  And, for thou shalt not die alone, I took it.
  If mankind had been in thee at this murder,
  No more to people the earth again, the wings
  Of old Time clipped forever, reason lost°
  In what I had attempted, yet, O Caesar,   75
  To purchase fair revenge I had poisoned them too.

VALENTINIAN O villain! I grow hotter, hotter.

ARETUS   Yes,
  But not near my heat yet. What thou feel'st now°
  (Mark me with horror, Caesar) are but embers°
  Of lust and lechery thou hast committed,   80

But there be flames of murder.

VALENTINIAN   Fetch out tortures.°

ARETUS Do, and I'll flatter thee—nay, more, I'll love thee.
   Thy tortures to what now I suffer, Caesar,
   At which thou must arrive too ere thou diest,
   Are lighter and more full of mirth than laughter.°   85

VALENTINIAN Let 'em alone. I must drink.

ARETUS   Now be mad,
   But not near me yet.

VALENTINIAN   Hold me, hold me, hold me,
   Hold me, or I shall burst else!

ARETUS   See me, Caesar,
   And see to what thou must come for thy murder:
   Millions of women's labours, all diseases—   90

VALENTINIAN O my afflicted soul too.

ARETUS   —Women's fears, horrors,
   Despairs, and all the plagues the hot sun breeds—

VALENTINIAN Aëtius, O Aëtius! O Lucina!

ARETUS —Are but my torments' shadows.

VALENTINIAN   Hide me, mountains,
   The gods have found my sins! Now break!

ARETUS   Not yet, sir.°   95
   Thou hast a pull beyond all these.

VALENTINIAN   O hell,°
   O villain, cursèd villain!

ARETUS   O brave villain!
   My poison dances in me at this deed.
   Now, Caesar, now behold me: this is torment,
   And this is thine before thou diest. I am wildfire.°   100
   The brazen bull of Phalaris was feigned,°
   The miseries of souls despising heaven
   But emblems of my torments—

VALENTINIAN O quench me, quench me, quench me!

ARETUS   —Fire a flattery°
   And all the poets' tales of sad Avernus°   105
   To my pains less than fictions. Yet to show thee
   What constant love I bore my murdered master,
   Like a south wind I have sung through all these tempests.
   My heart, my withered heart! Fear, fear, thou monster,
   Fear the just gods. I have my peace.
       He dies

VALENTINIAN   More drink!   110

314

A thousand April showers fall in my bosom!
How dare ye let me be tormented thus?
Away with that prodigious body.
    [Exeunt Attendants with Aretus' body°]
                                 Gods,
Gods, let me ask ye what I am. Ye lay
All your inflictions on me; hear me, hear me!   115
I do confess I am a ravisher,
A murderer, a hated Caesar. O!
Are there not vows enough, and flaming altars,
The fat of all the world for sacrifice,
And where that fails, the blood of thousand captives   120
To purge those sins, but I must make the incense?°
I do despise ye all: ye have no mercy,
And, wanting that, ye are no gods. Your parol°
Is only preached abroad to make fools fearful
And women made of awe believe your heaven.   125
O torments, torments, torments, pains above pains!
If ye be anything but dreams and ghosts,
And truly hold the guidance of things mortal,
Have in yourselves times past, to come, and present,
Fashion the souls of men and make flesh for 'em,   130
Weighing our fates and fortunes beyond reason,
Be more than all, ye gods, great in forgiveness.
Break not the goodly frame ye build in anger,
For you are things, men teach us, without passions.
Give me an hour to know ye in. O save me   135
But so much perfect time ye make a soul in.
Take this destruction from me. No, ye cannot.
The more I would believe ye, more I suffer.
My brains are ashes, now my heart, my eyes. Friends,
I go, I go! More air, more air! I am mortal.   140
    He dies
PROCULUS Take in the body.
    [Exeunt Physicians° with Valentinian's body]
                          O Lycinius,
The misery that we are left to suffer!
No pity shall find us.
LYCINIUS   Our lives deserve none.
Would I were chained again to slavery
With any hope of life.
PROCULUS   A quiet grave   145

315

Or a consumption now, Lycinius,
That we might be too poor to kill, were something.

LYCINIUS Let's make our best use. We have money, Proculus,
And if that cannot save us, we have swords.

PROCULUS Yes, but we dare not die.

LYCINIUS   I had forgot that.   150
There's other countries, then.

PROCULUS   But the same hate still°
Of what we are.

LYCINIUS   Think anything, I'll follow.
        Enter a Messenger

PROCULUS How now, what news?

MESSENGER Shift for yourselves, ye are lost else:
The soldier is in arms for great Aëtius,   155
And their lieutenant-general that stopped 'em°
Cut in a thousand pieces. They march hither.
Beside, the women of the town have murdered
Phorba and loose Ardelia, Caesar's she-bawds.

LYCINIUS Then here's no staying, Proculus!

PROCULUS   O Caesar,   160
That we had never known thy lusts. Let's fly,
And where we find no woman's man let's die.
        Exeunt

5.3

        Enter Maximus

MAXIMUS Gods, what a sluice of blood have I let open!
My happy ends are come to birth: he's dead,
And I revenged. The empire's all afire,
And desolation everywhere inhabits;
And shall I live, that am the author of it,   5
To know Rome, from the awe o' th' world, the pity?°
My friends are gone before, too, of my sending,°
And shall I stay? Is aught else to be lived for?
Is there another friend, another wife,
Or any third holds half their worthiness   10
To linger here alive for? Is not virtue
In their two everlasting souls departed,

And in their bodies' first flame fled to heaven?°
Can any man discover this and love me?
For though my justice were as white as truth, ˙15
My way was crooked to it: that condemns me.
And now, Aëtius and my honoured lady,
That were preparers to my rest and quiet,
The lines to lead me to Elysium,
You that but stepped before me, on assurance 20
I would not leave your friendship unrewarded,
First smile upon the sacrifice I have sent thee,
Then see me coming boldly. Stay, I am foolish,
Somewhat too sudden to mine own destruction.
This great end of my vengeance may grow greater: 25
Why may not I be Caesar? Yet no dying:
Why should not I catch at it? Fools and children°
Have had that strength before me and obtained it,
And, as the danger stands, my reason bids me:
I will, I dare. My dear friends, pardon me, 30
I am not fit to die yet if not Caesar.
I am sure the soldier loves me, and the people,
And I will forward, and as goodly cedars,
Rent from Oëta by a sweeping tempest,
Jointed again and made tall masts, defy 35
Those angry winds that split 'em, so will I,
New pieced again, above the fate of women,
And made more perfect far than growing private,
Stand and defy bad fortunes. If I rise,
My wife was ravished well. If then I fall, 40
My great attempt honours my funeral.

    Exit

5.4

    Enter Fulvius, Lucius, and Sempronius,° three Senators, with
    Affranius

FULVIUS Guard all the posterns to the camp, Affranius,
    And see 'em fast, we shall be rifled else.°
    Thou art an honest and a worthy captain.

LUCIUS Promise the soldier anything.
SEMPRONIUS   Speak gently,
  And tell 'em we are now in council for 'em,   5
  Labouring to choose a Caesar fit for them,
  A soldier, and a giver.
FULVIUS   Tell 'em further
  Their free and liberal voices shall go with us.°
LUCIUS Nay, more, a negative say we allow 'em.°
SEMPRONIUS And if our choice displease 'em, they shall name him.   10
FULVIUS Promise three donatives, and large, Affranius.
LUCIUS And, Caesar once elected, present foes,°
  With distribution of all necessities:
  Corn, wine, and oil.
SEMPRONIUS   New garments, and new arms,
  And equal portions of the provinces   15
  To them and to their families forever.
FULVIUS And see the city strengthened.
AFFRANIUS   I shall do it.
      Exit Affranius
LUCIUS Sempronius, these are woeful times.
SEMPRONIUS   O Brutus,°
  We want thy honesty again. These Caesars,
  What noble consuls got with blood, in blood°   20
  Consume again and scatter.
FULVIUS   Which way shall we?
LUCIUS Not any way of safety I can think on.
SEMPRONIUS Now go our wives to ruin, and our daughters,
  And we beholders, Fulvius.
FULVIUS   Everything
  Is every man's that will.
LUCIUS   The vestals now   25
  Must only feed the soldier's fire of lust,
  And sensual gods be glutted with those offerings,
  Age, like the hidden bowels of the earth,
  Opened with swords for treasure. Gods defend us,°
  We are chaff before their fury else.
SEMPRONIUS   Away,   30
  Let's to the temples.
FULVIUS   To the Capitol;°
  'Tis not a time to pray now. Let's be strengthened.
      Enter Affranius

318

SEMPRONIUS How now, Affranius, What good news?
AFFRANIUS   A Caesar.
FULVIUS O who?
AFFRANIUS   Lord Maximus is with the soldier,
   And all the camp rings, 'Caesar, Caesar, Caesar!'   35
   He forced the Empress with him for more honour.
LUCIUS A happy choice. Let's meet him.
SEMPRONIUS   Blessèd fortune.
FULVIUS [to the off-stage crowds] Away, away! Make room there!
      Room there, room!
            Exeunt Lucius, Sempronius, and Fulvius. A flourish is played
VOICES [within] Lord Maximus is Caesar, Caesar, Caesar!
   Hail Caesar Maximus!
AFFRANIUS   O turning people!   40
   O people excellent in war and governed,
   In peace more raging than the furious north°
   When he ploughs up the sea and makes him brine,
   Or the loud falls of Nile. I must give way,°
   Though I neither love nor hope this Caesar,°   45
         A flourish is played
   Or, like a rotten bridge that dares a current
   When he is swelled and high, crack and farewell.
            Enter Maximus, Eudoxa, Fulvius, Lucius, Sempronius,° and
            Soldiers
SENATORS Room for the Emperor!
SOLDIERS   Long life to Caesar!
AFFRANIUS Hail Caesar Maximus!
MAXIMUS   Your hand, Affranius.
   Lead to the palace, there my thanks in general   50
   I'll show'r among ye all. Gods give me life,
   First to defend the empire, then you fathers°
   And valiant friends, the heirs of strength and virtue,
   The rampires of old Rome, of us the refuge.
   To you I open this day all I have,   55
   Even all the hazard that my youth hath purchased.
   Ye are my children, family, friends,
   And ever so respected shall be. Forward.
         [He hands Sempronius a document]
   There's a proscription, grave Sempronius,°
   'Gainst all the flatterers and lazy bawds   60
   Led loose-lived Valentinian to his vices:

See it effected.
  A flourish is played
SENATORS   Honour wait on Caesar.
SOLDIERS [*to the off-stage crowds*] Make room for Caesar there!
  Exeunt all but Affranius

AFFRANIUS   Thou hast my fears,
But Valentinian keeps my vows. O gods,
Why do we like to feed the greedy ravin   65
Of these blown men, that must, before they stand°
And fixed in eminence, cast life on life
And trench their safeties with wounds and bodies?°
Well, froward Rome, thou wilt grow weak with changing
And die without an heir, that lov'st to breed   70
Sons for the killing hate of sons. For me,
I only live to find an enemy.
  Exit

5.5

Enter Paulus, a poet, and Lycippus, a gentleman
PAULUS When is the inauguration?
LYCIPPUS   Why, tomorrow.
PAULUS 'Twill be short time.
LYCIPPUS   Any device that's handsome,°
A Cupid or the god o' th' place will do it,°
Where he must take the fasces.
PAULUS   Or a Grace.°
LYCIPPUS A good Grace has no fellow.
PAULUS   Let me see.   5
Will not his name yield something? Maximus—
By th' way of anagram? I have found out 'axis':
You know, he bears the empire.
LYCIPPUS   Get him wheels too,
'Twill be a cruel carriage else.
PAULUS   Some songs, too.°
LYCIPPUS By any means some songs, but very short ones, 10
And honest language, Paulus, without bursting;°
The air will fall the sweeter.
PAULUS   A Grace must do it.

LYCIPPUS Why, let a Grace, then.

PAULUS   Yes, it must be so,
  And in a robe of blue, too, as I take it.°

LYCIPPUS [*aside*] This poet is a little kin to th' painter   15
  That could paint nothing but a ramping lion:
  So, all his learnèd fancies are blue graces.

PAULUS What think ye of a sea-nymph and a heaven?

LYCIPPUS Why, what should she do there, man? There's no water.

PAULUS By th' mass, that's true. It must be a Grace, and yet   20
  Methinks a rainbow—

LYCIPPUS   And in blue.

PAULUS   Oh yes.—
  Hanging in arch above him, and i' th' middle—°

LYCIPPUS A shower of rain.

PAULUS   No, no, it must be a Grace.

LYCIPPUS Why, prithee grace him then.

PAULUS   Or Orpheus,°
  Coming from hell.

LYCIPPUS   In blue, too.

PAULUS   'Tis the better.   25
  And as he rises, full of fires—

LYCIPPUS   Now bless us!
  Will not that spoil his lute-strings, Paulus?

PAULUS   —Singing,
  And crossing of his arms.

LYCIPPUS   How can he play, then?

PAULUS It shall be a Grace. I'll do it.

LYCIPPUS   Prithee do,
  And with as good a grace as thou canst possible.
  Good fury, Paulus; be i' th' morning with me,°   30
  And pray take measure of his mouth that speaks it.°
    Exeunt

5.6

Enter Maximus and Eudoxa, [with a Messenger]

MAXIMUS Come, my best loved Eudoxa. [*To the Messenger*] Let the
  soldier
  Want neither wine nor anything he calls for,

5.6

THE TRAGEDY OF VALENTINIAN

And when the Senate's ready, give us notice.
In the meantime, leave us.
    [*Exit Messenger*]
O my dear sweet.

EUDOXA   Is 't possible your grace   5
Should undertake such dangers for my beauty,
If it were excellent?

MAXIMUS   By heaven, 'tis all°
The world has left to brag of.

EUDOXA   Can a face
Long since bequeathed to wrinkles with my sorrows,
Long since rased out o' th' book of youth and pleasure,   10
Have power to make the strongest man o' th' empire,
Nay, the most staid and knowing what is woman,
The greatest aim of perfectness men lived by,
The most true, constant lover of his wedlock,
Such a still-blowing beauty earth was proud of,   15
Lose such a noble wife, and wilfully?
Himself prepare the way, nay, make the rape—
Did ye not tell me so?

MAXIMUS   'Tis true, Eudoxa.

EUDOXA Lay desolate his dearest piece of friendship,
Break his strong helm he steered by, sink that virtue,   20
That valour that even all the gods can give us,
Without whom he was nothing, with whom worthiest,
Nay, more, arrive at Caesar and kill him too,
And for my sake? Either ye love too dearly
Or deeply ye dissemble, sir.

MAXIMUS [*aside*]   I do so,   25
And till I am more strengthened, so I must do.
Yet would my joy, and wine, had fashioned out
Some safer lie. [*Aloud*] Can these things be, Eudoxa,
And I dissemble? Can there be, but goodness
(And only thine, dear lady), any end,   30
Any imagination but a lost one,
Why I should run this hazard? O thou virtue!°
Were it to do again, and Valentinian
Once more to hold thee (sinful Valentinian
In whom thou wert set, as pearls are in salt oysters,   35
As roses are in rank weeds) I would find
Yet to thy sacred self a dearer danger.

322

The gods know how I honour thee.

EUDOXA   What love, sir,
  Can I return for this, but my obedience?
  My life, if so you please, and 'tis too little.   40

MAXIMUS 'Tis too much to redeem the world.

EUDOXA   From this hour,
  Ye sorrows for my dead lord, fare ye well.
  My living lord has dried ye. And in token,
  As Emperor this day I honour ye
  And as the great caster new of all my wishes,°   45
  The wreath of living laurel that must compass
  That sacred head, Eudoxa makes for Caesar.°
  I am methinks too much in love with fortune;
  But with you, ever-royal sir, my maker,
  The once-more-summer of me, mere 'in love'°   50
  Is poor expression of my doting.

MAXIMUS   Sweetest.

EUDOXA Now, of my troth, ye have bought me dear, sir.

MAXIMUS   No,
  Had I at loss of mankind—
      Enter the Messenger

EUDOXA   Now ye flatter.

MESSENGER The Senate waits your grace.

MAXIMUS   Let 'em come on,
  And in a full form bring the ceremony.   55
  [*To Eudoxa*] This day I am your servant, dear, and proudly
  I'll wear your honoured favour.

EUDOXA   May it prove so.°
      Exeunt

5.7

      Enter Paulus and Lycippus

LYCIPPUS Is your Grace done?

PAULUS   'Tis done.

LYCIPPUS   Who speaks?

PAULUS   A boy.

LYCIPPUS A dainty blue boy, Paulus?

PAULUS   Yes.

LYCIPPUS   Have ye viewed

323

The work above?

PAULUS   Yes, and all up and ready.°

LYCIPPUS The Empress does you simple honour, Paulus.
The wreath your blue Grace must present, she made.   5
But hark ye, for the soldiers?

PAULUS   That's done too.
I'll bring 'em in, I warrant ye.

LYCIPPUS   A Grace too?

PAULUS The same Grace serves for both.

LYCIPPUS   About it, then.
I must to th' cupboard. And be sure, good Paulus,°
Your Grace be fasting, that he may hang cleanly.°   10
If there should need another voice, what then?

PAULUS I'll hang another Grace in.

LYCIPPUS   Grace be with ye.

        Exeunt

5.8

*Trumpeters sound a sennet. Enter in state: Lictors, bearing rods
and axes; Maximus and Eudoxa; Affranius, Soldiers, and
Gentlemen of Rome; Lucius, Sempronius, and Fulvius;
followed by Attendants, who set out a table with a banquet*°

SEMPRONIUS Hail to thy imperial honour, sacred Caesar,
And from the old Rome take these wishes.
You holy gods, that hitherto have held
(As justice holds her balance) equal poised
This glory of our nation, this full Roman,   5
And made him fit for what he is, confirm him.
Look on this son, O Jupiter our helper,
And Romulus, thou father of our honour,
Preserve him like thyself: just, valiant, noble,
A lover and increaser of his people.   10
Let him begin with Numa, stand with Cato;
The first five years of Nero be his wishes;
Give him the age and fortune of Aemilius;
And his whole reign renew a great Augustus.°
        [*Enter a Chorus of Singers. A Boy, in the costume of a Grace,
        descends,*° *carrying a wreath.*] *Hautboys play*

BOY [*sings*]   *Honour that is ever living,*   15
                        Honour that is ever giving,
                        Honour that sees all and knows
                        Both the ebbs of man and flows,
                        Honour that rewards the best,
                        Sends thee thy rich labour's rest: 20
                        Thou hast studied still to please her,
                        Therefore now she calls thee 'Caesar'.
CHORUS [*sing*]   *Hail, hail, Caesar, hail and stand,*
                        And thy name outlive the land.
                        Noble fathers, to his brows   25
                        Bind this wreath with thousand vows.
        [*The boy gives the wreath to the Senators, who place it on
        Maximus' head*]
ALL Stand to eternity.
MAXIMUS   I thank ye, fathers,°
    And, as I rule, may it still grow or wither.°
    Now to the banquet. Ye are all my guests.
    This day be liberal, friends; to wine we give it,   30
    And smiling pleasures. Sit, my queen of beauty;
    Fathers, your places.
            [*Eudoxa and the Senators sit at the table*]
                        These are fair wars, soldiers;
    And thus I give the first charge to you all.°
        [*He drinks; an Attendant pours him more wine*]
    [*To Eudoxa*] You are my second, sweet.
        [*He drinks again; the Attendant again refills his cup*]
                                    [*To the company*] To every cup
    I add unto the Senate a new honour,   35
    And to the sons of Mars a donative.°
BOY [*sings*]   *God Lyaeus, ever young,*°
                        Ever honoured, ever sung,
                        Stained with blood of lusty grapes
                        In a thousand lusty shapes,   40
                        Dance upon the mazer's brim;
                        In the crimson liquor swim;
                        From thy plenteous hand divine
                        Let a river run with wine.
                        God of mirth, let this day here°   45
                        Enter neither care nor fear.
                        Enter neither care nor fear.°

[*Speaks*] Bellona's seed, the glory of old Rome,
Envy of conquered nations, nobly come,
And to the fulness of your warlike noise   50
Let your feet move, make up this hour of joys.
Come, come, I say, range your fair troop at large,
And your high measure turn into a charge.
        [*The Soldiers dance. Maximus does not respond*°]
SEMPRONIUS The Emperor's grown heavy with his wine.
AFFRANIUS The Senate stays, sir, for your thanks.
SEMPRONIUS   Great Caesar—   55
EUDOXA [*aside*] I have my wish.
AFFRANIUS [*to Eudoxa*]   Wilt please your grace speak to him?
EUDOXA Yes, but he will not hear, lords.
SEMPRONIUS   Stir him, Lucius.
    The Senate must have thanks.
LUCIUS   Your grace, sir, Caesar.
EUDOXA Did I not tell you he was well? He's dead.
SEMPRONIUS Dead? Treason! Guard the court, let no man pass. 60
    Soldiers, your Caesar's murdered.
EUDOXA   Make no tumult,
    Nor arm the court, ye have his killer with ye,
    And the just cause, if ye can stay the hearing.
    I was his death. The wreath that made him Caesar
    Has made him earth.
SOLDIERS   Cut her in thousand pieces!°   65
        [*The Soldiers draw their swords*]
EUDOXA Wise men would know the reason first. To die
    Is that I wish for, Romans, and your swords
    The readiest way of death. Yet, soldiers, grant me
    (That was your Empress once and honoured by ye)
    But so much time to tell ye why I killed him,   70
    And weigh my reasons well, if man be in you;
    Then, if you dare, do cruelly condemn me.
AFFRANIUS Hear her, ye noble Romans. 'Tis a woman,
    A subject not for swords but pity. Heaven,
    If she be guilty of malicious murder,   75
    Has given us laws to make example of her,
    If only of revenge and blood hid from us.°
    Let us consider first, then execute.
SEMPRONIUS Speak, bloody woman.
EUDOXA   Yes. This Maximus

That was your Caesar, lords and noble soldiers, 80
(And if I wrong the dead, heaven perish me,
Or speak to win your favours but the truth)°
Was to his country, to his friends and Caesar,
A most malicious traitor.
SEMPRONIUS   Take heed, woman.
EUDOXA I speak not for compassion. Brave Aëtius 85
(Whose blessèd soul, if I lie, shall afflict me),
The man that all the world loved, you adored,
That was the masterpiece of arms and bounty
(Mine own grief shall come last)—this friend of his,
This soldier, this your right arm, noble Romans, 90
By a base letter to the Emperor
Stuffed full of fears and poor suggestions,°
And by himself, unto himself directed,
Was cut off basely, basely, cruelly.
O loss! O innocent! Can ye now kill me? 95
And the poor stale, my noble lord, that knew not°
More of this villain than his forcèd fears,
Like one foreseen to satisfy, died for it:°
There was a murder, too, Rome would have blushed at.
Was this worth being Caesar? Or my patience? 100
Nay, his wife
(By heaven he told it me in wine and joy,
And swore it deeply) he himself prepared
To be abused. How? Let me grieve, not tell ye,
And weep the sins that did it; and his end 105
Was only me, and 'Caesar'. But 'me' he lied in.°
These are my reasons, Romans, and my soul
Tells me sufficient, and my deed is justice.
Now as I have done well, or ill, look on me.
AFFRANIUS What less could nature do, what less had we done, 110
Had we known this before? Romans, she is righteous,
And such a piece of justice heaven must smile on.
Bend all your swords on me if this displease ye,
For I must kneel and on this virtuous hand
Seal my new joy and thanks.
    [He kneels to Eudoxa and kisses her hand]
                    Thou hast done truly. 115
SEMPRONIUS Up with your arms, ye strike a saint else, Romans.
    [The Soldiers sheathe their swords]

[*To Eudoxa*] May'st thou live ever spoken our protector.
[*To all*] Rome yet has many noble heirs. Let's in
And pray before we choose, then plant, a Caesar
Above the reach of envy, blood, and murder.   120

AFFRANIUS Take up the body nobly to his urn,
And may our sins and his together burn.

          Exeunt with Maximus' body. A dead march is played

Epilogue°

Enter the Epilogue

EPILOGUE We would fain please ye, and as fain be pleased;
'Tis but a little liking, both are eased;
We have your money and you have our ware,
And to our understanding, good and fair.°   5
For your own wisdoms' sake be not so mad
To acknowledge ye have bought things dear and bad;
Let not a brack i' th' stuff, or here and there
The fading gloss, a general loss appear.
We know ye take up worse commodities
And dearer pay, yet think your bargains wise;   10
We know in meat and wine ye fling away
More time and wealth, which is but dearer pay,°
And with the reckoning all the pleasure lost.
We bid ye not unto repenting cost:°
The price is easy, and so light the play   15
That ye may new-digest it every day.
Then, noble friends, as ye would choose a miss,
Only to please the eye awhile and kiss
Till a good wife be got, so let this play
Hold ye awhile until a better may.   20

          Exit the Epilogue

APPENDIX

Selected Textual Variants in *The Maid's Tragedy* and *The Maiden's Tragedy*

This is a supplementary list of important textual variants not recorded in the notes to this edition. It is not a full collation of the different surviving versions of these two plays. For *The Maid's Tragedy*, it records points where, contrary to my general procedure described in the Note on the Texts, I have adopted Q1 readings in preference to Q2, and where I have not followed Q1's omissions of Q2-only passages. For *The Maiden's Tragedy*, it records readings from the unrevised text (U) and material omitted from the censored text as it was eventually performed (P). For both plays, an asterisk signifies instances where my textual decisions have been determined by the presumption that censorship has occurred. All variants are quoted in modernized form.

The Maid's Tragedy

1.1.9 groom] Q1, bridegroom Q2   14 peace] Q1, peace at home Q2
34 solemnities] Q1, solemnity Q2   36 here] Q1, *not in* Q2   66 sir]
Q1, for Q2

1.2.38 a dozen . . . own] Q2, a dozen heads Q1*   67 quite] Q1, *not in*
Q2   71 Bate me] Q1, Bate Q2   153 *nobler*] Q1, noble Q2
164 his] Q1, thy Q2

2.1.5–6 That . . . do] Q1, *not in* Q2   154–5 or . . . come] Q2, *not in* Q1*

2.2.7–10 Make . . . miserable] Q2, *not in* Q1   84 What . . . ass?] Q2, *not in* Q1*

3.1.152 something . . . heart] Q2, *not in* Q1*   153 it is] Q1, I shall be
Q2   215–16 I . . . To] Q2, *not in* Q1*   248 were . . . fools] Q2, are
thousands Q1*   250 land] Q1, island Q2

4.1.1 God] Q1, *not in* Q2   83–8 He . . . canker] Q2, *not in* Q1*
134 Too late . . . it] Q1, MELANTIUS Too late you find it Q2   139
He's . . . soul] Q1, Could'st thee not curse him? Q2

4.2.259 Melantius] Q1, *not in* Q2

5.1.23 O God] Q1, Good heavens Q2

5.2.32 Yet . . . best] Q2, *not in* Q1*

5.3.18–19 but . . . matters] Q1, *not in* Q2   147–9 and . . . shed] Q2, *not in* Q1*

APPENDIX

The Maiden's Tragedy

1.1.61 title] titles U   80–98 Weighty . . . Stay!] *not in* P*   112
Whence] Black! Whence U
1.2.15 all . . . courtiers] *not in* P*   165 courtier's] brazen P*
2.1.1 Who is 't . . . us?] What's he . . . me? U   75 courtier] woman P*
164 path] way U
3.1.162 great men] some men P*   220–2 'Twas . . . for it] *not in* P*
4.1.74 knight's daughter] man's daughter P*
4.2.42–3 Run . . . cathedral] Run, Atranius, | Bring me the keys of the cathedral straight U
4.4.28 fearful] limber U   46 villain] stone-cutter U   67 Lay . . .
again] Where be these lazy hands again? U   101 most ladies] many ladies
P*
5.1.165 our weapons] two weapons U   193–4 Tyrant . . . myself] *not in*
P*
5.2.20–3 By . . . for 't] *not in* P*   30 fate . . . hinderer] fate's my hindrance U   34 For . . . schoolmaster] *not in* P*   47 And . . .
corner!] *not in* P*   71 at court] but few P*   117–28 O thou . . .
too?] *not in* P*   131 Frenchmen's] extremest P*   154 farther]
farther now U   158 Your King's] I am P*   164–8 Here . . . torments!] *not in* P*   170–85 I cannot . . . with him] *not in* P*   191–6
Here . . . spirit!] *not in* P*   202 virtuous] honest U

330

EXPLANATORY NOTES

ABBREVIATIONS

Countess	*The Insatiate Countess*
Maid	*The Maid's Tragedy*
Maiden	*The Maiden's Tragedy*
Met.	Ovid, *Metamorphoses*
Tilley	Morris Palmer Tilley, *A Dictionary of the Proverbs in England in the Sixteenth and Seventeenth Centuries* (1950)
Val.	*The Tragedy of Valentinian*

References to Shakespeare are to the *Complete Works*, ed. Stanley Wells, Gary Taylor, John Jowett, and William Montgomery (1986).

The Insatiate Countess

The Persons of the Play

Isabella, Countess of Swevia: the character is based on Bianca Maria, Countess of Challant. 'Swevia' does not exist, though the name may refer to Savoy, an independent state in north-western Italy, with perhaps a pun on *swive* (= copulate). The name may also possibly be a misprint for 'Pavia', as it certainly is at 2.1.227 (Q reading, corrected in this edition). However, Isabella seems to have no connection with Pavia before she absconds there with Rogero in 2.3.

Claridiana: the name has ironic connotations of chastity (via the goddess Diana).

Abigail: probably named after the biblical character who made peace between her churlish husband and the future King David.

Mizaldus, a Jew: 'Mizaldus' was the Latin form of the name of Antoine Mizauld (1520–78), a French physician and astronomer; the character has no other connection with Mizault. His racial origins are disputed, even within the play: he calls himself a Catholic at 1.1.354, and later refers to the Catholic practice of confession (4.1.23–4); but Claridiana repeatedly calls him a Jew. This has been taken to be simply a term of opprobrium, offensive because misapplied. However, Mizaldus has the red beard of the stage Jew (2.2.33), and even his wife plans to annoy him by demanding pork during her pregnancy (1.1.231); it seems likely that he is a baptized Christian of Jewish extraction, who may have kept some Jewish habits but evidently wishes to conceal his ethnic background. See also notes to 1.1.138 and 5.2.167.

331

Thais: probably named after the courtesan in Terence's *The Eunuch*.

Lady Lentulus: the name, with its masculine ending, is probably her dead husband's patronymic rather than her personal name; its suggestion of Lent, a period of fasting and self-denial, is relevant to her self-imposed state of widowed chastity.

Mendosa: possibly suggestive of mendacity.

Don Sago: the name may derive from the Spanish *saco* (the sack of a town); the modern connotation of tapioca is irrelevant.

1.1 S.D. *discovered*: revealed, by pulling aside the traverse curtains across a large recess (known as the 'discovery space') in the rear stage wall.

1 *dark hole*: referring to the black-draped discovery space, Guido establishes early on his tendency to make vaginal puns.

2 *turtle*: turtle-dove; the word did not refer to the aquatic turtle until later in the seventeenth century. In English folklore the bird was an emblem of wedded constancy, which only ever took one mate in its lifetime; hence the wooers have no prospect of success with Isabella.

3 *members*: (*a*) citizens, members of the commonwealth; (*b*) penises.

9 *Zounds*: one of the strongest oaths (contracted from 'by God's wounds'); in the period, swearing was most offensive when, as here, it invoked the crucifixion.

10 *simple*: with secondary meaning, 'foolish'.

12 *in a cloud*: because Isabella is dressed in black; cf. *Maiden*, 1.1.112.

15 *Man i' the Moon*: possibly implying that Roberto is a 'moon-man' (= fool, madman).

15–16 *astronomers . . . ditch*: referring to the traditional story of the astronomer who was so busy star-gazing that he forgot to look where he was walking. Here, again, there are vaginal connotations.

19 *the way . . . ladyship*: with yet another vaginal pun.

23 *That . . . it*: true love was understood to entail a gestalt-like commingling of souls, depicted in John Donne's poem 'The Ecstasy'.

25 *dove-like spleen*: in casting Isabella as the bird of love, Roberto implicitly denies the existence of the spleen he mentions: it was believed that doves' livers did not secrete gall (= spleen).

27 *check*: rebuke.

28–9 *But that . . . boldly*: because the gods have ignored (literally, shut their eyes at) Roberto's intrusion (rather than punishing it), he dares further presumption. Alternatively, Roberto draws encouragement from the fact that the classical gods set light by (and indeed participated in) this kind of offence.

42 *Sink . . . deeper*: into his grave; the cubit was an ancient measure of length, corresponding roughly to 20 inches.

43 *I may not fear*: 'so that I may not fear'.

47-9 *mewed . . . pleasure*: in classical mythology, Daedalus, imprisoned by the tyrant of Crete, eventually made his escape by constructing wings made of wax and feathers (*Met.*, 8).

50 *Argus*: in classical mythology, the all-seeing, hundred-eyed guard set by Juno to watch Io and prevent her from committing adultery with Jupiter, Juno's husband (*Met.*, 1).

53 *proper*: (*a*) own; (*b*) handsome.

51-5 *You . . . have*: Isabella encourages young women in the audience to promiscuity; chastity, encouraged by the official culture of the period, is seen as merely a function of sexual unattractiveness. Her theme of *carpe diem* (seize the day) was common in seventeenth-century erotic poetry.

56 *aspect*: looks, appearance.

57 *effeminate*: tender, gentle.

64 *hers . . . golden ball*: Venus, goddess of love, was awarded the golden apple by Paris as the most beautiful of the goddesses; in effect, Roberto's lips seem superlatively kissable.

59-65 *A donative . . . meet*: Roberto is conceived as an anthology of the best features of the classical gods.

66 *synod*: an assembly, often of clergy; also, in astrology, a planetary conjunction.

72 *love . . . oratory*: (*a*) Roberto has never before spoken of love to a woman; (*b*) love which now masters him was hitherto like a schoolboy under his discipline (from 'oratory' as a place where oratorical arts are studied).

73-4 *Leave . . . seas*: 'Leave' may be conditional or imperative. If conditional, Roberto is saying that if Isabella abandons 'pleasing' him (by kissing), she will add the pain of rejection to the pain of unfulfilled love (74); if imperative, the passage is a lovers' hyperbole expressing the limitless extent of his passion, which Isabella has no need to supplement by continuing to kiss him.

75-6 *Pray frown . . . bury me*: it was popularly believed that a man's wrinkles corresponded to the number of his wives; Roberto evidently has more than one, since Isabella suggests that he will outlive her to marry again.

78 *rest*: (*a*) of the soul after death; (*b*) from sexual exertion.

82 *another world*: i.e. the 'little world' of a single human being (in this case, Isabella, who will become subject to Roberto as his wife).

83 *the first*: in Christian mythology, the world as it was originally created by God, before the Fall of Man.

80-4 *By heaven . . . unto thee*: Roberto begins with a sacred oath by heaven and an affirmation of chastity, but ends with the blasphemous suggestions that his relationship with Isabella outdoes the blissful condition of unfallen Adam in the Garden of Eden, and that his love for her is comparable, and equal, to his love for heaven.

85 *falling hand*: losing side, with a pun on falling backwards for sex.

86 *come over*: (*a*) overcome, defeat; (*b*) lie on top of, in the 'missionary position' for sexual intercourse.

89 *I . . . you*: 'I have been thinking about you for a long time'.

90 *a . . . maidenhead*: virginity that is ready for sex.

93 *Virtue's man*: a servant of Virtue personified.

100–1 *bold-faced . . . heads*: the story was more usually told the other way around, with a wife forcibly married to her husband's murderer, and made to drink from a goblet made of her first husband's skull.

97–106 *I here extinguish . . . defame*: the extinguishing of the two black tapers begins as a ritual rejection of mourning, with the first taper representing the memory of Isabella's first husband, Viscount Hermes; but it becomes a rejection of the past more generally, the second taper representing Roberto's emotional immaturities which might threaten the happiness of his marriage.

109–10 *not unlike . . . pronounced*: Rogero also came to woo Isabella, so Roberto's success is like a sentence of death to him.

112 *Cyprus . . . willow*: 'Cyprus' puns on 'cypress', a fine transparent fabric often worn as a hatband or crest to denote mourning; the reference may be to Isabella, soon to be Countess of Cyprus by marriage, rather than to Roberto. Willow was the emblem of a forsaken or disappointed lover.

115 S.D. *Exeunt . . . discovery space*: it is possible that Roberto and Isabella are inside the discovery space and make their exit unseen after the curtains are closed. From this point, the location is undifferentiated until line 138.

117–20 *A player's passion . . . breast*: a passage indebted to *Hamlet* (2.2.553–62); here the player's grief (undoubtedly feigned in Shakespeare) seems more sincere than Isabella's mourning, since the latter has been concluded so speedily.

124 *Nature's . . . disease*: children were normally understood to be a comfort and support to their ageing parents; but women are a discomfort or trouble ('disease', antithesis of 'ease') to Nature the universal parent, and hence not her natural children.

138 *A quarrel*: the feud between Claridiana and Mizaldus turns on their different, but equally lowly, family backgrounds: each taunts the other with his father. Apothecaries were a despised profession and Jews the principal objects of racial hatred; both were also mistrusted as potential poisoners. Presumably the two men consider themselves to have risen in society, and resent being reminded of their origins.

138 S.D. *rosemary*: worn at weddings as an emblem of fidelity.

one door ... other door: little is known about the Whitefriars Theatre where the play was originally performed, but the play assumes two principal stage entrances with a large, probably central, discovery space.

Both ... Guests: the 'others' who help Rogero and Guido to intervene in the fight between bridegrooms. 195 S.D. establishes that Lady Lentulus and the brides are the only women present.

139 *tilt at*: attack with a lance or sword (or, in Rogero's reply, penis).

140–3 *ROGERO ... GUIDO*. Q misattributes these two speeches to the two bridegrooms; they are clearly intended for the principal male wedding-guests. The second, with its explicit bawdy, seems to fit the tone already established for Guido, to whom Mizaldus is on the 'other side' (i.e. opposing party). Thus each bridegroom is restrained by his own guest, while each guest addresses the other bridegroom, providing an initial instance of the inversions and 'cross-points' (cf. note to 2.1.174) which characterize the comic plot.

146 *Alcides*: Hercules, hero of classical legend who fought in the battle between the Centaurs and the Lapiths at the wedding feast of the latter's king (*Met.*, 12).

150 *thy ... circumcised*: i.e. his penis is shorter than it should be (and size is presumed to matter); alternatively, Rogero may be confusing circumcision with castration, a common mistake in the period.

151–2 *Begot ... caterpillar*: Claridiana probably alludes to a pagan kneeling towards Mecca (or to worship the rising sun), a posture which makes the body resemble a crawling caterpillar; the insult turns on the common use of 'caterpillar' as a term for a parasite.

155 *choler*: one of the four humours of Renaissance medical theory, which were thought to determine human behaviour according to their mixture in the bloodstream. An excess of choler, a hot yellow liquid, made a man angry and prone to violence.

156 *Mountebank ... pedantical action*: 'play the mountebank (one who sells quack-medicines in the street) with your over-precise rhetoric'. Apothecaries were notorious for their use of obscure terminology.

157 *bugle-ox*: a buffalo or wild ox; this and the rhinoceros both have horns (also said to grow on cuckolds' foreheads).

160 *metal*: punning on 'mettle'.

162 *Mercury's water*: (*a*) a wash for the skin, prepared from mercury; (*b*) a corrosive mixture of chemicals containing aquafortis (nitric acid).

163 *aspis*: the asp was considered the most poisonous of snakes.

164 *within*: near.

166 *anatomy*: (*a*) corpse used for dissection; (*b*) skeleton. Human skeletons were displayed outside the hall of the Barber Surgeon's Company in London; this is presumably the 'second viewing' (the first being a public anatomy lecture).

168 *tribe of Gad*: one of the twelve tribes of Israel, probably here punning on 'gad' (= goad).

168–70 *that ... dromedary*: Claridiana shrugs off Mizaldus' threat, saying that he (Mizaldus) would not kill him but bring him back to life ('teach ... breathing'), and that he would show less courage if they were alone together; instead he would run away at top speed. (Dromedaries were famous for their speed.)

171 *tallest*: boldest.

176 *still ... again*: with secondary meaning, 'three times distilled'.

177–8 *I'll ... revenged*: 'I'll be revenged even if I have to study the black arts' ('nigromancy').

186 *Capulets ... Montagues*: feuding Veronese families, dramatized in Shakespeare's *Romeo and Juliet* (1595–6).

191 *quicksilver*: mercury, probably punning on 'quacksalver'.

198 *a falling*: (*a*) a falling-out, a fight; (*b*) sex.

198–9 *Guido's faction*: since there is no other evidence of ill-feeling between him and Guido, it is likely that Mendosa is jocularly extending the feud between the two bridegrooms to include their guests: Guido, like Lady Lentulus, was one of Claridiana's wedding guests, whereas Mendosa attended Mizaldus' wedding. Since Guido was a would-be peacemaker, however, and in view of the textual complications regarding the characters' names (on which, see the Note on the Texts; here, Q reads '*Mizaldus* faction'), it is not impossible that the intended referent is Claridiana.

199–200 *from ... pincase*: the phrase 'from the bodkin [dagger] to the pike' was sometimes used in a formal challenge to fight. Here, Mendosa humorously adapts it via the other sense of 'bodkin', a thick sewing needle, and incorporates a secondary, sexual meaning ('case' being a term for the vagina).

205 *Saint Agnes' night*: 21 January; a popular superstition held that a girl who fasted on that night and slept on the floor ('the stones') would dream of her future husband.

216 *put ... hands*: 'trusted me with the knowledge'.

222 *the nick*: the nick of time, the crucial moment; with secondary meaning, 'vagina'.

229 *prick-song*: descant, added to the 'grounds' (plainsong); with obvious bawdy pun.

233 *the least belly-ache*: the smallest indication of possible pregnancy.

237 *by rote*: i.e. insincerely.

240 *She . . . mate*: 'you will marry the next person you look at'.

241 *Till . . . fire*: it was proverbial that a fire could as well be extinguished by foul water as fair (Tilley, W.92); Lady Lentulus applies this to the metaphorical fire of lust.

246 *ladders . . . reach*: qualities which should enable Mendosa to get a better partner; the phrase also contains a latent prolepsis of 3.1.

249 *the camel . . . puddle-water*: it was popularly supposed that camels preferred muddy water to clear.

251 *board*: (*a*) make advances to; (*b*) enter sexually; like several others in this exchange, the word also contains a nautical reference.

255 *gates*: (*a*) outer doors of the house; (*b*) vulva.

259 *princes*: royal heads of state.

258–9 *a fellow . . . invisible*: political assassination was endemic in late sixteenth-century Europe; this passage refers to the case of Juan Jauréguy, who attempted to murder William of Orange in 1582, and was reputedly told that, after the killing, he would become invisible and so be able to escape.

259 *spirit*: a magician's familiar spirit, which put his magic into effect.

264 *little . . . named*: Cupid, the diminutive classical god of love, had the power to induce love in anyone, and was therefore considered mighty in spite of his size.

268 *Furies' sister*: i.e. the cause of prolonged mental discomfort; on the Furies, see note to *Maid*, 5.1.32.

272–3 *your lordship . . . chin*: unlike most adult men of the period, Mendosa has no beard.

275–6 *women's . . . night*: because they will be pregnant.

276 *constant*: faithful; Thais means faithful to their friendship rather than to Abigail's husband (as Abigail takes it).

284–5 *if I were . . . terribly*: Claridiana's gnashing teeth are wittily presented as both cause and effect. According to Roman Catholic belief, the host administered at mass was the body of Christ; to chew it could therefore be understood as a blasphemous act, leading to damnation (and so to 'gnashing of teeth', the usual periphrasis for damnation in St Matthew's Gospel).

293 *stones . . . stock*: punning on penis and testicles ('stock and stones').

291–3 *to be reconciled . . . world*: if a reconciliation were merely for Mizaldus' benefit, Claridiana would not undertake it even if to do so would save humanity; he would let the human race die out and the world be newly

337

peopled by stones (alluding to the classical myth of the deluge, after which a new human race was made from the stones: *Met.*, 1).

299 *character*: handwriting (metaphorical: he intends to mark Mizaldus' fore-head with cuckold's horns).

302 *Cicero's tongue*: the political and courtroom speeches of Marcus Tullius Cicero (106–43 BC), Roman politician and orator, were regarded as the summit of oratory.

303 *Let*: this edn. (Q reads 'But').

305 *Without . . . heaven*. After this line, Q prints a prose line, 'That overgoes my admiration shall not undergo my censure', omitted in this edition; the line is unrelated to the context and was probably a marginal note included in error.

310–11 *I have not . . . monstrous*: Cf. line 157. In fact it was Claridiana who called Mizaldus an onocentaur (half-man, half-ass), though without using the word itself. The inconsistency is attributable to the text's rough, unfinished state; anyone using this edition as the basis for a performance may wish to substitute Mizaldus' actual insult, 'bugle-ox'.

317 *O devil!*: an imprecation, implicitly rejecting Claridiana's overture.

319–21 *Your mother . . . conception*: Mizaldus should take after his mother and show a milder disposition (mildness being a female trait; cf. note to *Maid*, 4.1.98); but even if he does not, his father (his mother's 'rival', i.e. partner) was not a savage animal, so his behaviour has no basis in heredity.

321–3 *You seem . . . meets*: this seems to be a confused recollection of the tra-ditional representation of Envy (= malice), derived from Ovid (*Met.*, 2.768–82), as an old woman eating snake's flesh, and in particular of Geoffrey Whitney's version in *A Choice of Emblems* (1586, p. 94), where the snake's head is shown pointing away from Envy's mouth so that it might appear to be coming out. Thus here Envy 'devours all he meets' in that he will even eat a serpent, but the serpent leaps out again as a hor-rible image of malicious slander.

324–31 *Had . . . sacrifice*: Thais could have persuaded him to silence even when he was in the height of his rage.

328–31 *the lion . . . proud sacrifice*: the goddess Diana was portrayed as a huntress; the lion was archetypally proud. The passage may derive from a confused memory of the incident in *The Faerie Queene* (1.3.5–7) when the lion is tamed by the good influence of Una, whom the satyrs later mistake for Diana (1.6.16.8). Alternatively, Diana may have been con-fused with Daniel, the biblical character who was miraculously saved after King Darius imprisoned him in the lions' den (Daniel 6).

337 *push of pike*: hand-to-hand fighting.

338–9 *At . . . Cadwalader*: as the challenger, Claridiana must accept Mizaldus'
choice of weapon. He implies that Mizaldus, as a Jew, will select weapons
used by heathen peoples: 'hooks' (billhooks) were used in battle by the
Welsh, and the sickle continues to be associated with the Turks, appear-
ing on the modern Turkish flag. I have found no evidence for a
saw as a distinctively Babylonian weapon; it is possible that the word is a
misprint.

339 *Cadwalader*: King of Gwynedd (North Wales), d. AD 634; a great military enemy of the English.

358 *the centre*: of the earth.

359–60 *memory . . . me*: i.e. he magnanimously offers to forget Claridiana's
insults.

362 *want*: lack.

389–90 *nor . . . horn*: Claridiana would not pretend to tolerate (bear) the
enforced truce with Mizaldus, were it not that he means to cuckold him
('sound . . . horn', punning on celebratory playing of wind instruments).

401 *read it fair*: i.e. read it after its own sense and don't infer villainy from it.

403 *stick with*: continue arguing with.

411–12 *Others . . . face*: beauty was often described in terms of light (cf. line
378); Isabella outshines all other women by as much as the full moon does
the stars. But there is an ominous subtext, for the moon was also archetypally changeable.

415 *one . . . edition*: a recently widowed woman.

417 *noble guest*: the soul, traditionally known as the body's guest.

421 *My door*: i.e. the closed door to her house; cf. line 255.

423 *abstracted presence*: absence; she would not have left her house were it not
for the weddings of Claridiana and (tomorrow) Isabella.

426 *tie . . . tackling*: 'hold you to your promise' (punning on 'tackling' = ship's
rigging).

431 *goat's blood*: it was popularly supposed that diamond could be softened
by soaking it in goat's blood.

440 *Apollo's oracle*: the oracle at Delphi was the most famous in classical
Greece, and might be consulted to establish a person's true character or
for a verdict in a disputed case. Its pronouncements were, however, notoriously ambiguous.

441 *branch*: make his head branch out with cuckold's horns.

444 *griping*: painful.

449 *a true Italian*: i.e. given to revenge and cunning stratagem; also implying
his own racial purity in contrast with Mizaldus.

2.1.3 *divine*: spiritual.

6 *Gordian*: King Gordius of Phrygia dedicated his wagon to Jupiter, and fastened the yoke to a beam with an intricate knot, which proved impossible to untie (it was eventually cut by Alexander the Great in 335 BC); hence it was often used as an emblem of marriage.

9 *darts . . . Jove*: thunderbolts.

infernal: hellish (rather than heavenly, because he is a pagan god in juxtaposition with the Christian God referred to in the previous lines).

14 *enforcedly*: perforce; it was proverbial (Tilley, W.650) that women would habitually do what they were forbidden.

16 *cucking-stool*: set beside a pond or river, the stool was used to duck the victim in the water, a traditional punishment for scolding wives.

27 *city show*: a civic pageant (in Jacobean London, procured and performed by the tradesmen's guilds), inappropriate for an aristocratic wedding.

35 *property . . . shower*: they thought the rainbow prop had been brought on stage too early (since a rainbow would usually appear after rain), and so expected a shower (of urine).

36 *feared no colours*: was bold (punning on the colours of the rainbow).

39 *Justice . . . conduit*: a statue of Justice (traditionally represented as a blindfold woman with a set of scales) at a public drinking-fountain.

41–2 *gave . . . handful*: i.e. handed out 'free samples'.

44–6 *he shall . . . short*: he will no longer embarrass himself (in shows or pageants), because he will recognize the superiority of the noblemen's inventiveness ('wit') to that of mere citizens such as he.

46 S.D. *the masque*: here, a show with masked participants and allegorical content, followed by dancing in which the masquers partner members of the audience.

Torch-Bearers: Isabella's later remark (105–6) that Cupid must be present, disguised as a torch-bearer, indicates that these characters are young pages.

47 *be my expositor*: Isabella asks for an explanation of the emblem on Rogero's shield.

49 *Sensi . . . calorem*: I myself felt the heat.

50 *intimates*: Q reads 'imitates', which might make sense as referring to Rogero's performance in the masque (acting being an art of imitation).

54 *must . . . sun*: the overt meaning is that the disappointed lover must look for another woman ('sun') to woo; the fact that the sun which rises again is the same as the one that sets implies an ominous secondary meaning.

56 *Vidua spes*: (*a*) the widowed hope; (*b*) the widow is my hope.

57 *forlorn hope*: the phrase was used to refer to (*a*) the despair of unrequited lovers, (*b*) the vanguard of an attack, and (*c*) lawless desperadoes; the third sense anticipates the role Mendosa adopts later in the play.

66 *well ballast*: low in the water (implying that it is weighed down with cargo).

70 *Adventurer*: playing on the name of the Merchant Adventurers (or Venturers), a trading company incorporated in England in 1564. Members of the company were typically portrayed as being especially eager to leave home in search of profit, which is why, in Abigail's reply, a ship which longs to reach the haven cannot belong to them.

72 *Ut . . . portum*: that I may touch the harbour (with sexual undertone).

75–6 *Aut . . . precibus*: either at a price or through prayers.

77 *common council*: the executive body of a corporate town, hence associated with citizens rather than noblemen; Abigail is saying that her husband's contribution is as 'common' as she feared (cf. lines 27–42).

79 *changed*: from marriage to widowhood.

80 *death's head*: representations of skulls (e.g. in rings, or as paperweights) were common in the period as *memento mori* (reminder of death) devices.

83 *sink apace*: (*a*) 'are quickly getting tired'; (*b*) punning on *cinquepace* (the name of a dance); (*c*) 'are rapidly becoming detumescent'.

84 *That . . . upholsterer*: codpieces (men's decorative pouches worn over the genitals) were padded; Mendosa is saying that his ardour is undiminished, despite any outward appearance to the contrary.

88 *Love makes . . . divine*: Claridiana is motivated by Love (a personification, like the other abstractions in this speech), and this sanctifies *any* love, even an adulterous one like this.

89–90 *Would . . . surfeit*: if 'divine', Claridiana would have greater self-knowledge and morality than to proposition another man's wife; but love typically makes people run to excess in their sexual behaviour.

90 *ere . . . eyes*: Cupid was traditionally represented as a blind archer; here the blindness seems temporary, and associated with the working of his power.

92 *unwilling*: involuntary.

93 *anatomized*: opened by a surgeon (i.e. exposing the heart to view).

95 *Apelles*: Greek painter (356–308 BC); none of his work is extant, but a celebrated picture of Aphrodite (Greek goddess of love) rising from the sea is described by Pliny (*Natural History*, 35.91). It did not incorporate the burning heart Mizaldus mentions, but this image frequently appeared in sixteenth-century emblem books, signifying the pains of love.

100 *th' eagle's*: the eagle's eyes were deemed superior because it alone could look at the sun; Abigail's eyes outdo even these.

103 *stones*: (*a*) a byword for unresponsiveness; (*b*) jewels, referring to the ring he has offered her; (*c*) testicles.

103 S.D. *falls in love*: presumably this could be conveyed by visual means alone, without dialogue. Probably their eyes meet, and she responds: the process of falling in love was sometimes understood in terms of beams projecting from the eyes, and striking one another.

104 *Change . . . robbery*: proverbial (Tilley, C.228).

107 *brand*: Cupid was often depicted with a firebrand, signifying passion.

109 *Etna . . . anvil*: Vulcan, the classical god of fire and metal-working, was husband of Venus and so the putative father of Cupid; his smithy was located under the volcano Etna in Sicily.

111–12 *beacons . . . powers*: the image is of a besieged town lighting beacons to summon military reinforcements.

119 *Murano*: an island in the Venetian lagoon.

121 *put in*: (*a*) enter the house; (*b*) enter sexually.

122 *stand . . . nick*: (*a*) 'are ready at the exact moment'; (*b*) 'are erect inside the vagina'.

126 *open all*: (*a*) arrange for the doors to be open to allow access; (*b*) reveal everything (because he will not be able to see); (*c*) 'open your legs'.

129 *Tie . . . fast*: to wear a tight ring (cf. Tilley, R.129) meant to undertake a task too difficult for oneself.

130 *brought . . . bay*: 'got me at bay' (hunting term).

135 *ploughs . . . quarry*: (*a*) attempts an impossible task; (*b*) 'tries to fuck a stone': Claridiana implies that Thais is sexually frigid.

136 *Pygmalion*: in classical mythology, a sculptor who fell in love with his own statue ('image') of a woman, Galatea; Venus brought it to life (*Met.*, 10).

142 *spheres*: in the Ptolemaic theory of the universe, between Earth and heaven there were seven planets (including the sun and moon) fixed to rotating crystal spheres; according to the Greek philosopher Pythagoras (sixth century BC), the harmonious movement of the spheres produced a beautiful melody. Although discredited by Copernicus, the system served as a metaphor for cosmic order in the work of many Renaissance writers.

143 S.D. *fall off*: leave the dance floor.

144 *begin a health*: propose a toast.

145 *MENDOSA, CLARIDIANA, and MIZALDUS*: this edn; Q calls simply for '3. or 4.' to speak this line. This might indicate a number of supernumeraries taking part in the masque, which would in turn require a corresponding number of additional ladies to dance with them. However, the stage is already crowded (the scene calls for two groups of supernumerary torch-bearers as well as the ten speaking parts), and, even if company

personnel stretched to six or eight more supernumeraries, to include them would make it even more difficult to focus on the characters who matter. Moreover, it would also make Rogero's silence, commented on by Isabella in the next speech, less remarkable in that the three other named masquers also fail to reply.

146 *pledge*: a counter-toast, often drunk from the same cup.

147-8 *'t may be . . . we*: the overt meaning is that it would be presumptuous of Isabella to choose Rogero a mistress more beautiful or of higher rank than herself; the latent meaning is that she is herself the mistress whom she would choose.

148 *we*: Isabella uses the royal plural.

149 S.D. *lavolta . . . galliard*: lively dances which entail leaping into the air.

158 *banquet*: a dessert, served in a separate room after a meal, and usually without servants to wait on the diners.

158 S.D. *Rogero . . . on*: Isabella mentions at line 188 that Rogero is still masked; his unwillingness to reveal his face is probably a mark of the shame he feels at his accident (162-4).

The seats are removed: the clearing-up cannot be left until the end of the scene, since the action continues immediately, so it must take place in the background at some point. The precise timing is open to interpretation, but the departure of the bridegroom in whose honour the masque has been performed seems an appropriate cue.

160 *put you in*: 'accompany you in to the banquet'.

161 *My lord . . . sociate?*: it is unclear to whom the line is spoken. As citizens, Claridiana and Mizaldus would not be addressed as 'my lord'. It is possible that Mendosa speaks to Rogero, whose lack of a partner has already been remarked upon by Isabella; if so, he must respond with only a look, which might not be inappropriate in view of his sense of shame expressed after Mendosa and the ladies have left the stage. Alternatively, Roberto, off-stage in the next room, is also notably unpartnered now that Isabella has walked out. It is also possible that a speech prefix is missing, and that the line is spoken to Mendosa by Lady Lentulus.

166 *stiffest*: (*a*) boldest; (*b*) most erect (with 'fall' in the next line implying 'detumesce').

169 *What . . . way?*: victims of accidents would say that the devil laid his horns in their way; Rogero's concerns are more secular, and more sexual.

174 *cross-point*: an *entrechon*, a dance step in which the legs are crossed and uncrossed while leaping in the air; also, more broadly, a metaphor for the play's comic action.

183 *Love*: i.e. the god of love.

184-6 *Than . . . serve*: Isabella's speeches form a single verse line, interrupted by her kiss and Rogero's aside.

188–9 *face . . . disgrace*. Rhyme was sometimes used to show lovers in almost telepathic sympathy with one another, most famously in the sonnet shared between Romeo and Juliet in Shakespeare's play (1.5.92–105); cf. also 4.2.208–11. Here, the rhymed asides show Rogero and Isabella closer than even they know.

191 *the Fates*: who determined human destiny in classical mythology, by spinning a thread representing a person's life (cf. 4.2.201).

190–3 *have you . . . with me*. This may be another inconsistency attributable to the play's unfinished state (cf. note to 1.1.310–11): it was Mizaldus who gave a gem to Thais, not Rogero to Isabella; the confusion may have arisen from the fact that Mizaldus was called 'Rogero' in the earlier draft (see the Note on the Texts). Alternatively, Isabella may herself be the gem, lost to Rogero not only through her marriage (as expressed in his masque *imprese*) but also because his accident made him look ridiculous in front of her (and therefore, to his mind though not Isabella's, unlovable).

194 *bends*: inclines.

198 *well*: appropriately.

205 *With . . . advantage*: only against the heaviest odds.

209 *beguile*: the word is governed by 'Though' in the previous line; some editors have considered emending to 'beguiled', but the movement from subjunctive to indicative may also serve as a kind of syntactical wish-fulfilment.

207–12 *Were I . . . thrall*: in classical mythology, Apollo fell in love with the nymph Daphne and pursued her; she fled until exhausted, and was turned into a laurel tree (*Met.*, 1). Isabella is saying that she would reject Apollo (the most beautiful of the male gods) but allow Rogero to catch her. Ovid's Daphne is warned that she may trip on briars in her flight (*Met.*, 1. 508–9); Isabella's will trip over the flimsiest obstacle (cowslip stalks are floppy), because she wants to be caught.

213 *chance*: fortune.

214 *satyr*: ugly, rough and lecherous creature in classical mythology, half-man, half-goat. Venus is shown accepting one as a paying lover in Hernando de Soto's *Emblemas* (Madrid, 1599). Isabella's point, however, is that even a goddess will choose any partner when in thrall to sexual desire; in Rogero (her 'fair aim', 215) she at least has a more attractive object than Venus' satyr.

218 *music*: i.e. Rogero's name.

221 *Worthies*: the Nine Worthies (men of renown), three biblical, three classical, and three medieval heroes (traditionally Joshua, King David, and Judas Maccabaeus; Hector, Alexander the Great, and Julius Caesar; and King Arthur, Charlemagne, and Godfrey of Boulogne); they were a popular subject for pageants.

224–5 *I have ... trussed up for*: the lines hint that Isabella's wealth is ill-gotten. In the source, William Painter's *Palace of Pleasure*, her father is a usurer; the 'proper men' may have been tied in the metaphorical bondage of debt. Alternatively, men were literally 'trussed up' prior to being hanged, so Anna may be suggesting that the goods are stolen (and perhaps given to Isabella by obsessive lovers who later paid the penalty for theft).

226 *take ... night*: the scene is set in Venice on the evening of Isabella's wedding day. Anna is to travel overnight to Pavia, a city in the Duchy of Milan in northern Italy, about 150 miles from Venice. Isabella will follow with Rogero the following day (231–4).

227 *secretary*: one entrusted with secrets.

229 *the King of Love*: Venus was known as the Queen of Love (cf. line 95); Isabella invents a masculine counterpart.

231–3 *Ere Phoebus' ... sea*: before tomorrow's dusk. Phoebus, the classical sun-god, was thought to drive the sun across the sky in a chariot every day; Thetis, a sea-nymph, is described as Phoebus' lover (a role she did not have in mythology) in that they spend every night together (because the sun sets into the sea).

235 *fleet*: the word could be either verb (= move swiftly) or adjective (= swift); if the latter, it could also imply 'inconstant', a relevant secondary sense albeit not one intended by Isabella.

240 *thought*: imagined, anticipated.

241 *Andromeda*: in classical mythology, the daughter of Cassiopeia who was offered for sacrifice to a sea monster, and rescued by Perseus (*Met.*, 4).

249 *Beams*: of the sun.

244–9 *Sullen Night ... shadowest*: it was conventional for lovers to wish the night extended in order to lengthen their love-making (cf. note to *Maid*, 1.2.200–4); Isabella, going to Roberto's bed, hopes her ordeal will soon be over.

252 *die*: experience orgasm.

2.2.5 *hole*: (*a*) either the ring which was the lance's target in a tournament (cf. 2.3.119–20) or the name of a card-game (cf. 3.1.24, 3.3.2, 4.1.29); (*b*) vagina.

7 *at the face*: (*a*) directly; (*b*) face close to face (during sex).

10 *done ... hand*: 'ready-made'.

14 *back and belly*: A strong back was considered the *sine qua non* of sexual potency; the belly is here metonymic for the appetitive urge.

15 *starved me*: Claridiana has not consummated the marriage.

17 *turn me*: the phrase develops from Abigail's statement of her own sexual flexibility ('pliant and yielding'), but also, more literally, implies that she would even consent to buggery.

345

18 *style . . . high*: (*a*) referring to the 'high style' of Renaissance rhetoric, used to define the status of both the speaker and the subject-matter; (*b*) punning on 'stile'.

20–1 *astonishment . . . creation*: compliments to Thais (*astonishment* = marvel).

22 *honest*: chaste.

23 *a woman . . . answer*: because silence implies consent.

25 *a white sheet*: (*a*) the sheet of paper on which the letter is written; (*b*) referring to the custom of dressing sinners (especially adulterers) in white sheets to do public penance.

26–7 *the shaking . . . sheets*: a popular dance tune, often applied punningly to sex in bed.

29–30 *dash . . . parentheses*: dashes and parentheses were used to signify words omitted for decency's sake. Abigail may mean that Mizaldus has included such words anyway ('he' being perhaps a misprint for 'lie', i.e. go to bed with, 'as' perhaps signifying 'arse'), but has enclosed them within the usually modest, but here bawdy, parentheses.

31 *prick*: mark of punctuation (with obvious bawdy pun).

31–2 *he . . . hand*: Mizaldus has submitted himself so absolutely to Abigail that any commitment *not* expressed in his letter would still be legally binding on him.

33 *I . . . Judas*: Judas Iscariot (who betrayed Jesus to the Jewish authorities in Jerusalem in exchange for thirty pieces of silver) was traditionally represented as having a red beard. Marston also had one, and his plays often mention this by way of a private joke.

34 *makes . . . me*: 'values me highly' (here ironic).

36 *drink*: poison.

on: of; a common Jacobean usage.

that he will: if he should.

39 *signed . . . woodcock*: (*a*) assented to Mizaldus' will (literally, accepted responsibility for paying his bill) like a 'woodcock' (a byword for a simpleton); (*b*) 'inscribed my name on his beak as if he were a woodcock (a long-billed migratory bird), thereby identifying him as my property'. 'Woodcock' refers to Abigail in the first sense and Mizaldus in the second, emphasizing the fact that it is really Mizaldus who is acting foolishly (hence the parenthesis that follows).

45 *I . . . red*: (*a*) referring to the ruby ring he gave her (2.1.98 S.D.); (*b*) his testicles flushed with excitement.

48 *hawking about*: (*a*) hunting; (*b*) propositioning.

49 *closely* (*a*) secretly, privately; (*b*) with bodies close to one another.

50 *knew*: i.e. sexually; Thais is afraid of being raped.

51–2 *they are . . . together*: proverbial (Tilley, B.393).

59 *cleanly conveyance*: smooth transference (of the husbands, from the doors to the bedrooms).

nigglers: the word may mean 'idlers' or 'lascivious people'. Given the emphasis on darkness in this passage, it is also possible that the printer's copy read 'niggers' (not then an offensive term), indicating that the maids are black; this would suit the Venetian context.

65 *garden-pales*: a fence or row of stakes separating the two back gardens.

69 *crack*: boast (punning on 'creak').

72 *maid*: implying 'virgin'.

74 *boarded*: with a sexual secondary meaning (see note to 1.1.251).

86 *speak*: i.e. by crying out in sexual excitement.

97–8 *Are . . . another?*: younger brothers are here understood to be archetypally prone to sleep with other men's wives. The idea originates in a contemporary joke used by Marston as the sub-plot of *The Fawn* (1605), in which a younger brother sleeps with his elder sibling's wife and fathers a child who displaces him as heir to the estate.

104 *Jaques*: the name has two syllables.

105 *vessel*: a gondola.

108–9 *tie . . . fare*: 'force you to eat an unpleasant diet'.

111 *defraud*: deceive; the line may also have a secondary meaning ('the first sex is the best') which Thais later disavows (4.3.28–30).

2.3.31 *lewd*: wicked.

46–7 *O my . . . feel*: the subject of the verb in this sentence is 'new thoughts', not 'brave sprightly lord'. In all four plays, singular verbs are frequently governed by plural nouns, and vice versa.

67 *the Trojan wanderer*: Paris, who abducted Helen of Troy, Queen of Sparta (hence 'the Greek').

69 *Danaë*: see note to *Val.*, 2.5.28–34.

75 *my lord*: this form of address implied 'husband' (hence the parenthesis that follows).

77 *Furies*: see note to *Maid*, 5.1.32; the allusion implies Isabella's latent sense of guilt at her extra-marital liaison.

81 *I'll . . . long*: a hexameter line.

90–1 *Now use . . . net*: Rogero does not kiss Isabella as soon as asked, but plays hard-to-get.

91 *Vulcan's net*: in classical mythology, Mars, god of war, committed adultery with Venus, goddess of love; her husband Vulcan caught them in bed

together, trapped them with a net, and shamed them by displaying them to the other gods (*Met.*, 4). Some versions of the story make the onlookers envious of Mars.

100 *the plot*: evidently this was suggested in Isabella's letter.

103 *gaze*: gaze at.

102–4 *thus once . . . sight*: in classical mythology, Orpheus, a poet from Thrace, visited the underworld to rescue his dead wife Eurydice; as a boon, Pluto (the ruler of the dead) permitted her to follow him back to the world of the living, on condition that he did not look back at her during the journey; he did, and consequently she died a second time (*Met.*, 10).

106 *I'd see*: 'I'd like to see' (i.e. a statement of defiance).

106 S.D. *Enter . . . Guido*: this is often marked as the start of a new scene, but the action is continuous and there is no change of location.

110 *Fly . . . six o'clock*: Claridiana is preoccupied with thinking ahead to his 6 p.m. date with Thais, and wants the day to be over quickly.

112 *Jove . . . Semele*: in classical mythology, Jupiter appeared to Semele, who was pregnant by him, in the form of a thundercloud, and she was killed by his lightning (*Met.*, 3). Claridiana is still thinking of the night to come: the line begins a syntactic unit continued, after interruptions, in line 115. The idea may develop from the thunderous sound of the horses' hooves and Guido's mention of the hurricane. In any event, it is typically self-regarding: Claridiana is more interested in identifying himself with a god than Thais with the doomed Semele.

119 *staff*: (*a*) lance; (*b*) penis.

the rest: (*a*) support holding the lance horizontal for jousting; (*b*) vagina.

120 *tilt*: (*a*) ride to attack in a joust; (*b*) have an erection.

crest: (*a*) heraldic device worn on a knight's helmet in a tournament; (*b*) cuckold's horns.

121 *cod's head:* (*a*) blockhead; (*b*) someone with his mind on his testicles ('cods').

129 *bravoes*: a prostitute's enforcers; Roberto is simultaneously calling Isabella a whore and worrying about the prospect of being assaulted or killed should he cross her. (However, 'bravoes' did not refer specifically to hired assassins until *c.*1620.)

149 *after ages*: future times.

147–51 *Since . . . shame*: Roberto is humiliated by Isabella's rejection of him on the day after their marriage.

155 *keep*: dwell.

166 *capuchins*: a breakaway order of Franciscan friars, formed *c.*1528, famous for its austerity.

348

3.1 S.D. *several*: different; obviously each of them will exit using the door through which the other entered.

Lady Lentulus' window: represented by the upper acting area where Lady Lentulus makes her entrance.

3 *melancholy*: one of the four humours (see note to 1.1.155), black in colour.

4 *Heaven's eyes*: the stars.

5 *sphere*: see note to 2.1.142.

9–10 *lower house . . . chaste Phoebe*: Lady Lentulus is envisaged as an astral body (Phoebe, an alternative name for Diana, goddess of the moon and chastity), and her dwelling as one of the astrological 'houses' of the planets.

11 *brings*: the subject of the verb is 'thoughts'; cf. note to 2.3.46–7.

19 *Endymion*: in classical mythology, a beautiful youth who fell in love with the moon and watched it in a trance from the top of Mount Latmus in Asia Minor. Here, the allusion draws on the two-level staging, with Lady Lentulus' window cast as Latmus, a point between heaven and earth.

22 *chaste-vowed*: vowed to chastity.

42 S.D. *He . . . falls*: Mendosa's fall presents a difficult staging problem: the actor needs to land in plain view on the stage and appear stunned; but without something to break his fall he risks injury. It is unclear how this would have been achieved in the original production.

45 *that Sestian dame*: Hero of Sestos, a priestess in classical mythology whose lover Leander nightly swam across the Hellespont (the strait separating Macedonia from Turkey), to meet her; eventually he drowned and Hero committed suicide when his body was washed up on the shore.

57 *Relief . . . shame*: if she opens her doors to help Mendosa, she breaks her vow; but if she keeps it she will be shamed (because her liaison with Mendosa will be discovered).

61 *viper envy*: a common metaphor, turning on (*a*) the extreme poisonousness of the viper, like the noxious effects of malice, and (*b*) the way an envious person is psychologically destroyed by his own malice, just as unborn vipers were believed to gnaw through the entrails of their mother.

62 *my soul's rest*: a vocative, referring to Lady Lentulus.

68 *two stars*: Lady Lentulus' eyes.

85 S.D. *the Watch*: a night patrol comprising, or paid for by, the householders of the parish, and empowered to arrest suspected malefactors.

88–9 *a cloak . . . spur*: Jacobean courtiers wore such items; the Watchmen have the power to challenge their social betters.

90 *cock of the game*: a fighting cock (armed with sharp metal spurs).

91–2 *for . . . voice*: i.e. as a penalty for not speaking out; appropriately, capons cannot crow.

95 *aloft*: (*a*) upstairs; (*b*) mounted for sex.

97 *halberdiers*: i.e. watchmen, who were armed with halberds (long-handled weapons combining an axe-blade and spear-head).

98 *tickle*: (*a*) catch; (*b*) chastise; (*c*) excite sexually.

100 *shevoiliero*: knight. The word mangles French and Spanish together: like his predecessor Dogberry in Shakespeare's *Much Ado about Nothing* (1598), the Captain is less fluent in high vocabulary than he would like to think.

102 *fees*: criminals had to pay a fee for their own imprisonment.

105 *Some two hundred*: alluding to the many knights created by James I as a money-raising device (each new knight paid a fee to the crown).

111 *Art*: skilled medical help.

114, 116 S.D.S *Exeunt some Watchmen . . . Exeunt the rest of the Watch*. The absolute minimum number of Watchmen required is four (two to remove Mendosa's body and one each to arrest the two husbands), but obviously the scene would benefit from having more.

116 S.D. *Claridiana's . . . houses*: i.e. the doors through which the two husbands exited at the start of the scene.

120 *itself's*: its own.

124 *Cross-ruff*: a card game, with a sexual secondary meaning ('ruff' refers to sexual passion).

Christmas: refers to the custom of 'letting in Christmas', whereby the first visitor admitted to the house at midnight on Christmas Day was an especially honoured guest. Other visitors at Christmas included mummers, who would perform a traditional play in the homes of the principal members of a community.

128 *an action*: legal proceedings for slander.

131 *Take law*: 'take the execution of justice into your own hands'; Mizaldus would then have to hang himself as a villain.

132 *she*: Abigail.

133 *dangerous*: because the French were thought to be syphilitic.

137 *new-christened*: with horns; Christian baptism entailed making the sign of the cross with holy water on the child's forehead.

150–2 *Hemp . . . ink-horns of*: he will be killed by the hangman's noose (which was made of hemp) rather than by the quacksalver Claridiana. The reference to posthumous recycling of his cuckold's horns may play on the common idea that apothecaries made their medicines from dead human bodies: at least hanging will spare him that fate.

3.2.7 *Fear . . . move*: 'Let fear remain with cowards; the airy nothings of imagination cannot disturb fixed stars like ourselves.'

10 *Fear's . . . nectar*: fear intensifies the heat of desire ('fervency'), which in turn intensifies the pleasure of love.

17 *time's scholar*: the phrase is obscure; perhaps 'time's' is a misprint for 'love's'. Isabella may be playing on the scholastic sense of 'oratory' (cf. note to 1.1.72).

19 *maintain*: support.

26 *period of . . . content*: the conclusive point at which content is attained.

29 S.D. *He kisses Isabella*: Gniaca later apologizes (51–2) for something he would not have done had he known Rogero and Isabella were attached. A greeting kiss seems probable, hence Rogero's statement (32) that he can conceive imaginatively the joy which Gniaca actually tastes.

34 *He's fairer than he was*: the first 'he' is Gniaca, the second, Rogero.

40 *eagle's eyes*: see note to 2.1.100.

44 *fumitory*: a weed, used medicinally to improve the vision (Pliny, *Natural History*, 25.99); Isabella is saying that Gniaca's beauty has given her the clarity of sight she describes in lines 38–41. (This edn; Q reads 'femelacy', a word not elsewhere recorded. The copy probably read 'femetary', an early seventeenth-century spelling of 'fumitory', easily misreadable as 'femelacy' in contemporary handwriting. Other editors have suggested that 'femelacy' is a nonce-word, possibly expressing male beauty in female terms; or that more serious textual corruption has mangled a line which may originally have read something like ' 'Tis shape makes man kill female constancy'.)

46 *quit*: requite.

60 *Aid . . . constancy*: 'May Rogero's love make him believe in female constancy.'

69 S.D. *with Attendants*: the supernumeraries who entered with Gniaca are presumably not present to witness his wooing by Isabella.

72 *love, . . . loving*: 'love me, my love (vocative), in return for my loving you'.

80 *violent*: excessive, intense (and therefore evanescent); cf. the proverb, 'Hot love is soon cold' (Tilley, L.483).

91 *soul-killing*: because suicide was a mortal sin.

99 *Love's Queen*: Venus.

114 *condescend*: accede, consent.

121 *Hippocrates*: the greatest physician of antiquity (459–*c*. 350 BC); the name has four syllables.

3.3.2 *noddy*: (*a*) a card game similar to cribbage (cf. 'cross-ruff', 3.1.124); (*b*) fool (referring to the husbands); (*c*) copulation.

3 *our . . . jury*: in their desire to be executed, they have pre-empted the verdict (delivered to the court by the jury's foreman).

4 *heretic . . . predestination*: John Calvin's Protestant theology held that all events had been predetermined by God, and that no human action could change destiny. This was considered heretical by the Catholic church which held sway in Italy.

4–5 *born . . . hanged*: it was proverbial that hanging, like marriage, was decreed by destiny (Tilley, W.232).

6 *judgement*: (*a*) judicial verdict; (*b*) sagacity, wisdom.

8–9 *his . . . down*: i.e. he became detumescent.

11 *They . . . action*: Abigail's marriage has still not been consummated; Thais's may have been (cf. lines 13–14).

19–20 *if . . . will*: 'if we, who have appetites ("stomachs") seek to have "strange flesh" (= (*a*) unusual food, possibly desired during pregnancy; (*b*) someone else's penis), whenever we desire it'.

23–4 *we . . . lives*: it was popularly believed that a virgin could save a condemned man from hanging by taking him for her husband.

27 *broad seal*: the great seal; supreme authority.

30 *but*: only.

35 *The Snarl*: satires were often said to snarl, playing on two contemporary senses of the word; to snare and to quarrel aggressively; Abigail adds the third sense (lines 37–8), implying that her husband is a snarling animal, and so incapable of salvation.

36 *book*: with secondary meaning 'literacy': condemned men could save themselves from execution by pleading 'benefit of clergy', if they could pass a literacy test; they were then branded and handed over to the church courts, which did not pass capital sentences.

37–8 *any . . . fashion*: i.e. misogynists. Such attitudes were common in the period (cf. 3.4.48).

41–2 *being . . . consumption*: i.e. he would fatally exhaust himself with too much sex; a variation on the idea (cf. note to *Maid*, 1.1.139–40) that sex shortens life.

43–4 *Make . . . wise*: 'value your husband despite the sexual enjoyment we get from adultery ("wanton prize"), thereby combining pleasure with prudence as the proverb [Tilley, G.324] advises'.

3.4.2–3 *bring . . . shoulders*: Aeneas famously carried his father Anchises from burning Troy; Isabella inverts the image so that Gniaca, a young man, is carried by old Father Time.

6 *lock*: Time was conventionally depicted with a long forelock and the back of his head bald, signifying the need to grasp opportunity in time.

8 *Medea-like*: in classical mythology, Medea magically rejuvenated her father-in-law Aeson; but she later became a notorious murderess, so the simile is ominous as well as inviting (*Met.*, 7).

16 *still to cover*: always to conceal.

26 *sphere-like*: see note to 2.1.142.

29 *Panchaia*: a legendary Red Sea island, famous for its balsam, cinnamon, and incense-bearing trees; mentioned in *Met.*, 10. 309.

31 S.D. *with a Page*. The page will be needed to sing at 81 S.D., after Gniaca and Isabella have exited to make love in 'privacy' (74); presumably he would already have appeared as one of the attendants who arrive with Gniaca in 3.2. If, like his master, he is dressed for hunting, then he will complement the scene's classical eroticism with a visual allusion to Cupid.

32–3 *His breath . . . consume*: now that Gniaca is present, Isabella's instructions to perfume the air are no longer necessary, nor is there any need to waste time as discussed in the scene's opening speech.

34 *Adonis*: in classical mythology, a beautiful young huntsman loved by Venus, and later killed by a wild boar (*Met.*, 10).

35 *goddess-tempter*: tempter of a goddess; Isabella identified herself with the love-goddess Venus at 3.2.99.

38 *Joy's*: this edn. (Q reads 'Ways'); Isabella is saying that, having Gniaca's love, her earthly condition exceeds the joys of the afterlife.

52 *Conditioned lover, Cupid's intelligencer*: these epithets refer to Isabella herself; 'Conditioned' means 'wanton, especially disposed to love'. (This edn.; Q's reading, 'Conditious . . .', is probably corrupt. The authors may have found the word 'conditioned' in the source, Painter's *Palace of Pleasure*, where the seduction of Ardizzino, the original of Rogero, is said to be a lesson 'to refrain the whorish looks of light conditioned dames'.)

55–8 *For women's . . . nature*: Women hold sway over men of all ranks and types; and though men are scornful and conceited in their assumed superiority, women are nature's supreme creation.

59 *admire*: wonder.

62 *Paphian*: venereal; from Paphos, a name for Cyprus where Venus was born.

77 *that fruit . . . wise*: in a startling transition from classical to Judaeo-Christian mythology, Isabella equates herself with Eve, who fed Adam the apple from the tree of knowledge, causing the Fall of Man and expulsion from Eden.

82 *I . . . captive*: because she has her arms around his neck.

free: (*a*) at liberty, unrestrained; (*b*) liberal (possibly implying licentious).

91 *deaths*: with secondary meaning 'orgasms'.

93 *delicates*: delicacies (metaphorically applied to Isabella herself).

98 *shame . . . diseases*: moral infamy and venereal diseases.

100 *you*: i.e. women, thought to be constitutionally more changeable than men.

108 *The serpent's . . . in me*: 'May I have the cunning which the serpent used in tempting Eve' (cf. line 77).

113 *under*: at ground level, whereas Isabella is going to the upper acting area (her 'window', 107).

114 *Ushers*: assistant schoolmasters, punning on her task as door-keeper (cf. line 16).

degrees: (*a*) steps or rungs on a ladder; (*b*) gradual stages; (*c*) academic qualifications (which make the difference between being an usher and a master).

133 *puritan*: follower of an extreme Protestant movement which advocated self-restraint. Puritans in general were often suspected of secretly indulging in sexual excess and perversion, but the line may also refer implicitly to the Family of Love, one of the most radical puritan sects, which believed that religion consisted chiefly in the practice of love, and which was accused of advocating absolute sexual freedom.

146 *family*: sect; from the Family of Love (see previous note).

148 *fee-simple*: absolute possession in perpetuity (legal terminology referring to the ownership of land).

149 *halt*: limp.

156 *but now*: only a moment ago.

159 *done*: finished, disappeared forever.

170 *Ushers . . . hair*: to have more hair than wit was proverbial (Tilley, B.736); the association with ushers may suggest panders 'of the hold-door trade' (Shakespeare, *Troilus and Cressida*, Additional Passage B.19) who have lost their hair through syphilis.

174 *private*: accessible to or patronized by only men of higher rank; as such, Isabella is worse than a common strumpet because of the greater status (and presumed virtue) of the men she corrupts.

176 *that . . . hell*: the seven deadly sins. These included pride and lust, but not murder (though contemporary thought considered it a natural consequence of lust, envy, and anger; and it is proleptic here; cf. 4.2.75, 5.1.25–6).

179 *without souls*: see note to 5.2.35–6.

184 *painting*: cosmetics.

189 *a . . . act*: punning on 'the act', the name for the break in the performance between the acts when music was played as the stage candles were trimmed.

4.1 S.D. *the rest of the Watch*: so Q; but only the Captain speaks, and the others may well be token representatives rather than the full complement.

2 *Senate*: the Jacobeans conceived the Venetian Senate as a judicial as well as a legislative body.

6 *cause*: legal case, subject of litigation.

9 *Subject authority*: the Senators, subject to the head of state.

1–12 *Justice ... mine own*: judicial corruption was a major topic of concern after the great extension of state power in sixteenth-century England. This passage rehearses familiar views on a ruler's proper administration of justice in order to establish Amago's credentials as a figure of unquestioned authority. See also 5.1.48–50.

20 *vipers*: vipers were a byword for ingratitude and betrayal (and so, by extension, treason) because they were thought to kill their mother in the act of being born (cf. note to 3.1.61); here, Claridiana and Mizaldus are called traitors in that they profess to have killed a member of the royal family.

27 *jealousy*: often considered a vice of the Italians in general, because Italian women were allegedly more prone than those of other nations to commit adultery; Venetian women had a particularly bad reputation for promiscuity, which may be why their men are singled out here.

29 *magnificoes ... stamp*: stamped as cuckolds.

29–30 *primero ... presence*: (*a*) a card game in the presence chamber at court, where the monarch would appear to receive official visitors; (*b*) sex in the vagina.

34 *needy*: lacking either money or original ideas for a plot.

34–5 *brought us ... stage*: a number of comedies performed by London theatre companies of the period were in fact thinly disguised retellings of real-life incidents illustrating the sexual mores of citizens.

44 *lanthorn and candle*: Londoners were required to provide street lighting by hanging a lantern (here given in its old spelling, to preserve the pun on the cuckold's horns) outside their front door at dusk. It is unclear how 'candle' (sometimes used to pun on the penis) might refer to Thais: Mizaldus may mean 'me and my wife' to refer loosely to their story; alternatively horns and (the temporary use of another man's) penis may be what husband and wife have respectively got from the incident.

51 *after*: subsequent.

55–6 *Grave ... earth*: underlying the passage is the biblical injunction, 'Judge not, that ye be not judged' (Matthew 7: 1): because sin is inescapable (as Reformation theologians taught with reference to 1 John 1: 8), Amago is aware that he has frailties comparable with the defendants', and so treats the normally serious matter of justice with a levity appropriate to the case.

60 *promoter . . . Lent*: it was forbidden to sell or eat meat during Lent; a 'promoter' (informer) would be rewarded with a portion of the fine levied. Mendosa was, of course, after 'flesh' (in the sexual sense), and 'Lent' carries a latent pun on Lady Lentulus' name.

61 *Venetian spirit*: both jealous (line 27 above) and vindictive (4.2.129).

65 *dart*: weapon (literally a spear, associated with Death personified in Renaissance iconography).

66 *lever*: crowbar.

66–7 *I brained him . . . Strike home*: Claridiana, who claims more legal knowledge, skilfully implicates Mizaldus: in English law, anyone present at and abetting a murder was a principal offender, not merely an accessory. (Mizaldus later shows himself ignorant of this point of law, lines 74–5.)

75 *gave consent*: was an accessory.

76 *cross*: contrary.

78 *slip*: (*a*) fail (literally, fall); (*b*) escape.

80 *jump*: (*a*) agree exactly; (*b*) literally jump, off the ladder of the gallows as they are hanged.

81 *I'll . . . cross-point*: he will arrange matters so that only he is hanged; here 'cross-point' (cf. note to 2.1.174) refers to the kicking legs of the hanged man.

83 *make . . . mouth*: 'making a mouth' refers both to a derisive face and the open-mouthed grimace of a hanged man.

86 *Jew*: the most provocative insult Mizaldus could offer the anti-Semitic Claridiana.

89 *Fencer*: professional swordsman; they were often thought to be either contemptible parasites or foolish.

91 *Hang . . . quarter*: referring to hanging, drawing, and quartering, the standard penalty in England for high treason.

96 *a turn*: the push given by the hangman, 'turning' his victim off the ladder.

103 *the . . . Judgement*: the last day on which, according to Christian belief, the dead would rise from their graves to be sent either to heaven or hell.

108 *King's . . . breath*: i.e. the sentence is irrevocable.

112 S.D. *the Captain of the Watch . . . returns*: Q requires the Captain to enter with Mendosa, even though he has already entered at the start of the scene and is presumably on stage when Mizaldus refers to him at line 24. The most likely solution is that he exits here to supervise the removal of his first set of prisoners, and then re-enters immediately with Mendosa.

133 *So*: provided that.

136 *that favour*: i.e. a quick death by beheading, rather than a slow one by strangulation at the rope's end. Decapitation was the prerogative of the aristocracy in Jacobean England.

4.2.7 *viper*: as well as envy (= malice), poison, and betrayal (all relevant here; cf. notes to 3.1.61, 4.1.20), the viper was associated with slander and calumny. However, the image also cuts back at Isabella herself: the female viper was thought to bite off her mate's head after copulation, just as Isabella now seeks to have Rogero killed.

   get: attack.

13 *Atlas' back*: in classical mythology Atlas held up the heavens, and so had the strongest back of all (cf. note to 2.2.14).

15 *renders . . . for*: gives Fidelity personified ('Truth') deceit in return for.

36 *Composed of me*: i.e. having the same flesh and blood.

53 *dart*: cf. note to 4.1.65.

58 *Phoenix*: a mythical Arabian bird which was reborn out of its own funeral pyre: only one existed at any one time, hence a byword for uniqueness.

62 *Lethy*: causing oblivion; from Lethe, a river in the classical underworld whose waters, when drunk, induced amnesia.

63 *useless*: unprofitable, worthless.

67 *mad'st 'em known*: in the libels Isabella has read.

79 *has*: who has.

85 *tending*: intending.

88–9 *I do . . . remove*: the sincerity and completeness of the friends' reconciliation is signalled by the way one effortlessly completes the other's sentence.

95 *Indian . . . treasure*: it was widely reported that uncivilized peoples such as the native Americans would exchange their valuable possessions for trinkets. Anna is calling Rogero's attention to the fact that she has not been adequately rewarded.

100 *Turned up . . . stock*: the passage refers to the card-game 'noddy' (see note to 3.3.2); the 'stock' is the portion of the pack which has not yet been dealt.

108 *bring . . . way*: 'accompany you part of the way, "see you off"'.

110 *flamed*: that flamed.

112 *screech-owl*: a bird of ill omen.

119 *crown*: English term for a foreign gold coin equivalent in value to the English crown (five shillings); not a handsome fee.

126 *When*: an expression of impatience.

127 *fear*: frighten.

131 *this . . . bone*: her arms; cf. 3.4.82.

134 *fame . . . acts*: murder committed personally (rather than by poison or hired assassin) was thought to be out of character in women.

135 *respects*: considers, takes into account.

136–8 *Their place . . . swells*: Rogero and Gniaca are men of rank, so their hatred is dangerously defamatory, whereas that of lesser people is just harmless name-calling. The 'high blood' of line 138 is theirs ('high' = aristocratic), while it is Isabella who swells with vindictive indignation.

147–51 *Forces . . . imbecilities*: a puzzling passage. 'Observation' may be used primarily in the sense of observance of rule or custom, punning on the alternative sense of watching. If so, the lines probably mean that keeping the army together as a single force will breed and nourish military discipline, through which the world may be conquered: those who would rule others must first rule themselves, so 'observation' will make it possible for the Spanish forces to control the weak native population of the city. ('Imbecilities' refers to weakness in general rather than to specifically mental debility.) Don Sago heads an army of occupation (historically, the Spanish army which occupied Pavia in 1525 after Charles V defeated the French king Francis I); thus the Pavians are 'strangers' (foreigners) to him.

165 *make . . . remove*: 'displaces our destinies'.

166 *o'er-rules*: holds sway over.

168 *he . . . him*: refers to Don Sago, whom Isabella seeks to use as an instrument of murder.

174 *'Tis but . . . them*: i.e. the only difference between intrusion and courtesy is how they are construed by the recipient.

182 *Thou abstract . . . storehouse*: Sago imagines Isabella as being the sum ('abstract') of every element in nature, leaving the storehouse empty (cf. 3.2.42); the conceit expresses the intensity of his experience.

192 *Hercules*: hero of classical mythology who killed his wife and children in his madness, and undertook twelve labours in atonement; thus purified, he achieved apotheosis.

196 *the . . . dart*: the Tartars were central Asian nomads known for aggressive barbarism.

200 *which . . . resisted*: the phrase refers to 'fear' rather than 'strength'.

201 *twisted*: spun like a thread; cf. note to 2.1.191.

221 *blood . . . white*: a blasphemous variation on the idea that Christ's blood shed at the atonement washed away humanity's sins; cf. John Donne, *Divine Meditations* 4.13–14: 'Or wash thee in Christ's blood, which hath this might | That being red, it dyes red souls to white.'

233 S.D. *She kneels*: Isabella returns blasphemy for blasphemy, identifying Sago as God and kneeling to him as if in prayer.

239–40 *Thus will I clip thy waist . . . dally with thy hair*: Isabella may rise before speaking these lines, but her embrace of Sago's waist suggests that she is still on her knees; in the next line, however, the action of fingering his hair requires her to be standing. If she rises while speaking, still embracing him, the stage image of her slithering up his body not only conveys her lasciviousness but also offers a visual reinforcement of the serpentine imagery associated with her in the later part of the play (see note to 4.2.7, and cf. 3.4.108, 5.1.10).

241 *Protean-like*: like Proteus, the shape-changing sea-god of classical mythology.

245 *revenge . . . rods*: the rods are probably the *fasces* (a bundle of rods and axes, symbolizing authority and the power to punish) carried ceremonially before ancient Roman magistrates; Sago appropriates the emblem to express his sense of the justice of Isabella's revenge (cf. 4.4.14).

247 *Mars . . . Vulcan*: see note to 2.3.91.

4.3.3–5 *If my husband . . . from another*: Mizaldus' inability to recognize his own wife makes him a fool, and so eligible to be committed to a guardian; in the case of rich fools, the office was sought after by courtiers wishing to milk the estate, but Mizaldus is not rich enough to interest them.

10 *will*: wish to.

14 *younger brothers*: because money and property were normally inherited by the eldest son, younger brothers were often impoverished. Going to sea with the Merchant Venturers (see note to 2.1.70) was one way of acquiring capital; another was to marry a rich widow, a staple theme of Jacobean comedy. See also note to 2.2.97–8: the younger brothers are probably responsible for cuckolding the dead husbands in the first place.

28–30 *the opinion . . . first*: cf. the French proverb cited by Randle Cotgrave, *A Dictionarie of the French and English Tongues* (1611), s.v. *premier*: '*Il n'est que les premieres amours*, The first love is the fastest, or faithfullest; no love's like to the first.'

31 *know*: have sex with.

36 *lively*: (a) living; (b) sexually potent.

44 *late*: i.e. too late to save her husband.

4.4.4–5 *The stage . . . tragedies*: Jacobean stages were traditionally hung with black for performances of tragedies; cf. 1.1, opening S.D.

6 *The . . . queen*: the moon.

10 *voice-killing mandrakes*: the mandrake plant was thought to emit a lethal scream when pulled up.

15–17 *her fame . . . Deemed*: the reputation ('fame') of her who is reckoned ('Deemed') to be the paragon ('life-blood', the most essential component) of deliciousness.

27 *leper*: leprosy is a disfiguring disease which eats away the skin leaving red lesions; it was often used as a metaphor for moral corruption (cf. *Maid*, 3.2.176, 4.1.199, *Val.*, 2.6.18).

28 *the . . . heav'n*: the sun. The reference is probably not ironic (even unintentionally on Sago's part); sunspots were only discovered in 1611 (by Johannes Fabricius in Holland).

44–5 *I'll make . . . gentleman*. Against these lines Q prints the mysterious instruction, '*Tell him all the plot*'. If it is a stage direction at all (rather than, for example, an authorial *aide-mémoire*), it is probably misplaced. It cannot be a direction for Rogero to tell his side of the story, since he subsequently offers to do that the following day (51–2).

50–2 *Murder . . . will*: Rogero offers to explain himself to Sago and, if he wishes, fight a duel. In effect, he is offering Sago an honourable alternative to committing murder.

53 *can*: who can.

56 *lead*: a byword for heaviness.

65 *powers*: the occupying Spanish army.

5.1 S.D. *A scaffold is discovered*: though time-consuming both to erect and strike, a physical scaffold is required by the text (128 S.D.). It would probably have been located in the discovery space at the rear of the stage: since that area is not used after the opening scene, the scaffold could be set up gradually (and therefore quietly) during the performance; after this scene the curtain would be drawn across it, obviating the need to remove it before the end of the play. (The alternative, of having a scaffold on the main stage, would significantly delay the subsequent action during its removal.) This would also make Isabella's on-stage execution feasible (see note to 224 S.D.). Since Rogero's body will be cumbersome to carry on (and later remove), it is possible that it and the other principal characters are discovered already in position on the scaffold.

1 *this spectacle*: Rogero's corpse.

4 *rest*: either (*a*) conclude ('blood' being metonymic for murder), (*b*) eventually achieve repose (with reference to the common notion, originating in Genesis 4: 10, that the victim's blood would cry to God for revenge; once vengeance is achieved, the blood can take a rest), or (*c*) be closely associated with.

3–7 *blood . . . bleed*: it was believed that murder was particularly hateful to God and would inevitably come to light through the miraculous operation of providence.

15 *cockatrice*: a legendary monster, hatched by a serpent from a cock's egg, which killed everything it looked at; also a slang term for a prostitute.

360

19 *reinspire*: breathe life back into.

Aesculapius: classical god of healing, killed by Jupiter when he discovered the secret of bringing the dead back to life.

20 *crimson conduits*: Rogero's empty veins.

16–21 *By this . . . horrid fact*: Sago would undergo the torments of the damned if doing so would enable Rogero to live again.

24 *bubbling wounds*: a popular superstition held that the wounds of a murdered body would bleed in the presence of the murderer.

29 *a free pardon*: scaffold pardons were a common judicial device in the period.

30 S.D. *Exit the Executioner*: the Executioner must leave the stage so that he can enter again with Isabella at line 66; it seems appropriate that he should do so now, at the point Sago ceases to be subject to his ministration.

40–4 *What Tanaïs . . . extant be*: Sago seeks larger and larger bodies of water to wash the blood off his hands: the Tanaïs (now the River Don) in Asia, the Nile in Egypt, the Tigris in Persia, the Rhine in Germany, and the Maeotis (now the Sea of Azov) adjoining the Black Sea, into which the Tanaïs flows. The passage is imitated from Jasper Heywood's 1581 translation of Seneca's *Hercules Furens* (lines 1323–9 of the Latin text), when the recovered Hercules expresses his guilt for the blood he has shed in his insanity. In Seneca, the Maeotis and the 'northern sea' are one and the same, though it is possible that the authors here intended reference to the North Sea, one of the world's roughest stretches of water.

52 *Croesus*: King of Lydia (d. 546 BC), whose vast wealth was legendary.

54–5 *Her lust . . . Italy*: she must die, or she'll betray more men: Isabella's sexual appetite is dangerous because apparently irresistible, and each change of partner marks the superseded lover for death.

61 *glass*: a looking-glass or magic mirror which shows things not visible to common sight; often used as a metaphor for an exemplum.

67 *the castle green*: the location parallels the venue for aristocratic executions in England, 'Tower Green' within the precincts of the Tower of London. In the next line Isabella imagines it as a village green at festival-time.

84 *Emperor*: the Holy Roman Emperor, ruler of central Europe.

85–6 *Didst thou . . . his lust*: because he would go to hell if killed whilst sinning.

95 *painted sepulchre*: gaudily decorated tomb; the image (from Matthew 23: 27) refers to the contrast between exterior beauty and inner corruption.

105–7 *Mine honour's . . . indeed*: Medina has given his irrevocable word of honour; Isabella pleads on the basis of her honourable rank; Medina points out that she has no more honour left.

113 *help*: 'I can help'.

128 *Tyrant of France*: Medina is Spanish; he is a tyrant in his military acts against the French (cf. note to 4.2.147–51). 'France' may also refer to the King of France, Francis I, who was captured by the Spanish after the battle of Pavia.

134 *both worlds*: earth and heaven.

137–8 *pardon . . . Medina*: lineation this edn., line-division after 'and' in Q.

143 *teacher . . . cruelty*: one who outdoes the Furies in cruelty; the teacher is understood to be more skilled than the pupil.

159 *take . . . time*: bring back the past; time is conceived as continually taking away present circumstances as if by act of war.

162 *of himself . . . enough*: refers to Death personified.

165 *instant morrow*: the next morning after.

173 *Petrarch*: Italian poet and scholar (1304–74), famous for his love poems, the *Canzoniere* (1342).

179 *For*: because.

182 *trance*: contemplation.

193 *example*: an exemplary instance of a truly penitent sinner.

194 *in the church*: at their wedding.

196 *accident*: event.

197–8 *your executioner . . . give him too*: the executioner customarily asked forgiveness of his victim, who would pay him to ensure a speedy death.

207 *got*: begot.

Muses: the nine Muses of classical mythology, goddesses of the arts, were a common symbol of poetic inspiration in both antiquity and the Renaissance.

211 *minutes of light*: either (*a*) the minutes she has left to live or (*b*) miniature lights (i.e. her eyes).

219 *ingrateful*: unproductive.

224 *Strike*: victims would customarily stretch out their arms as a signal for the executioner to strike.

224 S.D. *Isabella is executed*. On-stage beheadings such as this occur in at least five other plays performed during the period. Rudimentary special effects seem to have been available: T.B.'s play *The Rebellion of Naples* (written 1649, published 1651) was probably never acted but is written as for the stage, and includes the stage direction, 'He thrusts out his head, and they cut off a false head made of a bladder filled with blood.' (F5ʳ) Alternatively, Isabella may have been beheaded with her head upstage, the sight-lines masking the impact from most of the spectators; at the end of the scene the discovery space curtain would have been drawn across the scaffold to allow the actor to exit unseen.

229 S.D. *Exeunt . . . scaffold*: Isabella's body (and possibly also Rogero's) is on the scaffold and so does not need to be removed; cf. notes to opening S.D., 224 S.D.

5.2 S.D. *Enter . . . the Watch*: it is odd that the Captain of the Watch does not appear here. Possibly '*the Watch*' signifies him (with or without his men); certainly lines 5 and 12–13 require a speaker in authority. Alternatively, the role may have been intended for doubling with one of the characters who exit at the end of the previous scene.

2 *clew*: a ball of twine, used by Theseus in classical mythology to find his way to the centre of the labyrinth (*Met.*, 8).

10 *the Libyan shore*: the quicksands on the coast of Libya were a notorious hazard to navigation.

25 *I, O, U*: punning on 'Ay, oh, you . . .'.

30–1 *ride . . . dung-cart*: the customary punishment for whores.

32 *cucking-stool*: see note to 2.1.16.

35–6 *the opinion . . . souls*: the original proponent of this view was 'Ambrosiaster', the anonymous fourth-century author of commentaries on St Paul which were later erroneously attributed to St Ambrose. If they have no souls, Abigail and Thais will never go to heaven.

41 *taking*: (*a*) plight; (*b*) passion.

43 *cornutes*: horned cuckolds; this edn. (Q reads 'cornets').

50 *like a hanger-on*: (*a*) like a parasite; (*b*) by hanging, considered a shameful and plebeian way to die.

51 *wooden horse*: gallows.

scurvy faces: the contorted expressions of the hanged man.

57 *branches*: (*a*) in rhetoric, formal divisions of a speech; (*b*) cuckold's horns.

59 *true lover's knot*: an elaborate knot of ribbons worn on a wedding dress, symbolizing the bonds of love and marriage.

63 *Niobe*: in classical mythology, a mother whom the gods punished for her pride by killing her children; she was turned into a weeping marble statue. The story was best known from Ovid (*Met.*, 6), and Niobe herself was an archetype of weeping womanhood.

64 *crocodile*: famous for weeping insincerely.

66 *Agamemnon's daughter*: Iphigeneia, sacrificed at Aulis to appease Diana, who was holding back the Greek fleet with contrary winds (*Met.*, 12).

68–9 *I'd make thee . . . drum major*: i.e. he will beat her like a drum.

73–4 *Husband . . . nail*: lineation this edn.; line-division after 'I'll' in Q.

77–8 *come off . . . come off*: Abigail means 'be pardoned'; but Claridiana means that he will fall from the ladder of the gallows as he is hanged.

79 *Chirurgeons' Hall*: by a statute of 1540, the Barber Surgeons' Company had the right to the bodies of four executed criminals per annum for dissection and other experimental purposes; the bodies could be claimed by supplication at the gallows. To be selected for this fate was considered a great posthumous disgrace.

108 *the leopard*: reputedly fond of wine.

119 *enforcèd*: forced to assume an uncharacteristic appearance (of anger).

138 *a Jesuit's recantation*: in Jacobean England the Jesuits were considered to be crafty Roman Catholic subversives; Mizaldus probably refers to their fanatical loyalty to the Pope, taking them to be unlikely ever to recant in religion.

139 *the Great Turk*: ruler of the Ottoman Empire, Christianity's greatest political enemy (and hence the person least likely ever to be converted).

148 *common:* common to all men.

151 *writ of error*: legal document brought to procure the reversal of a judgement on grounds of error; but Claridiana means that the letter ('writ') is itself in error.

153 *brachygraphy*: shorthand; Mizaldus' letter-writing style is less fulsome than Claridiana's (cf. 2.2.28–30), possibly because, if it is the letter he gave Abigail at 1.1.395 S.D., it must have been hastily composed.

155 *Perseus' shield*: in classical mythology, Perseus killed Medusa the Gorgon, whose hideous face turned all who saw it to stone, and carried her severed head on his shield (*Met.*, 4).

154–9 *He's stung . . . caves*: each wife is watching, and refers to, her own husband. Mizaldus is stupefied, Claridiana furious.

160 *till . . . world*: until death.

167 *star-mark*: the reference to cuckold's horns contains another racial insult alluding to the Star of David (worn as an identifying badge on Jews' clothing).

170 *Muhammad*: the founder of Islam (*c.* AD 570–632); Mizaldus responds to Claridiana's anti-Semitic abuse by placing him even further outside Christendom.

171 *Termagant*: supposedly the god worshipped by Muhammadans; also a colloquial term for a violent person.

176 *scour . . . gorge*: to scour a hawk's gorge is to give it a bitter medicine, wrapped in a piece of hen's skin, as a purgative.

182 *Spice*: a slight trace; the husbands' continuing aggression will put their necks back into the noose ('halter').

193 *prepost'rously*: perversely (literally, back-to-front).

196 *Phalaris' bull*: Phalaris (reigned 565–549 BC), a Sicilian tyrant, roasted his victims alive inside a giant bronze bull; their distorted screams resembled

the sound of the bull roaring (itself an exceptionally unpleasant sound to seventeenth-century ears).

197 *Darius-like*: the Persian ruler Darius (d. 486 BC) presided over an empire that extended from Africa (the location of Mount Atlas) to Europe; the two 'wings' of the empire symbolize a giant pair of cuckold's horns.

204–6 *They spring ... crowned*: there seems to be no basis for this anecdote about Methuselah, a biblical figure known only for being the longest-lived human being (Genesis 5: 27 says he lived 969 years); the chronology established in Genesis indicates that he died in the year of the Great Flood. Mizaldus' reference to him as 'our Methuselah' may be a tacit acceptance of his own cultural identity as a Jew.

214 *Muscovia*: Russia, famous for the length and severity of its winters.

217 *jealousy*: watchfulness, vigilance.

221 *Argus' eyes*: see note to 1.1.50.

222 *Pandora*: the equivalent of Eve in classical mythology, the first mortal female. Jupiter gave her the custody of a box containing the evils of humanity (rather than, as here, virtues). She foolishly opened the box and released evil into the world.

231 *torches*: the stars.

232 *Mycerinus*: Egyptian pharaoh of the fourth dynasty; an oracle predicted that he had only six more years of life, and he contrived to double it by commissioning numerous lamps and treating night as if it were a second day.

The Maid's Tragedy

The Persons of the Play
Calianax: the name is stressed on the second and fourth syllables.

Melantius: the name acquires an ominous suggestiveness from the Greek *melan*, black.

1.1.1–4 *The rest ... your word*: when the characters enter they are already discussing an initially undisclosed subject, with the three courtiers vying for the ear of Lysippus; the subject of the discussion is evidently the arrangements for the wedding entertainments.

6 *a masque*: Jacobean masques were short dramatic performances given on significant court occasions such as aristocratic weddings. The stories were generally mythological, often involving classical gods; the enactment, usually by courtiers rather than professional actors, made great use of dance and scenic spectacle. The genre expressed the Stuart monarchy's sense of its own pre-eminence, hence Strato's charge of flattery (line 11).

365

13 *The land by me welcomes*: as the heir to the throne, Lysippus greets Melantius on behalf of the kingdom as a whole.

30 *Patria*: either Patara in Asia Minor (mentioned in connection with Rhodes in Acts 21: 1) or Patras, a fortified city on the west coast of Greece.

37 *gamesome*: frivolous; Melantius may be invidiously accused of neglecting his military duties to return to Rhodes for Amintor's wedding.

53 *virtue*: power, strength (here a physical rather than a moral quality).

59 *holy knot*: wedlock.

65 *they*: her fortunes.

74 *the light*: may refer to Evadne's blonde hair (cf. note to 2.1.253–5).

74–5 *strikes dead . . . her eye*: Evadne is wittily imagined in terms of the basilisk, a mythological reptile which killed all it looked at; in her case, however, it is a dangerous beauty rather than ugliness.

84 *call it back*: i.e. undo his misunderstanding with Aspatia.

91 *Stuck full of*: crowded with.

94 *strew her over*: scatter the flowers over her.

96 *strikes*: infects.

100 *in course*: by turns; group story-telling was a popular Renaissance pastime.

112 *My mouth . . . heart*: i.e. he cannot speak his true feelings.

116–18 *A sacrifice . . . safety*: Amintor's call for a sacrifice is the first explicit indication that the play is not set in a Christian society.

119 *build . . . dwell*: i.e. take up permanent residence.

121 *innocence*: moral purity (with connotations of artless directness).

127 *Fetched . . . away*: i.e. drew so many tears from him.

137 *'change*: exchange.

139–40 *lose . . . arms*: Amintor is saying either that losing his virginity will make a man of him, or that he will literally grow old because male orgasms were thought to shorten life (in which case, 'lusty youth' may imply semen).

141 *rage*: are impatient. In the next scene, Lysippus is not one of the on-stage audience for the masque, so presumably his presence is required because he is one of the performers. So too may be Cleon, Strato, and Diphilus, who are also notably absent from the next scene.

My lord . . . you. In Q2 this line is spoken by a messenger, who enters immediately before. This may represent the authors' original intentions, altered for theatrical reasons in the Q1 text: the next scene, the play's most demanding in casting terms, may have required all the company's minor actors to appear in elaborate costumes and make-up as the courtiers and masquers, in which case none of them would be available at this point (though cf. previous note). In any event, the detail also serves to establish Amintor's weakness of character: he is sent on an errand at his own wedding celebrations, and is distracted from his urgent message by his reunion with Melantius.

142 *Cleon, Strato, Diphilus*: a tacit order to accompany him, which may also serve to remind the audience of the courtiers' names; Cleon has hitherto not been named in the dialogue.

145 *rude carriage*: inappropriately uncultured behaviour.

147 *But . . . mistress*: war and love were conceived as opposite spheres of activity in the seventeenth century; Melantius is saying that he is not wholly devoted to the former.

151 *place*: i.e. in his mistress's heart.

1.2.1 *doors*: The Globe stage, and probably the Blackfriars, had three doors, all of which are required in staging this scene. One is used by Calianax for his exit and re-entry (lines 18, 45), and is unobstructed. The other two, used respectively for Melantius' entry at line 26 and his exit and return at lines 31 and 48, have (imaginary) crowds massing behind them. The knocking which harasses Diagoras probably comes from both doors at different points, creating the opportunity for a comic performance by the exasperated doorkeeper.

3 *the King . . . court*: Calianax wishes the King had decided to hold the masque elsewhere, either because there would be more room for spectators or because it would be less public and so entail fewer problems of crowd control.

9 *your looks*: Calianax has authority in his face; but Calianax takes Diagoras to mean that he is especially ugly.

15–16 *I sweat . . . office*: i.e. his court position puts him to excessive labour; the metaphor is of clothes made uncomfortable by heavy perspiration.

16 *made room*: kept the door, his present function (he 'makes room' by keeping the riff-raff out).

18 *Serve that will!*: Calianax abandons his responsibilities to anyone who will take them on; cf. line 8 above.

25 *troop*: crowd, with pun playing on Melantius' military occupation.

28 *above*: a gallery. There was probably no attempt to represent it in the original production: although Calianax indicates the lady at line 58, the text does not require her to re-enter in the upper acting area.

29 *and there's room*: Q1 reads 'there is no room', giving an entirely different tone to the line: in the Q2 reading adopted here, Diphilus cajoles Melantius into placing his lady above, where there will be space for her; in Q1 he assertively refuses her a place near the King, where there will not. 'There' signifies a different place in each version.

34 *itch*: (*a*) desire (to get in); (*b*) usual meaning.

35 *thrust and hang!*: 'fuck off' and 'go hang yourselves'.

42 *calves' heads*: calves' brains were a culinary delicacy, but also a byword for folly.

47 *a*: the unstressed form of 'he'.

53 *timeless*: untimely.

59 *So near ... King*: at Jacobean court masques, the social standing of members of the audience was reflected in their proximity to the King's seat.

61 *women ... worth*: Calianax implies that Melantius' lady is a loose woman; cf. 'wenches' (line 66), 'whore' (line 70).

64-5 *What ... tongue to*: i.e. it was senility, not Calianax, speaking.

71 *Bate me*: exclude.

flesh and blood: i.e. human, not divine.

72 *fifteen*: an age at which a young woman would still be sexually innocent.

73 *to her*: compared with her.

78 *troubled*: in war.

79-83 *Would ... more!*: a transfusion of Melantius' battle-shed blood would give Calianax some of his qualities, so that he would either be less talkative (because soldiers like Melantius were conventionally men of action rather than of words) or else better able to fight (and so to support— 'maintain'—his words with blows).

84 *a place ... wrong*: i.e. where wrongdoers can escape the consequences of their actions.

85 *you may ... pleasure*: Melantius' licence of speech (allowed because of his position of political favour as both Evadne's brother and the state's military commander) is for Calianax an example of the privileged wrongdoing just mentioned.

104 *you ... office*: i.e. 'take care to do your job properly': Calianax is to keep the door (with Diagoras) rather than join the audience to watch the masque.

109 S.D. *Recorders play*: in response to the King's command to begin the masque. They had a soft, bass sound and were often used in Jacobean drama to create a solemn effect.

111 S.D. *Night rises*: Night emerges through a stage trapdoor with smoke effects. She is probably represented in dark make-up (cf. lines 118, 122), like that worn by the female masquers in Ben Jonson's *Masque of Blackness* (1605).

114 *Cynthia*: the moon, whose light is 'borrowed' (by reflection) from the sun. She probably wears white make-up (cf. lines 116, 126, 140), creating a visual contrast with Night.

117 *horns*: of the crescent moon.

123–6 *This beauty . . . these eyes*: of the court ladies in the on-stage audience; cf. lines 119–21.

131 *reins . . . whips*: Night and Cynthia are conceived in antithesis to the sun god, who also drove a chariot in classical mythology.

139 *room*. Additional Passage A follows here in Q2 (10 lines).

144 *Endymion*: see note to *Countess*, 3.1.19.

146–7 *thy pale beams . . . make the day*: if the moon removes the beams, Endymion will no longer be fascinated by them and so will wake from his trance.

150 *rage*: are in the throes of poetic composition (often envisaged as a form of madness in Renaissance literary discourse).

153 *nobler*: than the one perpetuated by poets.

154–7 *Rise, rise . . . commanded*: the moon controls the tides (cf. lines 232–6); therefore Neptune, god of the sea, is at Cynthia's command. Like most English texts of the period, the masque uses the gods' Latin names in preference to the less familiar Greek pantheon (even though the action takes place in Rhodes).

157 S.D. *Neptune rises*: through a stage trapdoor. Neptune is an appropriate presence on Evadne's wedding day, since she takes her name from one of his daughters in classical mythology.

162 *Hie thee*: go (imperative).

163 *wind-god . . . den*: Aeolus, classical ruler of the winds, kept them in a cave on Sicily.

164–5 *Boreas . . . intentions*: Cynthia intends the winds to supply the music for the sea-gods' dance (line 170), but Boreas (the north wind) will be too rough for her purposes; cf. 4.1.75–6.

167 *vernal blasts*: spring breezes.

168 *blow*: cause to bloom.

170–3 *thy . . . brings*: the tritons or sea-gods (Neptune's 'wat'ry race'; cf. note to Additional Passage B.5) are to enter in pairs for dancing, wearing their finest clothes made from sea-shells or treasure from shipwrecks.

175 S.D. *a rock*: a piece of scenery representing Aeolus' cave (cf. line 163).

178 *Favonius*: the west wind.

190 *beaten*: by the waves.

196 S.D. *Enter Proteus . . . Music plays*: Proteus wears blue make-up (cf. line 188). The sea-gods enter two by two ('in couples', 171); their elaborate and suitably marine costumes are described at lines 172–3 and 188–90. The music is probably played by the winds.

200–4 *no day . . . befriended*: Jacobean masques often supposed the court to party on until dawn (e.g. Jonson's *Oberon the Fairy Prince*, 1611, ends with the break of day). In contrast, this masque turns on a postponement of dawn, requested in both songs, to give the newly-weds the opportunity to make love under cover of darkness; as in John Donne's poem 'The Sun Rising', the light of day will be an unwelcome intruder if it comes before the bridegroom has finished. See also lines 213–24.

207–8 *the galleys . . . beat*: the many oarsmen rowing a galley were kept in time by the beating of a drum.

221–2 *tears . . . denials*: the bride is unwilling to part with her virginity.

222 *often dyings*: multiple orgasms.

224 *help*: intervene. Additional Passage B follows this line in Q2 (14 lines).

227 *trident*: symbol of Neptune's power.

230–2 *We . . . gratulate*. This edition follows Q1 here; Q2 reads 'A thanks to every one, and to gratulate'. The Q1 text is corrupt, with the break in the rhyme-scheme indicating that one or more lines are missing. The Q2 version suggests revision at this point, which was either left incomplete or inadequately transcribed in the process of preparing the printer's copy.

237 *government*: Neptune and the Sea-Gods' control of the waters, their 'charge' (238).

238 *waste*: uncultivated land (here, the shore).

239 *the island*: Rhodes, where the play is set.

242 *my brother*: the sun.

246 *axle-tree*: of the chariot of the sun; Night hopes that it will break down and fall into the sea prematurely. The chariot had previously caught fire when stolen by Phaëthon, who lost control and scorched the earth.

250 *a greater majesty*: i.e. the King's.

252–3 *yon . . . south*: at court masques, the King was traditionally seated at the south of the hall. In another self-conscious acknowledgement of the audience (cf. lines 126–7), the masquers mistake him for the rising sun.

254 *into day*: as the moon's light virtually disappears when the sun lights up the sky.

256 *laid*: seventeenth-century weddings often ended with the bawdy custom of putting the bride and groom to bed together. The King's reasons for waiving this practice become clear later.

261 *Goodnight, Melantius*: the King's final salutation maintains the focus on the potentially threatening presence of Melantius.

261 S.D. *The seats are removed*: also any other special scenery for the masque; this will take place during the act-interval.

2.1 S.D. *other Ladies*: there are at least two other attendants; Dula still addresses them as 'ladies' (102) after Aspatia has left the stage.

NOTES TO PAGES 90–93

1–2 *fight . . . tonight*: the rhyme, which continues intermittently during the undressing sequence, gives the dialogue a stylized and comic effect; Aspatia's blank verse, beginning at line 40, displaces the mirth.

5–6 *That . . . do*: Dula wishes she could have sex with Amintor without endangering her reputation.

8 *done*: deflowered.

9 *Good . . . both*: wearing many clothes makes both undressing and sex more difficult.

15 *more*: more 'pricking' (sexually, by Amintor).

22–3 *take it . . . take it*: in Evadne's line, 'taking it' is simply the alternative to 'leaving it' (cf. line 18); Dula then changes the meaning to 'have sex' (implicitly with Amintor).

24 *give . . . o'er*: dismiss.

25 *ablest*: most sexually potent.

24–5 *So will . . . ache*: she will make him 'ache' either from exhaustion after having sex with her or with unsatisfied desire ('heartache') if she refuses him.

26–32 *I'll hold . . . that way*: this banter centres around the notion of a card-game as a metaphor for sex; Dula proposes to play alongside Evadne in the game (26–7), i.e. share her sexual partners; Aspatia, if assigned to her side, will lose her the game ('pluck down a side') because she has no experience of cards/sex ('does not use it'), unlike Evadne, who has more aptitude (32).

37–8 *Hang . . . country*: 'I might as well be hanged if I were in love, unless ("But") I could "run my country" (= "flee my domicile", but punning on "cunt", hence "give up my sexual desires")'.

40 *It . . . cheek*: 'it would be an untimely smile that attempted my cheek'.

42–4 *When . . . sacrifice*: at the most solemn religious ceremony.

45 *night*: wedding night.

66 *some*. Additional Passage C follows here in Q2 (23 lines).

72 *artificial*: skilful. Artifice was highly valued as a mode of expression in seventeenth-century aesthetics; the modern connotations of insincerity are not implied.

82 *Write . . . fortune*: in her masochistic grief, Aspatia applies to herself the common topos of inscribing a woman's wrongdoing on her body (cf. 4.1.31–5); her only fault is her romantic misfortune.

83 *by course*: in turn.

86 S.D. *the door*: a different door from the one through which Evadne has just exited.

97 *willow garland*: the willow was associated with forsaken women; cf. note to Additional Passage C.1.

111 *sensible*: sensitive.

119 *vapours*: mists; cf. Night's entry in the masque (1.2.111 S.D.).

127 *watch*: stay awake all night (because they will be making love).

136 *If ... not great*: 'It doesn't matter who'.

150 *unconquered*: he assumes that she is a virgin.

169-71 *If you ... a night*: the bride's coy desire to preserve her virginity on the wedding night was often considered an attribute of a truly chaste woman; cf. lines 264-6.

184 *the oracle*: see note to *Countess*, 1.1.440.

195-6 *make ... ceremonies*: dissuade later generations from marriage.

194-207 *Hymen ... issue*: like many Jacobean tragedies, the play keeps an ironic eye on the fact that in performance it is a re-enactment of past events (albeit, in this case, fictitious ones). In a distraught overstatement, Amintor wants to keep the story a secret for fear of its social effects: men will pursue sex like animals without any sense of subsequent responsibility to the woman or the issue. (The passage may alternatively contain darker implications of homosexual buggery and then—since even men are women's issue—bestiality.)

210 *break forth*: speak out.

213 *the form*: i.e. of the oath.

234 *never ... heaven*: being sinful vows, they are not heard by the gods, so there can be no retribution for breaking them.

240-1 *It is ... worth*: his good reputation is in Evadne's power.

253-5 *those hairs ... arms*: bracelets of hair were worn by lovers, but Amintor may also imagine a king's golden bracelet; if so, Evadne's hair is blonde, which was considered exceptionally beautiful in the period.

256-8 *thy tongue ... let out life*: the concern with orifices and penetration here latently emphasizes Amintor's sexual frustration.

271-2 *they ... Both*: her desire and her will have resulted in practical sexual experience (as distinct from mere sexual fantasy).

274 *second*: both second lover and second best.

279 *northern wind*: as in the masque, the roughest of the winds.

289-91 *Let ... wait*: according to Jacobean views on the morality of regicide, no subject might assassinate a monarch by legitimate succession; only the King's superiors (in effect, the Christian God) might effect his deposition.

292-3 *Why ... virgin*: popular belief held that a man could tell during sex whether or not the woman was a virgin; to deflower a virgin was considered an especial sexual delicacy. Evadne is saying that, since she is no virgin, Amintor should be less keen to go to bed with her.

296 *To father children*: to be legally presumed the father of the children she conceives by the King.

306 *rid . . . wretch*: set free (with a quick death) a wretch in the grip of a slow but mortal illness.

318 *blaze myself*: 'proclaim my true nature'.

320 *flesh*: human frailty.

329 *close*: secretly.

336 *practice*: do what he has said (with ironic sexual overtones).

2.2 S.D. *sewing box*: this contains Antiphila's sampler of Ariadne, and evidently other pieces of needlework (since at line 30 Antiphila has to clarify which piece Aspatia means).

4 *Yes*: Antiphila humours Aspatia (contrast line 13 below).

8 *miracles*: after her recent experiences, Aspatia assumes infidelity to be a general characteristic of all men; therefore the true lovers of the past seem to her miraculous.

12 *fit for stamp*: impressionable.

15 *was*. Additional Passage D follows here in Q2 (11¹/₂ lines).

19–20 *the nymph . . . Helen*: in classical mythology, the Phrygian nymph Oenone married the Trojan prince Paris, and committed suicide after he left her for Helen of Troy.

22 *the Carthage Queen*: Dido, who killed herself after being abandoned by her lover Aeneas, a refugee from the fall of Troy and ancestor of the Romans.

27–8 *some . . . marble*: the image draws implicitly on the classical story of Niobe (see note to *Countess*, 5.2.63); she is not named, probably because she was not abandoned by her lover.

30 *Ariadne*: in classical mythology, a Cretan princess who saved Theseus from the labyrinth and was later abandoned by him on the uninhabited island of Naxos.

31 *he's*: he has.

36 *spent*: wrecked.

40 *they . . . ill*: the classical gods were notorious for their casual sexual encounters with human women.

41 *go so*: leave the sampler as it is.

43 *smiling*: deceptively attractive; cf. 3.1.57–9.

44 *a Fear*: a personification (not of fear in Theseus but of its cause).

46 *wronged*: misreported.

wanton: because the poets have more interest in the man's sexual adventures than sympathy for the abandoned woman.

NOTES TO PAGES 101–105

52 *by me*: 'using me as a model'.

54 *all true . . . island*: Aspatia sees her plight as identical with that of Ariadne, except that she is on the civilized island of Rhodes.

57 *all about me*: her appearance and clothes.

61 *sorrow's monument*: a statue personifying sorrow.

65 *A . . . picture*: herself.

80–8 *a rogue . . . rascal*: Calianax refers to Amintor (80–6) and Melantius (86–8).

88 *twice*: we have seen one confrontation with Melantius, in 1.2; this line hints that their antagonism derives from another specific incident before that; cf. 1.1.81–3.

90 *take . . . withal*: take steps to deal with the matter.

3.1.5–6 *he ne'er . . . lives*: because most women have had sex before marriage; the joke is truer than he knows in Evadne's case.

9 *at your service*: with secondary meaning 'sexually available' (hence Diphilus' reply).

15 *brother*: brother-in-law (Diphilus).

17 *lost your eyes*: Amintor's eyes are half-closed with tiredness.

20 *twelve*: then, as now, an exceptionally young age at which to be a soldier, let alone a commander.

24 *Lethe*: see note to *Countess*, 4.2.62.

24–5 *made . . . heaven*: i.e. died; a person's life was commonly referred to as a debt which was discharged upon death.

26 *What's that?*: it was often assumed that other characters on stage could hear asides as indistinct mumbles.

28 *headsman*: punning on the (pretended) taking of Evadne's maidenhead.

29 *clap*: slap (sometimes an affectionate gesture).

37–8 *I'll . . . effects*: it is the innocent Amintor, not the guilty Evadne, who has suffered the sleeplessness traditionally associated with a guilty conscience.

61 *shoots . . . sun*: the metaphor stresses the waves' vertiginous height.

46–62 *I wonder . . . carries on him*: Amintor has made the traumatic discovery, frequent in Jacobean tragedy, that a person's face is not a reliable indicator of their true character. His misplaced trust in Evadne now makes him question Melantius' outward appearance of virtue.

68 *cunning*: ingeniously indirect.

90 *spoiled*: no longer a virgin; this is mere banter, with the irony that Diphilus' spurious method did not detect Evadne's actual deflowering before her marriage.

111 *thus*: as merry as Amintor is pretending to be.

122 *You'll . . . shortly*: a husband's interest in marital sex often wanes quickly—more so than his wife's, which is why he will thank her for allowing him abstinence.

123 *honest*: chaste. In his next line, the King asks Amintor's opinion of his first experience of sex; Amintor, of course, cannot give him a straight answer. The question is covertly sinister and needling; its outward tone can depend on whether the unmarried, childless King represents himself in public as being sexually experienced.

129 *it . . . name*: i.e. there is no polite synonym ('but' = only).

134 *as . . . delivered*: (*a*) 'as sexy as you said'; (*b*) 'as pregnant as you (may have) made her'. Amintor suspects the marriage may have been arranged because Evadne is already expecting the King's child (cf. 2.1.294–6).

176 *leprosy*: see note to *Countess*, 4.4.27.

188 *close with*: (*a*) embrace (sexually); (*b*) complete a contract (by consummating the marriage) with.

191 *You . . . King*: his rank would inhibit her from striking him.

196 *as*: this edn. (Qq read 'a').

199 *ruin thee forever*: either by rape or (more probably) disfigurement.

201 *dissembling*. Additional Passage E follows in Q2 (4 lines).

202 *ingenious*: honest.

209 *O God*: this and the first sentence of Amintor's next speech (213–15) might both be spoken as asides.

226–7 *Unless . . . myself*: he would seek not only to take the King's life but to destroy his and Evadne's reputation by publishing an account of their illicit relationship, which would justify the assassination.

230 *this*: the King's sword (symbolizing justice; cf. 3.2.158).

263 *private*: discreet.

264 *wink*: 'shut your eyes'.

276 *pull . . . me*: the period's criminological thinking understood murder to be an involuntary act (here, caused by Amintor's passions taking control of his will to action).

3.2.19 *name*: reputation.

30 *set a face*: assume a fierce look.

31–3 *When . . . fight*: to maintain his reputation, he behaved pugnaciously only when there was no chance of his actually having to fight.

50 *well dissembler*: good concealer.

51 *rareness*: i.e. the presumption that he is unique in his misfortunes.

54 *'change*: exchange.

58 *forced*: worked unnaturally into the conversation.

81 *chaste*: sexual activity within marriage was considered chaste.

82 *another*: different (from his appearance before marriage).

83 *Causes*: reasons (for his behaviour).

86 *idle*: frivolous.

87 *blasted*: astonished (literally, thunderstruck).

90 *that man*: Amintor's true self.

93-5 *I would . . . bosom*: Melantius would break a friendship roughly by 'giving the lie' (a grave insult, usually provoking a duel) rather than gently withdrawing intimacy as Amintor does with his distantly polite 'compliment'.

99 *played with*: (*a*) trifled with; (*b*) risked (literally 'gambled with').

103 *lose consideration*: cease to think carefully.

112 *old*: former.

117 *make way*: erode a larger opening.

118-19 *scape . . . fame*: retain either his life or his reputation.

130 *throwing down*: the image, from wrestling, expresses the struggle by which Melantius retains his self-control.

132-4 *After . . . unrevenged?*: 'After I have won honour by my deeds in battle, shall the fact of my friendship with Amintor allow him to get away with dishonouring my family and marking Evadne perpetually as a whore as if she had been branded?'

138 *basely*: i.e. without giving Amintor an opportunity to defend himself.

143 *eternally*: Amintor wishes to die, and to be killed by Melantius will save him from being damned for the sin of suicide.

146 *not blows but words*: cf. the proverb 'to come from words to blows' (Tilley, W.824); from Latin '*a verbis ad verbera*'.

154 *However*: in any event.

159 *cut . . . off*: sentence to death.

164 *I . . . you*: because he will be executed for the murder.

167 *searching*: keenly observant, questioning.

186 *house*: noble family.

189 *horrid*: causing horror.

196 *Still*: make still.

swelling: heaving with sobs.

206-7 *I will . . . part*: Amintor's sword is still drawn; his words carry a latent threat to cut the secret out of Melantius' body.

217 S.D. *drawing his sword*: this time Melantius draws not to fight Amintor but to express his readiness to kill the King and Evadne.

221 *birth*: inborn status, with associated family honour.

230 *I will not fight*: Melantius may sheathe his sword after this line, in which case it seems likely that Amintor will also sheathe his before he leaves the stage, possibly after line 235. Alternatively, both men may leave the stage with their swords still drawn and arms linked, an image expressing their joint commitment to violent redress.

231–3 *Though . . . to it*: anger, which caused Melantius to challenge Amintor, was a murderous but evanescent passion in Renaissance psychological thought; it has now worn off, leaving his rational faculties in control.

242 *bravery*: ostentatious splendour (which is all the family honour would be if Melantius were to act as he says).

244 *but rather*: it is better to.

246–8 *Faith . . . ease*: in this speech, Amintor's resistance to Melantius' regicidal determination seems broken; his 'leaning' on his brother-in-law may be literal, but seems more likely to be metaphorical, expressing his collapse into dependence.

261 *spleens*: Jacobean medicine identified the passions with specific bodily organs. The spleen was the seat of mirth; the King and Evadne risk breaking theirs from overuse.

285 *the fort*: a fortified stronghold, comparable with the Tower of London, to which a strategic withdrawal might be made.

288 *shaking*: i.e. with old age: either a palsied quivering of the limbs or an unsteady walk; cf. 4.2.254.

322 *red*: in contrast with her current grieving pallor.

4.1.3–4 *Come . . . else*: Evadne assumes Melantius intends to compliment her, whereas his true purpose is to shame her; both will make her blush.

9 *gallery*: a long room adjoining one or more private chambers.

12 *Milan skins*: Milan in Lombardy was known for its textile industry; the reference is to fine leather clothes (possibly gloves) such as a spruce courtier might wear; also used in *Val.*, 2.2.34.

11–13 *I will not . . . business*: Melantius does not want to be disturbed by the entrance of frivolous courtiers visiting Evadne.

18 *riddle*: express himself enigmatically, like a riddle.

27 *at these years*: 'old as I am'.

27–8 *through . . . scars*: scar tissue does not blush, having too few capillaries.

32 *written . . . forehead*: in Jacobean England, some criminals were branded with letters signifying their offence; contemporary writers developed the idea into a fuller account inscribed on the forehead. Melantius goes one step further in the next line.

35 *twins . . . her*: i.e. a significantly larger area of skin; refers to a multiple pregnancy.

42 *without enforcement*: of her own free will.

43 *swell . . . temper*: 'enrage me beyond my capacity for self-control'.

46 *seconds*: supporters, those who affirm it to be true.

52 *Forgetfulness*: disregard (of manners).

53 *mighty humour*: Evadne's haughty disposition.

56 *Though . . . blood*: even if he has to shed Evadne's blood to force her to reveal the name.

58 *when . . . reigns*: in the 'dog-days' (July and August, when Sirius the dog star is at its height), traditionally the hottest time of the year.

62 *wolf*: outlaw, banished from all human society.

66 *goat*: traditionally known as an exceptionally lascivious animal.

67 *cooler*: than Evadne.

72 *fighters*: a prostitute's bravoes or enforcers; cf. *Countess*, 2.3.129.

76 *heaven's fire*: a thunderbolt.

80 *dare not*: dare not be here.

84 *service*: in the sexual sense.

91 *pulled on*: provoked.

98 *women*: assumed to be gentler than men; Melantius wants to attack Evadne with full male ferocity.

100 *be thy lover*: i.e. 'penetrate your body'.

115 *speak truth still*: continue to speak truth.

122 *I'll . . . thee*: 'I shall make your death last all day'.

128 *it . . . King*: Evadne's use of the past tense suggests her developing penitence: she no longer envisages a future for the illicit relationship.

142 *play . . . out*: continue in wickedness.

153 *cool*: sexually sated.

157 *kiss him dead*: kill him with kisses.

160 *Found out*: pointed at.

168 *wealth*: her virginity, often described as a jewel in Jacobean drama.

176 *Dare*: who dares.

182 *wandered*: lost her way (morally).

186 *dare*: daunt, terrify.

194 S.D. *She prostrates herself*: Evadne, already kneeling, responds to Amintor's order to stand up by doing the opposite (cf. 'fall', 221).

203 *dazzle*: cannot see correctly.

214 *dull calamity*: insensible state of distress.

232 *Lerna . . . Nilus*: both homes to noxious reptiles: in classical mythology, the many-headed serpent, Hydra, lived in Lake Lerna until it was killed by Hercules, and the River Nile in Egypt was famous for its crocodiles. In performance, the comparison with these creatures is sharpened by her lying prostrate as she speaks.

248 *crocodiles*: see note to *Countess*, 5.2.64.

254 *many*: many days; Evadne means that she will not live long.

257 *it*: the good which she cannot absolutely achieve.

259 *Niobe*: see note to *Countess*, 5.2.63.

265 *made a star*: been stellified (as a consequence of her virtue).

4.2 S.D. *banquet*: see note to *Countess*, 2.1.158. The King's conversation with Calianax (1–32) may take place as the banquet is being set out.

13 *pawn*: offer as security; wager.

25 *am . . . enough*: 'is my unsupported word not adequate testimony'.

41 *councillor*: member of the Privy Council (in Jacobean England, the pre-eminent executive body).

43 *thou . . . bridegroom*: the scene takes place the day after the wedding (cf. 220).

44 *use thee so*: 'treat you like one' (i.e. in allowing him to sit first).

49 *chop . . . unseasonably*: blurt them out at an inappropriate time.

51 *'Tis . . . then*: Strato has told all his funny stories at the times the King mentioned, and now has none left with which to entertain the company.

60 *Such . . . are*: this line might alternatively be an aside, depending on how far Calianax feels that, with the King seeming to support his story in his previous remark, he can afford to be openly rude, and on the extent of Melantius' overt self-control under such provocation.

66 *have it*: referring to (*a*) the fort, and (*b*) his just deserts as a traitor.

68 S.D. *Strato . . . Amintor*: Amintor is to 'pledge' the King (return his toast) from the same cup.

77 *wear . . . sword*: i.e. 'kill us all'.

78 *the island*: Rhodes, where the play is set.

121 *ears*: spies.

128 *fenced*: defended (as by erecting a rampart); possibly punning on swordplay.

129 *gave . . . to*: believed.

131 *pardon*: licence.

379

158–9 *bestowed . . . blood*: i.e. in the King's service he has lost his blood (shed in battle) without caring; 'blood' may also carry the secondary sense of 'kindred' (i.e. Evadne).

160 *To think*: even to think, let alone do.

164 *for . . . King*: his valiant deed was done in the King's service.

165 *arm*. Two additional lines follow in Q2: 'This sword of mine hath ploughed the ground | And reaped the fruit in peace'. This somewhat literary elaboration of the preceding line risks losing the thread in performance; the lines may have been present in the authors' first draft and cut for performance.

167–8 *without . . . conquest*: Melantius' reputation alone is enough to make the enemies of Rhodes surrender.

226 *I sleep . . . hope*: he hopes he is dreaming.

241–3 *To poison . . . land*: a catalogue of serious crimes in the Jacobean mind: poisoning was considered even more heinous than other methods of murder; it was a grave offence wrongfully to accuse a married woman of unchastity; and the murder of child heirs to ensure that their wicked uncle would inherit land was an archetypal villainy exemplified in the Richard III story.

255–6 *hold . . . state*: 'continue in your accustomed court position'.

285 *wrought*: worked round.

286 *astronomers*: astrologers (who might pronounce the night inauspicious).

315 *uncollected*: not under rational control (and therefore prone to excessive passion).

319 *run*: driven (without his having actively willed it).

323–4 *There's . . . in't*: the King, by virtue of his royal status alone, has the power of quasi-divine retaliation (by thunderbolt).

5.1.3 *pleasure*: will (misunderstood by the Gentleman to mean 'sexual pleasure').

11–12 *all . . . purpose*: i.e. the 'horrible' nocturnal surroundings correspond with her 'black purpose'.

15–16 *Let . . . disloyal*: errant female characters in Jacobean drama often generalize their situation like this in order to point a moral for female members of the audience.

18–19 *that . . . fight*: the sea was a common image of the dominion of fortune, and war was also notoriously ruled by chance. In choosing to go to sea to fight, the fool unnecessarily subjects himself to a double risk.

21 *through*: go through.

23 *there*: in the King's bed, where it began.

32 *Furies*: the Furies of classical mythology punished wrongdoers and were often used as an emblem of a guilty conscience.

38 *a shall . . . him*: this edn. (Q1 reads 'I shall not . . . him'; Q2 reads 'I shall be strong enough.').

45 *pretty new device*: The King assumes Evadne has tied him up for a sado-masochistic bondage encounter.

48–50 *I'll be . . . embraces*: see note to *Countess*, 2.3.91.

51–6 *You are too hot . . . must bleed*: The King assumes that Evadne's 'physic' (medicine) is a metaphor for sex; but in fact she refers to the medical practice of 'bleeding' a patient to draw out an excess (or surfeit) of noxious substances.

67 *unprepared*: without having had the chance to repent his sins or take any last rites; the Jacobeans considered this an exceptionally terrible way to die, since it endangered the victim's soul.

69 *look*: look at.

86 *blessèd fires that shot*: stars that flared.

97 *Within*: within earshot of.

104 *brave*: in ostentation (refers to Evadne, not the King).

110 s.d. *Evadne . . . and exits*: Qq read '*Exeunt*', indicating that both Evadne and the King's dead body leave the stage; in the latter's case this would be effected by drawing the curtain across the bed.

111–12 *The King expects it*: presumably the Gentlemen's usual function is to clear up after the royal love-making.

142 *Must . . . stop*: must be quickly brought to a conclusion.

5.2.4 *ends*: deaths.

10 *for company*: i.e. as one of the conspirators, even though he has (or so he thinks) personally committed no treason.

13 *his full command*: all the soldiers whom he commands.

29 *left yourself*: 'acted against your nature'.

32 *best*. An aside from Calianax follows in Q2: 'When time was I was mad; some that dares fight, | I hope, will pay this rascal.' This continues the pattern of interruption established in lines 25–6, but also pulls focus away from Melantius and Lysippus at the fulcrum of their confrontation; its omission in Q1 may reflect a theatrical cut rather than authorial revision.

46 *mine own justice*: (*a*) 'judge in my own cause'; (*b*) executive agent of justice (in his own revenge).

58–9 *there . . . as this*: the disruption caused by the King's assassination and Melantius' rebellion could lead to even more serious insurrections.

59 *blank*: an official document, sealed but not filled in; Melantius can write in his own demands over the royal seal.

5.3.18–19 *have in charge*: have orders.

30 *all . . . so*: 'everyone will be the same (as us)'.

35–6 *O that . . . in it*: Aspatia still cannot believe that a man as beautiful as Amintor could have betrayed her.

40 *blemishes*: Aspatia now has scars on her face, presumably from self-mutilation, a symptom of depression especially prevalent in women and reflecting low self-esteem; cf. 2.1.82.

43 *so*: i.e. brother; he wishes he had married Aspatia.

64–5 *The . . . combats*: duelling was both a frequent recourse in aristocratic disputes (peaking in 1610) and a subject of intense ethical debate. King James I himself was passionately opposed to the practice: in 1600, he had made duelling without royal consent a capital crime in Scotland.

73–5 *Yet . . . what*: Amintor is so affected by the sight of Aspatia's 'brother', that he does not dare risk seeing her in person even if it were to possess the whole world.

88 S.D. *She strikes him*: to strike one's opponent was a sure way to provoke a duel; it was considered dishonourable to accept the blow without hitting back.

98 *flesh*: manhood (literally, penis).

103 *besides*: missing their target.

123 *knew ill*: began to do wrong.

147 *slow*: reluctant.

151 *O, O, O!*: a groan.

179 *her house*: the body, often described as the mansion of the soul.

195 *unsatisfied*: without (moral) payment, unavenged.

210 *abroad*: out of the body, its 'house' (179).

213 *The world . . . loss*: the world lacks sufficient beauty that it can spare Aspatia's, so her death is inexcusable.

217–8 *I would . . . then?*: Now that Evadne is dead, Amintor is free to marry Aspatia if she lives.

232 *bow*: bend down (to bring the blood to the head; it was also thought that this would staunch internal bleeding).

235 *out of . . . nothing*: human beings have no right to claim ('challenge') anything from the gods; they must request it.

264–5 *Here . . . had*: the bonds of Renaissance male friendship were often represented as being stronger than those of kinship or marriage.

284 *Amintor*: Melantius' intention is to join his dead friend.

289 *temper*: moderation.

Additional Passages A.11 *lend:* give; ironic in view of the fact that the moon's light is itself 'borrowed' (cf. 1.2.115).

12–13 *Gazed on . . . unquiet eyes*: only insomniacs see the moon.

B.1 *Queen of us*: cf. note to 1.2.154–7.

   3 *Amphitrite*: wife of Neptune in classical mythology; the name has four syllables.

   5 *Tritons*: the sea-gods, generically named from Neptune's son Triton, who was traditionally represented as a merman (half-man, half-fish) playing a conch shell as a trumpet.

11 *say a maid*: call themselves virgins.

12 *other*: otherwise.

C.1 *Lay . . . yew*: in the seventeenth century, a 'maiden's garland' decorated with symbolic herbs and flowers was carried on the hearses of unmarried girls; yew symbolized mortality. After the funeral, the garland would be hung in the church roof above the maiden's usual pew.

   7 *willow*: see note to 2.1.97.

23 *laid*: undressed and placed in bed, ready to receive her husband.

D.6 *wind . . . sails*: the comparison between swelling sails and a heavily pregnant woman was a commonplace, and is here extended by casting the wind, which makes them 'pregnant', as a wooer.

4–9 *rather believe . . . blasted*: each of the examples deals with a destructive force naïvely supposed benevolent: for example, the sea ruins the merchant by swallowing his cargoes.

   E By deepening the crisis of confidence between the King and Evadne, this passage strengthens the moment of Amintor's readmission to their conversation. This reflects the need for Amintor physically to cross the stage, and may have been required when performing the play in the Globe, which had a larger stage area than the Blackfriars.

The Maiden's Tragedy

The Persons of the Play

Govianus: probably pronounced 'Jovianus', alluding to Jove, ruler of the classical gods.

Memphonius: possibly implying one who voices complaints or grievances (cf. 4.3 and 5.2.177–84), from Greek *memphis*, reason for complaint, and *phone*, voice.

Sophonirus: the name's implication of wisdom (from Greek *sophos*, wise) is ironic.

Votarius, his resident friend: a well-to-do gentleman would sometimes house his best friend as part of his extended family.

1.1.2 *unmovèd stars*: in Ptolemaic cosmology, the stars were fixed to the outermost of the concentric spheres of the universe (see note to *Countess*, 2.1.142); it was hence the highest in relation to the Earth, and the only one which did not move.

9 *lay usurpers*: cause usurpers to lie.

10 *in warm beams*: in the sun.

14-15 *Now . . . us*: the Tyrant hopes that the Lady will emulate Evadne's promise in *Maid*, 3.1.170-4.

16-18 *Happier . . . kneeled to*: the Tyrant kneels to the Lady in a lover's supplication, the Lady to Helvetius as child to parent; this establishes a (nonconstitutional) hierarchy in which Helvetius is greater and happier than a king.

23 *that*: i.e. pride.

Be . . . in 't: normally to die in a state of sin was to risk damnation.

37 *stop her mouth*: (*a*) prevent her complaining; (*b*) literally stop up her mouth with kisses; (*c*) 'mouth' also has vaginal connotations.

38 *table*: board.

39 *stone-horse*: stallion, used for breeding (like the lover himself, as Sophonirus goes on to explain).

43-7 *He gets . . . one-and-thirty*: Sophonirus saves himself the life-shortening expense of having orgasms (to 'kick up one's heels' being to die); see note to *Maid*, 1.1.139-40.

58 S.D. *The Tyrant . . . Nobles*: the noblemen advise the Tyrant to banish Govianus, hence Govianus' attitude to them in lines 75-8. This is the Tyrant's first sign of weakness and political naïvety: to banish or kill a deposed king was the standard practice of Renaissance *realpolitik*, but he undertakes it only on his nobles' prompting.

64 *never weary yonder*: i.e. never tire of looking on the Tyrant.

80 *Weighty and serious*: an ironic explanation of 'ponderous'.

82 *sucked*: suckled, i.e. was an infant.

85-6 *construe . . . Pierce . . . decline*: a series of puns on the scholarly analysis of Latin grammar: *construe* = (*a*) analyse the syntax of, (*b*) interpret; *pierce* = (*a*) parse (describe the grammatical structure of a sentence), (*b*) penetrate sexually; *decline* = (*a*) inflect a noun, (*b*) impoverish.

87 *fines and rackings*: fees (other than rent) payable to a landlord, and excessive rent increases.

89 *living*: landed estates.

91 *mercers' books*: account books of textile dealers, recording sums owed; many Jacobean courtiers were heavily in debt to mercers.

94 *stuff*: with secondary meaning 'fabrics'.

100 *hell . . . him*: hell has a firmer expectation ('hope') of possessing the Tyrant after his death. (The form of words was more often used of a person due to receive an inheritance after the testator's death.)

112 *cloud*: the Lady's black clothing.

116 *Back!*: the Tyrant stops himself from thinking ill of the Lady.

118 S.D. *To Helvetius*: the Tyrant could also address Memphonius and Sophonirus, who have just fetched the inappropriately dressed Lady, but the most appropriate person to be told to bring her back dressed as a bride (if only metaphorically) is her father.

125 *this frame*: the Earth.

138–9 *there . . . here*: the Tyrant sits on the throne, which probably stands on its own dais towards the back of the stage; the deposed Govianus is at ground level. The Tyrant continues the stress on the vertical difference between them in his metaphor of valley and mountain in lines 142–3, and its ironic inversion at lines 208–10.

147 *What . . . here*: is any person here.

147–8: *What . . . on her*: the Lady's beauty is such that the male gaze lights on her even in preference to the King himself.

156 *wants*: lacks.

159 *use*: financial return on an investment.

174 *loose*: release, let go.

177 *sets . . . forth*: shows, reveals.

179 *progress*: a royal excursion through the kingdom. The monarch would be entertained in the houses of the local nobility at crippling expense; one way of staving off bankruptcy was to cut down the trees on the estate (a great status symbol in the period) and sell them for timber.

181 *game*: (a) scheme; (b) sexual pleasure.

182 *greatness*: Additional Passage A follows here in the unrevised text (4 lines).

184 *unkindly*: not as a father should.

198 *combination*: alliance.

204 *my liberty*: i.e. the Lady.

206 S.D. *with Memphonius*: it seems unlikely that Govianus and the Lady would be allowed to leave unattended; Memphonius, charged to see them committed, is the most likely character to attend them.

216–17 *'Tis true . . . command you*: the Tyrant starts to act on Helvetius' advice, and then changes his mind. The passage was added in revision.

227–34 *Nay, more . . . pricks me*: another passage added in revision, emphasizing the unpremeditated nature of the Tyrant's decisions.

234 *honour pricks me*: the phrase was a well-known Falstaffism (from *1 Henry IV*, 5.1.128–9), and hence would probably have carried an irony unintended by Helvetius.

238 *wards*: internal mechanism of a lock (with vaginal connotations).

1.2.1 *confine*: limit.

12 *in office*: in a position of authority, as a jailer.

15 *That . . . courtiers*: in contrast with the courts of earth, where many courtiers are corrupt.

25 *only think*: rather than know for certain.

28 *next . . . wives*: 'our wives make the next best fools of us (by being unfaithful)'.

34 *So . . . rest*: 'may I know the woman I sleep with to have the chaste thoughts just mentioned'.

36 *approved*: proven.

63 *interest*: influence.

67 *prostituted*: degraded.

73 *Falls in with*: is the same as (literally, takes its proper place alongside).

84 *natural touch*: touch of 'nature' (feelings expressing his bonds of kinship with Govianus).

100 *scarce . . . starlight*: it is so dark that the light of the moon is barely as bright as the stars normally are.

116–17 *one . . . bridge*: in early Roman history, Horatius Cocles prevented an Etruscan invasion of Rome by single-handedly defending the bridge over the Tiber. Anselmus' allusion is ironic: in this case there is no need of such heroic action.

122–3 *find . . . enough*: entail enough work for ten ages.

125 *a judge . . . on 't*: a judge's frown was reckoned a sure sign that the defendant would be sentenced to death.

124–7 *Bring . . . under-kingdom*: Anselmus' wife is so virtuous that she disables sinful intentions; this will mean no more souls going to hell (the 'under-kingdom').

138–9 *I thank . . . nothing*: Anselmus is glad that, through his mistrust of Votarius, he took steps to overhear the attempted seduction, because the result was to justify that mistrust: Votarius has betrayed him by failing to tempt his wife adequately.

140 *wipe . . . score*: forget this failed attempt.

147 *way*: opportunity.

148 *an absence*: Anselmus' own, not Votarius'.

150 *starting*: sudden displacement (from the Wife's bed, because Anselmus has come back unexpectedly).

154 *ground*: (*a*) foundation; (*b*) earth.

159 *his mind*: refers to Anselmus.

168 *left . . . untaken*: has not said goodbye.

171 *your lip*: to kiss her goodbye.

182 *whose will*: whosoever wants.

   rides: while Anselmus is riding his horse, someone else may as well be 'riding' his wife (sexually).

188 *together*: as a whole.

192–3 *You . . . you*: women in general.

194 *benefit*: gift conferred by God or nature.

199–200: *the general . . . gamester*: the time when everyone has sex, i.e. night ('gamester' = lewd person).

203 *observe*: pay due attention to.

205 *a dear year*: a year of dearth.

217 *retainer*: retainers wore a lord's livery but were not ordinarily resident in their master's household.

220 *work*: with secondary meaning, 'sex'.

221 *up*: (*a*) out of bed in the morning; (*b*) ready for sex, with an erect penis.

225 *Heart*: an oath (abbreviated from 'by God's heart').

229 *it's . . . relish*: it has a strange taste.

230 *time enough*: in time (not to fall in love with her; cf. note to *Countess*, 2.1.103 S.D.).

228–34 *I must . . . already*: both characters declare their intention to act, but remain paralysed in spite of themselves.

236 *fond boy*: love personified.

254 *naught*: wicked (stronger than the modern 'naughty').

   her: in the unrevised text Votarius adds, 'Sin's mere witchcraft. | Break all the engines of life's frame in pieces,' [i.e. 'may all the parts of my body shatter'].

255 *the boy*: Cupid, son of Venus.

256 *Face*: dissimulation; he is giving up on the stratagem which he has undertaken for Anselmus.

276 *have . . . wind*: the metaphor is from hunting: when the dogs have the quarry in the wind, its scent can be picked up; thus Leonella both understands what her mistress is implying and has the advantage of her.

281 *You*: Leonella (addressed rhetorically as if she is not present).

287 *high water*: when the water pressure will make it impossible to close a sluice-gate.

295 *most . . . heads*: men in fear of being arrested, particularly for debt, had to walk the streets of London 'muffled' to conceal their identity.

301 *one thing*: probably the Wife's adultery with Votarius, which will put her in Leonella's power; Leonella will then be able to entertain Bellarius openly.

305 *give . . . 'em*: do not step aside to let them pass.

306 *avoid the 'fool'*: avoid being called a fool, or becoming insane ('foolish') through unrequited love (cf. line 312).

311 *bear . . . another*: (*a*) tolerate each other; (*b*) both have sex (in which the woman conventionally bears the weight of the man).

2.1.3–10 *In despite . . . children*: this passage was added in revision, and establishes that the Tyrant's order for the separation of Govianus and the Lady has not been obeyed.

10 *jailers' children*: members of the tribe of jailers.

13 *constant suff'rings*: constancy in enduring suffering.

20 *Think?*: in the unrevised text, Helvetius adds, 'You come too late | If you seek there for me.'

29 *reversion*: since the Jacobean court did not have enough lucrative offices to go round, some courtiers would be granted offices in reversion (i.e. the right of succession after the incumbent's death); this would give them expectations against which to borrow. Helvetius will not actually be rejuvenated by the Tyrant's favour, but it will be the next best thing.

30 *dejection*: lowliness; cf. the Tyrant's metaphors of high and low in the opening scene.

32 *draws . . . question*: Helvetius suspects that his daughter's defiance is a mark of illegitimacy.

39 *eternal hazard*: damnation.

46 *Basely . . . thyself*: (*a*) 'serve yourself with one of lower rank' (i.e. Govianus); (*b*) do without servants like a base-born person; (*c*) 'follow your own base inclinations'.

59 *next*: second only to.

70 *light*: trivial (but with secondary meaning 'promiscuous' when used by the Lady in line 72).

71 *friend*: lover, partner in adultery.

75 *Push*: Middleton's distinctive variant form of the dismissive interjection 'pish'.

77 *flight*: (*a*) flock; (*b*) the height to which a bird can fly.

feathered: with rich plumage (metaphorical and human as well as literal and avine).

82 *one end on 't*: part of it (the implication is that she should bestow the other 'end' elsewhere).

94–5 *in . . . bargain*: 'entirely in addition to (the sex you receive as a result of) your original (or principal) contract (with a man, i.e. Govianus)'.

97 *suspect*: doubt (i.e. he is sure that she *is* wise).

100 *Make . . . market*: get the best price.

123 *a dead*: the merest.

134 *squire*: 'squire of dames' (=pimp).

144 *Sirens*: sea-maidens in classical mythology whose beautiful songs drew mariners off course, causing shipwrecks; here, a metaphor for worldly distractions from spiritual pursuits.

149 *thy . . . inward*: Helvetius has sunken eyes, or possibly has closed them in a sign of his developing sense of shame.

151–2 *miserable . . . kings*: a conscience that is so busy flattering kings that it cannot truly pray will only be able to manage a poor song of repentance.

153 *searched*: probed (as a surgeon probes a wound).

165 *both your hands*: the Lady's and Govianus'.

2.2.1 *There's . . . left*: referring to the biblical parable of the prodigal son who spent his substance on riotous living (Luke 15: 13).

4 *Pursuing sin*: a vocative.

shun: outrun.

15 *bowed*: bent.

17–18 *Most . . . to 't*: most other jobs are pleasing to do (which is the best thing about them).

26 *She's myself*: 'she can be trusted as if she were myself'.

32 *They're . . . twinkling*: probably Votarius and the Wife have sprung apart from an embrace at the news of Anselmus' return.

33 *Down . . . mainmast*: the sails suggest the Wife's skirts (hoisted for sex), the mainmast Votarius' erect penis.

35 *tossing*: (*a*) of a ship in a storm; (*b*) of the body during sex.

35–6 *I fear . . . still*: Leonella has a plan that will enable her to have sex with impunity; cf. note to 1.2.301.

51–2 *A second kiss . . . first friend*: it was customary for a wife to kiss her husband back, but Anselmus' wife fails to do so; Leonella interprets this as reserving the kiss for her lover, behaviour lacking in cunning in that the best way to conceal adultery is to dissemble affection for the husband.

53 *strangely*: as a stranger.

65 *slack*: with secondary meaning, 'detumescent'.

68 *advance my forehead*: because he has no cuckold's horns on it.

78 *like . . . dead*: too late; medicine cannot revive a corpse.

87 *to . . . hence*: 'for me to move out'.

89 *a degree kinder*: a closer bond.

99 *go so near*: become so intimate.

106 *shift of friends*: like a change of clothes.

109 *drink . . . mistress*: friends toasting one another, or their mistresses, would drink from the same cup (cf. note to *Countess*, 2.1.146); Votarius fears that he and his enemy may similarly be sharing the Wife's vagina.

111 *head physician*: Anselmus, who is of Votarius' and Bellarius' 'making' in that they have cuckolded him (hence 'head', suggesting his horns).

114 *stands next thee*: 'joins you', (*a*) in wickedness, and (*b*) in sex ('stands' = has an erection).

116 *breaking . . . money*: coins ceased to be legal tender when they became cracked.

131 *play 'em home*: take them as far as they could go ('home' also = on target, with bawdy implications).

139–40 *Are . . . aloft*: addressed rhetorically to the person heard upstairs.

147 *Confessed*: 'I have confessed'.

149 *Does . . . harm*: the harm a man sustains by pursuing revenge is greater than the good.

150 *mingled cup*: cocktail.

164 *offer*: attempt, i.e. with the dagger, which he has no doubt been brandishing as he interrogates her.

176 *You . . . business*: because she was forced to tell him her mistress's secret, and so can no longer use it for blackmail; cf. note to lines 35–6.

2.3.3 *miss*: want, lack.

   8 *Your . . . lies*: the Tyrant's behaviour here is provocative: to call someone a liar was a great insult which would normally result in a duel; the Tyrant's position prevents any such reprisal.

  13 *quickens*: (*a*) revivifies; (*b*) excites sexually.

  23 *sance bell*: used to summon people to church (also a small bell, sometimes a handbell, rung during the Sanctus at Mass).

24–5 *Let . . . one*: Sophonirus assumes that the best way to acquire honour is to give whatever answer the Tyrant expects or wants. ('Let me alone' = 'trust me'.)

  28 *tempt'st us*: 'try our patience'.

  37 *threescore hours*: since the recent deposition of Govianus in the Tyrant's favour.

  40 *prefer*: advance.

  51 *set by*: put aside.

50–2 *must I . . . place*: Helvetius' lordship is hereditary, not dependent on the royal patronage ('court grace') which was increasingly creating aristocratic titles in early Jacobean England. Consequently his office as the Tyrant's pander degrades him: it metaphorically associates him with 'base money' rather than honour, and lowers his status to that of a squire (a rank below a knight). See also note to 2.1.134.

56 *with him*. Additional Passage B follows here in the unrevised text.

58 *parts*: abilities.

68 *pass . . . time*: with Sophonirus' wife.

70 *however*: in any event.

69–71 *That may . . . nature*: the Tyrant does not share Sophonirus' self-confidence, but intends to support his uncertain abilities ('nature' = the inherent character of humanity, in the sense of human frailty) with the threat of force.

76 *great*: (*a*) ennobled; (*b*) pregnant.

77 *wide and strange*: distant and unfriendly.

   me: in the unrevised text, the Tyrant adds, 'Thou'lt feel thyself light shortly.'

78–80 *I'll not . . . miserable*: lineation this edn. (MS lines 78 and 79 end with 'thee' and 'name' respectively).

82 *a better workman*: God.

93 *close*: the most restrictive form of imprisonment, confined to one room and without the right to receive visitors.

119–20 *will . . . bottom*: will drink the best part of the wine themselves and serve their masters the lees.

123 S.D. *A flourish is played*: presumably to accompany the departure of the Tyrant (just off-stage); Sophonirus then hurries to join him, leaving his final verse line incomplete.

3.1.7 *This'*: this is.

17 *shall*: may.

22 *gi' 'm*: give him.

28–9 *set before . . . Fall to*: the imagery describes the killing of Sophonirus in terms of the start of a meal: food would be 'set before' a diner, and he would then 'fall to' it (i.e. begin to eat).

31 *Home . . . lodging*: to hell.

51 *banquet*: see note to *Countess*, 2.1.158.

60 *still*: constantly.

71 *think scorn*: consider it degrading.

74 *master*: the secondary meaning, 'sea-captain', serves to apply the Lady's simile directly to Govianus.

76 *Prevent*: anticipate, forestall.

83 *in soul*: in soul alone; in death, the Lady's soul will be released from her body and so escape.

85 *Or will it*: since otherwise it will.

92–4 *Thy . . . do 't*: Govianus' male reason, and not the Lady's weak female prompting, should incite him to kill her; it should not be the victim's role to urge him to act.

110 *Where . . . most*: i.e. in heaven.

117 *rise*: (*a*) from their sickbed; (*b*) up the ladder of the gallows.

146 *dying*: 'because I die'.

152 *gone*: dead, departed for heaven.

158 *Thou . . . thou*: the sword.

159 *preferred*: appointed.

171 *respectless*: disregardful.

179 *Spare not*: don't refrain from acting (addressed to himself).

184 *purple*: bloody.

185–6 *How . . . hand*: Govianus pretends to be the doorkeeper trying to stop the knocking. 'My lord' refers (with irony) to Sophonirus.

189 *All-Ass*: a derisive epithet, implying 'entirely foolish' and punning on 'alas'; presumably Govianus calls to Sophonirus, seemingly to establish whether he is still alive (and so to imply that he is innocent of the old courtier's death).

190 *inch-boards*: the thick boards of the door.

199 *inward*: intimate.

201 *You . . . her*: the Fellows have not made the connection between the dead female body and the Lady they have been sent to fetch.

211 *yonder*: in heaven.

220–1 *ladies In ordinary*: ladies-in-waiting at court.

222 *for*: because of.

223 *him*: Sophonirus.

229 *A vengeance of*: an imprecation (cf. 'a curse on').

231 *e'en . . . wives*: i.e. unsuccessfully; old men's wives were thought to go out in search of the sexual pleasure their husbands could no longer give them.

233 *her*. Additional Passage C follows in the unrevised text (12 lines).

236 *discreetly*: with judgement.

237–8 *ransack . . . deep*: 'even if in search of one you ransacked the places where jewels are found'.

243 *offence . . . kindred*: technically the Lady has no right to be buried in Govianus' family vault, because they were never married; however, his love for her makes her his wife in effect if not in legal fact (cf. 4.5.24).

4.1.9 *spring tide*: a high tide after the new and the full moon.

17 *twice*: a second time.

20 *Was . . . free?*: 'was it too easy to seduce me?'

24 *Where . . . lives*: 'whereas, if you women honestly examine your own habitual behaviour'.

25 *from*: absent from.

22–32 *A man . . . left you*: Votarius' tirade turns on the belief that weakness, both of mind and moral character, is inherently a female quality (cf. 1.2.58–9, *Maid*, 4.1.256); according to him, when men show weakness they must be borrowing it from women.

46 *moon*: lunar month; madness induced by the full moon would occur only once a month, and Votarius has already had his quota in arousing Anselmus' suspicions.

47–8 *any . . . funeral*: refers to a young man becoming irresponsible and self-indulgent after inheriting his father's money.

60 *lively*: authentic-seeming (used e.g. to commend an actor's performance).

64 *it*: the idea of her scheme.

67 *Pshaw ye!*: the line may be played in at least two ways: Leonella either impudently throws back her mistress's expression of contempt ('Pshaw ye!') or queries it ('"Pshaw ye"?').

74 *There's many . . . service*: the line refers to the contemporary practice among some aristocratic parents of sending their teenage children into service in another noble household; the overall implication is that Leonella, who is not a knight's daughter, enjoys better conditions of employment than many other servants of higher standing.

78 *long-nosed*: a long nose was considered a sign of a long penis.

95 *first*: best.

109 *set her forth*: informed on her.

113 *privy*: concealed under his clothes.

136 *weapon*: with secondary meaning, 'penis'.

137 *what follows*: (*a*) the rest of the scheme; (*b*) sex.

138 *without book*: without need of further instruction (literally, 'off by heart').

140 *ha' 't again*: be called the same name back.

164 *play*: (*a*) bout of sword-play; (*b*) feigned action (like a stage play).

393

4.2.6 *grace*: mercy.

9 *equality*: justice.

17 *exalted*: highly praised.

23 *stint*: allotted portion, allowance.

35 *of that sudden*: so suddenly.

35–6 *I'm . . . provision*: he is not ready to receive a (metaphorical) visitor (i.e. his new idea).

39–42 *Go . . . purpose*: added in revision; the passage serves to establish that Govianus is freed, as he needs to be for subsequent events.

46 *close lanterns*: sealed lanterns with a shutter enabling a beam of light to be shown or hidden at will; more commonly known as 'dark lanterns', they allowed people to move about at night without attracting attention.

52 *a widow's . . . policy*: in order to prevent a second husband from acquiring their estate (property inherited from the first husband), some widows would have it 'made over' (legally put in trust) to a nominee.

59 *to . . . church*: considered a great act of sacrilegious wickedness.

61 *What's . . . law*: ill-gotten gains are always used up in the payment of legal fees.

4.3 This short scene was added in revision, presumably to avoid the soldiers' having to make an immediate re-entry after their exit at the end of 4.2. Other editors have treated it as a coda to 4.2, which would imply that Memphonius has been eavesdropping; but it is as reasonable to assume that the news of the Tyrant's behaviour has simply travelled around the court.

2 *His soul . . . leader*: Memphonius implies that the Tyrant's actions are committed at the instigation of the devil; at the time this was one common way of explaining sinful or criminal behaviour.

4.4 S.D. *The . . . discovered*: traverse curtains on the rear wall of the stage are opened to reveal the tomb in the discovery space. The tomb is probably a stone sarcophagus, with the Lady's body buried in the horizontal position: the body is not visible to the audience until it is lifted out at 80 S.D., and in the next scene Govianus cannot immediately see that it is missing.

9 *monument*: tomb.

11 *springs*: eyes (from which tears spring).

10–14 *Now . . . dullness*: the tomb is wet (perhaps with condensation or nocturnal dew), which the Tyrant takes for tears; he thus thinks the inanimate tomb to be reproaching his own failure to weep.

29 *'Tis . . . element*: 'I am not accustomed'.

30 *open field*: battlefield.

32–3 *I beseech . . . hand*: 'Please don't ask this of me: find someone (morally) worse to do the job'.

36 *Of any*: out of all.

living: in the unrevised text, the Third Soldier continues, 'That's my humour, sir.'

47 *forfeit my lieutenantship*: because soldiers were notoriously irreligious.

56 *breach*: a gap in a city wall made during a siege; entering the breach was one of the most dangerous moments in siege warfare. The word probably also puns on 'breech' (buttocks), buggery being understood as a sexual perversion. Throughout the scene the bawdy but conventional sexuality of the First Soldier stands in contrast with the Tyrant's descent into necrophilia.

57 *stone*: with subsidiary meanings 'testicle' and 'jewel'.

60–1 *I never . . . see thee*: the Tyrant uses the register of conventional romantic love; cf. *Romeo and Juliet*, 2.1.216–20.

64–6 *She's . . . affect it*: exceptionally pale skin, with red cheeks and lips, was considered the summit of feminine beauty.

71 *here*: at this point the Tyrant is presumably some way from the body; the soldiers' ensuing dialogue between themselves (74–8) occurs as they walk across to the tomb.

79 *took up*: with secondary meaning 'possessed sexually'.

81 *the moon rises*: refers to the Lady's pale body being lifted from the tomb; appropriately, the moon was a symbol of chastity.

90 *prove*: attempt.

91 *pander's heels ache*: the laboured pun turns on the fact that panders kept guard while their clients had sex, and so were used to 'cooling their heels' (i.e. waiting).

107 *from*: alien to.

113 *house*: see note to *Maid*, 5.3.179.

116 *a Herod*: in Jewish legend, Herod loved Mariamne so immoderately that he preserved her body after death (according to some versions, expressly to facilitate sexual intercourse with it).

125–6 *All's . . . If*: 'your obeisance will be insufficient even if.'

129 S.D. *replaces the tombstone*: the text allows very slight opportunity for the actor to do this. The stone is evidently still displaced at lines 129–30; and since the tomb needs to be visible from the start of the next scene, it cannot be concealed and reset by stage hands without interrupting the performance. The likeliest stage action, assuming the stone to be made of some lightweight material, involves the soldier replacing it single-handedly while speaking lines 130–5.

133–6 *a great . . . cozen people*: cf. Lording Barry, *Ram Alley*, ed. Peter Corbin and Douglas Sedge (1981), 288–90: 'as a pie thrust to the lower end | That hath had many fingers in't before, | And is reserved for gross and hungry stomachs.' Some feasts had impressive-looking pies at the bottom of the table for show rather than eating, with only moss and stones under the pie-crust.

4.5.12 *bead*: tears are imagined as rosary beads, used by Roman Catholics to keep count of prayers said.

40 *everlasting harvest*: the Day of Judgement (see note to *Countess*, 4.1.103); Govianus' metaphor derives from the biblical parable of the wheat and the tares (Matt. 13).

42 S.D. *doors*: the stage doors by which characters enter and exit.

Enter . . . him: the unusual stage direction, '*Enter . . . standing*', seems to signify the sudden appearance of a motionless figure; the ghost probably appears through a stage trapdoor rather than entering conventionally and crossing the stage.

stuck: adorned.

59 *treads . . . do*: walks on the earth, is alive.

63–4 *run . . . eternity*: because sinful acts will have to be paid for in the afterlife.

65 *below*: in hell.

74 *hand of art*: a skilful artist.

79 *restore 't*: by reinterring the body.

80 S.D. *Exit . . . Ghost*: the ghost probably disappears in the same manner as it entered (cf. note to 42 S.D.).

89 *first rest*: original resting place.

5.1.15–16 *He's cleft . . . wide*: the metaphor is from archery: a bowman would shoot at a wand, trying to split it with his arrow; if he missed, his shot was 'wide' (of the mark).

22 *private gallant*: the best seats in the Jacobean indoor theatres were on the stage itself, giving 'gallants' (well-to-do, fashionable men-about-town) the opportunity to show off their finery to other members of the audience; Bellarius is a 'private gallant' in that his on-stage seat (in the gallery) is chosen with a view to his *not* being seen.

28 *action's*: one of the word's seventeenth-century senses, relevant here, was 'acting'.

34–5 *The . . . up*: the metaphor is of a siege, commonly used in Christian discourse to signify the human soul under temptation; here it has bawdy connotations too, with the gates of the castle signifying the Wife's vagina.

37 S.D. *He locks . . . closet*: the 'closet' (a small side room) is probably represented by one of the stage doors.

39 *she . . . lady*: there is no lady alive.

52–3 *if he . . . able*: St Paul states that God will not allow human beings to be tempted more than they are able to bear (1 Cor. 10: 13); here, the husband is identified as a divinity in relation to his wife.

58 *idle*: foolish.

59 *sad*: serious, earnest.

63 *of no religion*: and therefore without fear that his actions will have any consequences in the afterlife.

82 S.D. *Votarius . . . opens it*: He does not cross the threshold onto the stage until after line 90. (MS's stage direction reads '*Enter Votarius | to the doore | w^{th}in*'.)

83 *coming*: possibly with secondary meaning 'orgasm' (the usage is first recorded in 1650).

85 *duty*: respect.

86 *them . . . under*: (*a*) 'your own household servants' ('keep' = maintain); (*b*) sexual partners.

97 *prefer*: advance, proffer.

106 *upon going*: (*a*) about to leave; (*b*) about to die.

109 *My . . . afire!*: an intense burning sensation was commonly perceived as a symptom of poisoning.

111 S.D. *Exit . . . gallery*. Unless it is possible for Bellarius to descend from the gallery without exiting, he must leave at some point prior to his entrance onto the main stage at 113 S.D. The attack on Leonella is his likeliest inducement to intervene, and is also the point at which events cease to go according to his expectations. This gives him little time to make his descent (Leonella earlier managed it in eight lines, 30–7), but at this climactic moment the time could easily be filled with unspoken action representing Leonella's death-agonies. The important point is that Bellarius rushes down to defend Leonella, but arrives to see her already dead.

122 *I come*: she expects to be reunited with Votarius in the afterlife.

132 S.D. *Anselmus . . . pass*: the principal problem in determining how to stage the fatal exchange of wounds is the syntactic continuity of Bellarius' lines spoken before and after (130–3). If the audience is to follow the sense, this cannot be interrupted by an extended fight. Accordingly it seems likely that the two men wound one another in a single, carefully choreographed pass without any break in the dialogue.

136 *us both*: Bellarius and Votarius; the sword which wounds Anselmus is not poisoned (and so he takes longer to die).

144 *rage*: probably the burning effect of the poison, making Bellarius literally sympathetic to Votarius' death-agonies.

163 *cunning*: as well as crafty calculation, the word implies a woman who uses her 'cunney' (cunt).

165 *weapons*: with secondary meaning 'penises'.

174 *my . . . beggars*: because blood (representing life) is draining out of them.

177 *there*: in heaven.

167–80 *O thunder . . . women's lust*. This passage was added in revision, replacing Additional Passage D (nine lines). The excision creates a difficulty by removing the original text's provision for getting the bodies off the stage (D.9); this must then happen silently at the end of the scene. The result is that Govianus' elegiac critique of his brother becomes the more effective for being spoken over the body; however, with five corpses to be lugged off, there would also have to be a delay in starting the next scene. This was presumably the reason for Govianus' giving the order early in the original draft, and it is also possible that this line was retained in performance (after 180), despite being marked for omission.

192 *thorough*: go through.

193 *run*: force.

5.2 S.D. *Attendants*: possibly the soldiers who bring on the body at 13 S.D.

  3 *house*: see note to *Maid*, 5.3.179.

 13 S.D. *sets out*: emphasizes.

 14 S.D. *in voices*: with different vocal parts.

20–3 *By this hand . . . sought for 't*: the First Soldier has acquired just enough theological learning to know that the Tyrant's behaviour towards the corpse is idolatrous, and that he himself will be damned. There may be an element of anti-Catholic satire, suggesting that the common people are eschatologically disadvantaged by the practice of holding church services in Latin.

 25 *living*: in the unrevised text, he adds, 'And shall do seven year hence.'

 29 *colour*: in the unrevised text, he adds, 'And think it the best bargain that ever king made yet'.

34–5 *a court . . . forenoon tutor*: the art of applying cosmetics ('painting') was considered an important attainment for female courtiers. Middleton probably recalls Fine Lady Would-Be in Ben Jonson's *Volpone* (1605), who studies the subject 'i' the forenoons' (3.4.68).

 37 *him*: Additional Passage E follows in the unrevised text (8 lines).

 40 *privat'st*: see note to Additional Passage E.3.

 49 *security*: mistaken confidence.

 59 *thousand years' sleep*: the metaphorical sleep of death, lasting until the Day of Judgement when the dead will rise from their graves.

60–1 *All . . . masters*: some editors mark the Tyrant's rude remark about 'the painter' as an aside; but a man of his power has no need of courtesy; cf. 2.3.8 and note.

62 *has . . . film*: is covered too thickly (preventing clear sight).

65 *I am overmatched here*: 'it is too difficult for me (to make him understand)'; marked as an aside by some editors (cf. note to 60–1).

66 *lower chamber*: a grave.

69 *hired*: paid.

71 *trust*: extend credit (because courtiers were notoriously bad at paying their bills).

76–7 *thy reward . . . friend*: not only will 'the painter' be lavishly rewarded himself but so will his friends and even their friends.

103–4 *That's . . . approbation*: the job is only finished when the Tyrant likes the results.

117 *thou*: as the painter, Govianus addressed the Tyrant formally and politely as 'you'; in his own person he addresses him familiarly as 'thou'.

127 *ghosts*: spirits (of the damned).

131 *Frenchmen's*: the Tyrant refers to the terrible and protracted execution of the French king Henri IV's assassin, François Ravaillac, in May 1610, which concluded with the unfortunate man being torn to pieces by wild horses.

133 *one head*: a single force.

136 *lodging*: heaven.

137 *Doom*: condemn to death.

138 *noble*: here used adverbially.

140 *it*: the Lady's ghost.

143 S.D. *Enter the Ghost*: here the ghost enters conventionally through one of the stage doors in response to the Tyrant's call (contrast note to 4.5.42 S.D.). It probably had the 'gliding', noiseless movement noted in other stage ghosts of the period. Obviously ghost and corpse cannot both be played by the same actor; in the original King's Men production, the stand-in probably played the corpse (which, obviously, does not have to speak).

152 *to rise again*: (*a*) from its grave at the Day of Judgement; (*b*) after that, into heaven.

156–7 *O if . . . bosom*: the Tyrant cannot conceive of pains, even those of hell, that are worse than those of death.

158 *for*: ready for.

162 *all*: the unrevised version reads 'both'; presumably Middleton was trying to be frugal in his demand for supernumerary courtiers, and the company was able to spare more than two.

163 S.D. *The Nobles . . . throne*: by 'lay hands on him', the Tyrant obviously means to arrest Govianus; the nobles' response is to confirm Govianus as King. In the period, the election of a monarch by his nobles was usually understood to be done by vocal acclamation (as at line 169), but here they

evidently use their hands (hence Memphonius' sarcastic reply to the Tyrant; and cf. line 164); it seems most likely that they physically place Govianus in the seat of majesty.

165 *both mine*: i.e. clapping, a witty prolepsis of the audience's hoped-for response at the end of the play.

170 *that thunder*: probably the shout of acclamation rather than the flourish.

176 *mountain*: the throne; cf. 1.1.143.

188 *her . . . mistress*: the Lady's soul (mistress to the body).

201 *honour's rooms*: positions of honour; an implicit criticism of court ladies.

202 S.D. *Exeunt*: MS makes no provision for the removal of the Tyrant's body from the stage. It might be silently removed at some point soon after his death (thereby ensuring that he is physically as well as spiritually 'gone' in line 184), but one would expect this to be noted in a prompt-book. Alternatively, it could be carried off at the end, but this would inappropriately draw focus from the Lady's body. The only other option is for the characters contemptuously to leave it behind on the stage as a final image of the destructive power of lust.

Recorders: see note to *Maid*, 1.2.109 S.D.

Additional Passages A.1 *set light by*: think trivial.

2 *book*: source of instruction.

C.5–10 *In time . . . flew*: the man would rather live healthy than die; yet, having died and gone to heaven, he has no wish to return to earth.

D.2 *full time*: complete human lifetime.

3 *[blank]*: a word is missing in MS.

E.3 *To . . . hand*: to find a painter whose discretion could be relied upon ('some private hand'), and so suitable to participate in the Tyrant's secret actions ('close deeds').

7 *her*: i.e. art's; the Tyrant refers to the use of cosmetics.

9 *reckoning*: the sum of a woman's physical attractions.

10 *servants*: lovers, who are paid in their mistresses' beauties.

The Tragedy of Valentinian

The Persons of the Play

Aëtius: in the play, the name is usually trisyllabic, with the stress on the *ë*; it is pronounced with a soft *t* (cf. F's spelling, 'Aecius').

freedmen: F2 describes Chilax and the three Romans as 'noble panders', but its character listings are not always reliable; two passages (1.1.11–12 and 5.2.144) establish that they are freedmen (freed slaves who remain clients of their former master).

1.1.9 *course of practice*: practical experience (of working as a pimp).

12 *to . . . carry*: (*a*) as a servant; (*b*) as a procurer of women.

16 *affect*: live up to.

13–17 *Did you . . . honest?*: Proculus is saying that exceptionally beautiful women are almost always promiscuous.

23 *tried*: tested, put to the proof (here implying 'successfully tempted sexually').

24–5 *if . . . compass*: 'if I say I have experience with two hundred women, even then I understate my capacity'.

27 *degree or calling*: status or profession.

28 *fat*: plumpness was considered attractive and a sign of vitality in the period.
cunning: skill.

29 *not sweat for 't*: i.e. without undue effort.

30 *Were . . . again*: 'if I had to repeat the job'.

23–31 *For all . . . bedrid*: Chilax claims to be a highly skilful and experienced pander, who could successfully re-tempt every woman he has procured at a cost of less than £1,000.

32 *staggers me*: 'makes me stagger, defeats me'.

34 *Asia*: the Middle East.

43–4 *Cold . . . again*: crystal was thought to be formed from snow or ice hardened over many years.

48 *as much . . . have*: i.e. virtually none; cf. note to *Countess*, 1.1.25; 'spleen' here means vindictiveness.

49 *safe*: immune from prosecution.

51 *come near*: be comparable with.

58–9 *A new nature . . . all ages*: she would be so powerful that she would be considered the creator and progenitor of all future times, supplanting nature.

65 *held for*: considered.

71 *ashes*: a conventional term for the decomposed substance of the dead human body.

74 *I would . . . god*: Balbus wishes the Emperor were 'in her' sexually.

76 *Stoics*: adherents of a philosophy which demanded absolute mastery of desire and contempt for worldly things.
truth: integrity.

78 *intended*: conceived.

82 *Phoenix*: see note to *Countess*, 4.2.58.

88 *Like . . . against*: differs from as absolutely as may be (literally, moves away from at full speed).

92 *a Lucrece*: a picture of the early Roman heroine Lucretia, who committed suicide after being raped by the son of Tarquinius Superbus, the last king of Rome (reigned 534–510 BC).

94 *vestal*: chaste, like the goddess Vesta and her virgin priestesses; Vesta was goddess of hearth and home, so the adjective also underlines Lucina's status as a wife.

95 *posed in*: 'stumped by'.

101 *the tutor to great Alexander*: the Greek philosopher Aristotle (384–322 BC); his *Nicomachaean Ethics* includes the recommendation that young men should not study the subject, having too little worldly experience (though no specific age is given).

111 *what . . . purchase*: the panders, the Emperor's 'nets' (instruments for 'purchase', i.e. catching prey) fear for their position at court if they fail to procure Lucina.

113 *the first . . . tail*: eels are hard to catch, because they slip through the net (or the fingers); the panders are so skilful that, before Lucina, they have not lost even an eel. 'Tail' also has the secondary meaning 'pudenda'.

1.2.5 *saint*: an object of worship.

13–14 *bury . . . roof*: hide her beauty by burying herself in domesticity (literally, staying indoors).

15 *That . . . red*: Lucina's complexion; cf. note to *Maiden*, 4.4.64–6.

15–16 *That white . . . nothing*: beauty is in the eye of the beholder; therefore it does not exist unseen.

19 *That most unvalued horn*: the unicorn's horn was sought after, and therefore 'unvalued' (priceless), as a universal antidote to poison.

32 *I a man*: 'were I a man'.

34–5 *Come, goddess . . . for you*: a complex metaphor which conflates the concentric spheres or 'orbs' of Ptolemaic cosmology (see note to *Countess*, 2.1.142) with the classical goddesses after whom the planets are named. Lucina will take a higher orb in moving from her commoner husband to a royal lover; in so doing she will also leave the sphere of the moon (= Diana, goddess of chastity), which was closest to the earth, for the higher sphere of Venus (goddess of love).

36 *Be . . . 'em*: cf. the proverb, 'Maids say nay and take it' (Tilley, M.34).

38 *guilty of*: responsible for.

55 *coming . . . curses*: if Ardelia and Phorba have anything to look forward to other than being cursed (by their victims; the curses being theirs in that they are the recipients).

83–4 *Numa . . . Octavius*: Numa Pompilius (*c.*715–672 BC), the legendary second king and lawgiver of Rome, renowned for wisdom and piety; and Caius Octavius (63 BC–AD 14), later the Emperor Augustus. They are named as archetypes of great Roman rulers; Ardelia suggests that another will be produced if Valentinian inseminates Lucina.

91 *nothing . . . service*: with secondary meanings, 'vagina' and 'sexual intercourse' respectively.

102 *rarely*: exceedingly.

108 *imp*: add to, enlarge (literally, replace lost feathers in a falcon's wing).

110–11 *turns . . . itself is*: her mother's fame, which is good in itself, also has the property of making good the things it comes into contact with.

114 *happily*: 'haply', perhaps.

116 *ancient . . . ruins*: edifices so well built that even the ruins are attractive.

124–5 *Let . . . 'em*: let women make their own mistakes (rather than be persuaded into error by the panderesses).

135 *ravished*: stolen.

from anger: through her own anger; the burden of Phorba's speech is that even Lucina's anger has an aphrodisiac effect.

138 *hold from*: abstain.

141 *Runs . . . bones*: aching bones are one of the symptoms of syphilis.

155 *have here*: she has admitted the panders to her own home; cf. 2.2.4–5.

166 *and women thus*: if women are so chaste.

169 *halt*: limp; cf. line 23.

177 *rid . . . bit*: (*a*) ridden unbridled; (*b*) sexually possessed by their consent, without the use of force.

1.3.1 *the nations*: provinces of the Roman empire (cf. lines 172–5).

10 *made up*: gathered together, mustered.

10–11 *like . . . action*: the image is of barnacles attaching themselves to the hull ('walls') of a disused ship.

13 *larger means*: more powerful influence (literally, intercessor).

17–19 *Obedience . . . ours*: cf. note to *Maid*, 2.1.289–91.

25 *why we are*: 'for what purpose we were created'; Maximus extensively reapplies the question from line 35 on.

29 *Make but a rule*: are subject to a similar law.

33 *took surfeit*: (*a*) had too much of; (*b*) was led astray (literally, made sick) by.

40 *Gauls*: i.e. Gaul (France), divided into three provinces of the Roman empire.

quivers . . . Parthians: the Parthians, whose empire abutted Rome's on the eastern frontier, were famous for their archery (cf. lines 188–89); Maximus' metaphor suggests that, by condoning Valentinian's excesses and the empire's consequent decline, the Romans may themselves be the instruments of a Parthian conquest.

42 *curious*: fastidious.

47 *danger*: political danger, sedition.

51 *time out-daring*: challenging the oblivion that comes through the passage of time.

56–8 *the Emperor . . . worthiness*: Aristotle held that the youthful mind was influenced more by appetite than by intellectual faculties (*Politics*, 7).

59 *these . . . call*: these things commonly referred to as.

65 *depress*: make less excitable.

69–72 *all ears . . . heaviest*: not everyone will listen to Maximus with the same attention to his meaning; and many will encourage him to commit treason (by killing the Emperor) rather than try to restrain him.

81 *Brutii*: famous anti-monarchists of Roman history: Lucius Junius Brutus (consul, 509 BC), who expelled King Tarquin from Rome after the rape of Lucretia, and his descendant Marcus Brutus (*c.*85–42 BC), one of the republican conspirators who assassinated Julius Caesar.

77–86 *durst . . . example*: even if Aëtius were to allow himself to act in anger rather than out of virtue, the first person to die would not be the Emperor but the one who preached sedition, no matter how righteous his cause.

91 *The elephant . . . anger*: elephants were considered slow and long-lived, and consequently required skill and patience to train.

94–6 *Our honest . . . back*: the best way to restrain a prince is by honest service which may provide him with a good example.

101 *as . . . flourish*: 'may his fortunes correspond with our views of him'; *affect* = love, are disposed towards (possibly ironic in Maximus' case).

108 *defend*: forbid, prevent.

109 *shrewd*: unfavourable, hostile.

117 *hold the hammer*: endure rough usage.

118 *lusty*: spirited.

135 *suspicions*: obsessive, paranoid delusions.

140 *Fencers*: see note to *Countess*, 4.1.89.

regarded: esteemed, valued.

145 *Nero*: tyrannical Roman emperor (reigned AD 54–68), notorious for fiddling while Rome burned (in AD 64).

157–9 *A people . . . a-working*: it is not clear precisely what opprobrious court practice Aëtius means. The 'paper' of which the court bawds are said to be made probably refers to letters patent, crown legal documents authenticated with the royal seal and establishing a right, possibly to an aristocratic title or to a monopoly.

176 *eagles*: legions of the Roman army (which had eagles on their standards).

mew: shut up, confine (from the cage in which falcons are confined for moulting).

177 *wont*: were wont.

183 *shining brass*: armour.

186 *Lined*: together in a battle-line.

185–9 *Where . . . arrows*: the battle-hungry soldiers recall great military campaigns from Rome's history: the conquest of Spain by Scipio Africanus (210–206 BC), of Gaul (France) by Julius Caesar (58–51 BC), and of parts of Germany by Germanicus (AD 11–17). Mithridates was the personal name of three of the Arsacid kings of Parthia, but the most famous Mithridates was the King of Pontus in Asia Minor (120–63 BC), who fought three major wars against Rome.

191–3 *tell their wounds . . . glory in those scars*: Jacobean audiences would have known from Shakespeare's *Coriolanus* (1608) the importance which the Romans attached to wounds as marks of honour and civic responsibility. The contrast between the soldiers' Stoicism and their Emperor's epicurean pursuit of sensuality indicates for them the decline of Rome.

204 *Tiberius*: tyrannical Roman emperor (reigned AD 14–37), notorious for his suspicious nature.

Caligula: sanguinary and licentious Roman emperor (reigned AD 37–41), probably insane.

224 *that style . . . 'soldier'*: Valentinian gave Aëtius the honourable name of 'soldier' when endorsing the Empress's favourable report of him (118–19).

227 *looked*: appeared.

229 *the scape of*: escaping, surviving.

231 *purchase*: prey.

237 *I . . . Roman*: Aëtius asks to be allowed a dignified death by suicide (to the Jacobeans a distinctive aspect of Roman culture) rather than at the hands of an executioner.

238 *Reclaim the soldier*: 'restore the army (to its former state of loyalty and discipline)'; however, the line could also mean 'take back the style of "soldier" which you offered to pawn'.

245 *but*: with the exception of.

2.1.1 *set my hand out*: 'equal my stake'.

4 *good conditions*: promises.

7 *at*: 'have at' (cf. line 8), said with reference to the stakes when rolling the dice.

10 *Spaniard*: Spanish horses were especially prized for ostentatious riding.

22 *luck's sake*: this edn. (F reads 'luck sake'); the sense is obviously genitive, with the final -*s* elided.

33 *and above*: more than the pay they are due.

38-9 *only . . . lessons*: what they know has been learned word for word without understanding the sense, in the same way as birds have distinctive songs, but no theoretical knowledge of music.

47 *take*: succeed, 'bring it off'.

51 *a thought*: slightly.

2.2.7 *hatched hilts*: sword-hilts engraved with closely parallel lines; the reference is to the panderesses' wrinkles, and may also recall the phrase 'loose in the hilts' (= unchaste).

8 *painted*: covered their faces with make-up.

9-10 *One might . . . ages*: the panderesses are imagined as gilt iron, with the gilt wearing off in places.

11 *sheathed like rotten ships*: old ships were refurbished with a protective layer called 'sheathing' on their bottoms; with secondary sexual meanings (sheath = vagina, rotten = venereally diseased). Nautical imagery continues until line 23.

13 *passed the line*: crossed the equator (and so are a long way into their voyage).

16 *make a drollery*: not take life seriously, have a good time.

25 *To stand . . . A bow short*: in archery contests, 'markers' stood by the target ('mark') to judge the contestants' aim; 'bow' presumably means 'a bow's length'. The secondary meaning presents a no-longer-attractive woman who wishes herself to be the target (shot at with phallic arrows), obliged to tout for a man (or 'beau').

27 *five . . . pound*: possibly meaning 'expensive, high-class', by contrast with 'ten-a-penny', though the latter phrase is not recorded until the twentieth century.

28 *great . . . it*: good reason to think it; there may also be a secondary reference to a bawd's lighting the way to a nocturnal assignation.

29 *spring*: the mating season; Claudia is feeling lascivious.

33 *gilded*: embroidered with gold thread.

34 *Milan skins*: see note to *Maid*, 4.1.12.

35 *showed*: appeared.

37 *I know . . . last*: they are finely dressed (cf. 2.4.37); after the panders' doublets, Claudia's attention characteristically comes to rest below the waist.

45 *In's chamber*: (*a*) as a groom of the chamber (a high honour in the Jacobean court); (*b*) as a procurer of women for his bedchamber.

46 *Roman*: Roman citizen.

47 *Mantuan*: Lycias claims an especial honour: Mantua in northern Italy was revered in the Renaissance as the poet Virgil's birthplace.

48 *parents*: forefathers.

66 *ad unguem*: Latin: 'to the last detail' (literally 'to the fingernail').

70 *notice*: prior announcement, advance warning.

2.3.4 *Give me myself*: Maximus may be attempting physically to restrain Aëtius.

6 *and I living*: 'whilst I am alive' (and, it is implied, still in command: Aëtius is partly angry because his authority has been undermined).

8 *drawing out*: marching out of camp (here metaphorical).

16 *he's*: he has.

17 *that*: because.

19 *Consider . . . do*: 'consider the crime rather than your ability to punish'.

21 *may*: 'you may'.

37 *Hold . . . honesty*: Maximus wants to restrain his honesty from making him criticize Aëtius too harshly.

39 *bosom piece*: close personal friend.

46 *ye'd*: this edn. (F reads 'y'e had'); a contraction is metrically necessary, and may be signalled by F's misplaced apostrophe.

48 *seclude*: separate.

59 *with*: as.

69 *trees and roots*: natural sources of food.

70–2 *the charity . . . nurses*: the soldiers have prostituted themselves to sexually frustrated ('longing') women, who then kindly supplied them with accommodation and clothing.

76 *Heats*: fevers.

80 *hatched*: inlaid, decorated.

82 *daws*: jackdaws, considered contemptible in the period.

85 *years and beets*: old age and coarse, unappetizing fare.

94–5 *And . . . Rome*: 'and if you are willing to give me back my captaincy, I will prove, by fighting Rome's enemies (that I am honest)'.

99 *want*: material need (because, like the rest of the army, he has not been paid).

103 *Not . . . traitor*: the Romans held it dishonourable to be wounded in the back (i.e. while running away).

104 *cast*: cashiered (literally, discarded).

108 *talk but near*: say anything remotely like.

407

2.4.9 *Take no care*: don't worry.

14 *man yourself*: 'fortify your spirits', 'make yourself (sexually) manly'.

17 *cut off*: intercepted.

20 *waiters*: attendants.

34 *resolved*: resolved to be.

50 *will*: intends to.

58 *man*: with secondary meaning 'provide sex'.

61 *stand to 't*: (*a*) 'keep your promise'; (*b*) have an erection.

2.5 S.D. *with*: the F stage direction reads '*Enter Lycinius, and Proculus, Balbus*'; the emphasis on Lycinius probably indicates that he is the singer.

4 *Peace!*: i.e. 'Be quiet!' Presumably Lycinius countermands Proculus' order in the previous line: F clearly directs, '*Jewells shewd*', at line 84. An alternative interpretation might be that the jewels are discovered here, that Lucina affects to ignore them, and the panders eventually 'show' them by gesturing towards them.

6 *Green*: song MS; F reads 'Golden'.

8 *On every bush*: song MS; F reads 'Everywhere'.

10 *pull*: pick the flowers.

28–34 *Fair Callisto . . . shower*: the song refers to the sexual conquests of Jupiter in classical mythology: Callisto, an Arcadian nymph and companion of Diana, who demanded chastity of her (hence the anachronistic suggestion that she was a nun); Leda, raped by Jupiter in the guise of a swan; and Danaë, locked away by her father to prevent her conceiving offspring, but visited by Jupiter in a shower of gold.

37 *the boy*: Cupid.

38–42 *The chaste moon . . . dies*: even the classical goddesses known for chastity (Diana the moon goddess and Vesta the goddess of hearth and home) are subject to love.

43 *Ilion*: the city of Troy, razed to the ground at the end of the Trojan war.

44 S.D. *Enter . . . Lucina*: the songs are to be heard by Lucina as she approaches; there is no need to bring her on stage, as some editors have, earlier than indicated in F.

56 *triumph*: military victory, considered a source of great honour by the Romans.

72 *him*: the Emperor (mentioned in Proculus' whispered proposition).

90 *dying*: orgasm.

93 *Rushes*: fresh rushes were strewn on the floor for visitors. Claudia and Marcellina take no further part in the scene and, as mere servants, are sent to fetch them (really as a pretext to separate them from Lucina). The

panders then follow, as if on cue, as Lucina remarks; it is later implied (3.1.133–4) that they have had sex with the two waiting women.

97 *better fitted*: 'equipped with better company (than us)'; refers to Ardelia and Phorba.

101–4 *If thou . . . vices*: Lucina pronounces a curse on herself: whereas she will be buried after her death if she remains chaste, and her body will provide plants with moral as well as physical nourishment, may she remain unburied (a great dishonour) if she should fall from virtue.

112 *enjoy*: possess.

118 *it is*: 'you are' (baby-talk).

2.6.2 *worming of her*: insinuating their way into Lucina's confidence (in order to tempt her).

18 *leprous*: see note to *Countess*, 4.4.27.

25 *sailing*: overhanging; the cedar tree was noted for its tallness.

36–8 *I did . . . to him*: Valentinian claims to have been testing Lucina and to have found her chaste; he will now escort her to Maximus with all the 'commendations' (praises) which 'wait on' (belong to, are attendant upon) her chastity.

3.1.7 *Whose honesty . . . tissue*: a gift of tissue (a finely woven fabric) would override her chastity.

9–10 *an itching . . . get it*: the husband will be granted an honour in return for the sexual services of his wife, provided there is also a non-compromising reason ('ground') to bestow it.

13 *play*: have sex.

16 *motion*: sex.

21 *wholesome*: free from venereal disease.

45–6 *raze thee . . . vicious*: he will be expunged from the record of history, except as a vicious tyrant.

70 *gilded*: a further reference to the panders' fine clothes; but the F spelling 'guilded' could also suggest that Valentinian's regime legitimizes panders as if they had a livery company (guild).

79 *rods and axes*: the *fasces*; see note to *Countess*, 4.2.245.

88–9 *those . . . maids*: according to legend, in the time of Romulus (the founder of Rome, eighth century BC), the men of Rome abducted and married the women of the neighbouring Sabines, provoking an invasion of Roman territory (Livy, *Annals*, 1.9–10).

101 *Were . . . again*: if it were not yet done.

114–15 *Be . . . make it*: Valentinian offers to create for Lucina a political office superior to his own.

117 *use*: monetary payment.

121–3 *where . . . make it*: if the rape becomes public knowledge, Lucina's reputation will be damaged, but not the Emperor's.

130 *most*: greatest, highest.

143 *prize*: reward.

159–60 *Go . . . requiem*: referring to the belief that the swan sang immediately before its death; Maximus is implicitly telling Lucina to kill herself.

180 *obedience*: to the Emperor.

185 *dropped . . . marble*: refers obliquely to Niobe (see note to *Countess*, 5.2.63).

191 *Cassiopeia*: the mother of Andromeda in classical mythology, who was turned into a constellation after her death.

195 *must not*: cannot expect to.

222 *justice*: due penalty.

229 *them*: the gods.

233 *laid in*: inlaid.

236 *after issues*: the descendants of Maximus and Lucina.

258–9 *killing . . . neighbour*: the yew-tree is poisonous; Pliny (*Natural History*, 16.20) reports the belief that anyone who slept or picnicked beside one would die.

266 *this sad day*: i.e. on the anniversary of this sad day.

268 *full . . . self*: full of thoughts of Lucina.

untold: uncounted.

272 *what . . . lives*: historical accounts from which their lives may be reconstructed.

274 *stand to eternity*: survive forever.

275 *Elysium*: the islands of the blessed in the classical underworld, posthumous destination of the virtuous.

278 *bedrid justice*: Maximus may be making the conventional contrast between ideal justice in the afterlife and its imperfect (here, weak or crippled) equivalent on earth; but a more direct reference to Rome's justice, Valentinian (cf. line 34), and his activities in bed, also seems likely.

282 *fear him*: fear for him (in that he may be tempted to regicide, as previously discussed in 1.3).

285 *Beyond a man*: beyond human capacity.

288 *had her*: was able to provide her.

295 *not tied*: i.e. if it were not tied.

296 *to*: compared with.

301 *mentioned . . . tales*: go down in history for telling what happened (rather than acting to avenge it).

311 *a general ruin*: destruction of the state as a whole, rather than merely a single individual.

317 *i' th' heat on 't*: actually raping Lucina.

326 *much good may do*: may do much good to (ironic).

328–9 *More than the . . . lost*: more than the natural process of change and decay.

334 *from*: alien to.

338 *well-handled . . . breeding*: skilfully bred (during the century needed to produce it).

343 *flesh*: and therefore has sexual feelings.

353 *here*: within your breast (possibly accompanied by a gesture), and therefore a secret.

355 *bitten*: partially eaten (by someone else).

354–6 *She knows . . . knavery*: Maximus suspects that Lucina wants a divorce, and has falsely cried rape because she knows he will reject a wife whom another man has slept with.

380 *melted*: his entire body will turn to tears.

3.2.4 *But . . . master*: except Aëtius.

5 *he . . . he*: Valentinian . . . Aëtius.

11 *time*: this edn. (F reads 'tune'). Soldiers beat their targets (shields) to intimidate the enemy; Pontius turns this into a metaphor of a musician beating time.

13 *those*: martial subjects.

20 *Not . . . execute*: obey orders without pausing to consider what they mean.

22 *run empty-handed*: 'leave us unrewarded'.

32 *Men's . . . truth*: a good reputation.

33 *trial*: testing, putting to the proof.

56 *trim*: proper, fashionable (used ironically).

58 *a worse*: a worse course of life.

59 *ways*: roads.

66 *mend*: grow healthy.

   diets: customary ways of life.

71–3 *Yet may . . . velvets*: the image turns on the fact that the courtiers' garments are made of fine, soft materials that will not keep out the wind, unlike a poor man's coarse clothing.

75 *Put us . . . served him*: 'we were recommended, and have accordingly served him, as (morally) good men'.

82 *you . . . too*: the passage could mean either 'you shall live honestly at

court, as we do' or 'you shall live at court even though you are an honest man, and as such out of place there'.

88 *my good master*: Aëtius.

3.3.4 *This . . . opinion*: Aëtius' moral superiority, which keeps Maximus from redeeming his reputation ('opinion') by inhibiting his revenge. (This contradicts the previous line, and articulates the other horn of his dilemma.)

12 *in . . . me*: 'defeats me in the attempt'.

15 *this*: this edn. (F reads 'his').

20 *wither him*: should he wither.

24 *rumour*: reputation; some editors have emended to 'honour'.

28–9 *Can . . . has*: Aëtius has defended innocent men against false accusations made out of malice ('envy').

30–1 *Can . . . has*: Aëtius' skill at battlefield rhetoric can transform cowardly soldiers who want to fly away into fighting tigers.

32 *and . . . so*: 'and thereby had my life saved'.

45 *led away*: misled.

51 *Out . . . justice*: the line's syntactical position is ambiguous: it could relate to Aëtius' holding Maximus back (in the previous line) or his avenging the rape (in the next).

53 S.D. *Enter a Servant*: the servant's entrance at this point (the positioning is explicit in F) creates a momentary suspicion that Maximus may have been overheard while soliloquizing on the murder; the effect is to enhance our sense of its furtive and illicit nature.

54 *and I cold*: 'whereas I am cold' (= sluggish, not disposed to action).

62 *If . . . it*: this could alternatively be a subordinate clause of the following sentence.

63 *loose*: kill.

63–4 *'tis . . . difference*: Aëtius must be killed; Maximus' only options are when and how it happens.

66 *Take him directly*: kill him personally in single combat.

doubts: (*a*) fears, apprehensions (because he does not want to risk fighting Aëtius); (*b*) moral uncertainties (because he does not want to kill his friend in person).

81 *thoughts*: of revenge.

89 *fair*: morally unblemished.

114–15 *quit you . . . fetch ye off*: 'rescue you'.

118 *he*: Valentinian.

120 *black-eyed*: with especially lustrous eyes; implying the courtiers' hedonism.

e'er: this edn. (suggested by Michael Cordner); not in F.

122–3 *on . . . nothing*: Maximus would kill Valentinian even if doing so would destroy the world ('pile' = foundation, with secondary meaning 'hair').

124 *dames of hell*: the Furies; see note to *Maid*, 5.1.32.

126 *mankind more*: the continuation of the human race.

perished: should perish.

129 *no Roman*: a 'stranger' in the sense of foreigner (and also dissociated from the stoic virtues which were part of Roman national identity).

131 *so*: when alone.

133 *shadow*: double (literally, an actor playing the role).

148 *his . . . of us*: a commonplace of monarchist writing; cf. Anthony Munday, *A Watchword to England* (1584), L1ᵛ: 'the lives of Kings and Princes are the lives and souls of their kingdoms and commonweals'.

152 *as . . . disobedience*: because there is a rebellion in the provinces.

157 *ours*: legitimately succeeded to the throne (rather than by conquest); this had a bearing on the subject's right of resistance (cf. note to *Maid*, 2.1.289–91).

170 *Give . . . ruin*: 'even if I know for certain I shall be destroyed'.

4.1.13 *our maker*: in the sense that Valentinian is responsible for the panders' exalted position at court; but there is probably also a hint of idolatrous Caesar-worship (cf. lines 20–6).

19 *told*: fixed to a set number (literally, counted out).

41 *run me over*: 'given me exhaustive experience of'.

43 *fencers' whores*: the lowest members of an already lowly profession (cf. note to *Countess*, 4.1.89).

44 *nice*: wanton.

51–2 *Your . . . fillies*: Pliny (*Natural History*, 8.67) describes how Spanish mares were supposedly impregnated by the west wind; here 'proud' = lascivious.

54 *Messalina . . . Lais*: Messalina, the wife of the Emperor Claudius (reigned AD 41–54), was a notorious adulteress whose sexual insatiability was described by Juvenal (*Satires*, 6.115–33); Lais, a Corinthian courtesan, was famous for having slept with a thousand lovers.

55 *backs of bulls*: see note to *Countess*, 2.2.14.

57 *oracle*: truth; see note to *Countess*, 1.1.440.

58 *put by*: compared with.

62 *Rotten*: venereally diseased.

67 *common Pasquil*: general satirical comment (from an ancient statue erected in Rome in 1501, on which satires were posted).

68 *Since . . . wench*: since Valentinian's puberty.

413

70 *They . . . show*: probably the 'payment' was a dose of syphilis.

104–5 *If . . . fears*: if the letter does indeed contain private business and not treason.

116 *another*: another Emperor.

120–1 *should . . . dangerous*: if the Emperor were to demote him, it would enrage the people because it would not be of Aëtius' own choosing.

130 *Germanicus*: popular Roman general (*c.*15 BC–AD 19), adoptive son of the Emperor Tiberius; in AD 14 he refused the army's offer to make him emperor, and was poisoned five years later.

135 *Corbulo*: Roman general (d. AD 66) who distinguished himself in campaigns against the Parthians during the reigns of Claudius and Nero; he was forced to commit suicide after his son-in-law conspired to depose Nero.

138 *Arsaces' line*: Arsaces founded the Parthian empire, *c.*250 BC; his successors were called the Arsacidae.

144 *adventure*: appeal to (literally, try).

147 *laughed at*: be laughed at: to allow Aëtius to live, rather than nip the danger in the bud, is foolish and invites ridicule. Some editors have emended to 'laugh at'.

166 *this fellow*: the anonymous author of the letter.

167 *look about*: take care, 'watch out'.

4.2.40 *wither*: grow old.

44 *fall so happy*: die untainted by sin.

46 *as . . . enemy*: as if he had died honourably in battle.

53 *Cato*: Marcus Porcius Cato (95–46 BC), surnamed Uticensis; a Roman statesman and Stoic, who committed suicide rather than outlive the Roman republic.

4.3.12–13 *I ever . . . affection*: because Aëtius was so loyal (had 'too much affection') to the Emperor, Pontius feared he might provoke the army ('the soldier') to mutiny against him. But in the following lines Proculus takes him to mean that the army has undone Aëtius by making him ambitious.

22 *Out . . . merely*: for no good reason.

28 *main link*: of a metaphorical chain which holds the state together.

31 *all . . . be*: the same as being.

35 *Charon*: ferryman of the classical underworld, who carried the shades of the dead across the River Acheron to their final destination.

4.4.14 *humour*: sexual or emotional fancy; but F's reading, 'honour', could make sense as referring to a wooer primarily interested in a wife as an external ornament, without any real understanding of the nature of wives, or ability to foresee the tensions of marriage.

18 *stay*: await.

44 *a wilful death*: suicide.

56 *for want of will*: because they can't get their own way.

57 *poises*: weights (i.e. metaphorical gravity).

66 *what . . . been*: the memory of Aëtius' honesty.

68 *for*: because.

70 *traffic of my travails*: 'profit from my labour' (possibly punning on 'travels', with reference to Aëtius' military campaigns outside Italy).

71 *this silver*: his hair.

89 *it is . . . say so*: 'my saying that I am not afraid is itself a kind of fear'.

103 *my masters*: a familiar, 'hail-fellow-well-met' mode of address.

111 *used*: accustomed.

115 *give out . . . side*: 'claim that you supported me' (rather than obeying their orders).

117 *marked*: noted.

138 *but*: other than.

139 *A . . . fortune*: because he has been discarded by the Emperor as Pontius was cashiered by him.

147 *Heaven's angry flashes*: lightning.

163 *hatchment*: heraldic escutcheon (as distinct from a weapon actually used in battle).

165 *Chained all defence*: 'prevented me from defending myself'.

193–4 *no . . . 'em*: this may mean that the Romans have not rewarded the soldiers' military service because they only care about receiving the benefit of it; or alternatively that the only comfort for their injuries is the knowledge that they were sustained in battle (playing on the proverbial idea that virtue is its own reward, Tilley, V.81).

207 *a . . . sufferer*: Aëtius.

209 *end*: reason.

215 *one*: i.e. an appropriate epithet.

228 *any man would*: is there any man who would.

230 *favours*: (*a*) boons granted by a man in power; (*b*) objects worn in honour of a lover.

243 S.D. *Exit Aëtius*: F clearly positions this stage direction before the end of Aëtius' speech; presumably his next line is to be shouted from behind the tiring-house façade.

244 S.D. *Enter Proculus and three Men*: Proculus is in charge of the assassination. The other three men may have been brought as assassins (in which case he has doubts about Pontius' efficiency, possibly implicit in line 245), or to dispose of the body after Pontius has done his work.

250 *Shift for yourselves*: 'every man for himself'.

271 *His body . . . theirs*: Phidias and Aretus will want to give Aëtius an honourable burial.

273 S.D. *with Pontius' body*: the fact that Phidias, Aretus, and Maximus do not notice Pontius' body suggests that by the time they enter it is no longer on stage. F provides no S.D. for its removal; this seems the likeliest point.

278–80 *Is it . . . overthrow?*: is being a just man once again the only certain way of being killed, as it had been during the reigns of previous tyrant emperors?

282 *corruptions*: poison, rottenness.

286 *tokens . . . plague*: physical symptoms, buboes (swollen, infected lymph glands).

287 *owe*: possess.

323 *utter being nothing*: annihilation.

327 *made them means*: gave them an allowance.

332 *would*: should.

336 *cold*: (*a*) sluggish, slow to act; (*b*) lacking in humane feelings (here, grief).

347 *Meroe*: capital of ancient Ethiopia.

351–2 *force . . . sorrow*: will impregnate expectant mothers' wombs with sorrow, thereby causing each to have a miscarriage (by displacing the foetus).

353 *Scylla*: monster in classical mythology, who threatened Odysseus (Homer, *Odyssey*, 12), and was later turned into a reef whose rocks remained a danger to shipping (*Met.*, 14). Here the rocks are understood to be the most robust 'grave' in the world.

356 *Olympus, Ida . . . Latmus*: famous mountains in Greece and Asia Minor.

357 *gums*: fragrant sap, e.g. myrrh.

358 *Thessaly*: district of Greece, famous for its fertility and lush crops of flowers.

5.1 S.D. *Aretus poisoned*: the standard symptoms of poisoning in Jacobean drama were bodily swelling and an intense burning sensation (cf. lines 4, 14–15); in some cases it also produced inflammation of the skin, simulated by make-up.

21 *pleasure*: pleasure in death.

22 *as fools*: i.e. as fools fall.

 simple: (*a*) without advancement; (*b*) foolish.

23 *This . . . me*: the dagger stops up its own wound; Phidias will bleed to death only if he removes it.

5.2.3 *bedrid*: been rendered bedridden; ironically, it is Balbus who survived Pontius' attack, even though he thought himself wounded more seriously than Chilax (4.4.126).

13 *BOY*: no singer is indicated in F, but the musical setting by Robert Johnson (see the Note on the Texts) is written for a boy's voice.

21 *O gently, O gently*: song MSS; F reads 'O gently'.

24 *Scythian mountains*: the Caucasus mountains, east of the Black Sea, which were a byword for cold.

40 *Numa*: see note to 1.2.83–4.

41–3 *Like Nero . . . empire*: the Emperor Nero only burned the city of Rome; Valentinian threatens to incinerate the entire empire.

49 *oils and mithridates*: antidotes to poison.

50 *You . . . sickness*: the physicians are dealers only in medical terminology, not effective remedies.

65 *You . . . poisoned*: tempted him to the vices which led to his murder by way of reprisal.

70 *would*: that would.

73–4 *the wings . . . Time*: because time flies, its personification was represented as a winged man.

78 *near my heat*: 'as hot as I am'.

79 *Mark*: (*a*) attend, listen to; (*b*) observe closely ('with horror' because Aretus' present sufferings will also come to Valentinian in the later stages of his death).

79–81 *but . . . murder*: the pains Valentinian now feels are punishment for his sexual misdeeds, the more extreme ones yet to come are for Aëtius' murder.

85 *than laughter*: than laughter is.

94–5 *Hide . . . sins*: the cry of the kings of the earth when facing damnation on Judgement Day (Rev. 6:16); a rare Christian reference in this predominantly classical play.

96 *a pull*: superior force (literally, the power to pull rather than be pulled, i.e. by death).

100 *wildfire*: inflammable liquid used as a chemical weapon: when ignited, the fire could not be extinguished.

101 *Phalaris*: see note to *Countess*, 5.2.196.

104 *flattery*: something with little relation to reality (as fire has with the more intense heat of Aretus' body).

105 *Avernus*: the entrance to hell in classical mythology, featured in Virgil's *Aeneid*, 4.

113 S.D. *Exeunt . . . body*: F makes no overt provision for the removal of Arétus' body. It could be removed here, in obedient response to the dying Emperor's final order; alternatively, it is possible that nobody responds, underlining the dwindling of his authority even before his death.

121 *make*: be; Valentinian imagines his own body as a burnt offering.

123 *parol*: verbal promise (here, of an afterlife).

141 S.D. *Exeunt Physicians*: any attendants remaining on stage also exit here.

151 *other countries*: the option of going into exile.

156 *lieutenant-general*: their commanding officer; literally, their general's deputy (the general, Aëtius, being dead).

5.3.6 *from . . . pity*: Maximus anticipates the fall of Rome as a world power as a consequence of the Emperor's assassination; instead it will be 'the pity' of the world.

7 *of my sending*: 'sent by me'.

13 *their bodies' first flame*: of the funeral pyres.

27 *Fools and children*: probably referring to the Emperor Claudius, widely considered a fool, and Valentinian himself, created Emperor in AD 425 at the age of 6.

5.4 S.D. *Fulvius . . . Sempronius*: F gives the Senators' speech prefixes as '1', '2', and '3' throughout this scene; this edition uses the names they are ascribed in the dialogue. '1' answers when addressed as Fulvius at 5.4.24, while '3' is similarly addressed as Sempronius at 5.4.18. In 5.8, two of the three characters speak, and in F are initially assigned the speech prefixes '*Sen.Semp.3.*' (5.8.1 S.P.) and '*2. Sen. Luc.*' (5.8.58 S.P.).

2 *rifled*: pillaged (by the soldiers coming out of the camp).

8 *free and liberal voices*: unconstrained acclamations (for their choice of Emperor).

9 *negative say*: veto.

12 *present foes*: an immediate declaration of war, giving the army something to do.

18 *Brutus*: Marcus Brutus, principal assassin of Julius Caesar in 44 BC.

20 *consuls*: military commanders, who conquered the provinces which are now in revolt; also the highest political office of the Roman republic.

28–9 *Age . . . treasure*: old men, who should be treated with respect, will be slaughtered for their wealth in the same way that the earth itself is mined for precious minerals.

31 *the Capitol*: the citadel on the Capitoline hill in Rome where the Jacobeans understood the Senate to meet.

42 *north*: the north wind.

44 *the . . . Nile*: the cataracts of the River Nile were a byword for deafening noise.

45 *hope*: have good expectations of.

47 s.D. *Fulvius . . . Sempronius*: the F stage direction states merely '*Senat.*'; Sempronius is evidently one of them, and the other two may be inferred. It is possible that other, anonymous Senators are also intended.

52 *fathers*: the Senators (literally 'old men').

59 *proscription*: a formal document of outlawry; proscribed individuals were not protected by the law, and might legitimately be killed by any private person. (This edn.; F reads 'Prescription'.)

66 *blown*: either 'puffed-up' or 'rotten'.

66–8 *must . . . bodies*: must, in order to be secure in their eminent positions, throw away life after life and create (metaphorical) defensive trenches with violence.

5.5.2 *short time*: Lycippus is commissioning Paulus at short notice to provide a court masque for Maximus' inauguration as the Emperor.

3 *the god o' th' place*: the tutelary divinity of the building where the inauguration is to take place.

4 *fasces*: see note to *Countess*, 4.2.245.

   Grace: one of the three Graces, female personifications of grace and beauty in classical mythology.

9 *a cruel carriage*: a bumpy ride.

11 *bursting*: excessively strained diction (?).

14 *blue*: Paulus' choice of colour arouses Lycippus' mockery because it is inappropriate for a state occasion: in Jacobean England, servants' uniforms were blue, as were the dresses worn by convicted whores in houses of correction.

22 *him*: the Emperor.

24 *Orpheus*: see note to *Countess*, 2.3.102–4.

31 *Good fury*: Lycippus wishes Paulus a successful period of composition (fury = '*furor poeticus*', the condition of the inspired poet).

32 *take . . . it*: 'fit what you write to the limitations of the actor who will play the part of the Grace'.

5.6.7 *If*: as if.

29–32 *Can . . . hazard?*: 'would I have run the risk of having Valentinian assassinated for any end, or any motive (literally, thought) that was not damnable, other than to possess you?'

45 *caster new*: transformer.

46–7 *The wreath . . . head*: a laurel wreath was worn as an emblem of victory in ancient Rome.

50 *once-more-summer*: Eudoxa presents herself as an older woman restored to her prime by the love of Maximus.

57 *favour*: the laurel wreath she says she will make for him.

5.7.3 *The work above*: the mechanism for lowering the boy actor to ground level (cf. 5.8.14 S.D.).

9 *cupboard*: where the cups for the banquet are stored; Lycippus is evidently in charge of the catering as well as the entertainment.

9-10 *be sure . . . cleanly*: if the boy is overweight, the Grace's descent will be undignified.

5.8 S.D. *Attendants . . . banquet*: this presumably takes place in the background while the other characters watch the masque. F also calls for '*Hoboies, Musicke, Song, wreath*' at this point, but these evidently relate to the masque.

11-14 *Numa . . . Augustus*: a catalogue of good Roman statesmen: Numa Pompilius (see note to 1.2.83-4); Cato might refer either to Cato the Censor (234-149 BC), a distinguished soldier and politician and great advocate of public morals, or to his grandson Cato Uticensis (see note to 4.2.53); the Emperor Nero (see note to 1.3.145) reigned well under the influence of Seneca the Stoic until AD 59 when he had his mother murdered; Aemilius Paulus the younger (d. 160 BC), conqueror of Macedonia, praised in Plutarch's *Lives* as a model of virtue because of the age in which he lived; and the Emperor Augustus (reigned 30 BC-AD 14), who presided over a period of great stability and artistic achievement in Rome.

14 S.D. *descends*: the boy-actor is winched down mechanically; this signifies the Grace's divinity.

27 *Stand . . . eternity*: may the wreath (metonymic for the emperorship) remain on Maximus' head forever.

28 *it*: the wreath.

33 *charge*: the wine in his goblet (punning on a military charge in battle).

36 *the . . . Mars*: the army (Mars being the god of war).

37 *BOY*: this edn.; F does not identify the singer.

Lyaeus: a surname of Bacchus, god of wine.

45 *mirth*: song MS; F reads 'youth'.

47 *Enter . . . fear*: a refrain (song MS; not in F).

53 S.D. *The Soldiers . . . respond*: the soldiers' dance (likened to a military charge) is to be answered with a 'charge' (toast) from Maximus.

65 *earth*: dead matter.

77 *If only . . . from us*: albeit only an unedifying example of revenge and secret murder.

82 *but*: other than.

92 *poor*: mere.

96 *my noble lord*: Valentinian.

98 *foreseen*: preordained.

106 *'Caesar'*: the title, not the man.

    'me' he lied in: 'he lied in saying that he was motivated by love for me'.

Epilogue This semi-apologetic epilogue, printed in large type on the verso of the final leaf of the play, seems bizarrely unrelated to the preceding action. It is no more jarring than the epilogues to some other tragedies of the period, but some scholars have preferred to think it belongs to the comedy which follows in F, *The Fair Maid of the Inn*.

4 *to our . . . fair*: the players understand their play to have been 'good and fair' merchandise.

12 *which . . . pay*: time and wealth are worth more than the amount the audience paid for admission to see the play.

14 *unto repenting cost*: 'to regret your expenditure' (in paying for admission to the theatre).

GLOSSARY

a the unstressed form of 'he'

abroad away from home, out of doors

adamant a byword for impenetrable hardness

affect love, like, prefer

after subsequent, future

air tune

amain at full speed

Amazon member of a female warrior race in classical mythology

ambage quibble, equivocation

ambrosia the food of the classical gods

an if

annals historical record

antiquities old writers

apostata apostate

apostate one who abjures his religious faith or abandons a solemn commitment

approved proven

aquafortis nitric acid

a-ranging astray

art skill

ascribe submit (*Countess*, 1.1.111)

aspect looks, appearance, face

aspic asp

atone reconcile (*Countess*, 1.1.356, 358), unite (*Countess*, 3.1.111)

ave hail (Latin)

aware beware

axis axle

aye always, ever

Bacchus classical god of wine

baggage good-for-nothing woman, strumpet

balance set of scales, a symbol of justice

bane ruin, destroyer

bare-board playing without wagers

bark a small ship

barren unattractive

barricado defensive barrier, barricade

base apron (*Countess*, 2.1.29)

basis foundation

bass-viol stringed instrument, the ancestor of the modern cello

bate subtract

beadsman votary

beholding indebted

belike probably, in all likelihood

Bellona ancient Italian goddess of war

bend (vb.) incline; submit

beshrew curse

birth brood, progeny (*Maid*, 1.2.141)

blazon (vb.) proclaim, make publicly known

block stumbling-block

blow bloom

blunt rough, uncourtly

bodkin blunt needle; dagger

boisterous violently fierce

bolt thunderbolt

bolting sifting flour

bout set-to, fight

bowl goblet

brabble brawl

brack a flaw in cloth

brain-trick cunning stratagem

brave (vb.) flout, challenge; (adj.) excellent, ostentatious

bravery splendour (*Val.*, 2.6.7)

bridal (n.) wedding

broker bawd

buckler protector

bugle-ox buffalo, wild ox

but only

camphor an aromatic oil used as an antaphrodisiac

canker a rose whose petals have been eaten by a caterpillar (also used of the caterpillar itself)

cankerworm caterpillar

capon a castrated male chicken

carpet-friend a mere companion in pleasure (literally 'friend in the boudoir')

carriage behaviour, deportment

carver one who chooses for herself at her own discretion

case clothing

cast cashiered

catch (n.) a round, a merry song in which each singer begins at a different point

catching easily infected (*Maid*, 5.1.92); infectious (*Val.*, 4.4.43)

catchpole minor officer of justice with powers of arrest

catechize orally instruct

cates food, especially delicacies

Cazzo an expletive (literally a vulgar Italian term for the penis)

centaur half-man, half-horse in classical mythology

chaff light husks of corn left behind after winnowing

challenge claim

chamber bedroom (*Maiden*, 2.2.23)

chamb'ring sex

chance fortune

change a round of dancing

chaplet a wreath worn around the head

character handwriting

charge orders, responsibility; expense, cost

charily carefully

check rebuke, restrain

chimney-piece an ornament or hanging above a fireplace

chirurgeon surgeon

circumstance preamble (*Maid*, 4.2.5)

cite formally summon to appear in court

clear innocent

clip (vb. and n.) embrace

close private, secret

closet a small side room

Coads! a 'polite' oath derived from 'gods'

collop slice of meat for frying

colour reason, pretext

comfortable comforting

compass encircle

compeer equal

compulsive compelled

congratulate salute

conjure appeal to, solemnly charge

conjuror black magician

conster construe

consumption a wasting disease

contemn scorn, disdain

control challenge, reprove, contradict (*Countess*, 4.2.116)

cope engage in battle

cordage ship's tackling

corsive corrosive

couch lay flat

counterfeit dissimulate

County Count

courser swift horse

cousin-german close kinsman

covetise covetousness

coxcombly stupid

cozen deceive, 'con', cheat

credit reputation

cross-point a dance step in which the legs are crossed and uncrossed while leaping in the air

crusoile crucible

Cuds me a light oath, 'Cuds' being a minced form of 'God'

cunning (n.) skill

Cupid juvenile god of love in classical mythology

curious intricate (*Maiden*, 2.2.12); fastidious, excessively cautious (*Val.*, 2.1.19)

curry (vb.) ride rapidly away

Cynthia the moon

daintily finely, handsomely

Danubius the river Danube

darkling in darkness

date term (*Maiden*, 1.2.94)

deliver proclaim

Diana classical goddess of the moon and chastity

die have an orgasm

discourse gossip

discover make known

distract distress, unhinge

distracted (adj.) distraught

distraction madness

donative gift

doom judicial sentence

doublet a close-fitting garment for a man's upper body

down outright (*Val.*, 1.1.90)

drachma Greek silver coin used by the Romans for foreign trade

dress prepare food

dross dregs, worthless by-product

durance imprisonment

earthen earthly

easiness gentleness, indulgence

engine device, stratagem

enter instruct

environ surround

envy malice

equal just, impartial

eringo the root of the sea-holly, reputedly a powerful aphrodisiac

Etna a volcano in Sicily

fact criminal act (legal terminology)

faction profession (*Countess*, 4.2.96)

fain eager, eagerly

fast sound asleep (*Maid*, 5.1.117); loyal (*Val.*, 1.3.49)

fault moral transgression

favour an object worn in honour of a lover

fee'd paid

fell (adj.) terrible

femalist ladies' man

fit punish fitly

flourish fanfare of trumpets

fly flee; be sold

fond foolish

forbearance absence (*Countess*, 1.1.67)

forfend prevent

forsooth in truth (asseveration)

fosse trench used as a defensive barrier

fray frighten, scare off

friend lover

front forehead (*Countess*, 1.1.60)

froward perverse, refractory

frozen zone the Arctic circle

gallimaufry a hodge-podge of different materials

gamester lewd person; gambler

geld castrate

gentle of gentry status

ghostly spiritual

glass mirror

glozer flatterer, sycophant

goodman husband

grapple engage in hand-to-hand combat

gratulate reward, give thanks for

grounds plainsong, the melodic foundation of a tune (*Countess*, 1.1.227)

grudging slight physical pain

guerdon reward, payment

guise habitual behaviour

halt limp

halter hangman's noose

hand signature (*Countess*, 5.2.180)

hand-wolf a hand-reared wolf

hanging drape

happily perhaps

hautboys wind instruments with a shrill, reedy sound, usually played in a consort; the ancestor of the modern oboe

hazard (vb.) wager, risk

headsman executioner

heats exercise

Hesperus the evening star

hie (vb.) hurry

honest chaste

honour (n.) bow

hoodwink (vb.) blindfold

horrid causing horror

host army

hot passionate, lustful

house-tailor personal tailor maintained as a member of a household

humorous prone to quirky behaviour

humour disposition, quirk of personality

hurricano hurricane

Hymen classical god of marriage

hymeneal rites marriage ceremony

idle frivolous

inevitable irresistible

intelligencer spy, informer

inundation flood

invent devise

jakes-farmer lavatory attendant

jar (n.) quarrel; musical discord

jealous watchful, vigilant

jennet a Spanish breed of horse

joint (vb.) fit together

jointure provision made for a woman in the event of her widowhood

Jove alternative name for Jupiter

jubilee day of rejoicing

juggling deceitful

Juno the classical goddess of marriage and wife of Jove

Jupiter the classical god of thunder and ruler of heaven, also known as Jove

keep dwell

keeping possession

know have sex with

lay bet

lay about search

lawn fine linen gauze

legerdemain sleight of hand

level (vb.) equate, make the same as

lictor a Roman magistrate's attendant

light happy, merry; unchaste, promiscuous

limber limp, pliant, flabby

limn paint (often associated with miniature painting)

list (vb.) wish; attend, listen

loaden overloaded

looking-to attendance

lusty full of life

made-up utter, through-and-through

magnifico magnate, rich and powerful man

maid virgin

maidenhead virginity (literally a woman's hymen, pierced in her first sexual encounter)

main ocean

maintain support

make away kill

malapert an impudent or presumptuous person

martialist warrior

match marriage

mazer goblet

mean average, mid-point

measure stately dance

Mercury messenger of the classical gods

minion hussy

miracle a wonder, something not found in nature

miss kept woman, mistress

monument tomb

mote speck, tiny piece

move propose

muffler a scarf worn to conceal the face

muster join up, enlist in the army; gather the army together

myrrh a fragrant gum-resin used in perfumes

mystery trade

mystical secret

name reputation

nations provinces of the Roman empire

Neptune classical god of the sea

nerve tendon

nosegay posy

number rhythm (*Maiden*, 4.5.13)

number on add to

odoriferous diffusing pleasant smells

Oëta a mountain in Thessaly

offer attempt

on of

ounce lynx

overcharge excess, surplus

ox-head cuckold

paean a joyful song of celebration

painting make-up, cosmetics

palm first prize in a contest

party person

pass a bout of swordplay

passenger traveller, passer-by

patrician Roman aristocrat

patrimony estate inherited from one's father

Pavy Pavia

period full stop (punctuation)

persever endure, continue

petulance wantonness

Phoebus the sun god

physic medicine

phys'nomy facial features

pickthanks tell-tale

piece picture

pike a long pole with a sharpened end, used by footsoldiers to hinder cavalry charges

pile funeral pyre

pined starved (in monastic discipline), emaciated

pledge (vb.) return a toast by drinking from the same cup

poise weigh

politic cunning, crafty

ponderous weighty

post ride swiftly

GLOSSARY

postern secondary entrance, 'back door'
power military force
practice practical experience; skilful machination
praetor a Roman higher magistrate
presently immediately
pretty pleasing
prick (vb.) incite
proper handsome
Proteus a blue-skinned sea-god in classical mythology
publish make public
puke vomit
purblind quite blind
purchase (vb.) strive for
purling rippling, murmuring
quacksalver a pretender to medical knowledge
qualify appease, pacify, make less violent
quean strumpet, loose woman
quick alive
quicken revivify
quit requite, repay; acquit
quondam former (Latin)
race brood of children
racking an excessive rent increase
raggèd rugged, uneven
ramp (vb.) rear on the hind legs (heraldic)
rampire barricade, rampart
ram up block
rase erase by scraping
ravin gluttony, voracity
reasoning discourse
recantation withdrawal of a statement or abjuration of a belief
receiver debt-collector
reckoning bill
recreant one who breaks allegiance
regardant backward-looking
rehearse recount
rest pause in music (*Maiden*, 4.5.12)
resty indolent
rinatrix a venomous snake (from Latin *natrix*, a water snake)
Risus mirth personified (classical)
rivelled wrinkled, shrivelled
Romulus legendary founder of Rome
room place, space

sable black
Sancta Maria an oath by St Mary (Italian)
sanguinolent bloody
'sblood a strong oath (contracted from 'by God's blood')
scape escape
score (n.) twenty
screw stretch
second (vb.) follow
sect followers
secure over-confident (*Maid*, 4.1.117)
seed progeny, children
sennet a flourish of trumpets before the entrance of an important personage
sensible sensitive
sensibly physically, with one's senses
sessions trial
sesterces Roman silver coins
several different, separate
severally (in stage directions) at different doors
shadow (vb.) conceal; (n.) shade, ghost
shape (vb.) devise, concoct (*Maid*, 3.2.82); (n.) physical appearance
shelf shallow part of the sea-bed on which a ship might run aground
short-heeled wanton
smock-woman female bawd
sneap (vb.) snub, reprove
sociate companion
soldier army
somewhat something
spleen anger
spleeny full of spleen
sport (vb.) trifle, joke
sprite spirit (without supernatural connotations)
squaring adjustment
stale laughing stock (*Maid*, 2.2.85); unwitting instrument (*Val.*, 5.8.96)
stand withstand
standing (n.) position
stay detain
stillatory distillery
stirring meat aphrodisiac
strain pedigree (*Maid*, 3.2.268, 5.3.276); tune (*Maiden*, 4.5.10)
stranger foreigner

426

striker robber
stuff cloth
style title
Styx the principal river of the classical underworld
sumner summoner (court official)
surcease end finally
surge (n.) wave
swallow stomach, brook
swinge thrash
taffety taffeta, a glossy silk cloth
tainture stain, defilement
taper slender wax candle
target shield
tedious seeming excessively long
tell count
temper moderation, self-control
threescore sixty
throughly thoroughly
timeless untimely
tire broadside
toy whim (*Countess*, 1.1.270); penis (*Countess*, 1.1.271), trifle (*Val.*, 2.1.19)
tract (vb.) tread
traffic trade
train entice (falconry term)
translate transfer
troth (n.) betrothal promise; (asseveration) 'in truth'
trow? 'do you think?'
trull strumpet, trollop
trussed bound, tied up; hanged, 'strung up'
try (vb.) test
Uds life a minced oath (Uds = God's)
underbuy undervalue
unexpressed inexpressible
unfashionable inappropriate
unpossible impossible

use (vb.) characteristically or habitually do; (n.) custom
vail bow down, yield
vanity triviality
vendible saleable
venereal house brothel
venery sex
venture (vb.) try
Venus classical goddess of love
Vestal virgin priestess of the goddess Vesta
viands food
virtue power, physical or military strength (*Maid*, 1.1.53, 4.2.165, 211, *Val.*, 1.3.172, 3.1.30)
vizard mask
Volga river which flows into the Caspian Sea
voluntary wilful
waghalter gallows-bird, someone likely to be hanged
wait await
wall-eyed with glaring eyes
want (vb.) lack; (n.) hunger
wat'ry-coloured pale
weaking enervating, enfeebling
weeds clothes
weigh value
wherefore why
whiblin trick
wild-fire especially destructive fire, conflagration
winding-sheet shroud
wink shut one's eyes
withal with; moreover; with it
wort cabbage
zany (n.) comic performer (often used contemptuously)
zounds a strong oath (contracted from 'by God's wounds')

ANN RADCLIFFE	The Castles of Athlin and Dunbayne
	The Italian
	The Mysteries of Udolpho
	The Romance of the Forest
	A Sicilian Romance
FRANCES SHERIDAN	Memoirs of Miss Sidney Bidulph
TOBIAS SMOLLETT	The Adventures of Roderick Random
	The Expedition of Humphry Clinker
	Travels through France and Italy
LAURENCE STERNE	The Life and Opinions of Tristram Shandy, Gentleman
	A Sentimental Journey
JONATHAN SWIFT	Gulliver's Travels
	A Tale of a Tub and Other Works
HORACE WALPOLE	The Castle of Otranto
GILBERT WHITE	The Natural History of Selborne
MARY WOLLSTONECRAFT	Mary and The Wrongs of Woman

A SELECTION OF OXFORD WORLD'S CLASSICS

American Literature

British and Irish Literature

Children's Literature

Classics and Ancient Literature

Colonial Literature

Eastern Literature

European Literature

History

Medieval Literature

Oxford English Drama

Poetry

Philosophy

Politics

Religion

The Oxford Shakespeare

A complete list of Oxford Paperbacks, including Oxford World's Classics, OPUS, Past Masters, Oxford Authors, Oxford Shakespeare, Oxford Drama, and Oxford Paperback Reference, is available in the UK from the Academic Division Publicity Department, Oxford University Press, Great Clarendon Street, Oxford OX2 6DP.

In the USA, complete lists are available from the Paperbacks Marketing Manager, Oxford University Press, 198 Madison Avenue, New York, NY 10016.

Oxford Paperbacks are available from all good bookshops. In case of difficulty, customers in the UK can order direct from Oxford University Press Bookshop, Freepost, 116 High Street, Oxford OX1 4BR, enclosing full payment. Please add 10 per cent of published price for postage and packing.